YALE HISTORICAL PUBLICATIONS

Fighting for American Manhood

How Gender Politics Provoked the Spanish-American and Philippine-American Wars

KRISTIN L. HOGANSON

Yale University Press   New Haven and London

Published under the direction of the
Department of History of Yale University
with assistance from the income of the
Frederick John Kingsbury Memorial Fund.

Designed by James J. Johnson and set in
New Caledonia Roman by Running Feet
Books, Durham, North Carolina.
Printed in the United States of America

A catalogue record for this book is available from the British Library.

The paper in this book meets the guidelines for permanence and durability of the Committee on Production Guidelines for Book Longevity of the Council on Library Resources.

10 9 8 7 6 5 4 3 2 1

Library of Congress Cataloging-in-Publication Data

Hoganson, Kristin L.
  Fighting for American manhood : how gender politics provoked the Spanish-American and Philippine-American Wars / Kristin L. Hoganson.
    p.   cm. — (Yale historical publications)
  Includes bibliographical references (p.   ) and index.
  ISBN 0-300-07181-7 (cloth : alk. paper)

  1. Spanish-American War, 1898—Social aspects. 2. Philippines—History—Insurrection, 1899–1901—Social aspects. 3. Politicians—United States—Psychology. 4. Masculinity—Political aspects. 5. Sex role—Political aspects—United States—History—19th century. 6. Imperialism—United States—History—19th century. I. Title. II. Series: Yale historical publications (Unnumbered)
E721.H69   1998
973.8'91—dc21   98-13307

TO
My parents and Charles

Contents

Acknowledgments

Like all historians, I owe a tremendous debt to the institutions that hold my source materials and to the librarians, archivists, and interlibrary loan workers who helped me find them. This book was made possible by the staffs and holdings of the Yale University Sterling and Seeley Mudd Libraries, University of Virginia Alderman Library, Harvard University Houghton and Widener Libraries, Alabama Department of Archives and History, Cincinnati Historical Society, Connecticut State Library, Cornell University Olin Library, General Federation of Women's Clubs Archives, Historical Society of Pennsylvania, Library of Congress, Massachusetts Historical Society, University of Michigan Bentley and Clements Libraries, Minnesota Historical Society, National Archives, New-York Historical Society, University of North Carolina Wilson Library, Pettigrew Museum, Radcliffe College Schlesinger Library, Proctor Free Library, Smith College Sophia Smith Collection, Swarthmore College Peace Collection, U.S. Army Military History Research Institute, and the Western Reserve Historical Society.

I was able to research and write this book because of the financial support provided by an Enders dissertation research fellowship, Massachusetts Historical Society research fellowship, University of Michigan Bentley Library research fellowship, Andrew W. Mellon pre-dissertation research fellowship, North Caroliniana Society Archie K. Davis research fellowship, and an Andrew W. Mellon dissertation fellowship. A Charles Warren Center fellowship enabled me to revise the manuscript for publication in a thought-provoking and collegial environment. Subventions from my great aunt, Esther Nystrom, helped feed, clothe, and shelter me along the way.

[ix]

As I strayed from women's history to gender history to cultural, political, and international relations history in the course of writing this book, I sometimes had the sense of being in a kind of interdisciplinary no-man's-land, far from familiar landmarks. But enthusiastic friends, colleagues, and advisers reminded me that boundary crossing is both a worthwhile exercise and an exciting adventure. That I did not become hopelessly lost in this endeavor owes much to their encouragement and advice. My foremost intellectual debt is to Nancy F. Cott. I feel fortunate to have had the benefit of her astute insights and good judgment ever since my search for a senior essay adviser first led me to her door. David Brion Davis and Paul Kennedy also provided sage guidance as I embarked upon this project. That I did embark upon it is owing, in large part, to José, Varela Ortega and Robin Winks, who sparked my early interest in the Spanish-American War and imperial history.

I am indebted to Gail Bederman, Amy Kaplan, Walter LaFeber, Frank Ninkovich, and the anonymous readers who took the time to read the entire manuscript and suggest ways to strengthen and clarify my argument. The members of my Cambridge writing group—Elizabeth Abrams, Steve Biel, Jim Cullen, Hildegard Hoeller, Jill Lepore, Allison Pingree, Laura Saltz, and Joy Young—also suggested ways to make my chapters clearer and more compelling; they never failed to inspire a frenzy of rewriting. Joyce Berkman, Oscar V. Campomanes, Frank Costigliola, Peter Filene, John L. Gaddis, Akira Iriye, Ernest May, John Offner, William R. Roberts, Robert Rydell, and participants in the Yale International Security Studies round table, the Harvard Contemporary History Circle, and several Warren Center colloquia commented on papers that, sharpened by their remarks, have found their way into this book. Kathleen Dalton, Arthur P. Dudden, Rebecca Edwards, Ruth Feldstein, Laura McCall, Mark R. Shulman, Nina Silber, and Laurel Thatcher Ulrich also deserve thanks for commenting on parts of the manuscript. Chuck Grench and Otto Bohlmann of Yale University Press guided me through the publishing process, and Lawrence Kenney polished the book in the editing stage.

I have more general debts to Ed Balleisen, David Blight, Anne Erling, Emily Gammie, James Gammie, Emily Greenwald, Ann Hoganson, Edward Hoganson, Susan Hunt, Rochelle Kopp, Jane Levey, Elizabeth Rourke, Kathryn Schifferdecker, Bruce Schulman, and Lorraine Wang, who asked provocative questions, shared ideas, and put me up (and put up with me) as I researched, wrote, and revised this book. My parents, Barbara F. Hoganson and Jerome L. Hoganson, deserve particularly heartfelt thanks. They have contributed to this project in numerous ways, from commenting on rough drafts to providing me with a peaceful "porch of my own" where I could hide out with the manuscript. My last, and greatest, debt is to Charles F. Gammie, whose good humor, broad perspective, critical eye, and warm companionship enriched the process of writing this book as well as the final product.

Abbreviations

ADAH	Alabama Department of Archives and History, Montgomery
AHR	*American Historical Review*
CHS	Cincinnati Historical Society, Cincinnati
CR	*Congressional Record*
CSL	Connecticut State Library, Hartford
D	Democrat
DAR	Daughters of the American Revolution
GAR	Grand Army of the Republic
GFWC	General Federation of Women's Clubs Archives, Washington, D.C.
HL	Harvard University Houghton Library, Cambridge, Massachusetts
HSP	Historical Society of Pennsylvania, Philadelphia
JAH	*Journal of American History*
LC	Library of Congress Manuscripts Division, Washington, D.C.
LW	*Leslie's Weekly*
MHRI	U.S. Army Military History Research Institute, Carlisle, Pennsylvania
MHS	Massachusetts Historical Society, Boston
MNHS	Minnesota Historical Society, St. Paul
NA	National Archives, Washington, D.C.
NAR	*North American Review*
NAWSA	National American Woman Suffrage Association
NYHS	New-York Historical Society, New York
NYT	*New York Times*
PFL	Proctor Free Library, Proctor, Vermont
PM	Pettigrew Museum, Sioux Falls, South Dakota

Pop.	Populist
R	Republican
ROR	*Review of Reviews*
SCPC	Swarthmore College Peace Collection, Swarthmore, Pennsylvania
Silver R	Silver Republican
SL	Schlesinger Library, Radcliffe College, Cambridge, Massachusetts
SSC	Sophia Smith Collection, Smith College, Northampton, Massachusetts
UMBL	University of Michigan Bentley Library, Ann Arbor
UMCL	University of Michigan Clements Library, Ann Arbor
UNC	University of North Carolina Wilson Library, Chapel Hill
WCTU	Woman's Christian Temperance Union
WJ	*Woman's Journal*
WRHS	Western Reserve Historical Society, Cleveland

Fighting for American Manhood

Introduction

Newspapers published in the United States on February 25, 1895, gave no indication that the previous day had been an exceptional one, a day that would be enshrined in history books as a starting point, a significant moment, a date. They briefly mentioned a revolt of the "natives" in the distant Philippine island of Jolo against a Spanish garrison and another in Guinea against the British. In Boston, there had been a memorial service for the abolitionist Frederick Douglass, who had died a few days earlier, and in Baltimore, Mrs. Katherine Stevenson, corresponding secretary of the national Woman's Christian Temperance Union, had declared herself a "staunch woman-suffragist." The most sensational story of the day came from Chicago. Under the headline "LAST SHOT IS FATAL," the *Chicago Tribune* reported that "Prof." Alfred Rieckhoff, known as the champion rifle shot of the world, had killed his seventeen-year-old assistant in a public demonstration of his sharpshooting prowess. At the end of his "human target" act, the professor misfired, and his assistant, whose job it was to stand on the platform with a steel target strapped to his breast, fell to the floor crying, "My God, I am shot."[1]

More than a century later, these stories open a window on the past. They reveal a nation wary of the imperial endeavors that were reshaping the globe; a nation in which leadership was passing from the venerated Civil War generation to those who had grown up in the shadow of the Civil War; a nation in which assertive "New Women" were encroaching on men's traditional prerogatives and audiences were gathering to watch men prove their courage and martial capacity in death-defying and, in some cases, deadly acts. These events afford a glimpse into late-nineteenth-century U.S. culture, but they seem more evocative than informative—the unconnected incidents of a bygone day.

Yet however disparate, these incidents, together with a myriad other happenings, helped constitute the stuff of U.S. culture—that is, the common reference points, customary beliefs, and patterns of behavior that formed the framework from within which individuals perceived and responded to the wider world. As strands in a complicated cultural web, the stories of February 25 helped define a moment. But they still do not seem to illuminate the future. The nebulous thing we call culture might affect the way people engage the world around them, but it appears too amorphous to readily explain specific decisions and events. Even if we could grasp it in its entirety, culture might only complicate our understanding of historical causality, for it is never determinative. To the contrary, it encompasses differences and permits innovation. If the February news stories hint at the bellicose policies to come, their message is elusive, a mere whisper in the cacophony of the day's news.

On February 24, 1895, as the ill-fated assistant prepared to face the professor's fire, Cuban patriots resumed their struggle for independence from Spain. The news arrived too late to make the papers on the twenty-fifth, and when it did reach the United States, newspapers depicted the insurrection as just another of the periodic upheavals for which Cuba was famous. Seasoned editors predicted that Spain would quell the rebellion, as it had the Ten Years War of 1868–78 and subsequent uprisings. Headlines reassuringly announced, "The Trouble Thought to be Slight."[2] Yet this time the trouble in Cuba was not slight and Spain was not victorious. And this time the United States did not remain aloof. Three years after the uprising began, the United States enthusiastically entered the conflict, thereby joining European nations in the scramble for colonies, creating a new generation of veterans, deflecting public attention from women's demands, and giving American marksmen a new opportunity to test their skill. Looking back at a conflict that is not easily explained in terms of national self-interest, we cannot but wonder whether the roots of war were embedded in American culture. Seen from a later vantage point, do the scattered news stories from 1895 illuminate the events to come?

This book investigates the cultural roots of the Spanish-American and Philippine-American wars. It is based on the premise that the conduct of foreign policy does not occur in a vacuum, that political decision makers are shaped by their surrounding cultures. In trying to understand why the United States went to war at the turn of the century, it is tempting to overlook the cultural frameworks that shaped contemporaries' outlooks and instead to focus on precipitating incidents, political and diplomatic wranglings, closed-door meetings, and the like. But to focus exclusively on immediate causes is to skim the surface of the past, to assume that earlier generations understood their world as we understand ours. To fully understand the descent into war, we need to understand how contemporaries viewed the precipitating incidents, what seemed to be at stake in their diplomatic and political wranglings, and what assumptions they brought to their high-level meetings—and to do that, we need to understand something of their culture.

But as we have just seen, the challenge posed by a cultural approach is connecting the amorphous stuff of culture to something as concrete as policy decisions. Recognizing this difficulty, the following chapters concentrate on political culture, that is, the assumptions and practices that shaped electoral politics and foreign policy formulation.[3] Even more specifically, they focus on the gender convictions—meaning the ideas about appropriate male and female roles—that did so much to define the contours of late-nineteenth-century U.S. political culture.

It may seem implausible that such a seemingly personal phenomenon as gender convictions would have far-reaching political implications, but by stipulating social roles for men and women, gender beliefs have significantly affected political affairs. In the nineteenth century, middle-class Americans commonly believed that men and women had very different capabilities and destinies. Men were thought to be well-suited for "public" endeavors, chief among them politics, and women for the "private" realm of family and home. This is not to say that gender beliefs were universally agreed upon or that they went unchallenged, but that most nineteenth-century Americans turned to inherited ideas about gender to order their world. Although they differed on the details of male and female natures and spheres, most nineteenth-century Americans agreed that there were important differences between men and women and that these should affect individual identities, social practices, and political organization.

Especially before 1920, the year the Nineteenth Amendment granted women equal suffrage, gender beliefs fundamentally shaped U.S. politics. Arguing that electoral politics should remain male terrain, opponents of women's suffrage frustrated efforts to win political equality for women. Besides keeping women on the sidelines of electoral politics, gendered understandings of citizenship and political leadership affected men's political standing. Because political power was associated with manhood, political leaders faced considerable pressure to appear manly in order to maintain their political legitimacy. The ideas about gender that affected the allocation of political authority also affected understandings of American democracy. Late-nineteenth-century Americans commonly believed that their political system ultimately rested on manly character, something defined in different ways but generally in reference to contrasting ideas about womanly attributes.[4] This meant that policymakers tried to legitimize their policies by presenting them as conducive to manhood. The political pressure to assume a manly posture and appear to espouse manly policies gave gender beliefs the power to affect political decision-making. This book investigates how they helped lead the nation into war at the turn of the century.

At first glance, the Spanish-American War does not seem to be a particularly difficult war to understand nor does it seem that gender is an integral part of the story. The initial conflict pitted Cuban revolutionaries against their Spanish rulers. In 1895, under the leadership of the poet and political organizer José Martí and the Ten Years' War veterans Máximo Gómez and Antonio Maceo, peasants, patricians, and middle-class Cubans formed a heterogeneous coalition to fight for *Cuba libre*. In response, Spain turned to Gen. Arsenio Martínez Campos, who had defeated Cuban revolutionaries almost twenty years earlier. When the moderate Campos failed to establish peace, the Spanish government replaced him with Gen. Valeriano Weyler, who soon became known as the Butcher. After arriving in Cuba in 1896, Weyler established a "reconcentration" policy that involved forcing rural Cubans into Spanish-controlled towns, where they could be monitored. Then, to hamper the guerrillas who still occupied the countryside, Spanish troops destroyed crops and other goods that might prove useful to them. This policy turned fertile fields into desolate wastelands and overcrowded towns into pestilential prisons where tens of thousands of noncombatant Cubans, many of them women and children, died of disease and starvation. Horrific though it was, the reconcentration policy failed to end the conflict. In October 1897, Spain's new Liberal government, led by Práxedes Mateo Sagasta, who had replaced the assassinated Conservative leader, Antonio Cánovas del Castillo, recalled the ruthless Weyler and sent a third general, Ramón Blanco, to govern the island. But the damage had been done. Weyler's brutal tactics had driven rural fence-sitters into the revolutionary cause and hardened the revolutionaries' resolve.[5] They also had helped the beleaguered Cubans win American sympathy.

Cuba lies only ninety miles from Key West, Florida, and when the rebellion took root, it became a leading foreign policy concern in the United States. The underdog Cubans won a great deal of positive press coverage in the United States, to the immense satisfaction of expatriate Cubans who worked hard to disseminate stories favorable to the revolutionary cause. Although American filibusters smuggled arms to the Cuban patriots, and the Red Cross, under Clara Barton's guidance, distributed supplies to suffering civilians, the nation remained on the sidelines. In 1896, Congress overwhelmingly passed a joint resolution that called for the recognition of Cuban belligerency, but President Grover Cleveland refused to endorse the measure, explaining that the United States should remain neutral in a conflict involving a friendly state. Thinking it would help them in the fall election, both major parties put *Cuba libre* planks in their platforms, but the Republican presidential victor, William McKinley, continued Cleveland's neutrality policy. In 1897, Spain formulated an autonomy scheme that would grant Cubans control of their domestic affairs but preserve Spanish sovereignty over the island. McKinley endorsed this compromise measure in hopes of securing peace.[6]

As the Cuban revolutionaries continued to chip away at Spanish power and resolve, loyalist Cubans grew fearful that Spain would withdraw from the island. In January 1898, a group of Havana residents rioted against the autonomy plan and in favor of continued Spanish rule. Because McKinley had endorsed autonomy, there was an anti-American cast to these riots. Fearing for the safety of expatriate American citizens, McKinley sent the battleship *Maine* to Havana. After being moored in Havana harbor for almost a month, the *Maine* exploded and sank on February 15. Although Spanish guilt could not be proven, the U.S. press generally held Spain responsible. Public and congressional clamor for revenge continued to grow until Congress passed a war resolution on April 25. The resolution included an amendment, known as the Teller Amendment after the Colorado senator who proposed it, that denied "any disposition or intention to exercise sovereignty, jurisdiction, or control over said island [Cuba] except for the pacification thereof."[7]

Fighting commenced a week later. U.S. military strategists opted not to raid the Spanish coastline or take the Canary Islands (earlier plans had called for such steps in the event of a war with Spain), but they did decide to attack the Spanish fleet in the Philippines in order to weaken their opponent. On May 1, the Asiatic Squadron, commanded by Commodore George Dewey, destroyed the Spanish fleet in Manila Bay. Meanwhile, back in the United States, hastily mobilized troops prepared to embark for Cuba. On June 22, U.S. soldiers landed at the village of Daiquirí, near Santiago de Cuba. Two days later, U.S. forces defeated the Spaniards in a skirmish at Las Guásimas, and on July 1 they fought again at El Caney, San Juan Hill, and Kettle Hill, which lay between the American forces and Santiago.

After advancing to a position overlooking Santiago, Gen. William R. Shafter, the gout-suffering Civil War veteran who commanded the U.S. land forces, contemplated withdrawing. His poorly provisioned troops were exhausted from lack of food and wet, sleepless nights. On July 3, however, the North Atlantic Squadron's victory over the Spanish fleet outside of Santiago changed Shafter's mind. He realized that the Spaniards' defeat at sea had made their defeat on land just a matter of time, for their troops could not be reinforced or resupplied. Shafter demanded surrender. Recognizing the hopelessness of their situation, the Spanish forces capitulated on July 16. The following day, U.S. troops occupied the city. Shafter did not include his allies, the Cuban patriots, in the negotiations or the occupation; indeed, he forbade them from entering Santiago. Although the United States had entered the war proclaiming its intention to liberate Cuba, the U.S. military virtually ignored the Cuban forces.

As the United States and Spain negotiated an armistice to end the war, Gen. Nelson A. Miles took the island of Puerto Rico. On August 13, the day after the armistice took effect, U.S. soldiers, unaware of the peace settlement, captured the city of Manila. (Dewey had lacked the troops necessary to occupy Manila after his naval victory on May 1 and had just held the harbor until reinforcements arrived.)[8] The war against Spain lasted sixteen weeks. In its aftermath, Secretary of War Russell A. Alger reported 345 combat-related deaths among the U.S. forces and 2,565 deaths from disease. In spite of the fatalities, numerous Americans agreed with John Hay, the U.S. ambassador to England and later the secretary of state, that it had been a "splendid little war." It was, indeed, a fairly popular one. More men tried to volunteer than the armed forces could accept; contemporary observers exulted that the war had "brought us a higher manhood" and "compelled admiration for American valor on land and on sea."[9]

Following the armistice, Spain and the United States sent delegates to Paris to negotiate a peace treaty. The final draft stipulated that Spain would relinquish sovereignty over Cuba and cede Puerto Rico, Guam, and the Philippines to the United States. Because of the Philippine provision, the Treaty of Paris elicited keen debate when it came to the Senate for ratification in January 1899. Republicans supported the treaty—their fellow Republican President McKinley had appointed the negotiating team—but did not have the necessary two-thirds votes to ratify it. Democrats were divided on the issue and tilted in favor of the treaty only after party leader William Jennings Bryan endorsed it. Bryan argued that Democrats should ratify the treaty to end the war and then vote to give the Philippines independence. The treaty passed 57 to 27, one vote above the required two-thirds mark, but then, to Bryan's dismay, the Senate narrowly voted against Philippine independence.[10]

The end of the Spanish-American War did not mean a return to the prewar status quo. Neither did it mean peace. In addition to taking the territories ceded by the peace treaty, the United States occupied Cuba from 1898 to 1902. A measure introduced in Congress in 1901 by the Connecticut senator Orville H. Platt spelled out the terms for U.S. withdrawal. The so-called Platt Amendment stipulated that the United States could intervene to preserve Cuban independence or maintain a stable government. Realizing that acceptance of the amendment was a precondition for self-government, Cuban leaders included its provisions in their constitution, thereby leaving their nation vulnerable to future interventions, the first of which came in 1906.[11]

In the United States, a much more contentious issue than Cuba's fate was that of the Philippines. In February 1899, a skirmish between U.S. troops and Filipino soldiers on the outskirts of Manila sparked the Philippine-American War. Filipino nationalists, led by Emilio Aguinaldo, tried conventional warfare and, when that failed, guerrilla tactics to dislodge the American soldiers who had replaced their Spanish rulers. From 1899 to 1902, 126,468 American soldiers landed in the Philippines; 4,234 died. Filipino casualties were much higher: an estimated sixteen to twenty thousand Filipino soldiers and two hundred thousand Filipino civilians died in the war. After U.S. troops captured Aguinaldo in March 1901, the revolutionary effort fragmented. McKinley's successor, President Theodore Roosevelt, declared an end to the fighting on July 4, 1902, but the Moros, or Muslims, in the southern Philippine islands resisted American troops for more than a decade after that.[12]

The irony is hard to miss. After entering the Spanish-Cuban War with loud proclamations of its humanitarian and democratic objectives, the United States refused to cooperate with the Cuban revolutionaries and ended up fighting another war halfway around the world to deny independence to Filipino nationalists. One can imagine the Midwestern farm boys who found themselves creeping through tropical jungles and the Filipino villagers who found themselves relocated by American troops—much as Cubans had been forced into camps under the Weyler regime—wondering what historical forces had brought them face to face.[13] The question has also puzzled historians, who, in spite of their familiarity with the sequence of events that preceded the Spanish-American and Philippine-American wars, still argue over the motives behind U.S. policy.

Why did the United States go to war in 1898? The number of explanations offered by historians can boggle even the intrepid reader—economic ambitions, annexationist aspirations, strategic concerns, partisan posturing, humanitarian sympathy for the Cubans, a desire to avenge the *Maine,* a psychic crisis, and Darwinian anxieties all have been cited as causes of the Spanish-American War. Historians have added late-nineteenth-century racial convictions to this mix of motivations to explain the nature of American policies in 1898 and during the subsequent Philippine "pacification" efforts.[14] At first glance, these theories appear to offer a convincing rationale for war. Indeed, they seem to explain the Spanish-American and Philippine-American wars four or five times over.

Yet the very abundance of explanations raises questions as to how they fit together. Assuming that each of these explanations reflects the motivations of at least some of those who supported war, why did so many reasons for war converge at once? The multiplicity of reasons for wanting war makes us wonder whether advocates of bellicose policies had any common ambitions, expectations, or presuppositions. A cultural approach that looks for links between various motives can answer this question. Such an approach has the potential to show how seemingly rational economic, political, and strategic justifications for war were related to each other and to more emotional appeals.

If, at first, the various explanations for the Spanish-American War are unsatisfying because they do not seem to cohere, once one delves into the historical documents they become even more unsatisfying, for they do not fully explain why a diverse array of American men, labeled jingoes by their contemporaries, clamored for war in the late nineteenth century. These men did not form a coherent group in the sense that all had similar class, regional, or party backgrounds. Neither did they belong to a common organization or agree on every aspect of U.S. foreign policy. But they did agree that war had redeeming social implications, chief among them that it would bolster American manhood. What brought jingoes together was a shared enthusiasm for war, predicated on common gender assumptions.[15] Why, then, were jingoes so obsessed with manhood? Why did they look to war as a solution for their gender angst? Once again, a cultural approach seems in order.

Besides failing to account for the jingoist desire for war, existing explanations fail to explain the pervasiveness of gendered rhetoric in debates over war and empire. If national self-interest, political ambitions, and the other motives currently cited by historians were sufficient to lead the United States into war, why did bellicose congressmen, political commentators, and other late-nineteenth-century political activists feel compelled to assert that manhood was at stake in the Cuban and Philippine issues and that aggressive international policies would build character in American men? To understand why jingoes drew on gendered arguments to make their case, we must examine their assertions in light of U.S. political culture and, more specifically, the gender politics of the 1890s.

The questions raised above—How did gender affect the jingoist clamor for war? Why did jingoes draw on gendered arguments to make their case?—are intriguing in themselves. But they merit particular attention because considering gender can help connect existing explanations for the Spanish-American and Philippine-American wars. On the one hand, gender served as a cultural motive that easily lent itself to economic, strategic, and other justifications for war. On the other, gender served as a coalition-building political method, one that helped jingoes forge their disparate arguments for war into a simpler, more visceral rationale that had a broad appeal. As both motive and method, gender helped men from different regions, parties, and walks of life to come together to form a powerful political movement. The chapters that follow elaborate on the ways that gender worked as a motivating ideology and a political posture in debates over war and empire.

In so doing, the book raises yet another question: What difference did jingoes' gendered motives and arguments make? Causal questions are never easy to answer, and this one is especially difficult because gendered motives and arguments were so often intertwined with other motives and arguments for war. Jingoes did not hesitate to phrase economic, political, and other arguments in gendered terms. As a result, it is not always clear what lay behind their bellicosity. The promise of markets? The impending elections? Or the seeming imperatives of manhood? Neither is it clear which strands of their arguments were most persuasive. The statistics? The strategic calculations? Or the appeals to manly honor? Given that gendered arguments often intersected with other lines of thought, one way to assess how gender beliefs affected U.S. policies is to reconsider the existing framework for understanding the Spanish-American War with gender in mind. How does adding gender to the picture enrich or clarify older explanations?

To start with the economic and annexationist arguments, jingoes often claimed that the nation needed overseas markets and territories in order to provide an outlet for men's robust energies. In addition to promising material gains, expanded markets and colonial holdings seemed attractive as a means of preventing American men from falling into idleness and dissipation and enabling them to meet the basic male obligation of providing for their families, something that many men found themselves unable to do during the depression of 1893–1897. Economic and annexationist arguments reflected convictions about what it meant to be manly; their persuasiveness relied on a commitment to fostering manhood in the United States. Some advocates of assertive politics undoubtedly regarded Cuba primarily as an opportunity for markets or as a choice piece of real estate, but those who held that a war—any war—would be good for American men also saw it as an opportunity to build manhood. To these jingoes, the prospect of combat enhanced Cuba's allure.

Besides providing a richer cultural context for economic and annexationist arguments, adding gender to the picture can help explain why, rather than regarding the United States as a beacon for the world, as earlier generations of American foreign policy theorists had done, late-nineteenth-century strategists advocated a more active and aggressive role for the nation. Their writings reveal a fascination with power, something often understood in gendered terms. The most prominent naval theorist of the time, Capt. Alfred Thayer Mahan, called for a "manly resolve" rather than "weakly sentiment" in U.S.

policy. Force must be met with force, he argued, for "conflict is the condition of all life." In such a strife-ridden world, the nation must strengthen its navy, "the arm of offensive power, which alone enables a country to extend its influence outward." Mahan insisted that war, once declared, "must be waged offensively, aggressively. The enemy must not be fended off, but smitten down." Mahan's statements about hard-hitting offensive maneuvers suggest that strategic theorists had other issues on their minds besides defending the nation's borders.[16] In an age when even tiny Belgium had overseas colonies, it appears that a kind of empire envy underlay calls to join the rough and tumble ranks of the great powers, that strategic arguments rationalized a desire to join the fray. Mahan's call for the nation to follow a manly course of action suggests that gender concerns infused geostrategic thinking.

If we shift from economic, annexationist, and strategic arguments (that is, from what appear to be national self-interest arguments) to political explanations, gender appears even more germane. The late-nineteenth-century belief that "manly" character was a prerequisite for full citizenship and political leadership can explain why support for bellicose policies seemed politically astute at the turn of the century and why jingoes triumphed in political debate. The links between manhood, military service, and political authority led a number of political leaders to think that they would enhance their political standing if they supported martial policies. Those who did not jump on the jingoist bandwagon after the *Maine* disaster felt the power of the militant manhood / political authority nexus: jingoes derided men who hesitated to support bellicose policies, foremost among them President McKinley, for lacking manly character. Confronted by admonitions to act like men, McKinley and peaceable members of Congress realized that they would lose political credibility if they did not adopt a more militant posture.

Although gendered arguments for war often served partisan purposes, beneath the partisan posturing lay uneasiness about the American political system. In the late nineteenth century, men from across the political spectrum generally agreed that democratic government rested on the manly character and fraternal spirit of male citizens and political leaders. Because American men commonly associated the civic virtue necessary for democracy with the manly character exemplified by soldiers, the dwindling tally of Civil War veterans led a wide range of men to fear that unless the nation forged a new generation of soldier-heroes through war, U.S. politics would be marked by divisiveness, corruption, and weakness. Women's encroachments into electoral politics also created unease. Not only were women winning voting rights in a number of states (mostly the right to school board and local suffrage), but they also were active in reform movements and political parties. Women's political activism led traditionalists to worry that politics was becoming feminized and to dourly conclude that when manhood was no longer valued as a basis for full citizenship and political leadership, the nation would succumb to exterior threats or crumble from within. Fearing for the future of the nation, jingoes regarded war as an opportunity to shore up the manly character of American politics. War, they believed, would return the nation to a political order in which strong men governed and homebound women proved their patriotism by raising heroic sons. Echoing British imperialists' claims that empire built character, jingoes promoted their martial ideas by arguing that war would forge a new generation of manly, civic-minded veterans who would serve as the pillars of American democracy.

A look at the press coverage of the Cuban revolution suggests that gender also can illuminate the substantial humanitarian sympathy for the mixed-race Cubans, a surprising development given the racist sentiments common among white Americans in the late nineteenth century. In accounts of the Cuban revolution published in the United States, positive gender convictions often counterbalanced negative racial ones, thereby fostering sympathy for the Cuban cause. American correspondents frequently depicted Cuban women as pure and virtuous victims of Spanish lust and Cuban men as chivalric fighters who had proven their manly character and hence capacity for self-government in combat. Such accounts portrayed Spanish soldiers as effeminate aristocrats, best embodied by their queen regent or boy king, or as savage rapists who lacked the moral sensibilities and self-restraint of civilized men. The Spaniards' apparent lack of manhood seemed to indicate that they were ill-suited to govern. Taking advantage of these popular images, jingoes urged the United States to assume the role of the heroic rescuer to the Cuban damsel or loyal brother to the Cuban knights. A failure to intervene, they argued, would reveal a lack of chivalry in American men.[17]

Besides contributing to the political pressure to intervene on the Cubans' behalf, gender beliefs contributed to the jingoist clamor for war in the aftermath of the *Maine* disaster. Jingoes' insistence that the disaster was an insult to American manhood made war seem an acceptable response to the incident, if not an imperative one. Employing a men and nations analogy, jingoes maintained that just as an honorable man would fight if insulted, so should the nation. Such assertions helped persuade less militant men, including irresolute congressmen, to favor war, because it appeared that a failure to do so would signal a lack of manhood.

Gender seems equally relevant to the psychological and cultural explanations for the Spanish-American War. Significantly, all the causes that Richard Hofstadter cited for the "psychic crisis" of the 1890s (which, he argued, caused the nation to go to war) had a gender component. To begin with, the depression of 1893 exacerbated anxieties about manhood, for unemployment resulting from the depression led to fears of male dependency. Rather than providing for their families, as men were expected to do, thousands failed to fulfill this basic male responsibility. In response, some men turned to social protest. These included the Populists, who depicted their struggle as a battle between money and manhood. Wealthier men had their own apprehensions. Those who feared social convulsion feared it all the more because men of their class seemed to lack the vitality necessary to keep vigorous working-class men in line. The rich were not the only ones to fear that civilized comforts were undermining manly fiber — middle-class men who held "soft" white-collar jobs also worried about a loss of vigor, and those who worked in large, bureaucratized corporations felt they lacked the autonomy their fathers had enjoyed. Thus the rise of big business had important ramifications for nineteenth-century gender roles. So did Hofstadter's final explanation, the closing of the frontier, that mythical space in which earlier generations of American men supposedly had developed their manly fiber. It appears that the psychic crisis was, in many respects, a crisis of manhood.[18]

But why did the gender anxieties of the late nineteenth century lead to an unusually bellicose spirit? The Darwinian corollary to the psychic crisis addresses this issue. According to the Darwinian explanation, jingoes' tendency to regard international affairs as an area of intensifying struggle led them to conclude that Americans needed to become tougher in order to compete. They viewed war as an opportunity to build the fighting virtues that allegedly were being undermined by industrial comforts. Historians who have investigated how Darwinian apprehensions proved conducive to war have highlighted the racial and national elements of this thought. But Darwinian anxieties also had a significant gender component. Those who spoke of national struggle and national survival generally believed that these depended on powerful men who did not shirk arduous challenges and domestic women who dedicated themselves to raising the next generation of vigorous heroes. To Darwinian theorists, new gender arrangements prompted fears about Americans' evolutionary fitness. As muckraking newspapers started reporting on metropolitan vice establishments and homosexual practices, members of the middle class began to worry that male immorality indicated an advanced stage of degeneracy. When bicycle-riding, bloomer-wearing, college-educated, job-holding New Women refused to serve as foils to traditional masculinity, conservative men began to fret about the future of the "American race" and, beyond that, about their place in it. Disturbed by these changes and influenced by the popular notion that the Civil War had developed the mettle of the men who fought it, jingoes began to advocate bellicose international policies.[19] Once again, adding gender to the picture can flesh out an older explanation.

Historians have attributed the Philippine War that followed on the heels of the Spanish-American War primarily to economic and strategic motives. Put simply, after becoming involved in the Philippines as part of its war effort against Spain, the United States stayed there because of a desire to have bases close to the potentially lucrative China market. Adding racial convictions to these explanations, historians also have stressed the belief that the Filipinos were incapable of self-government and that the United States had an obligation to civilize and Christianize them.[20] These explanations provide a strong rationale for American policies in the Philippines, but they still leave questions. Why did the nation forsake its democratic precepts to fight a war of conquest thousands of miles away? How were imperialists able to enact their policies over the impassioned protests of anti-imperialists?

Given that the Philippine-American War followed close upon the Spanish-American War, one might expect that the anxieties about gender that proved so conducive to the war against Spain also contributed to the allure of the Philippines and that the assumptions about manly character and political authority that benefited jingoes in 1898 later benefited imperialists. A closer look at the Philippine debate bears out these suspicions. Thrilled with the challenge posed by the war with Spain, ardent imperialists did, indeed, look to the Philippines to furnish a long-term remedy for the apparent problem of degeneracy in American men. When confronted with stiff anti-imperialist protests, they effectively manipulated martial ideals of citizenship and political leadership (which had, to their delight, been strengthened by the Spanish-American War) to enhance their political standing and undercut that of the anti-imperialists.

Rather than making our understanding of the Spanish-American and Philippine-American wars more diffuse, reassessing the existing explanations for these conflicts with gender in mind reveals common cultural assumptions among jingoist businessmen, annexationists, strategists, politicians, *Cuba libre* supporters, psychic crisis sufferers, and Darwinian theorists. Because jingoes had anxieties about gender they thought war would address and because gender beliefs served as a powerful political tool, it comes as no surprise that they drew on gender convictions in their efforts to convince less martial Americans to support the prospect of war. In sum, adding gender to the existing framework buttresses a variety of current explanations and offers some thematic unity for the whole mélange. It does not, however, fundamentally change our understanding of the conflicts. Using gender merely to embellish existing explanations may mean treating a potential cornerstone as if it were mortar.

This leads to a second way of assessing the significance of gendered motives and methods in turn-of-the-century foreign policy debates. Rather than starting with the existing framework for understanding these conflicts and using gender to fill the gaps, what happens if we start from the beginning and reconstruct the narrative with gender as a basic building block? What happens if we start by grounding foreign policy decisions in their wider cultural context and, more specifically, in the gender politics of the turn-of-the-century United States, thus leaving economic, strategic, political, and other theories the task of filling in the gaps? This is the project undertaken in the following chapters.

These chapters show that gender deserves serious attention in its own right. They show that a cultural phenomenon—the renegotiation of male and female roles in the late nineteenth century—helped push the nation into war by fostering a desire for martial challenges. They also show that gendered assumptions about citizenship and political leadership affected first jingoes' and then imperialists' abilities to implement their martial policies. By retelling the story of the Spanish-American and Philippine-American wars so that gender is an essential part of the picture, these chapters challenge us to rethink the cultural roots of American foreign policy at the turn of the century and beyond that, the cultural roots of international relations more generally.

A note on method is in order. This book takes rhetoric seriously, treating it as something that illuminates motivations, convictions, and calculations of what is politically efficacious. It approaches its source materials—primarily political speeches, correspondence, tracts, and reportage—both thematically and topically. On the thematic side, it examines how gender convictions affected political leaders' views about themselves, their political system, and the wider world. On the topical side, it considers how gender convictions (particularly gendered understandings of citizenship and political leadership) affected several broadly conceived foreign policy debates. Given that political leaders drew on such themes as honor and degeneracy in a number of specific policy disputes, combining thematic and topical approaches prevents the book from becoming too repetitive; given that political leaders did not reveal their full range of convictions each time they engaged in debate, combining related policy disputes into broader topics provides for a thematically richer account.

Finally, this book is based on the premise that categories like gender, political, cultural, and international relations history break the past into tidy plots that may not follow the unruly contours of the historical landscape. Because this book crosses some of the boundaries that historians have erected to subdivide their field, it has implications that extend beyond its central topic—the Spanish-American and Philippine-American wars—to several neighboring plots. As it traces the cultural concerns that lay behind these conflicts, this book also shows how international relations affected ideas about gender, how gendered ideas about political authority affected American democracy in an imperial era, and how high politics served as a vibrant locus of cultural struggle.

1

....

The Manly Ideal of Politics and the Jingoist Desire for War

TOWARD THE CLOSE of the nineteenth century, many Americans believed that a new era of peace was dawning. The nation had not fought a major war since the Civil War, a generation earlier. Increased commerce appeared to presage an era of greater international cooperation. Perhaps the greatest harbinger of peace was the arbitration treaty signed by U.S. Secretary of State Richard Olney and British Ambassador Sir Julian Pauncefote on January 11, 1897. The treaty committed the United States and Great Britain to arbitrate all their disputes for the next five years. Supporters of the treaty heralded the protocol as the "crowning glory of this wonderous age." They hoped that it was the first of many such treaties, that arbitration would end the rule of force in international affairs.[1] Their dreams were soon shattered, however—first by the Senate's rejection of the treaty and then, slightly more than a year later, by war.

The arbitrationists who imagined that lasting peace was at hand underestimated the growing jingoist spirit of the 1890s. Jingoes argued that war would be beneficial to the nation. They came from different regions, classes, and parties. Some were Civil War veterans, others had come of age after the war. The most vocal tended to be politicians, strategic thinkers, and members of the press. What united this diverse group of belligerent men—most prominent jingoes were, indeed, men—was a commitment to martial political ideals. Whereas the arbitrationists, many of whom were women, advocated a genteel style of politics based on intelligence, morality, and self-restraint, jingoes championed a more robust style of politics that placed relatively greater emphasis on physical power. Jingoes maintained that war would strengthen

American democracy by building manly character in the nation's male citizens. Disgusted by what they regarded as effeminizing trends in American politics, they worked to promote a countervailing political vision, in part by opposing the arbitration treaty, which they deemed a symbol of larger political changes.

Although the burst of enthusiasm that greeted the treaty made the arbitrationists confident of victory, the treaty failed by a slim margin to win the two-thirds Senate majority necessary for ratification.[2] The events of the next few years showed that the jingoes had won not only the treaty vote but also the larger contest over the character of American politics. In 1898, jingoes got their war, and they used it to further popularize their martial ideals. Far from attaining their dreams, the stunned arbitrationists could only marvel at the jingoes' rapid ascendance, an ascendance that they unwittingly had helped bring about. Because the concerns about the manly character of American politics that helped sink the arbitration treaty also affected subsequent debates over war and empire, the arbitration issue serves as a good starting point for understanding why the United States embraced bellicose policies in the late nineteenth century.

In the early 1890s, the international arbitration movement consisted of a small number of dedicated peace reformers. It was the growing jingoist spirit of the decade that turned arbitration into a mass issue. The most notable outbreak of jingoism prior to 1898 occurred in 1895, over a boundary dispute between Venezuela and British Guiana. Jingoes held up the Monroe Doctrine and proclaimed that if Britain intervened in Venezuela, the United States would go to war. Just as they had focused on the issue of honor in an earlier crisis with Chile in the winter of 1891–92, in 1895 jingoes again drew on martial ideas of honor to make their claims. Bellicose constituents wrote their congressmen to demand that they defend the "NATION'S HONOR." Like-minded congressmen maintained that "sometimes a nation in defense of its honor and integrity must go to war." Jingoes argued that those who wanted to settle the conflict through arbitration had no understanding of honor, that they were not "true men." Many agreed with Sen. William M. Stewart's (Silver R, Nev.) proclamation: "I want American manhood asserted."[3]

The possibility that the United States might fight Great Britain, the world's leading power and a kindred nation, over a point of honor appalled those who did not think that honor was sufficient grounds for war. The Venezuela crisis thus gave the international arbitration movement a tremendous boost. In April 1896, about four hundred delegates attended a proarbitration conference in Washington, D.C. Support for the treaty continued to grow as Olney and Pauncefote concluded their negotiations and sent the treaty to the Senate for ratification. A poll conducted by the *New York World* shows the widespread public backing the treaty commanded—of four hundred newspapers surveyed, all but thirty-nine favored ratification. Prospects for the treaty looked good because both the outgoing president, the Democrat Grover Cleveland, and the incoming president, the Republican William McKinley, urged the Senate to ratify it.[4]

Although some labor activists, including Samuel Gompers, endorsed the treaty, the most prominent boosters tended to be middle- and upper-class men and women from the Northeast and the Midwest. They believed that the treaty reflected the refined values of polite society. With this in mind, they suggested that opponents adhered to the rougher standards of working-class men, whose morals supposedly reflected a lower state of evolution. The *New York Times* argued that silverites, that is, Populists and others who called for the coinage of silver, were the major force against the arbitration treaty. It questioned whether there was something in "the silver creed that brings out the natural savagery of its sectaries and makes them delight in the barbarous principles and rough ways of early men?" Other arbitration backers implied that their opponents resembled those who approved of the working-class sport of boxing. One woman wrote her senator to say that war was "as uncivilized as prizefights and that it degrades the world as prizefights do a community."[5] The arbitrationists who characterized their opponents as uncultivated men resembled other elite reformers who aspired to raise the tone of politics. Just as municipal reformers hoped to replace "brutish" machine bosses with "intelligent" public servants, arbitrationists hoped to replace boorish ways of settling international disputes with a more elevated system of international relations.

The problem with arbitrationists' class-based arguments was that many of their opponents were, like the arbitrationists themselves, upper crust. Hence, in addition to drawing on class prejudices, arbitrationists drew on the idea of evolutionary progress. They commonly argued that they were the harbingers of the future and their opponents relics from the past. According to this line of thought, those who still considered war a viable means of ending disputes resembled cavemen, and their opinions were those of the glacial period, "when chipped-flint spearheads were the arguments that closed debate and the man with the thickest pate and the largest club was the boss of the neighborhood." Arbitration supporters also compared their opponents to the duelists of bygone days. As an article in *Godey's Magazine* noted, "There was a time when duelling was considered the only means of redress for an insulted gentleman but now duelling is a crime and is resorted to by none but senseless hotheads."[6] Whether treaty opponents resembled savage cavemen or hothead duelists, the message was clear: civilized nations must learn to restrain their bellicose impulses, just as civilized men and all women presumably did.

Although many of the leaders of the arbitration movement were men, women activists were highly visible. The Woman's Christian Temperance Union (WCTU), the largest single U.S. women's association of the time, created a department of Peace and International Arbitration in 1887, well before the Olney-Pauncefote treaty. Under the leadership of Hannah Bailey, the department generated enthusiasm for arbitration among WCTU members. In 1895, the National Council of Women, another organization of reform-minded women, adopted a resolution calling for a permanent arbitration treaty. The following year, the National-American Woman Suffrage Association, the nation's leading suffrage group, also adopted a resolution in favor of it, and the General Federation of Women's Clubs, a league of club women from across the country, urged its member organizations to take up the issue. Activist women attended arbitration conferences and petitioned Congress on behalf of the treaty, saying that the matter was "of vital interest to women."[7]

Although some women supported arbitration for the same reasons as men, others viewed it as a women's issue. These women saw war as a sign of masculinity run amuck and arbitration as a triumph of feminine values. When these women depicted their opponents as brutish men, they emphasized their maleness more than their suspected working-class status. They insisted that the only way to secure peace was to fundamentally change men's character. Arguing that boys must be taught the same values as girls, they agitated against military training in public schools, a pet project of Union veterans, and for more peaceable values. As an article in the WCTU mouthpiece, the *Union Signal,* argued, to promote peace, mothers must teach boys and girls that "true glory consists not in physical feats of warfare, but in mental and moral ability." The article went on to say that children should no longer be taught to "honor the military man above any other." Frances Willard, the leader of the WCTU, was so committed to extirpating male brutality that she proposed the following debate topic: "Resolved, that differences between Harvard and Yale be settled by arbitration, without resort to football."[8]

Even those who did not regard arbitration as a women's issue per se often did see it as a triumph of the moralistic values that were associated with women. The comments made by the president of Amherst College, Merrill E. Gates, at an arbitration conference illustrate this tendency. Gates remarked that, as men had come to see, the true strength of a nation lay in its moral power. Then he checked himself: "Did I say, as *men* have come to see? As men *and women* have come to see where true strength lies!" The greater women's influence, the more would moral ideals guide political affairs, argued Gates. Cartoons that depicted arbitration as a woman furthered the idea that it represented the moral virtue associated with women rather than the physical power connected with men (fig. 1).[9]

1. "Civilization Demands Arbitration and Peace." *Judge*, February 20, 1897.
Courtesy of Cornell University Library.

Many who espoused arbitration did not mind that the movement appeared moralistic or feminine because they supposed that societies guided by
moral principles or seemingly feminine virtues were at the forefront of civilized progress. According to this logic, civilized societies had to restrain men's
primitive impulses in order to advance. In the words of the arbitration activist
Philip S. Moxom, a minister from Springfield, Massachusetts, societies that
wanted peace had to control the "big beast" that lurked in men. To attain
peace, he said, "this beast must be chained and subdued, and then by some
subtle process sublimated to the force of a disciplined and powerful manhood."[10]

In order to subdue the male beast and end the paramountcy of force in international relations, arbitrationists proposed replacing old standards of combative honor with new standards defining honor as peaceful submission to law. Benjamin Trueblood was one exponent of arbitration who tried to redefine honor to imply intelligence and self-restraint. "If nations still have differences which an intelligent and peaceful diplomacy can not dispose of," he wrote, "there remains but one honorable appeal, that to arbitration. This method will always bring peace with honor; no other in our time will." "Old ideas of martial glory must fade," insisted another advocate of arbitration, who went on to say that "great leaders that owe their prestige to the old order of things must be deposed."[11] As these statements indicate, arbitration supporters proposed to neuter, if not feminize, ideas about male honor.

Arbitrationists' objectives caused dismay among those committed to the old order of things, meaning those who looked askance at efforts to discipline the male beast. "The new danger will be peace rot," wrote an essayist in the upper-crust periodical the *Arena*. If men did not preserve their pugnacious instincts, warned an article (tellingly titled "On Being Civilized too Much") in the equally highbrow *Atlantic Monthly*, they would die off. Sen. John T. Morgan (D, Ala.), a former Confederate officer, agreed with these thoughts: "Whenever we get to that period in our history that it is perfectly understood that we are never going to have another war," he said, "from that moment of time this Republic is going to degenerate, and her sons are going to forget the lessons and duties of patriotism."[12] Arbitration had little appeal for those who assumed that the character and policies necessary for national well-being were of a more martial nature.

A Senate amendment that exempted matters of honor from the treaty's provisions lessened anxieties that the Republic would degenerate. But even after the amendment had eviscerated the treaty, detractors derided arbitration as an "exhibition of pusillanimity" and its proponents as effeminate "gentlemen" who were "deluded by sentimental gabble and persuaded to advocate the theories of gush."[13] Such gibes were more than a rhetorical strategy to discredit the arbitration forces. They reflected genuine preoccupations about the character of American democracy, for a number of arbitration opponents were convinced that nations guided by "sentimental gabble" could not survive in a world based ultimately on force.

Those who regarded arbitrationists' proposed changes to men's character and to political arrangements with unease looked to jingoist policies to counter what they saw as the growing effeminacy in political life. Arbitration opponents were not necessarily jingoes, and jingoes were not necessarily treaty opponents, but jingoes and arbitration opponents generally shared certain assumptions about male character and government. Just as jingoes believed that the nation's foreign policy should rest on demonstrations of force and militant standards of honor, many arbitration opponents hoped to prevent arbitrationists' seemingly feminine values from triumphing in politics. Theodore Roosevelt, at the time president of the New York City board of police commissioners, illustrates this inclination. He did not think that arbitration was inherently objectionable, but he did worry that the "futile sentimentalists of the international arbitration type" would produce "a flabby, timid type of character, which eats away the great fighting features of our race."[14] Like other jingoes, Roosevelt regarded the popularity of the arbitration movement as a sign that American politics was losing its manly character.

The great irony of the arbitration movement is that it prompted men like Roosevelt to trumpet the value of a martial spirit even louder, to insist that if the nation did not support dynamic leaders whose policies would toughen the nation's male citizens, the United States inevitably would decay. The arbitration issue did not create the jingoes' anxieties about male character, citizenship, and political leadership, but it did bring them into focus. Jingoes saw arbitration as a symbol of what was wrong in U.S. politics and as a sign that the manly style of politics that had flourished in the aftermath of the Civil War was in a state of flux. To understand their apprehensions, it is necessary to step back from the arbitration debate and consider late-nineteenth-century U.S. political culture—meaning the practices and assumptions that defined political life—more generally. The wider political context can explain why misgivings about male character and governance were so salient in the arbitration debate. Beyond that, it can illuminate the cultural roots of the Spanish-American War, for the concerns about male character and governance that shaped the arbitration debate explain the appeal of jingoism.

Eighteen ninety-five, the year of the Venezuela crisis, was the thirtieth anniversary of the end of the Civil War. As Sen. George Frisbie Hoar (R, Mass.) noted in a eulogy for William Cogswell, a Union veteran and Massachusetts congressman who died in May of that year, the majority of men who had served in the Union and Confederate armies were dead. Surviving veterans were entering into an "honored old age," and the generation of men who had grown up in the aftermath of the war were taking their places at the forefront of public life.[15] Hoar and his political associates were highly conscious that a generation that had played a defining role in the nation's history was passing from the national stage, and they realized that this had profound implications for American politics.

The Civil War intensified the emphasis on manhood in U.S. politics that had emerged in the early nineteenth century, first with the extension of white male suffrage through the elimination of property ownership requirements and then with the growth of popular politics in the log cabin campaign of

1840. The postwar era was a time of mass male political participation. Whereas before the Civil War, both race and gender determined political rights, after the war, gender became the central basis for enfranchisement. This became clear in a Kansas referendum of 1867 in which white male voters preferred a measure that would enfranchise black men to one that would enfranchise women. The Reconstruction amendments to the U.S. Constitution underlined the point made in Kansas. The Fourteenth Amendment, adopted in 1868, allotted representation according to the number of eligible male voters, thus putting the word *male* into the U.S. Constitution for the first time. The Fifteenth Amendment, adopted in 1870, eliminated, at least on paper, racial restrictions to voting, thereby opening up electoral politics to virtually all men. After the war, eleven midwestern and western states permitted even male aliens to vote, provided they had declared their intention to become citizens.[16]

Manhood suffrage contributed to the markedly fraternal character of late-nineteenth-century American politics. Many factors, including class, region, race, ethnicity, and religion, divided men in this period. But as Paula Baker has noted in her work on gender and U.S. political culture, nineteenth-century political parties united men from different walks of life, thereby reminding them of their shared interests and brotherhood. Men's ability to participate in electoral politics brought them together not only within parties but also across party lines on the supposedly equal grounds of citizenship. Especially in the years immediately following the Civil War, when black men participated meaningfully in southern politics, electoral politics helped teach men that despite their many differences, they formed a privileged class relative to women. Late-nineteenth-century men turned to electoral politics as they turned to fraternal organizations and volunteer militia units to help develop their identities as men.[17]

In the postwar era a few women, such as the Republican orator Anna Dickinson, were active in party politics, but women typically won only ceremonial or symbolic roles in political gatherings. Women who appeared in public events represented such abstract ideals as liberty and justice or womanhood itself. The penchant for presenting women as symbols of the common good conveyed the message that they transcended class, party, and indeed politics. Most postwar Americans thought that women's political role was not to engage in party strife but to inculcate disinterested virtue in their husbands and sons. Just as women were expected to inspire men in battle, they were to do the same for the peacetime army of voters. As one women's suffrage opponent wrote, "It is a grand position, that of standing outside of strife and using moral power alone, keeping alive patriotism, inspiring valor, holding up the highest aims, animating sons, husbands, fathers, and breathing an atmosphere of pity and heroism, aloof from the perils of camp life. This is a noble sort of disfranchisement."[18]

The widespread belief that women stood for the common good helped exclude women from a political system seen as inherently partisan and war-like. Elihu Root, a corporation lawyer who later became secretary of war, demonstrated this point in 1894 when he said, "Politics is modified war. In politics there is struggle, strife, contention, bitterness, heart-burning, excite-ment, agitation, everything which is adverse to the true character of woman." In circular fashion, women's exclusion from partisan politics made that activity seem all the more manly, and the manly character of politics made it even harder for women to push for inclusion. The political satirist Finley Peter Dunne summed up the assumption that electoral politics rested on powerful, partisan manhood: "Polytics ain't bean bag. 'Tis a man's game; an' women, childher an prohybitionists do well to keep out iv it."[19]

As Dunne's inclusion of "prohybitionists" in his list of political outsiders indicates, the assumption that electoral politics was an essentially male en-deavor affected men's political prospects as well as women's. To win political authority, men had to appear manly. The partisan press thus went to great lengths to portray its favored politicians as magnificent specimens of manhood and their opponents as unmanly. Party loyalists were exceptionally hostile to men who joined third parties or switched party affiliations in hopes of lifting political life to a higher moral plane. These men appeared to lack the fraternal loyalty and hearty camaraderie that bound their fellows to the two major par-ties. They seemed suspect as citizens and as men. Rep. Henry R. Gibson (R, Tenn.) expressed this conviction in a speech made in 1896: "Partisanship is but a preparation for patriotism, and they who are partisans when the country is at peace are almost sure to be patriots when danger threatens. A man who has not enough zeal to make a partisan is not apt to have enough to make a pa-triot."[20]

The belief that a man's party loyalties reflected on his character made men who joined third parties subject to ridicule as men. In addition to stig-matizing members of the Prohibition Party as unmanly, party loyalists labeled male Populists "she-men." They were even more vehement in their denuncia-tions of mugwumps, a term first used to describe Republicans who crossed party lines in 1884 to vote for the Democrat Grover Cleveland because he ad-vocated civil service reform, and later used to describe almost all elite political reformers with questionable party loyalties. Realizing that mugwumps were trying to change the character of partisan politics, party regulars responded by calling them "eunuchs," "man-milliners," members of a "third sex," "political hermaphrodites," and "the neuter gender not popular either in nature or soci-ety."[21] When Republican and Democratic loyalists proclaimed that Prohibition Party members, Populists, and mugwumps lacked the manly character necessary for political authority, they reinforced the conviction that electoral politics rested not just on men, but on a specific kind of manly character.

Foremost among the character attributes valued by late-nineteenth-century political activists was honor. As Bertram Wyatt-Brown and Kenneth S. Greenberg have shown in their histories of honor in the antebellum South, links between honor and manhood were long-standing. Men associated manly honor with valor, particularly in exacting revenge on their enemies. Honor represented men's status and entitlement in a male hierarchy. Men of honor were convinced that, come what may, they must defend their reputation and manhood. Catherine Clinton has elaborated on the gendered character of honor in an essay on Southern dishonor. Honor, she argues, "was wholly a male domain—a man's to bestow and a man's to withdraw." Men accorded honor to women based on their sexual purity and fidelity—that is, based on their relationships with men. Whereas women's honor was intertwined with their sexual virtue, men's honor involved a demonstration of self-worth before the public.[22]

Honor fell into a temporary eclipse in the mid-nineteenth-century North, as Yankee men found dignity and self-restraint more conducive to success in a relatively egalitarian, industrializing society. The Civil War, however, brought honor into national vogue again, for the celebration of soldiers' heroic deeds gave chivalric ideals a new prominence. In the postwar period, popular novels, above all ones that romanticized antebellum plantation life, advanced the ideal. They defined an honorable man as one who demonstrated his superiority by treating the weak—a category understood to include women—with paternalistic solicitude. He was loyal to his fellows, fearless, and belligerent. An honorable man would tolerate no insult and would fight to preserve his reputation. Honorable men won deference from their subordinates and respect from their equals. If, on the one hand, the hierarchies embedded in the standard seemed in keeping with the growing inequalities of Gilded Age America, on the other hand, honor appealed to men frustrated by the restraints of an ever more corporate economy and the commercial values of the era. It also proved enticing to those who were disturbed by changing gender roles, for honor served as the keystone of a chivalric edifice that enshrined men's public authority and women's domesticity.[23]

The epitome of honor and the model of manly character in the post–Civil War period was the veteran. Even ex-Confederates, who had been humiliated on the battlefield, insisted that they never had surrendered their honor. The respect accorded to veterans led some observers to conclude that the greatest legacy of the war had been manhood itself. In the years following the war, political leaders honored veterans by favoring them in patronage appointments.

Voters honored them by electing them to office—indeed, all the presidents from Grant to McKinley, with the exception of Grover Cleveland, were Union veterans. In addition to winning a disproportionate number of offices, veterans filled an important symbolic role in postwar politics. In his reminiscences of life in the 1870s and 1880s, the political reporter Henry L. Stoddard recalled that at all important civic gatherings at least one veteran was present on the platform.[24] Veterans won seats on the platform for the same reason they won elections—because they appeared to represent the highest standards of male character and civic virtue.

Postwar politics had a markedly military cast not only because of the prominence of veterans but also because participants, whether veterans or not, conceptualized politics in military terms. The party system advanced the military style of politics, for political parties posed as armies of soldiers engaged in battle against political foes. Campaign clubs created uniformed marching companies that disguised their torchlights as bayonets and fired cannons in political assemblies. These parading armies sometimes brawled with their political opponents. Hence when politicians referred to party workers as "lieutenants" and "fighters" or described the voting booth as "the field of duty . . . from which none of us must skulk," their metaphors had substance. The political prominence of veterans and the military metaphors that pervaded politics highlighted the idea of politics as a manly endeavor—one that called for the same discipline, strength, courage, and fraternal loyalty required in battle.[25]

The military style of politics promoted the idea that the state rested ultimately on soldier-citizens, an idea that resonated among a generation that had seen its national government maintained by force. In speeches honoring veterans, political leaders reminded their audiences that in the time of crisis the nation had turned to its manliest men—to the "able-bodied, patriotic, brave-hearted heroes" who were strong enough to carry a canteen, knapsack, ammunition, and musket. Veterans cited their military records to prove their fitness for elected office, and they argued that they should be preferred over college-educated "dudes" in patronage appointments.[26] Although veterans benefited most from the links between military service and political participation, many civilian men also profited from militaristic political theories, for it was the soldiers' apparent manhood that justified their political status. Civilian men found they could prove they had the requisite manhood for political authority by citing the military valor of men from their class, race, region, or ethnicity or their own soldierly attributes. Political activists conflated martial and manly character so often that the two came to seem indistinguishable.

By associating political rights with manly character, the military style of politics made American political culture more inclusive for men. But it had exclusionary implications for women. Drawing on the idea that the primary characteristic needed for full citizenship was the manhood exemplified by soldiers, women's suffrage opponents argued that women should not vote because they did not bear arms.[27] To the dismay of women's rights activists, the wartime association of manly character, military service, and political authority continued to reverberate in American politics long after Appomattox. Martial ideals of citizenship and political leadership survived well into the 1880s, and in some circles the echoes of the Civil War lingered even longer.

The convictions about male character and political authority that defined American politics in the period following the Civil War help explain why jingoes placed so much emphasis on combative male character in the late nineteenth century. More than twenty-five years after the war, jingoes expressed a passionate commitment to the martial ideals of citizenship and political leadership that had flourished in the postwar period. They firmly believed that the fraternalism and honor embodied by soldiers gave American politics the manly character so necessary for national well-being. Although their martial vision of politics harked back to fading practices, their bold assertions that war was desirable for its own sake, as a character-building exercise, represented a departure from post–Civil War disillusionment. If elderly jingoes were seduced by nostalgia, young ones advocated a belligerent style of politics that was more an expression of militant new ideals of manhood than a memory. As the Civil War generation aged, jingoes clung to the manly ideal of politics all the more tenaciously, defending it against such perceived threats as the international arbitration movement. But in spite of their victory on the arbitration issue, jingoes realized that the martial values that had made politics seem so manly were losing their hold over U.S. political culture.

In the late nineteenth century, as the Civil War receded further into the past, the manly ideal of politics became ever more elusive. Growing class and racial divisions sapped the spirit of fraternalism that had permeated postwar politics, and self-interest appeared to replace honor as the driving force in public affairs. As the number of Civil War veterans dwindled, the argument that military service had proven the right of all men to participate in politics lost credibility, for the vast majority of men who had matured since the war could not demand political rights based on such service. Rather than reflecting on the shared experience of combat, political commentators paid an increasing amount of attention to the differences that divided immigrant and native-born men, working-class and wealthier men, and black and white men.

One symptom of the collapse of the manly ideal of politics was elite men's increasing tendency to question the idea that all men should participate in electoral politics. They downplayed popular claims to civic virtue based on military service and argued that the physical power represented by soldiers

was less relevant to governance than the intelligence and moral integrity supposedly demonstrated by white, native-born, wealthy men. At times they even
added well-to-do women to their list of virtuous citizens. Their reform efforts
undercut fraternalistic military-style campaigns, which began to give way to
more educational and merchandising forms of politics in which party organizations tried to teach their principles or sell their messages to individuals with
weak party loyalties. The new political style resembled that of organized
women, who had concentrated on education and lobbying since the early
nineteenth century because they could not vote.[28]

The "best" men's growing disdain for the fraternal character of postwar
politics was not only a sign but also a cause of significant political change. In
the late nineteenth century, elite men tried to shift more political power to
educated, presumably virtuous men like themselves. One tactic was to encourage upper-class men to claim their rightful positions of leadership. Reformers exhorted men "of the better class, who by virtue of intelligence, integrity, and business training are specially equipped for the responsibilities of
office," to become politically active, and they struggled to secure more civil
service positions for such men. Another tactic was to restrict male suffrage. In
the 1890s, wealthy white southern men worked to disfranchise poor white
men and all black men through legal means. (Earlier efforts to disfranchise
black men had relied more on violence and fraud than statutory or constitutional measures.) In the North, reformers tried to hamper illiterate voters by
introducing the Australian (meaning secret) ballot, literacy tests, and more
stringent registration requirements. Starting in 1894, states that had permitted aliens to vote began to restrict suffrage to citizens.[29] These measures
weakened the fraternal character of politics. The line between who could participate in electoral politics and who could not depended increasingly on race
and class, rather than just sex.

Elite reformers were not solely responsible for the declining fraternalism
in politics. The growing class divisions of the Gilded Age made it harder for
wealthy men and workers to regard themselves as brothers. Working-class
leaders increasingly rejected the idea that the wealthy shared common interests with the laboring masses, and they worked to mobilize men from different ethnic groups on a class basis. In 1892, delegates from Farmers' Alliances,
the Knights of Labor, and smaller labor parties gathered in Omaha, where
they formed the People's (or Populist) Party. Populists rallied behind the cry
that monopolies, trusts, and Wall Street effectively disfranchised working-
class men by manipulating state legislatures, controlling U.S. congressmen,
and rendering the masses of American men economically dependent on the
rich. The new party polled a million votes in the election of 1892.[30]

Class tensions increased as the nation sank into a depression in 1893. By the election of 1896, it was clear that the old politics of fraternalism that ostensibly united men from different classes within the two major parties had suffered a severe blow. The Democratic Party refashioned itself as a workingmen's party when it nominated William Jennings Bryan and backed an inflationary free silver policy. Mugwump reformers and businessmen who favored the gold standard fled the Democratic fold for the Republican one; silver Republicans shifted allegiance to the Democrats. The Republican candidate, William McKinley, drew on the language of fraternalism as he insisted that all Americans had common interests—indeed, he won on this platform—but his contention was a defensive response to charges that he represented the rich. During the campaign, his followers exacerbated the growing sense of class divisions by accusing Bryan of waging a war on property and trying to "array class against class."[31]

The ascendant understanding of politics as a struggle between irreconcilable class interests was related to the passing of the Civil War generation. Within the Union and Confederate armies, military service had brought men from different walks of life together in a shared enterprise. After the war, veterans continued to refer to the military as a great leveler in which men were judged on their manliness rather than on their class status. But when veterans started to fade from the American political scene, they took with them the idea of politics as a unifying male fraternity. The growing sense that there were more differences among men from various classes than similarities led President Grover Cleveland to call for the development of a "feeling of sincere brotherhood" among American men shortly before the election of 1896.[32]

The dwindling pool of veterans affected not only the fraternal character of American politics but also the conviction that American men were well-suited for the responsibilities of citizenship and political leadership. By the 1890s, the aging Civil War generation began to wonder if their sons and nephews had the character necessary to govern. Southern champions of the "Lost Cause" feared that young men would never be as noble as their heroic fathers. Northern critics viewed the souvenir dealing that accompanied the dedication of Grant's tomb in 1897 as a sign of the triumph of the profit motive over the virtue represented by the departed hero. In the North and South, men who remembered the war feared that the younger generation cared more about moneymaking than honor. Veterans implored their contemporaries to remember the selflessness and civic virtue demonstrated in the Civil War. They urged the American people to remember the example set by veterans who had risen above "the dictates of private ambition, selfishness, and greed of gain" and devoted themselves to an honorable cause. By the 1890s, however, such lofty exclamations rang a bit hollow, for there were increasing complaints that pensions for unneedy veterans burdened taxpayers.[33] Once veterans started to lose their position of honor, there was no group of men who could represent civic virtue to men from different classes.

As politics appeared to lose the underlying sense of commonality and civic virtue needed to unite men from different classes, political commentators began to assert that manly honor was disappearing from political life. In its place, they found self-interested materialism. Wealthy reformers vehemently deplored the greedy corruption of machine bosses, accusing them of lacking the integrity, fair-mindedness and honor that constituted manliness. Echoing their rhetoric in the 1896 campaign, McKinley denounced Bryan's free silver policy as a self-interested measure that would destroy the nation's honor as it vitiated its currency. He called on American men to "lift up the standard of national honor" and oppose the free silver policy. "We must pursue no policy that will ever degrade American manhood," he said, "for when we degrade American manhood, we degrade American citizenship (great applause and cries of 'that's right') and in the end degrade our country."[34]

Populists and Democrats responded in like terms. They, too, criticized the materialistic values that appeared to be triumphing over honor in political life. Rep. John Sharp Williams (D, Miss.) revealed this disgust with the base character of politics in a congressional speech: "The trouble is, Mr. Speaker, that the controlling element in this country has changed. From 1776 to 1865 the dominant spirit which controlled in this Republic was one of honor, glory, chivalry, and patriotism. The dominant spirit of to-day is the pride of gold, of palaces, of marriage alliances with dukes, and princes, and counts, and an exercise of the whole power of the Government in the interests of money changers, millionaires, and monopolies."[35] Republicans, Democrats, and Populists may have disagreed over who was at fault, but they all voiced the same concerns: the American political system was rotting from within because of an absence of manly honor. This conviction fueled the jingoist desire for war, for jingoes presented war as an opportunity to reinvigorate the manly ideal of politics.

Jingoes despaired over the manly character of electoral politics because the nation's political system was not only changing from within, it was being assaulted from without, by activist women. Besides pressing for a greater role in political life, activist women were critiquing the assumptions about male honor and valor that had played such a prominent role in postwar politics. In the last two decades of the nineteenth century, stalwart defenders of the old political order looked on aghast as women's tentative forays into electoral politics turned into assertive charges. "Whatever may be the future of the suffrage movement in this country," ran an article in the *Review of Reviews*, a periodical that hoped the future of the women's suffrage movement would be grim indeed, "there can be no doubt about the rapidly growing influence of women in our public affairs."[36]

By the 1890s, women were accustomed to participating in a wide range of political activities. Urban women gave naturalized citizens instructions in voting, canvassed neighborhoods on behalf of favored candidates, formed civic-minded municipal organizations, and attended political rallies. A mass meeting in New York City in support of an anti-Tammany mayoral candidate attracted so many women that they could not all fit into the building. The overflow crowd stood on the sidewalk for hours, applauding the remarks made inside. It was a "monster matinee" reported the *New York Times*.[37] Across the country, prohibitionist women gathered at the polls on election day to influence male voters. Populist women such as Mary Elizabeth Lease of Kansas and Cleora Eugenia Coke of Maryland made stump speeches. Women served as state legislators and jurors in Colorado, and elsewhere they won election to school boards and municipal offices, including mayor. Women's growing political activism led a hostile cartoonist in *Judge* to imagine a future political parade composed entirely of women (fig. 2). His vision was not far from reality—in Colorado, women voters marched in their own political parades, and the town of Spring Hill, Kansas, elected an all-woman municipal government in 1894.[38]

Women attained new heights of political visibility in the presidential campaign of 1896. That year, ten states sent representatives from women's Republican clubs to the Republican national convention, and Utah sent a woman as a delegate to the national Democratic convention. Women participated as delegates and speakers in the Populist convention, and a woman from Colorado seconded Bryan's nomination. Delegations of women visited McKinley at his home in Canton, Ohio, to show their approval. Bryan, in turn, spoke to women's gatherings, including one of two thousand women in Minneapolis. In New York, Republican women distributed campaign literature, in Boston, women publicly debated free coinage versus the gold standard, and in the Midwest, women wrote partisan pamphlets on the money question. J. Ellen Foster, leader of the Woman's National Republican Association, made speeches across the country, and Helen M. Gougar, a candidate for attorney general in Indiana, won recognition as "one of the foremost workers for Bryan in the present campaign" after she organized mass meetings for the Democratic candidate and spoke on his behalf. Every woman had a duty to inform herself on political issues, proclaimed the Nebraska resident Addie M. Billings in her pro-Republican speeches.[39]

During and after the election, the press commented on women's unprecedented political visibility. News stories drew attention to women's im-

2. "It's Coming. A campaign parade of the 'new woman' on the eve of a great
political battle." *Judge*, August 31, 1895. Courtesy of Harvard College Library.

portant role in the campaign, even in the states where they could not vote.
Perhaps the most sensational story of the election came from Utah, where the
Democrat Martha Hughes Cannon defeated her Republican husband in a
race for a state senate seat. After the election, an editorial in *Judge* remarked
that "the women of this country will have more to do with its politics, year by
year. That is apparent from the interest they had and the work they did in the
late campaign." The men of Idaho helped fulfill that prediction when they
voted to grant full suffrage to women that fall. Needless to say, women's political gains did not always win acclaim nor were women always successful. In
Chicago, a male police court candidate was praised as the "emancipator of his
sex" when he defeated a female contender.[40]

The hostility toward the woman police court candidate serves as a reminder that politically active women encountered great resistance. Detractors
deplored those "bustling, hustling busybodies who force themselves into public notice," and they worked to keep women at the fringes of politics. Such
hostility to women's activism helps explain why, despite their incursions into
electoral politics, late-nineteenth-century women remained far from political
equality. But even in the face of such opposition, activist women were extend-

ing their political reach. Once exposed to politics, women often pressed for a greater public role—including, in many cases, full suffrage. Politically active women boosted the suffrage movement in two ways. First, women who thought the ballot was necessary to accomplish specific political objectives swelled the ranks of the suffrage movement. Second, as growing numbers of women became politically active, women's suffrage started to lose its radical cast. Filled with a sense of momentum, suffragists pursued their goals with vigor in the 1890s. They put referenda on ballots, addressed state legislatures, testified in congressional hearings, raised the issue in southern constitutional conventions, and presented their cause to party platform committees. By 1896, four states had granted women full suffrage and twenty-one others permitted women to vote in local, mostly school board, elections.[41]

Women's growing political activism had powerful implications for male electoral politics not only because women were gaining entrance to a previously male activity, but also because of women's stated desire to change the political system. Whereas early women's rights activists had emphasized their shared humanity with men, late-nineteenth-century activists increasingly argued that they should be included in electoral politics because of their differences from men. The Reverend Ida Hultin spoke of this objective at a suffrage convention. Women, she said, wanted to vote in order to stamp the "womanliness of our nature upon the country, even as the men have stamped the manliness of their nature upon it." To reinforce their position that women's contributions were needed in government, suffragists and other reformist women often questioned men's character and hence their ability to govern well. "Man morally is in his infancy," opined the women's rights essayist Sarah Grand in an article published in the *North American Review*. Continuing to cast a critical eye on men's capacities, she later wrote, "In this mismanaged world it looks as if we should soon be obliged to do their work as well as our own, or nothing will be done." Politically active women maintained that, as one woman put it, men had made "selfishness, greed, and intemperance" prevail at the expense of patriotism—that they had corrupted politics.[42] Their criticisms heightened fears that the men who had come of age in the aftermath of the war lacked the character to govern.

In contrast to their unflattering depictions of men, late-nineteenth-century women's suffrage exponents and reformist women embraced commonly held ideas about women's superior morality. As the pool of Civil War veterans dwindled, women laid claim to disinterested civic virtue. Elizabeth Cady Stanton conveyed the views of numerous activist women when she called women the "most highly educated, moral, virtuous class in the nation." Taking advantage of women's status as symbols of moral virtue, suffragists argued that politically active women would uplift the state. "Might it not be better for the sex which furnishes nine-tenths of the criminals, to give to the sex which furnishes two-thirds of the church members an equal share in the duties and privileges of citizenship?" questioned a women's suffrage advocate.[43] Activist women believed that they were needed to clean up traditional male politics and purify American political life.

At the same time the champions of women's suffrage argued that women should vote because they were more virtuous than men, they promoted the idea that morality, and the intelligence that guided it, should be the cornerstone of political participation. In a direct assault on the manly ideal of politics, suffragists argued that ballots did not rest on bullets, as their opponents maintained, but rather, on the moral character best exemplified by women. Because the nation had not fought a major war in several decades, women's rights agitators found it credible to argue that "if there ever was a time when the argument of 'no fight, no vote' held good, that time has certainly passed." Suffrage leaders insisted that those who considered military service relevant to the ballot were oblivious to present conditions. "Time was when voting was done by the clash of the spear upon the shield," wrote one suffragist. "The ballot originally was the substitute for this demonstration, but now the state does not limit suffrage to warriors, and qualifications of voters are never physical. . . . The basis of the modern state is intelligence." To bolster their critique of the ballots and bullets equation, suffrage supporters said that because the world was entering an era of arbitration, physical power had become an anachronistic base for political rights. Suffragists' arguments resembled those of elite male reformers, who did not think that soldiers' physical power should justify their political power. Hand in hand, reform-minded men and women undercut political ideals based on soldierhood and promoted greater domestic imagery in politics.[44]

According to those who fought for women's suffrage, the state's shift from a military to a social emphasis meant that women must be included in governance. As Anna Garlin Spencer, a Rhode Island minister and social reformer, said, "Government is not now merely the coarse and clumsy instrument by which military and police forces are directed; it is the flexible, changing and delicately adjusted instrument of many and varied educative, charitable and supervisory functions." Spencer concluded that the changing character of government made women's participation imperative. It was increasingly apparent, she argued, "that for these wider and more delicate functions a higher order of electorate, ethically as well as intellectually advanced, is necessary." If, on the one hand, activist women took it for granted that civilized governments needed women's contributions, on the other hand, they were confident that granting women a greater political role would elevate government even further. Hannah J. Bailey, the head of the WCTU's department of Peace and

International Arbitration, expressed this conviction in an arbitration confer-ence. "When women shall have a direct voice in politics and in determining the continuance of carnal warfare," she said, "doubtless the former will be-come more purified and the latter be abolished altogether."[45] Bailey hoped that the desire for peace would win women a greater political role, but in spite of the high-minded nature of her vision, it was not universally acclaimed.

Some men regarded women's growing political activism as a sign of na-tional degeneracy and a threat to American government. Not all these men were jingoes, but jingoes tended to agree with a much wider pool of men (and less progressive women) that politically active women threatened American democracy. These detractors argued that the feminization of politics would lead to political corruption rather than to political purity. They maintained that women's entry into what William Croswell Doane, the Episcopal bishop of Albany, called the "rough strifes and contests of political life" threatened chivalry itself.[46] Doane and others like him suggested that if men seemed to be forgetting the meaning of honor, if they were characterized by rampant self-interest, it was because women were no longer filling the role of non-partisan political muses. Men who were uncertain of their political authority —because they had been slurred as unmanly or dishonorable—found it ad-vantageous to declare that the real threat to male politics was women. By de-crying women's activism, men from differing walks of life and various political parties could join with their fellows in a common struggle to defend the manly ideal of politics.

Men's political anxieties are only part of the reason that activist women elicited such a powerful reaction in the 1890s. More generalized concerns about American manhood also prompted uneasiness about the new political arrangements. Men hit hard by the depression of 1893 found that their self-respect had suffered along with their ability to provide for their families. As hard times raised doubts about the evolutionary fitness of struggling men, the comforts of the wealthy raised questions about upper-crust men's continued vitality. The apparent overcivilization resulting from an increasingly industri-alized, urbanized, and bureaucratized society elevated fears of weakened manhood among the growing cohort of middle-class men who held soft white-collar jobs. If white, middle-class men were beset by uncertainty about their ability to compete against hardened working-class men, they worried equally that seemingly degenerate lower-class men would reduce the virility of the national "stock." Mired in the pervasive racism of the time, a number of white people feared that, in the absence of the allegedly civilizing influence of slav-ery, black men were regressing toward their "natural" bestial state, turning into savage rapists. In addition, many native-born Americans regarded the in-flux of immigrants as fraught with peril for American manhood, for they inter-

preted immigrant men's social customs, labor protests, and support for machine bosses as signs of unmanly character. Reports of homosexual acts, impotence, mental deterioration, and a loss of vital energy suggested that the social
changes of the 1890s were causing degeneracy in middle-class as well as
lower-class men, an alarming thought in a world assumed to be governed by
Darwinian laws.[47]

What made these apparent changes exceptionally worrisome for the
northern middle- and upper-class men who fretted most about American
manhood was the lack of a remedy. Casting about for solutions, they concluded that old methods of inculcating manhood were becoming increasingly
obsolete or inefficacious. The aging pool of veterans meant that there were
fewer robust heroes to serve as models for younger men, and the apparent
closing of the frontier meant that young men had to search for new tests to
replace the challenges of the wild West. Perhaps most significantly, assertive
New Women, highly visible on their bicycles and in their forthright business
attire, seemed determined to elide gender differences, thereby making it
more difficult for men to define themselves relative to women. To those late-
nineteenth-century Americans who worried about the character of American men, it appeared that modern times demanded new ways of inculcating
manhood.[48]

Because many Americans assumed that the health of the nation rested on
the robust character of its men, doubts about men's character intensified apprehensions about the soundness of the U.S. political system. Those who
clung steadfastly to the manly ideal of politics commonly feared that temperance advocates, civil service reformers, arbitrationists, and others of their ilk
would effeminize American men. Even when women were not the sole causes
of their anxiety, men often conceptualized threats to traditional pursuits in
feminine terms. This proclivity can be seen in the complaint that "old women,
of either sex" were passing moralistic legislation that restricted such male
vices as smoking. The old order had deteriorated so much, wrote one cur-
mudgeonly essayist in the *North American Review,* that the smaller towns of
America were ruled by "old women of both sexes, shrieking cockatoos that
will by-and-by make life well-nigh intolerable to any man of self-respect and
make him wonder whether he lives in a free country or not."[49] But if politics
was part of the problem, it was also part of the solution: troubled men regarded electoral politics as one of a dwindling number of activities that could
enable American men to assert their manhood.

Jingoes emerged from this wider social and political context. Like many men,
they worried that organized women and their moralistic allies were undermining the manly basis of politics, if not manhood itself. What distinguished

jingoes from other stalwart defenders of male prerogatives was their militaristic solution. They wanted American men to rebuild their manhood and, as a
result, the manly style of politics by asserting their physical power. Jingoes
scoffed at suffragists' claims that "a government of reason will supersede a
government of force." Instead, drawing on the idea that nations were involved
in a Darwinian struggle for survival, they argued that physical power was still
of paramount importance in international affairs.[50]

The naval theorist Alfred Thayer Mahan spoke for many jingoes when he
said that "no greater danger could befall civilization than the disappearance of
the warlike spirit (I dare say *war*) among civilized men. There are too many
barbarians still in the world." Mahan, who secured a large following after publishing *The Influence of Sea Power upon History* in 1890, played on American
men's Darwinian anxieties. Regarding the luxury and comfort he saw in
Gilded Age America as signs of effeminacy, he urged his countrymen to build
up their navy. According to Mahan, naval power was not only a means to extend the nation's commercial reach, but also a remedy for male degeneracy. A
career naval officer who advocated vigorous daily exercise, Mahan maintained
that servicemen were exemplars of heroism, honor, and a fraternal spirit.
Even though he suffered from nervous headaches so debilitating that he
feared a breakdown, Mahan was convinced that naval service built manhood,
that it inculcated a strenuous ethic and self-discipline.[51]

Mahan found a ready audience for his avowals that a loss of the warlike
spirit would lead to male and national decay. In Congress and elsewhere, jingoes asserted that aggressive international policies would serve as a path to
male and political regeneration. Implying that war would produce a generation of tested soldiers who would preserve democratic government, Rep. Vespasian Warner (R, Ill.) asserted, "War is healthy to a nation." Rep. Albert S.
Berry (D, Ky.) also greeted the prospect of war with enthusiasm. "I think a
little blood-letting would be an admirably good thing about this time for
the people of the United States," he declared in a debate over U.S. Cuban policy. War, he maintained to prolonged applause, would advance manhood and
honor.[52] As these remarks suggest, jingoes regarded war as an opportunity
to develop such "soldierly" attributes as strength, honor, and a fraternal spirit
in men.

Jingoes' misgivings about American men were magnified by venturesome
New Women. Captain Mahan, for one, relished the male camaraderie of the
navy and regarded the sea as a welcome retreat from women's society. When
he did spend time with women, he preferred ones who were good-looking and
deferential. Suffragists filled him with horror. Mahan feared that women's suffrage would break down the "line of demarcation" that separated the "respective spheres of men and women," that it would destroy the "constant practice

of the past ages by which to men are assigned the outdoor rough action of life and to women that indoor sphere which we call the family." Not only would suffrage desex women, who were certain to leave their homes and children for the "outside hurly-burly of masculine life," but admitting women into political life also would hurt the state, for women lacked the physical power to back up their will by force.[53] Mahan was not the only advocate of assertive international policies who thought that seemingly feminine morality and sentiment had little place in political affairs. Fearing women's encroachments into men's sphere, jingoes looked to martial policies to shore up the virile character of electoral politics. Because they believed that changing gender roles posed a political problem, jingoes did not hesitate to seek a political solution.

In calling for belligerent overseas policies as a way to reinvigorate American men and their political system, jingoes were influenced by the Civil War veterans, who, thinking of the manly character supposedly exemplified by soldiers, insisted that war, "horrid and hideous as it is . . . has, nevertheless, its compensations." Jingoes were likewise influenced by British assertions that imperial endeavors elevated men's character. Henry Cabot Lodge (R, Mass.), a member of the Senate Foreign Relations Committee, supported jingoist policies for both of these reasons. In his public addresses, Lodge recalled feeling inspired by the sight of soldiers marching off to fight in the Civil War. He also spoke admiringly of the spirit shown by imperialistic Englishmen. With the Civil War and British examples in mind, Lodge maintained that combative international policies would build strength and character in American men.[54]

Lodge thought that it was imperative to build manly character in American men because he feared that immigrant men were threatening the "quality of our citizenship." They threatened to debase what he considered to be the attributes of "Anglo-Saxon" men: "an unconquerable energy, a very great initiative, an absolute empire over self." If this were not bad enough, Lodge feared that white, native-born men, especially the wealthy men of his class, were paying so much attention to material matters that they were losing the respect of the masses of American men. His desire to build manly character led Lodge to urge the Republican Party to focus on objectives besides business matters, namely, "patriotism, love of country, pride of race, courage, manliness, the things which money cannot make and which money cannot buy." Lodge even exhorted Harvard, his alma mater, to bolster its athletic program. "The time given to athletic contests and the injuries incurred on the playing-field are part of the price which the English-speaking race has paid for being world-conquerors," he said at an alumni dinner.[55] (Clearly, Lodge would have thought little of Frances Willard's proposal to replace football with arbitration.) But preaching the importance of robust character was not enough for the senator—he advocated assertive foreign policies as well. "While I do not seek war, I do not fear it," he wrote at the time of the Venezuela crisis, "and it is much better to fight than to be degraded and to sacrifice our best interests. . . . War is a bad thing no doubt, but there are worse things both for nations and for men."[56]

Many jingoes maintained that two things worse than war were weakness and corruption, and that prolonged peace fostered both of these. As Captain H. C. Taylor of the Naval War College put it, war, though "cruel and brutal," had redeeming qualities, for it saved nations from "corrupt ease" and "luxurious immorality." Disgusted by the commercial values of Gilded Age America, jingoes looked to war to break their hold. Sen. Roger Q. Mills (D, Tex.) had this goal in mind when he exclaimed, "If it were not for the boards of trade and the stock exchanges and the commercial gamblers in the great cities who are interested in the exports and imports, it might be possible for the Government of the United States to show some virility all over the earth."[57] Hoping to counter what they saw as the effeminizing tendencies of too much money-making, jingoes urged war for its own sake.

Needless to say, arbitration backers were appalled by militaristic claims. Carl Schurz, for example, was astounded at the number of his contemporaries who expected that war would elevate men's character. He was particularly disgusted by a conversation he had with a man who said he longed for war—if not with England, then with another power—"to lift the American people out of their materialism" and awaken their heroic spirit. In response to the assertions that the nation needed a war to prevent effeminacy, Schurz replied, "The idea that the stalwart and hard-working American people, engaged in subduing to civilization an immense continent, need foreign wars to preserve their manhood from dropping into effeminacy . . . or that they must have bloodshed and devastation as an outdoor exercise in place of other sports—such an idea is as preposterous as it is disgraceful and abominable."[58] But even as he protested jingoist ideas, Schurz inadvertently showed their reach. His remark that continental expansion (which involved "subduing" Native Americans as well as the landscape) served as a remedy for effeminacy showed that, like the jingoes he condemned, Schurz regarded martial struggles as a means of fostering manhood. Schurz might disagree over the severity of the problem, but he did not completely reject the jingoist solution.

In addition to holding that war would develop a robust kind of character, jingoes argued that it would bring about a greater sense of fraternity. The conviction that war would deepen "social solidarity" is not surprising, given that veterans and political commentators often applauded the Civil War for having united American men through the shared experience of combat. (Incredibly, some commentators argued that the Civil War had united even northern and southern men. As one nostalgic minister maintained, it had "brought together in manly conflict the citizens of different sections of the country and left them with that mutual respect that brave men always feel for one another after a trial of strength and courage.") Sen. Marion Butler (Pop., N.C.) was one jingo who longed for fraternal unity. Butler asserted that congressmen, "irrespective of party," had rallied behind the president when he stood up to Britain during the Venezuela crisis. This extraordinary unity filled him with a sense of exultation: "When I saw Senators of all parties rise on this floor and echo and reecho the patriotic sentiments of the President in upholding the great doctrine of self-defense and independence laid down by our forefathers, I also began to hope that American pride, that American honor, American patriotism, and American independence were still in the ascendency."[59] Jingoes such as Butler assumed that if a mere war scare could lead to unity, then surely a real war would help deflect attention from social and political divisions.

As Butler's remarks suggest, jingoes wanted to develop a martial kind of manly character and fraternity not just for their own sake, but for the sake of American democracy. They believed that war would benefit the state by reinvigorating the nation's male citizens. One of the most prominent advocates of this line of thought was Theodore Roosevelt. Roosevelt praised military heroes as model citizens, every one of them equal to the greatest civilian statesmen. "The men of Bunker Hill and Trenton, Saratoga and Yorktown, the men of New Orleans and Mobile Bay, Gettysburg and Appomattox are those to whom we owe most," he wrote. "None of our heroes of peace, save a few great constructive statesmen, can rank with our heroes of war." In another essay, Roosevelt maintained that the nation was "incalculably richer" because of its memories of the Civil War. Rather than dwelling on the death and destruction of the war, he asserted that its character-forming battles had benefited the nation. The following year he reiterated this conviction: "I should welcome almost any war, for I think this country needs one." Roosevelt's martial ideals of citizenship led him to agree with his close friend Senator Lodge that a war might be beneficial to the nation. At the time of the Venezuela crisis he wrote to Lodge, "Personally I rather hope the fight will come soon. The clamor of the peace faction has convinced me that this country needs a war."[60]

That conciliatory policies would undermine American men and their government seemed as self-evident to jingoes as the corollary that spirited policies would strengthen them. As Senator Stewart of Nevada hotly asserted in the Venezuela debate, "There can be nothing more injurious to the American people than to submit to the arrogance of Great Britain. It breeds toadyism; it breeds dependence; it destroys American manhood." Almost as pressing as their fears about manhood itself were their fears that American men would be perceived as unmanly. According to jingoes, some things were worse than war, including, as Rep. James B. Clark (D, Mo.) put it, "to play the cry-baby act until we are despised of all nations and kindreds and tongues." Jingoes regarded war as preferable to dishonor because they saw dishonor as a precursor to national decay. Rep. Joseph Wheeler (D, Ala.) made this clear in a statement on the nation's Cuban policy: "Unless the world believes we are ready and willing, able and determined, to sustain our convictions, our policies, and our principles by force and by the sword," he said, "we must lose the prestige we have so long enjoyed and drop from the high place of the first nation on the earth."[61] What made jingoes' claims so urgent was the nagging fear that the nation had already started to decline because American men were losing sight of the honorable character so crucial to national well-being.

Distress over the perceived debasement of American manhood and American government accounts in part for what the late-nineteenth-century political commentator Robert O. Law described as the desire for "war with anybody anywhere." This sanguinary state of mind had important policy implications. It underlay the naval buildup of the 1880s, the outbreak of jingoism over a quarrel with Chile in 1891–92, the demands during the Venezuelan crisis that the United States be, as the *New York Tribune* put it, "more manfully and honorably represented in foreign relations," and, to return to our starting point, the jingoist opposition to the international arbitration treaty.[62]

To be sure, not all arbitration treaty opponents were jingoes. Yet even those who cited specific points of policy to explain their opposition to the treaty seemed to have additional motives that led them to regard militant policies with enthusiasm. This receptivity to aggressive policies can be seen in a *Chicago Tribune* editorial that presented the possibility of an armed conflict with Britain as a great opportunity for the United States—the nation it thought sure to triumph—to prove its might to the world. "Pow-wows and palavering are not the way to settle disputes with England," it said. "The only way is for us to be in a position to hit back. Then we can settle disputes, we can talk as we please, we shall not have to ask any odds, we can demand our rights and insist upon them because we shall be prepared to insist." The editorial curtly dismissed the obstacle to this demonstration of U.S. prowess, the arbitration treaty, saying that it was "unmanly to potter over it longer." Opponents of the treaty gathered in New York City for a meeting were even blunter. "Hurrah for War!" they cried.[63]

Historians have attributed the treaty's failure to Anglophobia, to a commitment to an independent foreign policy, and to the desire to protect senatorial prerogatives. But these only partly explain the treaty's failure. The full explanation is rooted in late-nineteenth-century U.S. political culture. Numerous arbitration opponents saw international arbitration as an effort to strip foreign affairs of its manly character. It threatened to bring women who were openly critical of men's style of governing into foreign policy discussions. Women who spoke out on foreign policy crossed the boundary that stipulated that if women had no role in politics, they certainly had no role in diplomatic or military matters. It was one thing for women to agitate for better schools and something else entirely for them to question the assumptions about male honor and force that guided international relations. Furthermore, the arbitration issue undercut the manly ideal of politics because civic-minded women used it to press for a greater political role. Most notably, women's suffragists argued that if the nation really wanted to adopt arbitration, it would have to give women a greater political voice. Those who were confident that the treaty would pass argued that *because* the world was entering a more peaceable age, women's political participation was more appropriate than before. And finally, the arbitration movement threatened the manly ideal of politics because of its supporters' stated objective to do just that. Arbitration supporters argued that peace would be possible only if the assumptions that traditionally had undergirded male politics were discarded.[64]

When the arbitration treaty came to symbolize the erosion of the manly ideal of politics, jingoist senators joined with Anglophobes and other treaty opponents to protest what they believed the treaty represented—the feminization of American politics. To preserve the role of honor as a guide to international affairs, senators amended the treaty so that questions affecting the nation's honor were exempt from its provisions. The amended treaty would not have tied the nation's hands. Even those in favor of the treaty admitted that the nation could abrogate it whenever such action appeared to be in the national interest, for the treaty provided no enforcement mechanisms other than a sense of moral obligation. "The glorious privilege of fighting still exists, treaty or no treaty," wrote one of its proponents.[65]

Yet senators did not stop after gutting the treaty. They proceeded to reject it by a three-vote margin. The treaty failed to pass less because of its specific policy implications (it was, in its final form, an innocuous document) than because of the shift in U.S. political culture that it symbolized. As the *Review of Reviews* noted, most senators "regarded much of the talk in favor of it as mere gush."[66] Senators who felt that manly standards of honor should guide the nation used their votes on the arbitration issue to show that sentimental gush had no place in electoral politics.

Yet even the defeat of the arbitration treaty did not stop the jingoist surge in the United States. The currents in U.S. political culture that helped sink the arbitration treaty continued to swell the jingoist tide. The deeply felt concerns about male character and electoral politics that underlay the opposition to the arbitration treaty also gave rise to the amorphous desire for war that surfaced in foreign policy debates in the 1890s. The arbitration debate (like the Venezuela crisis) provided an opportunity for jingoes to articulate their ideas, but it was the Cuban issue that eventually formed the inchoate jingoist spirit into a powerful battle cry.

2

....

Cuba and the Restoration of American Chivalry

AFTER LAUNCHING their war for independence from Spain in 1895, Cuban revolutionaries won widespread support in the United States. Men and women from across the country wished the Cubans well. Sympathizers contributed funds, prayed for Cuban liberty, and took to the streets in pro-Cuban demonstrations. A meeting of two thousand supporters in New York City shows the passion the Cuban cause elicited: while the men stood on their seats cheering the patriots, the women, clad in evening dresses, jumped up and down waving their handkerchiefs and fans. Realizing the popularity of the Cuban cause, Republicans and Democrats included planks supporting Cuba's freedom in their platforms in 1896.[1]

Although many Cuban sympathizers thought the United States should offer only moral and material support, jingoist sympathizers pressed for U.S. intervention in the Spanish-Cuban War. Waving constituent petitions, jingoist congressmen introduced resolutions in favor of recognizing Cuban belligerency and independence (steps that, by enabling the United States to sell arms to the insurgents, seemed likely to embroil the United States in the conflict). In towns across the country, jingoes organized military companies and pledged to fight in case of war against Spain.[2] For three years before the battleship *Maine* sank in Havana harbor, jingoes took advantage of the widespread sympathy for the Cubans to promulgate their martial ideas. By the time of the *Maine* disaster, they had created a large following receptive to their claims that war was a reasonable, if not a desirable, course of action against Spain. Because jingoes gained greater political visibility and widened their appeal by grafting their bellicose ambitions onto the Cuban cause, to understand how they spread their martial vision, it is first necessary to understand the nature of the Cubans' appeal and the jingoes' ability to manipulate it for their own purposes.

Why did *Cuba libre* strike such a powerful chord in the United States? The leading explanation offered by historians is that humanitarian sentiments and democratic principles of self-government underlay the broad backing commanded by the Cubans. This explanation clarifies why Americans sided with the Cuban revolutionaries over their Spanish opponents, but it does not account for the depth of Americans' commitment to the Cubans, for destitute and disfranchised residents of the United States failed to provoke a comparable outpouring of support. As one prolabor essayist noted, "The poor in the tenement houses of our cities are in worse extremes than the down-trampled population of Cuba, but what patriot suggests war to free them?"[3]

The sympathy extended to the Cubans seems particularly incongruous when race is added to the picture. In the late nineteenth century, white Americans frequently invoked racial beliefs to justify denying self-government to people of color. Why, then, were so many white Americans distraught over the Cubans' political status? Sen. Orville H. Platt (R, Conn.) drew attention to this incongruity when he pointed out that men who did not seem outraged at the news of a recent lynching in Texas (in which a man was covered with kerosene and burned to death on a public platform in the presence of seven thousand cheering witnesses) were now "shedding tears over the sad fate of Maceo [a mixed-race Cuban general]." Although there was some debate over the whiteness of the Cuban revolutionaries, it was quite clear that whatever they were, "Anglo-Saxons" they were not. Taken as a whole, the Cuban revolutionaries undoubtedly had more African blood than their Spanish rulers. Given the racial prejudices, poverty, and political injustice tolerated within the United States, it appears that something more than humanitarian sympathy and democratic principles lay behind the outpouring of support for the Cubans.[4]

The key to the Cubans' appeal can be found in the numerous press accounts that treated them and their cause sympathetically: many of these portrayed the Cuban revolutionaries in chivalric terms. Michael Hunt and Amy Kaplan have considered one aspect of this in their respective studies of U.S. foreign policy and romance novels. Both find that nineteenth-century Americans often viewed Cuba metaphorically, as a maiden longing to be rescued by a gallant knight. Strange though it may seem, this interpretation fit into a larger chivalric understanding of Cuban affairs, for favorable accounts also characterized the Cuban revolution as a heroic crusade that merited the fraternal assistance of American men. In their effort to cast the Cuban revolution in chivalrous terms, sympathizers did not stop at presenting it metaphorically

—they also portrayed real Cuban men and women as if they were the protagonists of one of the adventure-filled romance novels that were so popular at the time. The tendency to depict Cuban revolutionaries as if they were the heroes and heroines of a chivalric drama helps explain why so many white Americans were well-disposed toward the mixed-race Cubans. To many Americans, chivalric standards represented the highest ideals of manhood and womanhood. Hence, the Cubans' positive gender images deflected attention from negative racial stereotypes.[5]

If it seems odd that Americans strongly sympathized with the Cubans, it seems especially odd that they insisted on viewing a national liberation movement in chivalric terms. They did so because of domestic concerns: sympathizers looked to the Cubans as models of gallantry because they feared that chivalric standards were endangered within the United States. Many of those who fretted about a decline in chivalry regarded the assertive New Woman as evidence of that decline, for at the heart of chivalry was the juxtaposition of feminine vulnerability and masculine power. An essay in *Popular Science Monthly* illustrates this conviction: "We know that the tenderness, affection, and sympathy which are the essential grace and charm of womanhood, as well as the courage, disinterestedness, and chivalric sentiment which form the nobility of manhood, have sprung from that very relation of strong to weak, protector and protected, which have for ages subsisted among all the civilized races." In the chivalric paradigm, women were the protected, men the protectors. Women were, in the words of the antisuffragist Helen Kendrick Johnson, "the inspiring force," men, "the organizing and physical power."[6] Because the chivalric paradigm enshrined men's monopoly on political power, women who pushed for a greater public role seemed to pose a fundamental challenge to the standard.

When reminded that they were violating the tenets of chivalry, activist American women responded in two ways. Women involved in purity (meaning antiprostitution) campaigns and other social reforms justified their activism by saying that men were unable or unwilling to fulfill their chivalric responsibilities. Apparently regretting the decline in chivalry, they presented their work as an effort to compensate for its demise. But some suffragists cast a more critical eye on the standard. Realizing that knightly ideals served to justify women's exclusion from political life, they wished chivalry good riddance. Women's abdication of power in exchange for protection was an arrangement that benefited men, they contended, and the sooner chivalry died, the better. The suffragists who rejected chivalry altogether declared that modern women considered "the language of mediaeval romance" obsolete. They preferred justice to the privileges conferred by chivalry and were too busy participating in public affairs to spend their time "leaning from their casements, waving adieux to plumed knights."[7]

Because American women seemed ever less inclined to assume the role of an appreciative audience for male exploits, aspiring American knights and women who preferred pedestals to politics turned to Cuban women as models of femininity. In contrast to activist American women, Cuban women often appeared to be ideal romantic heroines. Americans found evidence for this view in narratives that described Cuban women as natural "home-bodies" and "chaste spouses and slaves to duty." Those who fretted about assertive New Women were captivated by reports that Cuban women, "the most feminine and simple women in the world," spent their time worshiping their husbands rather than meddling in men's affairs. As the *New York Tribune* reported, "The 'New Woman' is altogether unknown in Havana. There is not even a woman's club there. In fact, in this regard the city is actually mediaeval."[8] Their images as acquiescent, traditional women made Cuban women seem to be perfect feminine foils for assertive American women.

In addition to appearing well worth defending, Cuban women appeared eager for rescue. Realizing that stories of suffering women struck powerful emotional chords, Cuban sympathizers highlighted Cuban women's vulnerability. Innumerable stories of Spanish atrocities against Cuban women suggested that beleaguered Cuban women would appreciate male protectors. At times Cuban women themselves reinforced this message. One sent a letter to Sen. Joseph B. Foraker (R, Ohio) in which, purporting to speak on behalf of "all the women of Cuba," she beseeched Foraker to "help our people who kneel with their hands out to you." Her effort to prompt a chivalrous response concluded with the line, "Noble Senator I kiss your hands."[9]

Although some sensational tales of the Cuban revolution described Cuban Amazons who fought alongside men, the chroniclers of the Amazons were careful to note that it was only the exigencies of war that turned Cuban women into fighters: ordinarily they were extremely feminine. The author Nathan Green effusively described Cuban women's fury in battle but then depicted the women as pitiful wrecks as soon as the fighting was over. "While the fighting lasts they show no emotion," he wrote, "but when the last shot is fired, I have seen women throw themselves on the ground and give way to a delirium of grief." Rather than fighting because of an aggressive or heroic spirit, the Cuban women in these narratives joined the insurgent forces for safety after their male relatives had enlisted or been killed. As the correspondent Murat Halstead wrote, "It shows the state of the Island that the women find the Army the safest place for them." Halstead buttressed his theory that the Amazons had joined the army for protection by claiming that "Cuban ladies are not advanced in the modern woman sense."[10] Accounts of Cuban Amazons implied that the exigencies of war had forced Cuban women into unwelcome roles and that the sooner the fighting in Cuba ended, the sooner

Cuban women would return to their homes, where they happily would remain.

If the first reason for the chivalric paradigm's powerful appeal was apprehension about the assertive New Woman, the second had to do with American men. Those who bemoaned the decline in chivalry often held American men partially accountable, their logic being that if men had upheld their side of the chivalric pact, then women would not be so eager to enter public life. According to this line of thought, the seeming decline in gallantry reflected a deterioration in manly character. Rep. John S. Williams (D, Miss.) drew attention to men's failings when he exclaimed, "In this latter end of the nineteenth century, men seem to think not only that 'the age of chivalry has gone,' but that this magnificent piece of humanity that God has created and which we call man . . . is nothing but a miserable money-making machine. . . . Poetry goes out from him; imagination ceases to exist with him. Chivalry is dead; manhood itself is sapped."[11] Just as those who regarded American women as unfeminine busybodies turned to Cuban women as foils, those who regarded American men as money-making machines turned to Cuban men as foils. In contrast to American men, who seemed to be losing sight of knightly values in their single-minded pursuit of riches, Cuban men appeared to exemplify chivalric character.

To men frustrated by the standardized routines of an ever more industrialized society, Cuban men represented adventure and male display. To those disturbed by the prospect of degeneracy in a world of civilized comforts, Cuban men stood for a hardier manhood. And, perhaps most important, to those concerned about the civic virtue that American democracy was thought to rest upon, Cuban men seemed ideal citizens: fraternal-minded men willing to sacrifice themselves for a noble cause. Recognizing the appeal of such chivalric attributes as respect for women, martial prowess, and honorable objectives, sympathetic authors did their best to make the revolutionaries' story appear, as one article put it, "more like the wonders of a romance than like the authentic annals of our time."[12]

Like true knights, the Cuban men depicted in favorable American publications often drew their inspiration from women. One popular history of the Cuban cause told of a revolutionary leader who kept some mementos from his mother in his wallet. Whenever he needed encouragement, he turned to these talismans of feminine virtue. Other sympathizers suggested that, in keeping with their respect for women's influence, Cuban men treated women honorably, that they offered due regard "for the sacred persons of women and children." In stark contrast to the Spanish soldiers, who, according to pro-Cuban dispatches assaulted virtually every woman they encountered, Cuban men supposedly offered protection to women, regardless of which side they were on. Even in the heat of action, they gallantly assured panicked women that they would not be harmed.[13] Their willingness to admire and protect women seemed to explain Cuban women's reluctance to meddle in public affairs: because Cuban men shouldered the role of gallant protectors, Cuban women had no need to enter public life.

Cuban men's reported courage served as further testimony to their chivalric character. Those who regarded American men's lives as sadly devoid of heroism were captivated by accounts that depicted Cuban men as fearless. The popular author Richard Harding Davis made this point in his description of a captured patriot known simply as Rodriguez. As the condemned Cuban took his place before a firing squad, Davis was thrilled to see that "he held a cigarette between his lips, not arrogantly nor with bravado, but with the nonchalance of a man who meets his punishment fearlessly, and who will let his enemies see that they can kill but can not frighten him." No doubt inspired by such accounts, one sympathizer wrote a ditty titled "The Insurgent," which proclaimed, "Match him, ye proud Castilian, if ye can. / This man is every inch a man."[14]

Strangely, given the racial convictions of the time, white Americans did not limit their admiration to white soldiers. Rep. John S. Little (D, Ark.) called the mulatto general Gómez "a man whose patriotism and courage rank high among the patriots and soldiers of any age," and Sen. William E. Mason (R, Ill.) applauded Gómez, "brave man that he is," for "fearing neither death nor the Spaniard." The *New York Sun* described the revolutionary commander at Guantánamo as "black as a coal, with the stature and muscles of a Hercules. He is afraid of nothing, a man of nerve." In the South, the *Atlanta Constitution* weighed in with an article calling the mulatto general Antonio Maceo one of the world's greatest warriors. Despite Maceo's African and Weyler's German ancestry (though born in Spain, Weyler was of Prussian descent), it called Maceo "infinitely a greater man" than the "contemptible Weyler."[15]

One might think that chivalrous knights, however manly, would be better suited to feudal regimes than to democratic states, but the late-nineteenth-century Americans who regarded Cuban men as knights thought that their chivalric attributes testified to their qualities as citizens. As chivalric knights, patriotic Cuban men appeared to embody heroism, honor, and a commitment to noble ideals, the same qualities that had won Civil War veterans recognition as the pillars of American democracy. The admiration for Cuban men's standing as citizens can be seen in a resolution passed by an assembly of Cuban supporters in Bloomington, Indiana: "We rejoice in the lofty heroism that is being displayed in Cuba every day, and which covers the patriots with a banner of glory. Their undaunted perseverance and daring courage challenge the admiration of a watching world and prove their right to self-government."

Those who believed that American men were so consumed with profit-making that they had lost a sense of common purpose with their fellows found a welcome counterexample in Cuban men. Favorable reports suggested that instead of putting their own interests first, Cuban men exhibited a deep sense of fraternalism, as evidenced in rich and poor men's willingness to rough it together in the field. Sympathizers saw their noble objectives and fraternal unity as a reminder that, as the *New York Sun* put it, "even in a . . . material age there are spirits that can give all for their principles without thinking of any selfish return for themselves." Cuban men's bravery and fraternalism seemed particularly indicative of their capacity as citizens because it was exhibited in the service of a noble cause—the defense of manly honor. Said an article in the *Chautauquan*, "Above all, we see in the Cubans men struggling for the rights of men—for the right to be men, the right to be free, the right to govern themselves."[16]

According to the conventions of chivalric novels, only a fiend would deny such heroic men that which they so valiantly struggled to attain. Cuban sympathizers did not disappoint these expectations in their descriptions of the Spaniards. Their critical assessments of the "proud Castilians" led numerous American readers to conclude that Spanish men, once known for their chivalry, had degenerated since the days of Don Quixote. The author Stephen Bonsal contributed to the Spaniards' degenerate image in his book *The Real Condition of Cuba To-Day* (1897). "It is not alone in prowess or in success that Spanish arms have fallen since the days they fought the Moors," wrote Bonsal. ". . . The decay has been even more strongly marked in the decadence of their chivalry." The most glaring evidence of Spanish men's decadent chivalry was the atrocities they committed against helpless civilians. American publications commonly presented the Spanish-Cuban War as a war waged against noncombatants, primarily women and children. As Davis said in reference to the Spanish policy of reconcentration, "In other wars men have fought with men, and women have suffered indirectly because the men were killed, but in this war it is the women, herded together in towns like cattle, who are going to die, while the men, camped in the fields and mountains, will live."[17]

If the shocking stories of starved and butchered civilians that frequently appeared in pro-Cuban newspapers left any doubts about the Spaniards' chivalry, stories that depicted the Spanish soldiers as sexual predators worked to put these doubts to rest. One chronicle said that during General Valeriano Weyler's command (Weyler was in charge of the Spanish forces in Cuba from 1896 to 1897), "women dared not leave their homes. In many cases they were dragged out by the Spanish and by the drunken rabble of the town, who had license given to them at the same time that protection was withdrawn from the homes." Similarly, the author James Hyde Clark maintained that licentious

Spanish soldiers violated and then killed "scores of young women," and Green contended that Weyler used his women prisoners in orgies, forced women to dance naked before his troops, and raped daughters in front of their parents. Accounts of bestial Spanish rapists paralleled the contemporary image, assiduously promoted by white supremacists, of dark-skinned rapists. But gender and racial stereotypes were at odds with each other in these stories from Cuba, for it was the white, Germanic Weyler and his Spanish associates who apparently brutalized women and the mixed-race Cuban men who respected them.[18]

Although many stories of Spanish assaults were so lurid they strained credulity, pro-Cuban congressmen lent credence to stories of Spanish sexual misconduct (as they did to other stories of Spanish misdeeds) by repeating them in political debate. Sen. William V. Allen (Pop., Neb.) told his colleagues that the Spanish military was "gathering up the little girls in that island and selling them into a species of slavery, the worst conceivable in the human mind, selling them to lives of shame." Rep. Alexander Hardy (R, Ind.) painted an equally sensational picture: "The Spanish soldiery at home and abroad have never hesitated to snatch the sucking babe from its mother's breast, dash its brains out, and then outrage the shrieking mother," he said in a congressional speech. Stories of Spanish rapes were so common that Cuban sympathizers came to expect such behavior. In a hearing on Cuba, Sen. Cushman K. Davis (R, Minn.) questioned, "How do [Spanish] soldiers treat women when they catch them?" The newspaper correspondent Frederick W. Lawrence answered, "Oh, insult them." Davis responded, "Do you mean by insult them they ravish them; do you know anything of that kind?" "Yes, sir," answered Lawrence.[19]

Whereas some pro-Cuban accounts depicted Spanish soldiers as bestial, others portrayed them as childlike or feminine. Instead of exemplifying the martial capacity expected of chivalrous men, the Spanish soldiers in these tales appeared weak and cowardly. Like the stereotypically savage Spaniards, the seemingly childlike and feminine Spaniards seemed to exemplify perverted gender roles. Bonsal drew this distinction between manly Cubans and unmanly Spaniards when he contrasted the Cuban general Gómez, "a man born to command," with the "half grown and immature boys, the raw recruits which Spain has sent to the island." Likewise, an article in the *Arena* portrayed the Spanish army as childish. "I have seen a whole company crying like children because one of their number had received a letter from home, and the rest were homesick," noted the author. The Spaniards' supposed lack of self-control made them appear feminine as well as youthful. Richard Harding Davis evoked both of these attributes in a description of Spanish soldiers who "giggled" at the clumsiness of one of their fellows. Whether childish or feminine, the giggling Spanish soldiers stood in sharp contrast to the martyred Rodriguez, whom Davis had described in the preceding passage.[20]

Accounts depicting Spanish soldiers as more devious than courageous provided further evidence of their lack of chivalrous character. Pro-Cuban publications accused Spanish soldiers of winning skirmishes through trickery, not bravery. They expressed outrage at the news that the Spaniards had tried to buy off insurgent leaders rather than fight them. Perhaps the most convincing evidence of Spanish cowardice was the contention that they "dare to make war only on women." Representative Hardy voiced the widespread contempt for Spanish military prowess when he said that General Weyler had "never fought a battle in honorable warfare."[21] Pro-Cuban news items insinuated that the Spaniards' lack of honor on the battlefield reflected Spain's fundamentally dishonorable objectives—to subjugate and exploit a noble people.

The favorable descriptions of Cuban men and women and unfavorable descriptions of Spanish soldiers led a number of Americans to empathize with the Cubans as if they were the heroes and heroines of a romance novel. Those who had read the adventure stories serialized in popular periodicals or published in book form had a rich imaginative context within which to position the Cubans. Sympathizers from different walks of life hoped for a Cuban victory because the Cubans' apparently noble personal characteristics indicated the worthiness of their cause. Furthermore, numerous supporters believed that a Cuban victory would represent the triumph of chivalric values, for they saw the Cuban revolution allegorically—as a struggle to restore a chivalric gender order to the island.

Building on the many stories of victimized Cuban women, writers who endorsed the Cuban cause characterized the colonial relation between Spain and Cuba as one of lustful bondage. These accounts portrayed the entire island as a pure woman who was being assaulted by Spain. One such narrative described Cuba as "a country that Spain has never loved, but has always wished to hold in bondage for lust and brutality."[22] A drama on the Cuban revolution (presented in Yiddish to enthusiastic audiences in the Bowery) based its plot on this allegory: it featured a dastardly Spanish villain who tried to force himself on an attractive Cuban maiden. The political cartoons that depicted Cuba as a ravished woman also promoted the idea of rape as a metaphor for the Spanish colonial endeavor (fig. 3). To add to the drama of the story, sympathizers played on Cuba's sobriquet, Queen of the Antilles, in their pleas on behalf of the revolution. "'Queen of the Antilles!' Beautiful Cuba! For ages she has writhed under the oppression of the haughty Castilian," exclaimed one pro-Cuban account.[23] Picturing the Spaniards as unchivalrous ravishers made their power seem immoral and illegitimate—a challenge to the principles of chivalry, which held that true women should be venerated and protected. It made the Spanish presence in Cuba appear to be an insult to the honor of Cuban women and the Cuban men charged with protecting them.

3. "Peace—But Quit That." *New York World*, in *Review of Reviews*, April 1898.
Courtesy of Harvard College Library.

In addition to insulting Cuban men through their women, the Spaniards
appeared to insult Cuban men directly by refusing to grant them the respect
that all honorable men merited. Rather than acknowledge that Cuban men
had shown themselves worthy of self-government, the Spaniards dishonored
them by keeping them in a politically submissive position. Spanish power appeared particularly egregious because instead of representing manly character, it appeared to be the inherited legacy of, as Rep. James M. Robinson (D,
Ind.) put it, an "effete and declining dynasty." To make the point that Spanish
power lacked manly character, political cartoons took advantage of the fact
that the king of Spain, Alfonso XIII, was still a boy and that his widowed
mother, María Cristina, was acting as queen regent. With the royal family in
mind, cartoonists depicted Spain as a spoiled mama's boy or as an aging mother
country that could no longer restrain her colonies (figs. 4, 5).[24]

4. **"Secretary Sherman Talks to the Boy-King."** *New York Tribune, Twinkles* supplement, May 15, 1897.

Although activist American women often claimed that female power was
inherently virtuous, the Cuban adherents who depicted Spain as an effete
aristocrat or overbearing mother suggested that feminine power was more
likely corrupt. Those who felt threatened by American women's encroachments into electoral politics turned to the Spanish occupation of Cuba to show
the dangers of feminization. If Spain seemed duplicitous, it was because she
was feminine, "as full of smirks and smiles, of courtesies and tricks, as a co-
quette of six seasons at least." Accounts that called Spain "the most effete of
European powers" and that traced Spanish policies to the "boudoirs of the
feminine leaders of the most dissolute society in Europe" implied that feminine influences rendered Spain incapable of good government.[25] Such statements denigrated Spanish power as an inversion of the chivalric order of male
power and female submission. They implied that backing the Cubans would

5. "She Is Getting Too Feeble to Hold Them." *Puck*, November 18, 1896.
Courtesy of Harvard College Library.

be equivalent to taking a stand in favor of men's political prerogatives. If, as the participants in a pro-Cuban meeting in Kansas City resolved, a free government "should be the heritage of all men," then helping the Cubans attain self-government meant helping men secure their manly rights. Rep. Charles W. Woodman (R, Ill.) underscored this idea when he said that recognizing the Cubans' independence would help Cuban men "defend themselves and their families and possessions like men."[26]

The Cuban sympathizers who portrayed the Cuban struggle as a struggle over chivalry tapped into Americans' anxieties about themselves. Whether Spain appeared to be a degenerate rapist or a manipulative mother country, it served as a warning of what could happen if chivalric standards continued to deteriorate in the United States. The Spanish case apparently showed that a land without chivalry would be a land of rapacious relations between men and women, a land in which a lack of manly character in government corrupted the nation's political system. The Cuban drama captured Americans' imaginations because the well-being of American chivalry seemed to be in question. A number of Americans rooted for the Cubans in order to express their commitment to chivalric principles.

This is not to say that the chivalric paradigm was the only way Americans read their concerns into the Cuban cause. Farmers and workers often conceptualized the Cubans' struggle as a battle against exploitative elites, and African Americans often saw it as a fight for racial justice. Some immigrants regarded it as analogous to the liberation movements in their homelands, some ex-Confederates depicted the Spaniards as exploitative carpetbaggers, and some northern reformers saw their struggles against political corruption reflected in the Cubans' struggles to free themselves from corrupt colonial rulers.[27] But behind these specific interpretations of the Cuban revolution lay a common predisposition to regard the Cubans favorably. This predisposition owed a great deal to the chivalric paradigm, which contributed to the Cubans' far-reaching appeal by providing a common framework that people from different walks of life could draw on to make sense of the Cuban revolution, even while leaving room for more nuanced interpretations.

That the chivalric paradigm left room for more nuanced understandings of the Cuban revolution can be seen in the different inflections put on *Cuba libre* by older and younger men. Many of the petitions to Congress that favored recognizing Cuban belligerency came from veterans' organizations. Petitioning veterans regarded the Cuban patriots as modern exemplars of their own virtues. (The tendency to regard Civil War veterans as valiant knights can be seen in eulogies that portrayed them as "a champion in the lists" and a "gallant knight of modern day.")[28] The veterans who feared that their chivalric deeds were being forgotten as the Civil War slipped further into the past regarded support for the Cuban patriots as an opportunity to honor their own legacy. Whereas grizzled veterans believed that siding with the Cubans meant honoring military heroes such as themselves, younger men expressed their sympathy for the Cubans in hopes of proving that they had not lost sight of their fathers' chivalric ideals. As one presumably younger man wrote to President Grover Cleveland, "Our sires were noble minded and high strung and what we have from them we come by honestly; if we are less noble than our sires it is rather from a lack of opportunity."[29] Spurred by mournful protestations that chivalry was departing along with the Civil War generation, younger men clamored for *Cuba libre* to deflect charges of degeneracy.

Although the seemingly chivalrous Cuban cause captured Americans' imaginations because of domestic concerns, the chivalric paradigm had powerful foreign policy implications. By casting the Cuban revolution in metaphorical terms, it helped Americans make the leap from sympathizing with individuals to opposing Spanish colonial power. By making Spanish power seem thoroughly corrupt, the paradigm suggested that humanitarian aid or limited political reforms were inadequate to settle the Cuban issue. It thus helped jingoes build their case for U.S. military intervention. This was no accident. The chivalric understanding of the Cuban revolution appealed to people who were

not jingoes, but jingoes embraced chivalric imagery and metaphors with singular enthusiasm. They turned to the chivalric paradigm to deepen Americans' interest in Cuban affairs and to propose a course of action for the United
States.

The chivalric paradigm appealed to jingoes for two major reasons. First,
it helped them propose an active role for the United States in the Cuban conflict: rescuer of helpless Cuban maidens or ally to embattled Cuban men. In
both cases, the romantic veneer made the unsavory prospect of war more
palatable. By coating their sanguinary ambitions with the cloak of chivalry, jingoes could pose as the defenders, rather than the destroyers, of high ideals.
The second reason the chivalric paradigm appealed to jingoes was because it
dovetailed with their goal of revitalizing the manly ideal of politics within the
United States. Jingoes believed that if American men embarked on a crusade
aimed at restoring chivalric values in Cuba, they would end up strengthening
chivalry at home. By posing as rescuing knights, American men could remind
women of men's political efficacy. By joining with their embattled fellows in a
heroic and noble struggle, they could develop fraternalism, honor, and martial
capacities in American men. With these objectives in mind, jingoes worked to
write the United States into the Cuban romance.

The first way that jingoes tried to incorporate the United States into the
Cuban romance was by arguing that truly chivalric men would not knowingly
countenance such gross insults to women as the Spaniards supposedly committed in Cuba. To generate a sense of responsibility for Cuban affairs, jingoes
claimed that the United States resembled a man who encountered a brute
pounding a helpless woman. Failure to intervene, they said, would be dishonorable and cowardly. A *New York World* editorial made this point in a hypo-
thetical scenario of a man (the United States) encountering a ruffian (Spain)
attempting to murder a woman (Cuba). It concluded that a "pusillanimous
cad" who sneered at such chivalric standards as "duty and honor and courage"
would run away but "a *man* would interfere." This and other accounts made it
clear that as long as women could be assaulted with impunity "under the
shadow of the American Republic," American pretenses to chivalry would be
empty.[30]

To further implicate the United States in the unfolding Cuban drama,
jingoes declared that the United States was more than a spectator—that it
had a role in the romance. After the *New York Journal* reported that the
Spaniards had strip-searched three Cuban women on an American vessel, jingoes called for recognition of Cuban belligerency, even for U.S. intervention,
to end such unchivalrous deeds. Rep. David A. De Armond (D, Mo.) was one
of the jingoes who pressed for a strong response. "Young ladies stripped and
searched on board an American vessel by Spaniards, bearded, booted, and

spurred!" he exclaimed in his plea for action. What made the strip-searches particularly offensive was not so much their effects on Cuban women—after all, the press reported more horrifying stories of rape and murder—but that they occurred on American ships. Jingoes presented them as insults to American men's ability to protect the honor of women. Senator Allen made this clear when, after describing the strip-search, he said he found it "absolutely humiliating" that the Spanish could commit such atrocities while American leaders "sit idly and supinely here." Richard Harding Davis, the writer who broke the story, agreed. Even after admitting that a female detective, not male soldiers, had stripped the young women, he continued to regard it as a grave affront to American honor. The true issue, he said, was that the demonstration of Spanish power on the American ship undercut the dignity of the United States. Davis was so ashamed by the incident that he cited it as grounds for intervention in the Spanish-Cuban War.[31]

As they voiced their outrage over the nation's reluctance to protect victimized Cuban women, jingoes were mindful of the sympathy shown by a number of American women for the beleaguered Cubans and particularly for Cuban women. The same interest in women's well-being that led thousands of American women to join temperance and purity crusades in the 1880s and 1890s contributed to American women's empathy for their Cuban "sisters." Women who sympathized with the Cubans made their sentiments known in a variety of ways, starting with letters to political leaders. A *Christian Herald* leaflet that implored mothers to "think of the wretchedness of these poor, heart-broken mothers of Cuba" motivated one woman to write her senator to urge him to do something to end the suffering on the island.[32] Women also indicated their views from the galleries of Congress. Perhaps most noticeable were the members of the Daughters of the American Revolution (DAR), who applauded congressmen who made assertive speeches on Cuba. Some of the women who sympathized with the Cubans were in political leaders' own households. A handful of prominent political wives in the nation's capital made their sympathies clear by establishing the National Relief Fund in Aid of Cuba. Other political wives expressed their positive feelings for the Cubans more discreetly in Washington social functions.[33]

Women who sympathized with the Cubans did not hesitate to question congressmen's chivalric character when the atrocities in Cuba dragged on. They called the government's policy cowardly and they questioned the honor of American leaders. As an article in the *American Home Magazine,* a Chicago periodical edited by Marie Madison and aimed at women, said, "Shame, shame that [President Cleveland] has allowed the wholesale butchery of women and children at his very door."[34] Such criticisms aggravated jingoes' suspicions that women no longer trusted men with the sole responsibility to govern. Jingoes

believed that men could not afford to be seen as shirking their protective responsibilities lest they give women greater cause to protest men's hold on political power. They feared that if American men tolerated Spanish atrocities
against Cuban women (especially on board their own vessels), the American
women who sympathized with the Cubans might conclude that chivalry was
dead, that men no longer offered protection in return for their power, and
therefore that men's exclusive claims to power were illegitimate.

Senator Mason played on this fear when he drew attention to the presence of "our wives and our children" in the galleries before making a plea for
helping Cuba. In effect, he warned his colleagues not to lose the esteem of the
watching women, for without that esteem they would lose the privileged position they enjoyed in political life. This rationale apparently proved convincing
to other members of Congress. Rep. Alston G. Dayton (R, W.V.) explained his
prowar stance by saying he wanted to be able to look his wife and boy in the
eye without feeling ashamed. "I do not want them to think that I can stand by
and see other wives and children starved and strangled without a word of
protest," he said.[35] Dayton invoked his wife and child to demonstrate that the
honor of American men was on the line.

Jingoes reasoned that if failing to act on behalf of Cuban women and children could cost American men the respect of women, then assuming the role
of rescuer could win them women's esteem. The well-publicized Cisneros
case conveyed this point. Evangelina Cosio y Cisneros came from a prominent
Cuban family. After the Spanish imprisoned Cisneros, suspecting her of aiding the Cuban revolutionaries, the jingoist New York Journal ran a slew of stories describing how she had been incarcerated for trying to protect herself
from the assault of a lustful Spanish officer. It reported that the virtuous
young woman had been put into a cell full of prostitutes. In lurid and somewhat conjectural articles, it announced that she was to be sentenced to the
Spanish penal colony in Ceuta, Morocco. The Journal noted that "no woman
prisoner has ever been sent to this African hell," populated by the murderers,
robbers, and "ravishers" of Spain. Her banishment, it said, meant "dishonor
first and death within a year." More respectable papers, including even the
WCTU's Union Signal, repeated the Journal's sensational stories, thus broaden-
ing their reach.[36]

In relating the young maiden's tribulations, the Journal encouraged
Americans to view Cisneros as a representative of all outraged Cuban women.
It maintained that all true women and men should feel for her in her plight.
As one article said (in an effort to discredit the manhood of the Spanish general Weyler at the same time it prompted Americans to support the Cuban
cause), "The only minds [the Cisneros story] does not revolt belong to creatures that are neither men nor women but Weylers."[37] Cisneros's story appar-

ently struck a chord among readers, for the issues of the *Journal* that high-lighted her travails sold exceptionally well. One reason her story proved so compelling was that the *Journal* wrote it as a romance. The newspaper's atti-tude can be seen in the introduction to its book-length history of the episode:

> In its setting and background, in its *dramatis personae,* in its dash, intrigue, and cumulative interest, it is almost ideally perfect. The desirable component elements are all present. A tropic island, embosomed in azure seas off the coast of the Spanish Main; a cruel war, waged by the minions of despotism against the spirit of patriotism and liberty; a beautiful maiden, risking all for her country, captured, insulted, persecuted, and cast into a loathsome dun-geon. None could be more innocent, constant and adorable than she; none more wicked, detestable and craven than her enemies. All is right and lovable on the one side, all ugly and hateful on the other. As in the old Romances, there is no uncertainty as to which way our sympathies should turn.[38]

Recognizing Cisneros's popularity in the United States, William Ran-dolph Hearst, the brash young editor of the *Journal,* resolved to free her. First, he mobilized American women in a letter-writing campaign. He sent copies of a petition to more than two hundred correspondents in towns across the nation with instructions to hire a carriage, secure the signatures of promi-nent women, and telegraph them to New York as soon as possible. Within twenty-four hours, thousands of telegrams poured into the *Journal* office. Ac-cording to the *Journal's* figures, fifteen thousand women, including prominent political wives and President McKinley's mother, signed a petition asking for Cisneros's release. Goaded by Hearst, well-known women also wrote letters on her behalf. Varina Davis, the widow of Jefferson Davis, appealed the Cis-neros case to the queen regent of Spain; Julia Ward Howe, the author of the "Battle Hymn of the Republic," wrote an impassioned letter to the pope: "How can we think of this pure flower of maidenhood condemned to live with felons and outcasts, without succor, without protection, to labor under a torrid sky, suffering privation, indignity and torment worse than death? Public opin-ion, it is said, cannot avail against this act of military vengeance—vengeance to be wreaked upon an innocent victim. To what and to whom, then, shall we appeal? To the sense of justice of the civilized world; to all good men and true women; to every parent to whom a child's honor is dear; to every brother who would defend a sister from outrage." Women's organizations, including the Woman's National Relief Association for Cuba (an organization that raised money for the Red Cross activities on the island) joined in the outcry by ca-bling the queen regent and begging Fitzhugh Lee, the American consul gen-eral in Havana, to exert every effort to save Cisneros.[39]

The *Journal* presented the appeals that it had solicited from the women of the United States as an implicit criticism of men's conduct of foreign affairs. Even as it celebrated American women's willingness to defend a persecuted sister, it implied that American women had to press for Cisneros's release because American men had failed to end the atrocities in Cuba. This critique of American men's chivalry can be seen in the remarks of Mrs. J. Duer, the general superintendent of the Christian Rescue Temperance Union in Brooklyn. The *Journal* quoted her as saying, "I rejoice to see the women of America coming forward to the rescue of the gentle Cuban girl. For once in my life I wish the reins of government were in the hands of noble women like Julia Ward Howe and others who are fearlessly doing their duty at this time, while Government officials are sitting with folded hands."[40] Duer's effusive praise for American women only made men's inaction on the Cuban issue more glaring.

Although the letter-writing campaign mortified chivalric-minded American men, all was not lost. As long as Cisneros continued to languish in prison, they still had a chance to redeem themselves. Hearst arranged for them to do so. After the letter-writing campaign failed to secure Cisneros's freedom, Hearst assigned one of his reporters, Karl Decker, the role of knight-errant. Decker bribed the prison guards to let her escape and then fabricated an elaborate rescue plan to exonerate the guards and furnish newspaper material. Fearful that the Spaniards would release Cisneros voluntarily, thereby ruining his chance to free her, Decker acted hastily. He rented the house next door to the prison, bridged the chasm between the two buildings with a plank, sawed through the prison bars, and, as the guards looked the other way, spirited Cisneros to liberty.[41]

According to the *Journal's* version of the rescue, Decker was plagued by one great anxiety as he embarked on his perilous quest: what if Cisneros turned out to be less beautiful than had been alleged? What if she failed to "come up to the fairy-tale standard," to play the traditional female role? Fortunately, the *Journal* concluded, these fears were ill-founded. After seeing Cisneros, Decker joyfully concluded, "No fairy princess could be more lovely than this fairy-like little Cuban maiden." Cisneros appeared to be a model woman: beautiful, charming, and compliant. Decker's backers at the *Journal* also were pleased to learn that she was appreciative. In its coverage of Cisneros's arrival in the United States, the *Journal* unblushingly reported her praise for her rescuers.[42]

As it idealized Cisneros as a model woman, the *Journal* held up Decker as a model man. "You might pass him in the street without noticing that he was anything more than tall and good-looking; but a man must be a great deal besides that before he can perform such a feat as that which stands to Karl Decker's credit. He must be a man from every point of view," gushed the *Journal's* book-length account of the rescue.[43] To support its enthusiastic praise for

Decker's great accomplishment, the *Journal* printed letters by appreciative women who applauded Decker as a model of chivalry. One such letter said that the episode reminded the writer "of the chivalry of the knights of old, who rescued fair damsels in distress"; another said that the rescue had shown "that even in this time of lust for gold men are still good and brave, that their hearts are still human and healthy, and the fires of chivalry still burn with undiminished flame."[44] The *Journal* depicted Decker as the American every-man turned chivalric hero. It used his example to show that the masses of American men were not as dishonorable as they appeared, that they were fundamentally manly and needed only an appropriate cause to demonstrate their latent gallantry.

The *Journal's* coverage of the Cisneros case made it clear that Cuba was the cause that American men had been waiting for. After Cisneros arrived in New York, the newspaper questioned, "We have freed one Cuban girl—when shall we free Cuba?"[45] Whereas other allegorical interpretations of Cuba as a suffering maiden merely hinted at the implications of intervening in the Cuban romance, the Cisneros case spelled these out. Above all, it presented U.S. intervention in Cuba as an opportunity to promote chivalric relations between men and women in the United States. By protesting Spanish atrocities against women and children, American men could refute American women's charges that men were immoral, abusive, and self-interested. By a noble demonstration of self-sacrifice, they could prove that American men embodied the civic virtue that American women had been claiming. Instead of being the objects of reform movements, such as temperance and purity, they could be the heroic uplifters. Indeed, they could prove that women's virtue was contingent on male power. By posing as rescuers of distressed Cuban women, American men could, like Decker, show that men's bold action was more efficacious than women's moralistic pleading. This message had implications both for U.S. foreign relations and for American politics. In the first case, it suggested that military action would be more effective than diplomacy in settling the Cuban issue. In the second, it suggested that American men deserved to wield political power because they got results.

By appealing to American men to take a stance in favor of chivalric principles, jingoes couched the Cuban issue as one for men to resolve. The emphasis they placed on brotherhood and male honor helped to keep women on the sidelines of the Cuban debate. The chivalric paradigm implied that American women should plead on behalf of their Cuban sisters but that they should not lead rescuing crusades, much less fraternal expeditions. These, it implied, were men's responsibility. Indeed, according to the paradigm, the Cuban issue was nothing less than a test of American manhood. If American men were truly chivalrous, they should enter the lists.

Significantly, when jingoes held up American men as knightly rescuers, they often wrote Cuban men out of the romance. They implied that intervening American men would take the place of Cuban men who were unable to protect Cuban women because they were at the front, had been killed, or lacked the ability to do so. By removing Cuban men from the picture, the rescue paradigm sketched a hierarchical relation between the United States and Cuba. Viewing relations with Cuba as a chivalric rescue implied that the maidenly Cubans would submit to American governance just as the heroines of chivalric novels voluntarily submitted to their heroic rescuers.[46] The rescue paradigm thus lent itself to imperial ambitions for Cuba as well as to the jingoes' desire to foster chivalric relations between men and women.

But not all jingoes were driven by imperial ambitions. Impressed by the images of heroic Cuban men, many favored Cuban independence. These jingoes feared that the annexation of Cuba would only exacerbate the profit-mindedness that corrupted and divided American men. They considered the rescue paradigm useful for generating American commitment to the Cubans, but to promote their fraternal objectives, they shifted the focus of the chivalric paradigm, picturing intervention as a brotherly act. A *New York World* cartoon that depicted Uncle Sam shaking hands with a Cuban soldier conveyed this point (fig. 6). "You've Earned Your Independence," ran the caption. According to the cartoon, Cuban men's military prowess had established their right to self-government.[47] This interpretation implied that U.S. intervention would have two major consequences. It would help Cuban men secure independence and help American men develop a greater sense of fraternalism and honor.

To build support for their martial objectives, jingoes who adhered to the fraternal vision of U.S. intervention asserted that a failure to intervene would demonstrate that American men had, indeed, lost sight of fraternalism and honor in their obsessive pursuit of profit. When the *Atlanta Constitution* attributed the hesitancy to recognize Cuban belligerency to the "commercial spirit" that had "sapped and destroyed the foundations of patriotism and brotherhood on which the Republic was builded [*sic*]," it suggested that staying on the sidelines would signal a triumph of that commercial spirit. Sen. Wilkinson Call (D, Fla.) argued that a failure to support the Cubans would show that the profit motive had triumphed over nobler sentiments. As he said in reference to the Cuban issue, "If this god of business is to be allowed to . . . suppress the manhood and courage of our people, if we were to take this low ground and say that cowardice, the lack of public spirit, was to be preferred to the danger of war, it would be an unwise and ruinous policy." Concern for manly honor led a Michigan man to complain to President Cleveland that other countries viewed the United States as a nation of "barter and money but never of honor

6. "You've Earned Your Independence." *New York World,* in *Review of Reviews,*
April 1898. Courtesy of Harvard College Library.

and self-respect." "I want my government to be a strong government and in the
hands of dignity," he wrote. "I desire the freedom of Cuba."[48]

Jingoes contended that the failure to intervene would betray more than
the Cuban revolutionaries—it would also betray the principles inherited from
earlier generations of American men. Sen. William V. Allen (Pop., Neb.) conveyed this point: "Are we, the sons of such an ancestry [the Revolutionary fa-
thers], to become pusillanimous and contemptible in the eyes of the world by
deserting the Cubans, our neighbors and friends, who have been inspired by
our achievements, and who are now seeking the liberty we enjoy?" Claude
Matthews, the governor of Indiana, raised a similar point in a gathering of
Union veterans. He said that failing to aid the Cuban patriots would be tantamount to forgetting the lessons taught by the brave men who died at Antietam. It would betray their legacy of freedom.[49]

According to jingoes, American honor was on the line not only because of American men's obligations to support their Cuban brothers and the principles inherited from their own fathers, but also because the Spaniards insulted American men to their faces. As evidence for this point, jingoes often cited the cases of American citizens charged with abetting the Cuban insurgents. One such case was that of Julio Sanguily, a naturalized U.S. citizen who was arrested in Havana on charges of rebellion. In disregard of his U.S. citizenship papers, the Spaniards tried him in a military rather than a civilian court and, on the basis of very little evidence, sentenced him to life in prison. The incident led jingoes to deplore the Spaniards' supposed belief that they could "maltreat Americans with perfect impunity."[50] If the Spaniards could insult one American man without retribution, they contended, then none of his countrymen were safe. This fear seemed to be borne out in reports that no American men in Cuba were free from insult. Even Fitzhugh Lee related feeling humiliated in Cuba. His "American blood" had begun to boil from the moment he landed on the island, he said, for Spanish sympathizers trampled on the American flag and hissed Americans on the streets. "Never before in the history of the country has the American name been brought to such a low state abroad," he told the press.[51]

Jingoes insisted that if American men did not respond to such insults, their honor would be discredited overseas. As Rep. James B. Clark (D, Mo.) argued, "Our foreign policy is so feeble, so cringing, so cowardly that even old and decrepit Spain insults our flag, maltreats our citizens, and searches our ships with perfect impunity; and President McKinley, instead of sending men-of-war to protect our honor, assert our supremacy, and teach the insolent and impotent 'Dons' a lesson [applause] they would never forget, passes the hat around and invites the American people to contribute alms for the starving and dying Cubans." The belief that unless American men assumed a more assertive role, they would be humiliated in the eyes of the world appears in a political cartoon that depicted a slouching Uncle Sam being jeered by puny figures representing Spain and other countries and wrapped in the British flag for protection. "Our Weak Foreign Policy—Its Inevitable Result" ran the caption (fig. 7).[52] The message was clear. If Uncle Sam did not stand up to "Spanish insolence," he would lose his standing among the world's powers. He would be dishonored before his peers. But challenging Spain would enable American men to manifest their chivalric character and thereby remedy this deplorable state of affairs.

Hoping to show that intervention would foster chivalric relations among men by deepening American men's sense of fraternal loyalty, jingoes often presented intervention as a brotherly act. A Pennsylvania chapter of the United American Mechanics petitioned Congress to intercede in Cuba "in behalf of

7. "Our Weak Foreign Policy—Its Inevitable Result. The American citizen abroad will be compelled to seek the protection of the English flag." *Judge*, August 24, 1895. Courtesy of Yale University Library.

our Cuban brothers." Similarly, Rep. William H. King (D, Utah) urged his colleagues to do their duty to "our brothers who fight in freedom's holy cause." Jingoes maintained that by standing with their Cuban "brothers," American men would strengthen their own sense of honor. When the *Chicago Tribune* argued that the United States should "make common cause with those gallant men who are fighting for freedom and independence," it intimated that aiding the Cubans would let American men share in their gallantry.[53] Similarly, when Senator Call proclaimed that the Cubans "have a right to honor and respect from all men who honor heroism and the sacrifice of personal ease and enjoyment for principle and right," he suggested that supporting the Cubans would testify to American men's appreciation of manly character.[54]

Above all, jingoes asserted that aiding the Cuban fighters would teach American men not to be so narrowly self-interested. Richard Harding Davis conveyed this idea in a passage that compared the martyred Cuban patriot Rodriguez to "that statue of Nathan Hale, which stands in the City Hall Park, above the roar of Broadway, and teaches a lesson daily to the hurrying crowds of moneymakers who pass beneath."[55] The youthful Nathan Hale, the Revolutionary War hero who gladly gave his life for his country, found his modern incarnation in the Cuban patriots. By joining their struggle, American men could prove that they were not completely absorbed by moneymaking and that they had not lost the sense of virtue that earlier generations of men supposedly had demonstrated.

In contrast to the less bellicose champions of *Cuba libre,* jingoes argued that the United States could no longer stand aloof from the conflict. The choice that faced American men, they maintained, was one between standing by the defenders of chivalric standards in Cuba and the United States or allying themselves with the unchivalric Spaniards and their American proponents. The pro-Cuban author Clarence King conveyed this point by questioning, "Which cause is morally right?—which is manly?—which is American?"[56] Jingoes thought that American men's position on the Cuban issue would have implications not only for their character, but also for the well-being of the nation, for if American men lacked manly character then their political system would be marked by dissension, self-interest, and dishonor. The nation would follow Spain's degenerate path. Rather than being a cynosure for democracy, it would lose the respect of the watching world.

The linkage between pro-Cuban policies and chivalry was so pervasive that political leaders who did not want to intervene in the Spanish-Cuban War considered it necessary to deny that chivalry was at stake in Cuba. President Cleveland's postmaster general, William Wilson, rejected the chivalric understanding of the Cuban struggle when he criticized stories about the war for having "all the earmarks of a manufactured romance." In the Senate, George L. Wellington (R, Md.) accused a pro-Cuban colleague of "wandering in the land of romance and fiction created by himself." Unlike his jingoist associates, he dismissed the applicability of romantic sentiment to international questions. In the House, Charles A. Boutelle (R, Maine) rejected the idea of Uncle Sam as a heroic knight: "It is not our duty to be the Don Quixote of the earth."[57]

Anti-interventionists asserted that the central issues at stake in Cuba were economic, political, and legal, rather than chivalric. After the former Confederate general Sen. John T. Morgan (D, Ala.) made an impassioned speech on the Cuban issue in which he laid his sword on the table and challenged Spain to take it up, Sen. George Frisbie Hoar (R, Mass.) urged his colleagues not to be carried away by passion but to act in a "calm, dignified spirit," motivated by "gravity" and "deliberation" rather than emotion. "It is not a question of valor," said Sen. David B. Hill (D, N.Y.) at the Democratic national convention. "The majority platform speaks of the subject as though it were simply a question as to whether we were a brave enough people to enter upon the experiment. It is a question of business. It is a question of finance. It is a question of economics. It is not a question, which men, ever so brave, can solve, as a mere matter of bravery."[58] Hoar, Hill, and like-minded leaders regarded the Cuban issue not as a crusade but as a policy issue to be settled by sober statesmen and foreign policy authorities. In effect, they contended that the kind of manhood that should govern foreign policy debate was not that of the chivalrous knight but that of the dispassionate, educated expert, someone who exercised restraint and sober judgment.

Anti-interventionists' scornful references to chivalry and their calls for judicious self-restraint helped keep the United States aloof from the Cuban conflict by undercutting the idea that chivalry was at stake in Cuba and, more fundamentally, by countering the idea that chivalric standards should outweigh careful deliberation in the conduct of foreign policy. Many Americans thought there was something to the jingoes' argument that aiding the Cubans would foster American chivalry, but they did not think that it was in such a deplorable state that the nation needed to fight for that purpose. Neither did they think that the United States was sufficiently implicated in the Cuban romance to justify war. Although numerous Americans shared the jingoes' domestic concerns, jingoes had a hard time convincing their compatriots that the best way to resolve these anxieties was through foreign crusades. Jingoes used the Cuban romance to attract an ever-greater following, but to lead the nation into war, they needed an issue that would resoundingly convince the general public that national honor demanded a martial response. The sinking of the *Maine* provided that issue. The fervent cries for war that followed the disaster owed much of their passion to the jingoes' assiduous efforts to associate war with the restoration of American chivalry.

3

. . . .

"Honor Comes First":
The Congressional Debate over War

O N THE NIGHT of February 15, 1898, the U.S. battleship *Maine,* which
had been sent to Havana to protect American citizens after an outbreak
of riots, exploded and sank in Havana harbor. Two hundred and sixty-six men
died in the disaster. President McKinley responded to the crisis by appoint-
ing a court of naval inquiry. The court's report, submitted on March 25, attributed the explosion to an external source. Although the commission admitted that it could not determine who was responsible, suspicion came to
rest on Spain. Not only did Spain have a reputation for perfidy, but, to many
Americans, it appeared that only the Spanish government had the technolog-
ical capabilities to commit such an act. Americans were outraged at the
thought of the Spaniards striking in the dark without giving the sleeping crew
a chance to fight. "Splendid sport, indeed! How chivalric!" exclaimed one
senator, who, well-versed in the chivalric paradigm for understanding the
Spanish-Cuban war, interpreted the incident as yet another manifestation of
Spanish treachery.[1]

Americans who blamed the disaster on Spain regarded it as a challenge
to American men, particularly because Spain refused to apologize or offer
reparations and instead suggested that the men of the *Maine* were at fault.
Sen. Richard R. Kenney (D, Del.) captured the leading sentiment of the day
in his response to the supposed Spanish insult: "American manhood and
American chivalry give back the answer that innocent blood shall be avenged,
starvation and crime shall cease, Cuba shall be free. For such reasons, for
such causes, America can and will fight. For such causes and for such reasons
we should have war."[2]

The desire to assert American manhood and chivalry was highly conspic-
uous in Congress, the most bellicose branch of government in the early months
of 1898. As it waited for the investigators' report on the cause of the incident,
Congress passed a $50 million defense appropriation to move the U.S. mili-
tary to a wartime footing. Congressmen were eager to show their support for
the measure. The Senate did not debate the issue at all, passing the $50 mil-
lion bill without discussion or an opposing vote. In the House, which also
passed the bill unanimously, one word surfaced repeatedly in the discussion
over the appropriation—*honor*. On the Democratic side of the House, Rep.
John F. Fitzgerald (D, Mass.) announced he would vote for the appropriation
"to defend the honor and maintain the dignity of this Republic. [Great applause.]" From across the aisle, Rep. Stephen A. Northway (R, Ohio) proclaimed that, if necessary, "we will vote to spend not only this appropriation,
but millions more in defense of our country and our country's honor. [Ap-
plause.]"[3]

After the *Maine* report had been submitted, congressmen continued to
invoke honor in debates over the appropriate response to the presumed attack. "I am one who believes in peace with honor, and I say now and again
there can be no peace with honor until Cuba is free and the crime of the
Maine is atoned," said Rep. William Sulzer (D, N.Y.). "I have been and am for
peace," said Rep. David B. Henderson (R, Iowa), but not, he insisted, at
the expense of his country's honor. Sen. George Turner (Pop., Wash.) joined
in the clamor by calling for a "declaration of war, pure and simple," because
"every dictate of national honor" demanded it.[4]

Many of the congressmen who cited honor exhibited an unfettered enthusiasm for war, but even those who professed to want peace often admitted
that war would be preferable to dishonor. Rep. James A. Norton (D, Ohio)
said that although he deplored "the infinite woe of war, yet better far that this
war should come, though at the cost of untold treasure, of countless wealth,
and human life, than the degradation of our country's honor." In a similar vein,
Rep. Mahlon Pitney (R, N.J.) said he hoped that there would be no conflict.
"We desire peace with honor," he said, "but we lay a solemn emphasis upon
the word honor. Honor comes first. It is most important; it is the end ever to
be held in view. [Applause.]"[5]

Republicans, Democrats, and Populists alike used the chivalric standard
of honor to explain their support for a militant response to the supposed Spanish insult. Although concerns for the Cubans continued to fuel prowar sentiment, in the aftermath of the *Maine* incident American honor superseded
Cuba libre as the leading justification for war. The frequency with which congressmen invoked honor to justify their bellicose stances testifies to the
strength of the chivalric paradigm for understanding the Cuban revolution.

By inserting the *Maine* disaster into the chivalric framework first applied to the Cuban revolution, jingoist congressmen made it appear to be yet one more example of Spanish villainy rather than an isolated, and perhaps accidental, incident. Not surprisingly, this framework proved conducive to the jingoes' martial objectives, for the chivalric standards that implied an obligation on the part of the United States toward Cuba implied an even stronger obligation toward the dead men of the *Maine*. According to jingoist congressmen, a slight of honor as great as the *Maine* incident must be avenged. This claim was more than a rhetorical flourish—jingoes regarded honor as a legitimate and persuasive rationale for war. To understand how their commitment to honor and their manipulation of the standard affected the war debate, it is first necessary to look at what the term meant to the congressmen who used it.

Although *honor* had a feminine component—in 1895 the *Century Dictionary* defined it as "loyalty and high courage in men and chastity in women, as virtues of the highest consideration"—in the context of the debate over war in 1898, *honor* implied male courage rather than female virtue. It referred to a male code of behavior; being honorable meant being manly. Congressmen showed that they connected the chivalrous standard of honor with ideals of manliness by declaring that the opposites of honor were effeminacy and childishness. As Rep. John J. Lentz (D, Ohio) questioned, would the nation defend its honor or "remain impotent"? Earlier Lentz had associated dishonor with childishness: "We have not yet awakened to a realization of what 'national honor' means when we can go waddling and wabbling along, day in and day out, refusing to hear the cry of the people—'Remember the *Maine!*' "[6]

That congressmen connected manliness and honor is also shown by their tendency to use the word *honor* alongside words that evoked manly qualities, such as *bravery*, *liberty*, *glory*, and *manhood* itself. Sen. George F. Hoar (R, Mass.) implied that honor was related to manhood when he expressed fears that "manhood and courage and honor will follow athletics to Yale" if Harvard men did not repudiate Charles Eliot Norton, a professor who discouraged Harvard students from enlisting. At times, congressmen substituted the word *manhood* for *honor* with no perceptible change in meaning, as in a speech by Rep. James R. Mann (R, Ill.): "We do not fight for a fancied slight; we do not fight for a commercial wrong; we do not fight for an increase of territory; we do not fight because our commercial spirit has been outraged; we do not fight because our land has been invaded; we fight because it has become necessary to fight if we would uphold our manhood."[7] In sum, as used in Congress in 1898, *honor* referred to a male code of valorous and self-respecting behavior. Honor was an attribute of a potent, mature, and chivalrous man, of a man who wielded power, who was poised to fight.

The militant understanding of honor that guided the war debate reflected the new standards of passionate manhood that were in the ascendance in the late nineteenth century. As E. Anthony Rotundo and other men's historians have noted, at the end of the century, older standards of self-controlled manhood were giving way to ideals that exalted aggression, toughness, and physical prowess. Late-nineteenth-century standards of manhood valued combativeness; new words like *sissy, pussy-foot,* and *stuffed shirt* expressed the rising disfavor with self-restraint. According to the new standards, it was not so much his specific objectives that signaled a man's character but his willingness to fight for whatever he believed in. An advertisement published in the *Boston Journal* at the time of the war debate conveyed this point. The pitch for Dr. Pierce's patent medicine (which promised to cure white-livered men) ran as follows: "A woman judges a man from appearances. If he is energetic and forcible she doesn't always stop to reason why. She . . . applauds the man who fights bravely. He may win, he may lose; but he must never flag; he must fight." The idea that bellicosity was, in itself, a mark of manliness also surfaced in late-nineteenth-century political reporting. A glowing profile of Rep. Charles H. Grosvenor (R, Ohio) published by the *Washington Post* in late February 1898 illuminates the enthusiasm shown for militant qualities in political leaders. The article, tellingly titled "A Manly Fighter is He," said that Grosvenor "delights in crossing blades with those worthy of his steel. . . . He prefers the battle-ax to the broadsword; yet he can use the rapier with exquisite skill. . . . He's ever rambling in the arena of discussion, looking for a fight, and he usually gets it." The valorization of militant qualities in men benefited jingoes after the *Maine* disaster, as an appreciative editorial from the *Rochester Democrat and Chronicle* attests: "We may call these war orators, 'hotheads', but what would a nation be without hot-heads? . . . Impatience that needs restraint is better than sluggishness that requires prodding."[8] The late-nineteenth-century propensity to prefer hotheads to sluggards gave rise to and legitimated jingoes' martial understanding of honor.

The congressmen who cited honor as a rationale for war were highly vested in the term because it represented their self-worth and identity as men. They used the concept of honor to connect deeply held individual ideals to public policies. What made this tactic effective was the widespread conviction that the standards that guided individual men should be the standards that guided nations. This certainty led jingoist congressmen to draw on a men and nations analogy to argue for war. The analogy was often only implicit in jingoes' prowar arguments, but at times they stated it straightforwardly. As Rep. Lorenzo Danford (R, Ohio) maintained, "No man ever went to the assistance of a weak and defenseless fellow-being who was being tortured by a brutal master and did not feel that he had done a good act, and did not receive the encouragement and plaudits of manly men; and so, no nation that goes to the relief of an oppressed people but will grow in the respect of other nations, and what is better than all, in the self-respect of its own people."[9] In his men and nations analogy (clearly a reference to U.S. intervention in the Spanish-Cuban War), Danford suggested that intervention would reflect positively on both American men and their nation, for the virtues admired in one were the virtues admired in the other.

Taking the men and nations analogy to heart, jingoist congressmen applied their personal standards of behavior to international affairs. One congressman who concluded that violence was the only appropriate response to the *Maine* incident was Representative Sulzer. "I am no jingo crying for war for the sake of war," he said, "but there are things more horrible than war. I would rather be dead upon the battlefield than live under the white flag of national disgrace, national cowardice, national decay, and national disintegration." Sulzer invoked the specter of male cowardice and disgrace to convey the magnitude of the nation's cowardice and disgrace should it fail to intervene. He cited his personal convictions to justify war. Assertive personal standards also led a number of Sulzer's fellows to conclude that it was better to be too precipitous than too prudent in a case involving honor. "I have no sympathy with those rash, intemperate spirits who would provoke war simply for the sake of fighting," said Rep. Joseph W. Bailey (D, Tex.), "and yet I would rather follow them, and suffer all the miseries and misfortunes their heedlessness would bring than to follow those other contemptible and mercenary creatures who are crying out for 'peace at any price.' [Great Applause.]" Bailey elaborated on this point in a later speech: "If in order for a man to preserve his equanimity and to appear cool he must allow insults to pass unanswered, then I prefer to be classed with those who lose their heads. I would infinitely rather lose my head in resenting an insult than to lose my self-respect by submitting to be insulted."[10] Believing that the nation should live up to his personal code of conduct, Bailey called for war.

The conviction that an affront to honor mandated combat led jingoist congressmen to conclude that submitting the *Maine* and Cuban independence issues to arbitration would be unacceptable. "There can not be and must not be any arbitration," Rep. William C. Arnold (R, Penn.) said to loud applause. "Our honor is at stake and our flag insulted. If I insult any gentleman in this house should there be arbitration to decide and inform that gentleman whether or not he has been insulted?" Sen. George C. Perkins (R, Calif.) agreed. Although he had voted in favor of the arbitration treaty the previous year, he said he could not countenance arbitration of the *Maine* issue. "There are questions that do not admit of arbitration," he said. "Men do not arbitrate questions of honor. Neither do nations." The problem with arbitration in a case of honor was that it could not address the core of the grievance: the implication that the aggrieved party could not command respect. Arbitration could lead to conciliation, but it could not reinstate the insulted party before his peers. To the contrary, it would undercut his position by implying that he was unable to settle his own affairs without assistance. War, in contrast, promised to demonstrate that the nation was not devoid of honor. Indeed, according to the jingoist logic, war would foster greater honor among American men. By building their character, it would strengthen their political system, bringing it closer to the manly ideal of politics. The belief that war would benefit American men and their nation led jingoes to regard the likelihood of war with enthusiasm. As Representative Norton said, "I welcome war."[11]

The first reason jingoist congressmen welcomed war was that they thought it would expose the hollowness of mercenary values. Rep. James Hamilton Lewis (D, Wash.) avouched that war would show "that the wealth of our nation's Treasury is not in the gold of her chests, but in the glorious patriotism of her noble sons." Sen. Hernando de Soto Money (D, Miss.) agreed. He averred that "any sort of a war is better than a rotting peace that eats out the core and heart of the manhood of this country. [Applause in the galleries.]" He continued:

> . . . War brings out not the commercial trait, not the business instinct, not the training faculties, not the skill to corner articles of general consumption at the cost of the consumer, not short cuts to wealth, but war brings out all the best traits of character.
>
> It teaches us devotion, self-abnegation, courage. It teaches us to offer upon the altar of our country everything dear to us—sons and brothers and fathers and all that goes to make life happy and holy. It teaches us to rise above the petty, the unworthy, the selfish. It broadens our nature, and in my opinion a wholesome war, like one for human liberty and human life, will have its purgatorial effect upon this nation and we will come out of it, like the Phoenix from its ashes, renewed and with glory.[12]

As this panegyric to war suggests, Money regarded war as a means to replace ascendant commercial values with honor, to the mutual benefit of American men and their nation.

What made a militant defense of honor particularly appealing to jingoes was their assuredness that such a noble undertaking would foster a greater sense of brotherhood in American men. Rep. Mason S. Peters (Pop., Kans.) conveyed this idea in his statement that war would bring men from different parties together "as one man in defense of our country's honor." Other congressmen predicted that war would lead wealthy men to enlist alongside poor men and northern men to serve alongside southerners. The remarks of Rep.

Reese C. De Graffenreid (D, Tex.) illustrate the conviction that war was an opportunity to foster brotherhood: "The boys who wore the blue and the boys who wore the gray, reconciled and reunited in the great and grand bonds of true brotherhood and love, side by side, heart in heart, and hand in hand, will go marching on with the one purpose, the one intention, and one exclamation, that is, woe, irretrievable woe, shall betide that country, that nation, and that people against whom a brother American's blood shall cry to us from the ground."[13] Congressmen like Peters and De Graffenreid welcomed the prospect of a war waged in the name of brotherhood because they thought it would engrave the value of fraternalism on American men's hearts.

Along with reminding American men of their common citizenship, war promised to draw attention to the differences between men and women stipulated by the chivalric paradigm. Rep. Joseph Wheeler (D, Ala.) declared that war would enable American men to recapture a bygone era, an era in which mothers "taught their sons that the highest possible honor and greatest possible privilege was to fight for [their] country, its safety, and its honor . . . that an ounce of glory earned in battle was worth more than a million pounds of gold." After the applause had died down he continued: "This is the teaching which we must continue to impress upon our children, and it is the best heritage we can give to those who are to follow after us. This and this alone will cause the flag of our country to continue to soar higher and higher and the prestige of this great Republic to extend its power for good in the farthest corners of the earth. [Applause.]"[14] Wheeler believed that war would restore an imagined past in which women dedicated themselves to their families and men won political authority on the battlefield, a past in which women respected men because of their fighting capacities and male honor reigned supreme in public life. According to jingoes, war would keep American politics virile.

The final reason jingoist congressmen welcomed war was that they thought it would increase their standing in the eyes of the watching world. For Sen. William E. Mason (R, Ill.), one of the most steadfast jingoes in Congress, this matter was of great personal interest: a Spanish nobleman had challenged him to a duel over his assertions about Spanish atrocities in Cuba. Rather than fight this individual challenger, Mason urged the nation to take on the entire Spanish army. Mason's jingoist colleagues, too, were eager to stand up to Spain because they believed that Spain had issued a collective challenge to all American men. Newspaper reports that Spanish men taunted American men as cowards and blustering braggarts, as men of commerce "wholly unacquainted with the martial spirit," buttressed this conviction. Congressmen who were convinced that Spain had impugned the honor of American men thought war was necessary to demonstrate both their own and their constituents' honor. The desire to win respect for American men can be seen in Representative

Lentz's proclamation, in support of an appropriation to ready the nation for war, that he wanted to "lift our American manhood high upon that appropriation as upon a pedestal, there to unfurl our flag."[15] Lentz regarded the prospect of war with enthusiasm because he expected that the watching world would see that American men did not value money more than manhood, that they had not lost their sense of fraternal obligation, and that they were not degenerate or effeminate. By conveying these points, war would secure American men a preeminent place in the hierarchy of nations. By proving their honorable character, it would prevent future insults.

Claiming a desire to defend and strengthen the honor of American men, jingoist congressmen rejected further deliberation. As Rep. Levin I. Handy (D, Del.) exclaimed in the middle of a pension discussion, "I am restraining and holding back the thoughts that swell in my breast lest I might inquire whether the honor of the Government of the United States has been upheld and is likely to be upheld in that matter [the sinking of the *Maine*]. I trust the gentleman will not appeal to my patriotism. I am wild when I get on that subject. I am not safe in a body like this." Rep. Ferdinand Brucker (D, Mich.) also voiced a strong preference for action. "This is no time for discussion," he impatiently said in reference to the Cuban issue. "That time has passed. This is the time for action, and 'vigorous action,' too, at that." The belief that men must aggressively defend their honor filled some jingoes with an almost overwhelming sense of frustration with the slow pace of congressional proceedings. Convinced that the manly response to an insult such as the *Maine* was, as Sen. Lee Mantle (Silver R, Mont.) put it, "open, aggressive, decisive action," jingoes clamored for war.[16]

The overwhelming desire to act made it impossible for some congressmen to continue sitting at their desks, legislating, in the middle of such a crisis. Motivated by their commitment to martial ideals, several congressmen offered their services to the military. At the start of the war, Representatives Sulzer and Lewis accepted positions as colonels. Lewis was such a firebreather on the war issue that a fellow congressman, Henry U. Johnson (R, Ind.), jested that the best solution to the crisis was to "harness up the gentleman from Washington [Lewis] and turn him loose upon Spain." Johnson then went on to note a possible objection to his proposal: "We are a Christian nation. We should not engage in a war of absolute extermination."[17] Another leading jingo, Joseph Wheeler, a former Confederate general, took command of a cavalry division in Cuba during the war. This surprised no one, for the general-turned-congressman, craving a fight, had offered his services to the military in earlier diplomatic crises, even stating a willingness to serve as a private if that would secure him a position.[18]

Although the congressmen who entered the military demonstrated an unusual commitment to action, they were not alone in their desire to fight. One senator who confessed a strong temptation to volunteer was Henry Cabot Lodge (R, Mass.). "It is most splendid and most uplifting the way our boys are going in everywhere, and it makes one love the country better than ever," he wrote to his friend Henry Lee Higginson. "I want to go, but I should be a fool, I suppose, and only fill a place some younger man could fill better, while here I can be of use." The strange proceedings in the Capitol lobby on the night of April 18 also illustrate the general desire to jump into the fray. Knowing that war was imminent, a large group of congressmen gathered to sing "Hang General Weyler to a Sour Apple Tree as We Go Marching On."[19] These legislators saw the war issue less as a matter to be soberly decided after lengthy deliberation than as an opportunity to rally with their fellows, to imagine themselves marching among the ranks in defense of the nation's honor. Their undisguised enthusiasm for war indicates that their insistence on action was not just a rhetorical ploy but a reflection of their personal codes of behavior. After weeks of deliberating the *Maine* issue, these congressmen could restrain themselves no longer.

The most vivid demonstration of the belief that action was the manly response to a slight of honor was the hullabaloo in the House on April 13. On that day, according to the *New York Times*, the House was in a state of "frenzied excitement" as it considered the prospect of war. Representative Henderson "made an impassioned appeal to the men of the American Congress to act like men. This remark was met with a storm of hisses." Democrats and Republicans accused each other of playing for political advantage. In the discussion, Rep. Charles N. Brumm (R, Penn.) called Rep. Charles L. Bartlett (D, Ga.) a liar. "Instantly," ran the description in the *New York Times*, "Mr. Bartlett reached for a large bound copy of the *Congressional Record* in the desk before him, and, raising it aloft, hurled it at his adversary. It fell short and then the two antagonists rushed for each other."[20]

The House was immediately in an uproar. Some of the ladies in the galleries screamed. Congressmen crowded into the aisles, "clinching, tugging, hauling at each other like madmen. It was like free fight in the street." Congressmen Bartlett and Brumm tried to "get at each other over the benches, but they were borne back by friends." In the end, the Speaker commanded the sergeant at arms to restore order. Armed with the great silver mace, he "repeatedly charged the thick mass of struggling members, but was as often swept aside." Another House employee was "felled by a blow on the jaw." Finally, a dozen "muscular members" of the House separated the belligerents and a semblance of order was restored. As the House again considered the resolutions before it, Representative Henderson said the Republicans were "overwhelmingly in favor of action, not talk." His Republican colleagues applauded his pronouncement.[21] The brawl in the House suggests that congressmen's aggressive personal standards of honor helped make fighting seem a legitimate, if not a desirable, option for the nation. Congressmen who saw violence as an appropriate response to personal insults viewed war with Spain as an appropriate way to resolve international disputes.

Not surprisingly, those who opposed U.S. intervention in the Spanish-Cuban War responded to the outbreak in Congress with horror. After the incident, the Boston reformer Henry B. Blackwell questioned, "How can we expect a Congress which in a grave national emergency resorts to blows and personal violence, to exercise national self-restraint and intelligent adaptation of means to ends?" Blackwell interpreted the nation's path toward war as the result of misguided standards of manly behavior. An ardent women's suffrage supporter, he thought the war debate demonstrated the need to enfranchise women. That, he opined, would shift the tone of political debate from aggressive posturing to intelligent reflection. As the language of honor drowned out other ways of viewing the war issue, thus leading the nation into war, his daughter, Alice Stone Blackwell, the editor of the prosuffrage *Woman's Journal*, cited the war debate to prove suffragists' point that Congress did not represent American women. "Congress is composed exclusively of men," wrote the younger Blackwell, ". . . the chosen representatives of all the men of the nation. Assuming for the sake of argument that this war is . . . utterly inexcusable . . . it is a Congress of men that has declared it. We must all admit that there is much division of opinion among the women of our acquaintance, while Congress is practically unanimous for war."[22]

Alice Blackwell's assertion that the jingoist Congress did not represent American women appears well-founded, for women were more visible on the anti-interventionist side of the debate than the jingoist side. Politically active women who belonged to groups such as the WCTU may have sympathized with the Cubans, but, as Judith Papachristou has argued in a study of American women and turn-of-the-century foreign policy, activist women generally viewed the prospect of a war between the United States and Spain as a reflection of male values.[23] The lack of modern polling data for this period makes it difficult to gauge the sentiments of women (and of men, for that matter) who did not take public stances on the issue, but it does seem likely that women were less enthusiastic about war than men because women experienced the dictates of honor differently. If a women and nations analogy had guided political debate, war would have seemed absurd, for chivalric traditions did not teach women to respond to insults with violence. To the contrary, one mark of a true woman was that she did not engage in fisticuffs. Furthermore, as the protected class in the chivalric paradigm, women had little reason to think that the *Maine* issue had bearing on their self-worth and identity as women. Unlike men, they were under little pressure to assume a bellicose stance.

In contrast to women, men faced considerable pressure to assume a bellicose stance on the *Maine* issue because of the standard of honor. Jingoes regarded honor not only as a guide for their own behavior, but also as a potent political tool. They realized that honor signified the manly character so necessary for wielding political authority and thus invoked the term to push their associates toward war. Reversing the men and nations analogy, they proclaimed that an honorable man should act according to the standards of his nation. When, in patent disregard for anti-interventionist men, jingoes contended that the nation stood "as one man" for war, they implied that any man who failed to join with his bellicose peers was no longer part of the men and nations analogy. He would lose his political status and suffer a kind of social death. If the nation as a whole determined that its honor had been affronted, then every man in the nation had an obligation to rally behind the flag. Failure to do so would betray a lack of manly character.[24]

Jingoes' efforts to present war as the manly course of action can be seen in Rep. David A. De Armond's (D, Mo.) claim that warlike sentiments represented "an assertion of American manhood by American representatives." It also can be seen in pleas exhorting men to act like men by supporting war. Representative Sulzer conflated fighting with manly character in his appeal: "Let us be men. Let us do our duty. Let us be true to the people and to our constituents." Rep. Samuel B. Cooper (D, Tex.) suggested that fighting was as necessary to men's honor as marriage was to women's in his assertion that men from his state would "rush to the nation's defense as swiftly and as cheerfully as ever maiden rushed to the marriage altar." Political cartoons that depicted effeminate or puny men trying to stop the nation (depicted by a tall, resolute Uncle Sam) from going to war buttressed the contentions that war was the manly course of action (figs. 8, 9). By portraying themselves as honorable men and their opponents as "nervous old ladies," jingoes inside and outside of Congress equated martial policies with manly character.[25] They left no place in this dichotomy for men to oppose war, or, for that matter, for women to support it.

Jingoes' conflation of military intervention and manly character can help explain why women were not very visible on their side of the war debate. Although few women clamored for war in the aftermath of the *Maine* disaster, thousands of women later mobilized to aid the war effort. The discrepancy between women's eventual support of the war effort and their earlier reluctance to join the jingoes can be explained by their ability to manipulate honor in political debate. Prior to the *Maine* disaster, women cited the honor of Cuban women to plead for intervention, but when attention shifted to avenging the

8. "Oh! Don't Go to War, Sam. It Would Just Kill Me." *Cincinnati Post*, in *Review of Reviews*, May 1898. Courtesy of Harvard College Library.

dead men of the *Maine*, Cuban women's status became a secondary concern. As jingoes proclaimed that the main issue in the war debate was manly honor, they implied that vengeance was a matter best left to men. At times they explicitly stated that war was a matter that men alone should decide when they said that they sought the approval of "good men" or that a failure to act would reveal American men to be "lost to all sense of brotherhood." Rep. Harry Skinner's (Pop., N.C.) remark that those who would resolve the war issue were "standing on an isthmus connecting the dead and unborn—the fathers of liberty who have gone before us and the sons that are to come after us," reflected the jingoist view that deciding whether or not to declare war was a choice that only men could make.[26]

Jingoes' efforts to associate intervention with militant standards of honor made interventionist women reluctant to call for war. Such hesitancy can be seen in the women assembled for a DAR convention a week after the *Maine* incident. Some of the delegates urged their organization to protest the "outrage" and advocate war, but the assembled women decided that it was not

9. "Urging the Old Man to be Calm." *Chicago Chronicle*, in *Literary Digest*, March 12, 1898. Courtesy of Harvard College Library.

women's place to call for vengeance. Rather than passing a prowar resolution, they discussed how to render "womanly assistance" in the event of war.[27] By setting up the war issue as a matter of male honor, male jingoes inhibited like-minded women. In turn, women's inclination to express militant views privately or not at all helped jingoes argue that militancy was the manly approach to take toward Spain.

Building on their argument that true men advocated war, congressional jingoes urged their less bellicose colleagues to show their manhood. It was time for "the doubting, the hesitating, the opposing to go to the rear," announced Sen. Joseph B. Foraker (R, Ohio), "while the virile, strong-minded, patriotic, liberty-loving masses" should rally around the military. Imbedded in

Foraker's exhortation was an implicit threat—a man who did not rally around the military would no longer seem virile. The threat was not always so veiled. Sen. William V. Allen (Pop., Neb.) said that men who failed to heed the nation's honor would prove themselves unfit to continue the nation's political traditions. Deserting Cuba, he said, would be "base cowardice"—a cowardice that "the men of other generations would not palliate or excuse." In addition to proving themselves cowards, those who contemplated arbitration supposedly would reveal a mercenary streak at odds with manly honor. "No man who loves the flag of his country, no man who loves its honor, believes that the outrage can be wiped out by the payment of money," said Sen. William B. Bate (D, Tenn.). "It is the trembling coward, the sordid huckster, who teaches such doctrine."[28] In the hands of jingoes, honor served a coercive function, for the claims that men who shirked war would appear to lack honor implied they would face a grim political future.

Lest the links between honor and political authority be overlooked, jingoes reminded their colleagues that the masses of American men demanded militant honor in their leaders. Representative Lentz conveyed this point when he said, "Our American manhood—the youth of this country—will not rest until that matter [the *Maine*] has been adjusted to their satisfaction, and to the honor of this country." Lentz implied that if Congress failed to declare war, then restless American men would seek new leaders. Constituent letters underscored Lentz's point that voters demanded leaders who would uphold the nation's honor. As one Ohio man wrote his senator, "Nine-tenths, yes 99% of the voters of this country want done what you have been driving at—the upholding of American honor and manhood through thick and thin."[29]

Lentz's jingoist associates also drew attention to the links between honor and political viability by saying that the men they represented were committed to defending the nation's honor. Rep. James T. McCleary (R, Minn.) pledged immigrant men's support for honor: "Every man beneath the flag, whether native born or naturalized, will, with genuine pleasure, contribute of his substance and his strength that the honor of the nation may be vindicated." In response to stories that Catholics would not support their government in a war against Catholic Spain, Representative Fitzgerald testified on their behalf: "If war does come, no more valiant, brave and heroic defenders of the national honor . . . will be found than the members of the Catholic church." Congressmen also hastened to show that no state or region was deficient in honor. Said Rep. Albert S. Berry (D, Ky.), "We who were defeated in the late unpleasantness will be glad as citizens of a common country to touch elbows with the men of Massachusetts and see who can go farthest for the honor of our country." Rep. Samuel S. Barney (R, Wis.) expressed similar sentiments when he said that the "sons of the old Badger State will do their full measure in maintaining our national honor," and Rep. James G. Maguire (D, Calif.) spoke for the Far West when he said that the men of California would not tolerate a "dishonorable peace."[30]

Assertions that men from various walks of life valued honor as a standard for individual and national behavior made it clear that a man who denied that honor was at stake or who hesitated to defend it would no longer represent American men. Such assertions made it seem politically imperative to join the jingoes in their defense of honor. Their manipulation of honor had partisan implications—clearly, if one party seemed to disregard honor, it would lose the respect of American men—but jingoes also manipulated honor to sway individual men, irrespective of party. Recognizing that the Republican, Democratic, and Populist parties all had jingoist members, jingoes maintained that honor outweighed partisanship. Honor, they held, should transcend ideological differences and unite all the men in Congress. Rep. George E. Foss (R, Ill.) revealed this conviction when he said, "To-day, when the honor of our country is at stake, we know no party." Rep. Alexander M. Dockery (D, Mo.) agreed: "Divided we may be, among ourselves, upon questions of domestic policy; as to our relations toward other nations we present an unbroken front. [Applause.] Party lines fade away, and we are ready on this side of the Chamber to join the other side in support of all proper measures to protect the country and to uphold the national dignity and the national honor. [Applause.]"[31]

According to the jingoist line of argument, the fact that honor was at stake made war politically imperative not only for individual men and their parties, but also for the nation. All men, they implied, had a shared interest in preserving the nation's honor, for honor underlay their common status as men and as Americans. The belief that honor and the manhood it signified were more fundamental than partisanship can be seen in Rep. Thomas C. McRae's (D, Ark.) appeal: "In this hour of threatened and impending war, every man who claims to be an American, and who would desire to exalt American manhood, should bury his partisanship and . . . say that the honor of this Government and the liberty and rights of our citizens everywhere shall be protected by it without regard to cost. [Loud applause.]"[32]

When jingoes spoke of exalting American manhood, one of the referents they had in mind was American women. Thinking that the war issue had bearing on men's privileged political position relative to women, jingoes warranted that women would lose their respect for American men if they failed to act. Senator Mason reckoned that a failure to fight would cause American men to be disgraced in the eyes of the wives and mothers rendered bereft by the *Maine* disaster. Rep. Samuel J. Barrows (R, Mass.) went a step further and claimed that *all* American women were "weeping in sympathy with the mothers and sisters of 266 unavenged American citizens." He thus implied that no women would excuse inaction. The suspicion that American women expected action underlay Senator Lodge's assertion that Congress could not "anymore negotiate about it [the *Maine*] than a man can negotiate about an insult to his mother."[33] Such a man would be scorned by all women because of his patent inability or unwillingness to uphold his end of the chivalric bargain: protection in exchange for power. To prevent women from publicly denouncing American men and taking the matter into their own hands, American men had to act.

Just as jingoes argued that American men were obligated to fight lest they lose standing relative to women, they argued that they must fight to avoid dishonoring American men in the eyes of the watching world. Senator Foraker spelled out the implications of failing to resent such an insult. It would lead the United States to be "written down before all the nations of the earth as pusillanimous—as wanting in pluck and courage." Representative Sulzer echoed these thoughts: "We must fight now for the independence of Cuba and our national honor, or we must retire in disgrace. We must bring about the freedom of Cuba and wipe out the stain Spain has put on our flag, or we must forever hereafter hold our heads in humiliation and shame before the civilized powers of the world." He continued, "Unless something is speedily done to vindicate American honor and the glory of our flag, unless something is speedily done for the freedom of Cuba, unless something is speedily done to demonstrate that we are a brave people and a great people, conscious of our rights and willing to maintain them, the world will charge us with cowardice. We are no cravens, no cowards. Let us prove it now. [Applause.]"[34] Sulzer presented the vindication of American honor as a collective responsibility, one that implicated all American men.

Jingoist congressmen took the threat of international disgrace as seriously as they took the threat of disgrace in women's eyes. They regarded it as nothing less than a danger to national integrity, for they believed that just as a dishonored man would suffer a kind of social death, a dishonored nation would cease to exist. As Sen. Edward O. Wolcott (R, Colo.) said, "This national honor which we evoke is intangible. . . . The existence of it makes nations survive and fit to live. The loss of it, or the trading upon it, or the abandonment of it, makes nations fit to die and perish from the face of the earth." Senator Turner employed equally florid prose to contend that without honor the nation would die. "There is a crucifixion of the soul when honor dies," he said, "there is a death of a nation 'when the jingle of the guinea heals the hurt that honor feels;' there is an existence, when patriotic pride is dead, 'that doth murder sleep' and life becomes a horrid nightmare, and men shun their fellows, and the laugh of little children becomes a taunt and a mockery. True, there have been men who could exist and thrive and fatten without national honor or pride or patriotism, like worms in a muck heap, but that nation has been the scorned of all time and has quickly died."[35] Jingoes drew on the idea of honor as a bedrock of male and national character to cast the debate over war as nothing less than a debate over the viability of American men and their nation.

The certitude that honor was at stake made it politically foolish to argue that a naval accident of uncertain provenance was insufficient grounds for war, because honor made the issue seem essential to the preservation of American manhood and the American political system. Jingoes were convinced that if the issue were understood as a choice between war and dishonor, American men would conclude, as Representative Lewis did, "there is no choice left us."[36] According to Lewis, war was not a choice but an obligation. American men had a responsibility to uphold their manhood because of its larger political implications.

Admonitions to follow the honorable course of action resonated among congressmen because honor was too important a component of male identity and political authority to take lightly. Congressmen hastened to prove that their honor was sound by citing their commitment to the principle. The desire to appear manly by associating themselves with honor helps explain why Representative Pitney asserted that "honor comes first" and Representative Norton avowed that war was preferable to dishonor. Such invocations of honor displayed congressmen's respect for the standard. Congressmen also were quick to assert that their political parties were committed to honor. Speaking for the Democrats, Rep. Leonidas F. Livingston (D, Ga.) said that every member of the party would rise to "defend the flag and the honor of this country." On behalf of the Republicans, Senator Hoar emphasized that he and his associates would follow their fellow Republican, President William McKinley, "an honorable American patriot," as he acted to resolve the issue in a way "creditable and honorable to American manhood."[37]

Jingoes' concerted effort to paint the *Maine* issue as a choice between fighting and dishonor proved so persuasive that few congressmen expressed strong opposition to war in congressional debate. Because congressmen faced so much political pressure to support war, much of the argument against it was developed not on the floors of Congress but in the press and among the wider public. When it came time to vote on a declaration of war, both houses of Congress voted unanimously in favor of it—the Senate in a closed executive session, the House in a resounding chorus of ayes that sparked a round of applause and some cheers from the floor and the galleries.[38] The congressmen who had reservations put them aside lest they or their nation appear less than completely committed to honor.

Anti-interventionists' tendency to agree that honor mattered strengthened the standard. But although anti-interventionists accepted the importance of honor and its relevance to international affairs, they differed over what the standard implied. In the debate over war, anti-interventionists tried to promote a more restrained definition of honor. As Rep. Albert J. Hopkins (R, Ill.) contended, "Moderation and firmness . . . will accomplish quite as much as bustle and bravado." Sen. Orville H. Platt (R, Conn.) also presented self-control as a higher virtue than passion. "Hot talk," he said, "should give way to calm judgment and dispassionate utterances."[39] Anti-interventionists argued that honorable nations, like honorable men, should exercise self-control and avoid using force if other means were available to settle disputes. An editorial in the *Boston Journal* made the point as follows: "An honorable nation, like a manly man, fights only when forced to fight." Only robbers, tyrants, and pugilists, it declared, fight for the sake of fighting. Writing in *Harper's Weekly*, the Republican senior statesman Carl Schurz maintained that honor did not require the nation to "swagger about among the nations of the world with a chip on its shoulder, shaking its fist under everybody's nose, and telling the world on every possible occasion that we can 'whip' any power that might choose to resent this, that we would be rather glad of an opportunity for doing so." Arguing that "a private individual taking such an attitude would certainly not be called a gentleman . . . [but] a vulgar bully," Schurz went on to say that the same would be true for the nation. Drawing on the men and nations analogy, anti-interventionists reasoned that because men no longer subscribed to a dueling mentality, neither should nations. "Why should not the policy usually adopted by the sensible men in their private affairs also govern in public controversies?" questioned an article in the *New York Times* which maintained that war over a point of honor was akin to murder.[40]

Because anti-interventionists criticized bellicose standards of honor, women did not feel as excluded from their side of the war debate as from the jingoist side. Like anti-interventionist men, women who opposed intervention tried to promote a more restrained definition of honor. May Wright Sewall, a women's club movement leader and suffragist, sent a letter to President McKinley arguing that just as the defense of honor among men no longer justified killing, neither should honor justify war. Similarly, the author Elizabeth Stuart Phelps Ward wrote to President McKinley, "'Honor' can no longer mean killing and being killed. . . . the honor of a nation must hereafter be rated by its success in the exertion of the peace-compelling power."[41] Unlike interventionist women, anti-interventionist women did not view their position on the war issue as unladylike; rather, they deemed it an expression of feminine values.

Anti-interventionists buttressed their argument that war was not the honorable course of action by describing Spain as a weak and unworthy foe. They argued that just as an honorable man would not fight an inferior opponent, neither should a nation, for no honor was to be gained from such a conflict. "What will we gain by war?" questioned Sen. George L. Wellington (R, Md.). "Glory? Nay; there can be no glory in defeating a nation than whom we are stronger as 5 to 1." Indeed, it would dishonor the nation to demand satisfaction from such an unworthy adversary. "Saying that our honor in the bellicose sense requires us to fight Spain is absurd," ran an article in the *Nation*. "It is like saying that a brawny pugilist's 'honor' requires him to meet a slight and consumptive youth in the 'twelve-foot ring.'" According to anti-interventionists, instead of demonstrating the nation's honor, war would reveal the nation to be a dishonorable bully.[42]

The anti-interventionists who said that fighting a weak opponent was dishonorable and hence unmanly may have disagreed with the jingoes' argument that American honor demanded war to avenge the *Maine,* but they sometimes conceded the underlying point that a truly honorable war would prove manly character. As a letter in the *New York Times* said, "It is much better to maintain a dignified peace than to rush into a conflict with an arrogant and emasculated race, a race entirely unworthy [of] a great Nation's hostile anger. If the country must have war—and, unless all signs fail, it will come sooner or later—let it be a contest with a power equal to our own, and one which it will be an honor to meet in respectable combat, rather than with an effervescent and quixotic race, whom it would be no credit to ourselves to thrash."[43] The letter disapprovingly hinted that honor, rather than a specific policy objective, was driving the nation into war. Even as it denounced the possibility of a war with Spain, however, it suggested that once the nation found a worthy opponent, it should not shirk battle, for a good fight would redound to the nation's credit.

As this letter indicates, although both interventionists and anti-interventionists cited honor in the debate over war, jingoist congressmen benefited from the assumption that honor must not be impinged, for implicit in the term was a willingness to fight. Because bellicose standards of manhood were in the ascendance in the late nineteenth century, congressmen who appeared cowardly ran a greater risk of losing political authority than congressmen who seemed too aggressive. More congressmen spoke in favor of bellicose manhood than against it because the political system equated a fighting spirit with leadership. Try as anti-interventionists might to redefine the term, most Americans thought that *honor* implied the inability to let pass an affront as grave as the sinking of the *Maine*. The belief that "men do not negotiate questions of honor" enabled jingoist congressmen to manipulate the standard of honor to limit dissent and present war as a desirable option. Anti-interventionist congressmen realized that they had to support war or be stigmatized as dishonorable. They feared that a failure to fight would undercut their own standing, that of their parties, and, indeed, their entire political system. The coercive use of gender ideals in political debate made war seem imperative to the reluctant congressmen who joined their jingoist fellows in voting unanimously for war.

4

······································

McKinley's Backbone: The Coercive Power of Gender in Political Debate

IN ASSESSING President McKinley's role during the months between the sinking of the *Maine* on February 15, 1898, and the U.S. declaration of war against Spain on April 25, 1898, historians have debated whether McKinley was courageous or spineless, strong or weak, a "chocolate éclair" or a "clever statesman." This debate echoes the rhetoric of the late nineteenth century, when McKinley's refusal to clamor for war led his contemporaries to both question and defend his backbone. Historians who have evaluated McKinley in the terms used by his contemporaries without stopping to question these terms have judged his character without fully understanding the political pressures he confronted. Furthermore, those who have focused attention on McKinley's courage or strength (attributes that may lie as much in the eye of the beholder as in the individual in question) have deflected attention from a more significant issue: how did U.S. political culture, especially the need to appear manly in order to wield political authority, affect what seemed to be viable policy alternatives in the aftermath of the *Maine* disaster?[1]

This is not to say that historians have ignored the political pressures faced by McKinley or the specific policy concerns that may have influenced his thinking. But those who have cited political considerations to explain McKinley's reluctant steps toward war have not fully explained why war seemed politically imperative to the president. The claim that McKinley joined the congressional jingoes to preserve his stature as a leader and his party's popularity at the polls still leaves questions about the political pressures he confronted. Why did McKinley think his party's future or his position as a leader were at stake? To answer this question, it is necessary to return to the debate over

McKinley's backbone, but to do so as observers, not participants. When seen from a critical distance, the attention paid to McKinley's backbone in the wake of the *Maine* disaster illuminates the coercive power of gender in political debate. It shows how assumptions about manly character limited the president's options in the spring of 1898.[2]

Like other nineteenth-century politicians, McKinley, a loyal Republican who had served as a congressman and governor before his presidential victory in 1896, was accustomed to being evaluated in terms of his manliness, for manliness served as a prerequisite to political leadership in the late nineteenth century. But two incidents in the early months of 1898 focused an extraordinary amount of attention on the president's manhood, much of it aimed at pressuring him to assume a more assertive position toward Spain. The first was the de Lôme letter. In December 1897, Enrique Dupuy de Lôme, Spain's ambassador to the United States, wrote a personal letter to a Spanish friend characterizing President McKinley as "weak and catering to the rabble, and, besides, a low politician." It also suggested that Spain was not taking its reform commitments in Cuba seriously. The letter fell into the hands of a Cuban patriot who sent it to the notoriously jingoistic *New York Journal*. The *Journal* published the purloined letter on February 9, 1898, and newspapers across the nation carried the story.[3]

The initial press accounts focused on de Lôme's slight to the president, rather than on his statement about Spanish duplicity in Cuba. "Spanish Minister Alleged to Have Insulted Mr. McKinley," ran a headline in the *New York Times*. "Insults for M'Kinley . . . Characterized as 'Weak,'" proclaimed the *Chicago Tribune*. De Lôme's aspersions echoed those made by McKinley's political opponents within the United States, but they hit a nerve because de Lôme was an outsider. In insulting the president's manliness, the ambassador insulted the men whom McKinley led. The author's nationality magnified the insult because Spanish men generally were viewed as either brutes or effeminate aristocrats, not manly fighters. As a Spaniard, de Lôme appeared particularly unworthy of evaluating the president's character. Rep. John J. Lentz (D, Ohio) expressed the sentiments of many Americans when he described de Lôme as "the chief representative of that effete and barbarous Government called Spain" and said that his insult to McKinley had impugned the nation's honor. A day after the story broke, de Lôme resigned, leaving the issue to fizzle out. But as tensions continued to build in the coming months, a number of Americans remembered the insult. Even in late April, Rep. Charles H. Martin (Pop., N.C.) recalled the letter and rhetorically questioned, "Did he not, in the person of the President, insult every American citizen?"[4] McKinley's supporters and detractors agreed that the insulting letter reflected poorly on the state of Spanish chivalry. But even as they deplored the insult, McKinley's opponents regarded the president's reluctance to fight as evidence that de Lôme's assessment was not entirely off the mark. If McKinley was unwilling to challenge affronts to himself and the men he represented, then was he not, as charged, "weak," a "low politician," implicitly devoid of honor?

Those who believed that the manly response to Spanish insults was war won a significantly wider following after the *Maine* disaster, which occurred a week after the de Lôme incident. McKinley appointed a court of naval inquiry and urged Americans to suspend judgment until the investigators had reported on the cause of the explosion. Yet even after the investigators submitted a report saying that an external mine had triggered the explosion, McKinley continued to urge restraint. He praised the country for its self-control as he continued to seek a peaceful resolution to the conflict. He told his callers that he wanted to avoid war. Instead of assuming a belligerent stance in his message to Congress of March 28, he asked for continued deliberation. Through the American minister in Madrid, McKinley tried to settle the issue without resorting to war. He asked Spain for an armistice in Cuba, negotiations between Spain and the Cuban insurgents mediated by the United States, and a revocation of the Spanish "reconcentration" policy that had caused so much suffering in Cuba. He hinted at the need for Cuban independence but did not demand it outright.[5]

When the Spanish government replied on March 31, it offered to arbitrate the *Maine* incident, abolish reconcentration, and submit the Cuban problem to an insular parliament. But Spain would not suspend hostilities or accept American mediation. After the Spanish reply, McKinley prepared another message to Congress, which he delivered on April 11. In this message, McKinley still did not ask for war. He asked for discretionary power to use the nation's military force, but he kept the possibility of further negotiations alive. Jingoes voiced disappointment with his continued restraint.[6]

McKinley's adversaries responded to the president's refusal to declare war by questioning his manhood. Editorials from the *Atlanta Constitution* illustrate this tactic. One described McKinley as a "goody-goody man," a disappointment in comparison to more militant versions of manhood. Another said that the Cuban crisis revealed McKinley's inability to fill the executive chair. "At this moment there is great need of a man in the White House," it opined. "The people need a man—an American—at the helm." A later editorial continued the theme. It said the people wanted a "declaration of American virility." Only the president, it concluded, was indifferent to the people's demands.[7]

Across the country, antiadministration newspapers joined in the chorus. The *New York Journal* looked forward to seeing "any signs, however faint, of manhood in the White House." "There are manly and resolute ways of dealing with treachery and wrong. There are unmanly and irresolute ways," said a *New York World* editorial which argued that McKinley had not been manly and resolute in his speech to Congress on March 28. The *Chicago Tribune* called McKinley's Cuban policy "a weak, ineffectual, pusillanimous policy," thereby impugning the character of the president. Perhaps de Lôme had been right in his estimate of McKinley, brazenly asserted the Sioux Falls *Daily Press*. These papers wielded the aggressive working-class standards of manliness that were gaining popularity among middle-class men in the late nineteenth century to contend that the president's self-restraint indicated a lack of manly fiber. They downplayed the moral dimension to manliness and proposed that a real man settled disputes with force; he did not hesitate to use military power.[8]

The press was not alone in questioning the president's manhood. Constituents wrote to their congressmen to complain about McKinley's character. One voter heatedly declared, "It is the verdict of the people that we have an executive whose timidity and lack of nerve and bravery and appreciation of American honor and dignity unfit him for the presidency in such a crisis." Bellicose congressmen agreed that McKinley was not demonstrating enough manliness. Sen. John W. Daniel (D, Va.) accused the administration of having lost the "virile instincts of the American people." Sen. George Turner (Pop., Wash.) described the administration's response to the crisis as "lame, halting, and impotent," characteristics that seemed as likely to refer to the president as to his policies. "He wabbles, he waits, he hesitates. He changes his mind," said Rep. William Sulzer (D, N.Y.) in disgust.[9]

The critics' various complaints—that the president was weak, indecisive, effeminate, cowardly, and ineffectual—were encapsulated in the contention that he lacked backbone. Theodore Roosevelt's remark that "McKinley has no more backbone than a chocolate éclair" is the best-known evaluation of McKinley's spine, but it was by no means the only disparaging one. In early April the president of a Wisconsin savings bank groused in a letter to Sen. John C. Spooner (R, Wis.), "Our president has no backbone."[10] A few days later, a New Hampshire man wrote his senator, William E. Chandler (R, N.H.), that McKinley should step aside because he did not have "the nerve and backbone to resent such damnable insults." After commenting that the president did not seem to have "sufficient backbone even to resent an offense so gross as this," the *New Orleans Times-Democrat* said that all was not lost, for Congress could declare war without him.[11]

The term *backbone* focused attention on the president's manhood because it not only referred to character traits that were valued in men, but also evoked images of the rigidity or flaccidity of his body. A *Chicago Chronicle* cartoon illustrates how the term conflated men's physical stature and character. The cartoon, exploiting less than subtle phallic imagery, depicts Uncle

10. "Uncle Sam—'All that you need is backbone.'" *Chicago Chronicle, in Cartoons of the War of 1898 with Spain* (Chicago, 1898). **Courtesy of Harvard College Library.**

Sam shoving a rifle down McKinley's coat to provide him with a backbone. The tall, lean, erect Uncle Sam of the cartoon towers over the short, pudgy (his stomach protrudes so much that he appears pregnant), slouched President McKinley, who is rendered helpless by Uncle Sam's weapon (fig. 10). According to McKinley's opponents, to have backbone meant to have a bold, masterful character and the physical capacity to enforce one's will. This was a robust ideal of manhood, one that valued self-assertion more than moral character and self-control, the characteristics that had been most highly valued in men (particularly northern, middle-class men) at the time of the Civil War, when McKinley's generation came of age.[12]

To underscore their point that McKinley was unfit to lead, his opponents argued that the great leaders of the nation's past had embodied the character-istics McKinley seemed to lack. After McKinley tried to ally himself with Washington by praising the first president's dedication to peace and his "sober and dispassionate" character, the *New York Journal* claimed that McKinley was no Washington. According to the *Journal*, Washington loved a good fight. He thus set an example that would survive "as long as men are men," unlike McKinley, who hesitated to declare war.[13] In addition to contrasting McKinley with Washington, McKinley's opponents frequently contrasted the president with the former president Andrew Jackson, who had fought the Spanish in Florida in 1818. The comparisons revealed McKinley's inadequacies as a man and a leader. "William McKinley is certainly not an Andrew Jackson," con-cluded one editorial in the *New York World*. In a later editorial, the *World* said, "What a pity it is that some such man as Andrew Jackson wasn't in the White House when the *Maine* was blown up."[14] By presenting the bellicose Jackson as a political paragon, such comparisons conveyed the point that con-temporary political leaders should demonstrate an equally combative spirit.

The critics who contrasted McKinley to past presidents intimated that he was unworthy of his position, that in failing to live up to the legacy of his heroic predecessors, he had betrayed the nation's principles. McKinley's de-tractors called for a leader who exhibited the firm character they deemed nec-essary to govern. "I wish to God we had a Andy Jackson . . . at the head now," wrote a Chicago resident to the secretary of the navy. "Had we an Andrew Jackson for President, redress [for the *Maine*] would have been had before this late day," wrote a constituent to Senator William E. Chandler (R, N.H.). "Oh, for one day of an Andrew Jackson in the White House, with his courage, his backbone, his nerve, and his patriotism!" exclaimed Representative Sulzer. "If a man like Jackson were at the helm of the ship of state there would be no more delay, no more hesitation, no more apologies." Sulzer went on to threaten the president: "There is nothing the American people despise so much as a weak and impotent foreign policy. It will wreck any administration." By hold-ing up assertive military heroes as ideal leaders, McKinley's jingoistic detrac-tors strove both to reinvigorate the military style of politics that was fading along with the Civil War generation and to lead the United States into a war against Spain.[15]

Realizing that the crisis lent weight to the aspersions cast upon McKin-ley, the president's allies responded by attributing to him qualities—such as bravery and strength—that even his opponents associated with manhood. The president's self-control, wrote one supporter, demanded more courage than "any which is needed amid the excitement of battle."[16] The *Los Angeles Times* praised McKinley for his "stamina, nerve, and backbone," and the *Balti-more Sun* applauded his "firmness and strength of character" and said that at times the "moral courage not to fight" should be valued more highly than the "physical courage to fight." As the positive references to McKinley's courage, strength, and backbone indicate, McKinley's defenders drew on the same terms used by his critics. They, too, recognized the importance of appearing manly to wielding political power, and hence they tried to refute the slurs against McKinley. A letter published in the *New York Times* that urged Americans to "uphold our President, for he is no coward" articulated the logic of the day: to defenders and detractors alike, the president's character reflected the worthiness of his policies.[17]

In the days following the sinking of the *Maine*, McKinley's supporters avowed that waiting was the most manly and courageous thing to do. They accused the jingoes of being hysterical, a word that connoted a feminine loss of self-control. They presented McKinley as a model of a more statesmanlike version of manhood, which they linked to the peaceful settlement of the Cuban issue. McKinley's backers urged the public to hold its condemnation and grant the president time to act. "Then," said Sen. Henry Cabot Lodge (R, Mass.) (who was restraining his jingoist ambitions in the name of party loyalty), "if there is any failure on the part of the Executive or of Congress to maintain the national honor, will be the time to condemn, and should such failure occur, which I do not believe for a moment possible, the condemnation will be heavy indeed." Those partial to McKinley agreed with his critics that "a weak or vacillating policy would mean the overwhelming defeat of the Republican party and everlasting repudiation of the administration."[18] They conceded to Sulzer that action perceived as unmanly could wreck the administration, but they expressed confidence that the president could be trusted to act in a manly fashion.

The fact that both sides of the war debate employed ideals of manliness leads to the question, Why did they reach such different conclusions about McKinley's "backbone"? Did political convictions determine their character assessments or did their character assessments determine their political convictions? Undoubtedly, political activists who had strong party preferences, sympathies for the Cubans, or convictions about American interests used gender ideals as a convenient tool, to be manipulated in the most advantageous fashion. But the different ways the two sides defined *manliness* also suggests that gender beliefs may have affected political activists' views of the president and his policies.

Significantly, those who championed McKinley often drew on old middle-class ideals of manhood that placed more emphasis on self-control, moral virtue, courage of convictions, and strength of principle than on violent outbreaks or bellicose posturing. They applauded McKinley's "firmness and strength of character" and cited the president's "dignity," "firmness," and "statesmanlike" behavior to prove that he had the manly character necessary to lead. The restrained version of manliness that many McKinley loyalists endorsed was consistent with their circumspect approach to international relations. Those who valued mental and moral rather than physical power in their leaders were more likely to consider the president's course to be, as one adherent described it, "wise, manly and just."[19]

Although many of McKinley's champions frowned upon aggression, they realized that late-nineteenth-century American men harking back to romanticized recollections of the Civil War generally regarded support for the military in times of crisis as the ultimate test of male character. They understood that many jingoes were benefiting from new standards of passionate manhood that glorified action and a fighting spirit as ends in themselves. Hence, McKinley's peace-loving supporters joined with his more bellicose followers, who stood by him more from party loyalty than personal or ideological affinity, to insist that President McKinley's manly character was beyond doubt because he had proven it in the Civil War. Sen. Edward O. Wolcott (R, Colo.) leapt to the president's defense by reassuring the country that McKinley had the "courage of a man who has known the smoke of battle." Rep. Charles H. Grosvenor (R, Ohio) stated that the president's Civil War record made aspersions on his manhood ludicrous: "Hesitation about the character of the Executive! A man who marched and fought at Antietam and in the Valley of Virginia, who followed the fortunes of Sheridan in the great actions of that ever-memorable campaign, who stood from his boyhood of 18 years to his manhood in the face and fire of battle—does anybody doubt where his loyalty is, where his patriotism is, where his courage is?" Similarly, the *Rochester Democrat and Chronicle* cited McKinley's military record to prove his worthiness to lead. After noting that the president "has a splendid record as a soldier," the paper concluded, "He has all the necessary courage for the great office he so nobly fits."[20]

Supporters invoked McKinley's war record not only as an indicator of past valor but as proof that the president's future course of action also would be manly. The *Sacramento Bee* asserted that McKinley would act "as firmly and as unflinchingly as when he went down into that murderous sea of hell in the Civil War. . . . We have no doubt that William McKinley will prove American to the backbone, staunch and true, every inch of him." Likewise, the *Los Angeles Times* argued that because McKinley had "proven his valor and patriotism in the fires of war . . . the great, patient, reasoning people of this mighty country should lean in confidence upon his manhood and integrity."[21] Those who cited the president's military record hoped that it would convince even the most skeptical jingoes that he had the manly attributes necessary to lead. They used McKinley's record to characterize him as manlier than his critics, many of whom were too young to have fought in the Civil War. Their tendency to portray military service as a crucible for manhood, however, undercut claims that seeking peace was manlier than jumping enthusiastically into war. After all, if military endeavors forged manly character, why would a manly man oppose them? The late-nineteenth-century revival of the Civil War–era belief that military endeavors and manliness were linked made it difficult for McKinley's defenders to refute the charge that McKinley's deliberative approach toward Spain reflected a lack of character.

Ironically, prior to 1898, McKinley had benefited from the association between military service and manliness. In his run for the presidency in 1896, McKinley called the Union veterans who visited his house in Canton, Ohio, comrades and spoke nostalgically of his military service. "It is a great thing to have been a soldier in the Civil War," he proclaimed.[22] The printed Republican record of these speeches referred to McKinley not as congressman or governor, his recent civilian titles, but as major, his old military one. His campaign biographies also stressed his war experience as proof of his manly character. One described his Civil War record as "full of heroic incidents" and emphasized that McKinley had known the hardships of a private before rising through the ranks. McKinley had the "same courageous characteristics as a boy soldier that he now has as a leader of the people," noted another. A third biography described McKinley's gallantry in the field and pointed out that he still wore the bronze badge of the Grand Army of the Republic. These biographies included photographs of the rifle McKinley had used in the Civil War and the candidate in his military-style Knight Templar's uniform (fig. 11). McKinley and his promoters implied that the former soldier could be counted on to act firmly in national crises. As an election-year pamphlet declared, "When battles were fought or service was to be performed in warlike things, he always took his place."[23]

In the campaign of 1896, McKinley's opponent, William Jennings Bryan— the youngest candidate who had ever been nominated for the presidency by a major party—demonstrated enormous vitality and indefatigable vocal chords as he crisscrossed the country by train, but only McKinley could claim to have proven his manliness as a military hero. Bryan, nicknamed the Boy Orator of the Platte by Republicans who wished to draw attention to his youth and inexperience, had been a small child during the war. A cartoon printed in *Harper's Weekly* shows how McKinley's adherents used his war record to enhance his political standing. It juxtaposed McKinley in his military uniform, rifle in hand, with Bryan in a cradle, rattle in hand. The caption said that McKinley was continuing to uphold the nation's honor, and Bryan, to shake his rattle. Out on the stump, Republican speakers dwelt on this theme. A passage from a campaign speech by the prominent lawyer Chauncey M. Depew illustrates this

11. "M'Kinley as a Knight Templar." Reprinted from Robert P. Porter, *Life of William McKinley* (Cleveland, 1896). Courtesy of Harvard College Library.

point: "Against the misinformation, the inexperience, the unfitness for the greatest office of the world of William Jennings Bryan, we place this type of our best citizenship, this model soldier, statesman and man, Major McKinley." Depew then described McKinley's military record in greater depth.[24]

Bryan's followers insisted that their candidate was an athlete, that he had shoulders "broad enough to excite the approval of a Norse viking," that there was "nothing soft, yielding or effeminate about him." They contended that he "eats thrice a day, scoffs at dyspepsia, and sleeps soundly at night."[25] They said that unlike McKinley, who had Marcus Hanna (his campaign manager) to "go to the front" for him, Bryan did his own fighting. McKinley's partisans held their ground, however, resolute in their faith that their candidate, the bona-fide soldier, was "one of the best examples of courageous, persevering, vigorous manhood that the nation has ever produced."[26]

Although his Union record won McKinley few votes among ex-Confederates, in the North, it helped him present himself as a man of the people rather than a tool of corporate interests. Even though wealthy capitalists lined McKinley's campaign coffers, his military service made him a comrade. His supporters held that just as McKinley had stood as an equal among the masses of men during the Civil War, he would continue to stand with his fellows in the peacetime Republican army. In the Republican state convention in Ohio, the former governor Joseph B. Foraker (then running for the U.S. Senate) proclaimed on his behalf, "Shoulder to shoulder with him we have been fighting the battles of Republicanism in this state for a generation. We know him and he knows us. He has been our soldier comrade, our representative in Congress, our governor." In another campaign speech, Rep. Theodore E. Burton (R, Ohio) praised McKinley as a man who, "as soldier or citizen," had proven himself "a patriot and a man. (Applause.) And when you have said that, you can say no more for any man. I love to read of his record: Going into the army as a mere boy, and identified with what is best and greatest in this country; identified with its bone and sinew."[27] Republican campaigners reasoned that because McKinley had fought shoulder to shoulder with the masses of American men, he was worthy to lead them. McKinley was a lawyer backed by the trusts, but as a military hero, he seemed to embody civic virtue. The masses of voters could trust him as a man.[28]

During the campaign of 1896, the visitors who paid their respects to McKinley at his home in Canton, Ohio, honored him as a military hero, thereby indicating that they did, indeed, consider his army record relevant to the political campaign. One visiting supporter, the spokesman for a group of Pennsylvania Republicans, said that he and his fellows had traveled to Canton to pay their respects "to him whom the great Republican Party has lifted upon its shield and who will guide the Republican hosts to victory." He promised that the Union veterans "who love to speak of you as Comrade McKinley" would be found "in the mighty phalanx which you will lead to victory next fall." Elsewhere, his admirers altered the words of "Marching Through Georgia," a Civil War song, so that the lyrics praised McKinley's bravery in war and predicted a Republican victory in 1896.[29] Republicans' eagerness to view McKinley's leadership in military terms signaled that their acceptance of him as a leader was connected to their vision of him as a military hero.

McKinley's military service made him appear a viable leader to the legions of military-minded campaign workers who considered themselves "the privates of the Republican army." The political warriors who marched to McKinley's porch dressed in military regalia, carrying tattered flags from Grand Army of the Republic post rooms and singing the party's martial songs to the accompaniment of military bands undoubtedly regarded McKinley's youthful record as relevant to the current campaign. Likewise, the men who spoke of the campaign as "the battle field" and who assured McKinley that they had "enlisted for the war," meaning for the duration of his campaign, respected McKinley because, as a tested military man, he appeared an apt commander. McKinley's military service made him accessible to the masses of voters, and it proved his worthiness to command a political system that, although more domesticated than in the postwar period, still relied heavily on military rituals, imagery, and metaphors. Indeed, following his victory, the Republican periodical *Judge* printed a cartoon of President-elect McKinley dressed as Napoleon, surrounded by the prominent men of his party, all dressed in military uniforms. "The triumphant return of the victorious Republican army," read the caption (fig. 12).[30]

When McKinley presented himself as a worthy presidential candidate because he had demonstrated his manhood in war, he reaffirmed the importance of a military style of manhood to political leadership, something that was beginning to fade as the Civil War slipped ever further into the past. But the military style of politics that helped McKinley win election in 1896 limited his options in 1898, when the *Maine* crisis drew even greater attention to martial ideals of manhood. Most American men did not demand a constant clamoring for war, but they did demand a willingness to fight in response to a slight of honor. McKinley had proven his manliness by serving in the military, but to continue to appear manly, he had to continue to stand by the military in times of crisis. He could not appear to betray the dead men of the *Maine*. Neither could he appear less aggressive than the masses of American men. As McKinley advocated restraint, he began to lose his martial image, to appear a doddering old man to combative younger men. The *New York Journal* conveyed the growing sense of disgust with the president's manhood when it said it could imagine McKinley "leading a delegation to a Grand Army parade, but not to anything more fierce."[31] Such gibes had powerful implications, for questions about his heroism and commitment to the military could undermine McKinley's position as a leader.

As he contemplated how to respond to the sinking of the *Maine*, McKinley faced a number of issues: humanitarian concerns, the interests of American businessmen in Cuba, the impact of a war on the entire American economy, and the potential for coaling stations and strategic bases. Added to these were concerns for his reputation and credibility as a leader and the implications of his image for his party. McKinley suffered the constraint of being a first-term president in a political system that valued a military style of manliness in its leaders. McKinley was deeply sensitive to public opinion.[32] As he

12. "The triumphant return of the victorious Republican army." *Judge*, November 21, 1896. Courtesy of Cornell University Library.

assessed the tenor of the war debate, he undoubtedly realized that his perceived cowardice in foreign affairs was undermining his credibility as a leader, that it threatened to sink his administration along with the *Maine*.

The president had good reason to be apprehensive about charges of cowardice because, regardless of his youthful Civil War record, he was not universally esteemed as a great military hero or a forceful leader. The up-and-coming Theodore Roosevelt was not alone in thinking that despite his military record, McKinley was "not a strong man." The sedate McKinley did not embody the new standards of active, athletic, aggressive manhood. He had never enjoyed hunting, and when he tried fishing once as president, in his frock coat and silk hat, he capsized the boat and ruined his shoes and pants. The clean-shaven McKinley was the only president between Andrew Johnson and Woodrow Wilson not to have a beard or mustache, signs of masculinity.[33]

In 1896 his campaign biographies were defensive about his soft image. They emphasized that even though he had been a studious child, he was nonetheless "a real boy, enjoying his sports with other boys, always popular with them." They insisted that, in spite of rumors to the contrary, McKinley was "possessed of great physical strength," that he was naturally muscular and had "strong lung capacity." But the campaign testimonials did not end discussion of McKinley's manliness. In 1898 the *New York Journal* contrasted the "squat and pursy" McKinley to the "tall and lean" Thomas Jefferson. Whereas Jefferson's "whole build [was] that of a man," McKinley's "pudgy" hands revealed that he had never done hard work. Jingoes argued that instead of embodying the robust energy associated with young men, McKinley appeared stodgy. As tensions with Spain mounted, detractors accused McKinley of running an old folks' home in the White House. All but two of his cabinet members were over sixty, and the two exceptions were fifty-four and fifty-nine. Although his adherents asserted that McKinley was "in the very prime of a splendid physical and mental manhood," the lack of vigor among his advisers made McKinley seem feeble by association.[34]

Besides appearing physically soft, McKinley appeared to lack the independence central to manliness. His opponents ridiculed him as a puppet of Marcus A. Hanna, who had risen to the Senate after running McKinley's campaign. A joke of the time questioned whether Hanna would still be president if McKinley died. Detractors accused McKinley of being a tool of his Wall Street advisers. "Take my word for it," said Representative Sulzer, "the American people will never consent to be governed by any man who is not big enough to own himself." McKinley seemed not only overly dependent on Hanna and other wealthy backers, but also incapable of managing his own finances. Nineteenth-century men were expected to provide for their families, but McKinley had gone bankrupt in 1893. Although his Republican biographers maintained that McKinley had handled his business failure in a "manly way," their praise was defensive.[35]

McKinley was known as a humane man, a Christian man, a man who was solicitous of his invalid wife. He was a domestic man who preferred home comforts to coarse male camaraderie. Press accounts labeled McKinley a "mother's boy." Even his military record evoked domesticity, for McKinley had won his reputation as a military hero by serving coffee to beleaguered troops. In telling this story, McKinley's supporters stressed his bravery under fire; his opponents chuckled at the nature of the mission and made invidious remarks about his commissary assignment:

> . . . being unprepared to go to hell
> He told the general he could cater well.
> At last, at last he had a bomb-proof place,
> And ruled the pantry with right queenly grace;
> Indeed, one day so well he served the food
> They voted him a major, where he stood.[36]

During the campaign of 1896, Republicans had responded vigorously to such aspersions. One the one hand, they had worked to subordinate his domestic image to his martial one, while on the other, they had advanced the notion that some domestic attributes were desirable in a peacetime leader. McKinley's victory testified to their success in portraying him as having the character necessary to lead.

But in the spring of 1898, as frustration over McKinley's delaying tactics grew, the president seemed to lose his martial veneer at the very moment that martial characteristics seemed most imperative. Critics warned that if the president "shows the white feather to Spain," he would lose his heroic reputation. As tensions rose, old gibes resurfaced, more powerfully than before. The *New York Journal* accused McKinley, when young, of sitting behind a haystack "making coffee while the fighting went on." The article implied that McKinley had not changed in the ensuing decades.[37] Advocates of a bellicose foreign policy took advantage of the *Maine* disaster to demand a more belligerent leader.

A calculating politician, McKinley no doubt realized that he needed to demonstrate he still had backbone lest he lose his ability to lead a political system that equated military valor and leadership. Highly conscious of public opinion, he surely knew that many American men thought war was necessary to defend American honor and avenge the dead sailors from the *Maine*. In Congress, Republicans and Democrats alike were citing their constituents' eagerness to fight. Rep. Joseph Wheeler (D, Ala.) announced that the "chivalrous men who fought in that terrible conflict from 1861 to 1865, and their equally noble sons, inspired as they are by the fame earned by their sires, all stand ready to place their lives and treasure on the altar of duty." Rep. David H. Mercer (R, Neb.) joyfully described the military enthusiasm of American men to prove that true men welcomed the prospect of a fight:

> What a patriotic scene confronts us at this hour! Old veterans, representatives of the "blue and gray," all vying with each other in the expression of loyal sentiments as they will vie with each other on the field of battle to protect the honor and dignity of our Government, if the President of the United States shall make a call to arms. Surrounding them are men equally patriotic, representing every section of the Union, but who were too young to participate in the late war, while the cheers from the multitude indicate that the whole country is full of faith in the Administration and full of fight if the needs of the hour demand it.[38]

Congressmen who portrayed their constituents as eager to fight insinuated that backing a military solution to the crisis would mean being in step with the masses of American men. Their claims were substantiated by the president's mail. Every night McKinley's assistant secretary, George Cortelyou, showed the president some of the tenders of service pouring in from across the country. Even newspapers that praised McKinley's caution informed their readers that men were keen to serve in the event of war.[39]

Assurances that men were eager to fight made efforts to avoid war seem incongruous with manly sentiment. If the masses of American men wanted to fight, why didn't McKinley? A *New York Journal* cartoon that depicted McKinley in a bonnet and apron futilely trying to sweep back a stormy sea conveyed the spreading (and, to McKinley, threatening) conviction that if the president countered the will of American men, he would become as politically potent as a feebleminded old woman (fig. 13).[40]

In addition to worrying about losing the respect of the masses of American men, McKinley worried about losing leadership to Congress. After McKinley's message of March 28, the *Washington Post* reported that the president was afraid he would not be able to prevent Congress from acting on its own. On March 30 the *Post* noted, "If the President desires to lead the procession . . . he will be accorded every opportunity of doing so. If not, the ranks will be closed and the President will be under the necessity of falling in behind." Congressmen underscored the point that the president must act or lose his stature as a leader. In a letter of April 4, Sen. Joseph B. Foraker (R, Ohio) said that Congress had been waiting for the president to take the lead on the war issue, to no avail. The president, said Foraker, "disappointed all of us very seriously with his message about the *Maine* disaster and we made up our minds that we would not wait on him any longer." "The responsibility is now

13. "Another Old Woman Tries to Sweep Back the Sea." *New York Journal*, in *Review of Reviews*, **May 1898. Courtesy of Harvard College Library.**

on Congress," said Sen. Marion Butler (Pop., N.C.) on April 12. "We must re-move the humiliation that is upon us as a nation."[41]

As Congress grew increasingly restive, even the president's erstwhile supporters began to question the manliness of his policies. Senator Spooner commented that "we have borne the methods of Spain in Cuba with patience approaching pusillanimity. We can tolerate it no longer." Republicans begged the administration to make war for party survival.[42] McKinley could appear to exhibit backbone by searching for a peaceful settlement for a while, but he could not hold back indefinitely. He knew that if Congress took the initiative in pressing for war, he might not regain his stature as a leader. A president who reluctantly followed the ranks into war would find it difficult to regain the confidence of men who interpreted politics in terms of military metaphors.

It is difficult to determine the degree to which McKinley's need to main-tain his manly image affected his decision to push for war because he did not record his reasoning. He wrote few letters, left almost no personal papers, and said little in conversation. But friends believed that McKinley did not want

war. They viewed him as a man who deeply desired peace. McKinley's associates were convinced that the president was pushed into war to satisfy Congress and public opinion. Senator Chandler believed that the president ad-
vised delay because he was unwilling to give a war message to a Congress he
knew would accept nothing else. Chandler attributed the president's increasingly bellicose attitude toward Spain to "the rising temper of the country and
Congress especially."[43] Although Chandler did not mention the aspersions on
McKinley's manhood, these were an important component of the country's
"rising temper." Placing the assaults on the president's manliness in the larger
context of a political culture based on military manhood leads to the conclusion that the need to appear manly to an aggressive constituency helped make
war seem politically necessary to the president.

On March 30 McKinley burst into tears as he told a friend that Congress
was trying to drive the nation into war. He remembered the Civil War as a
horrible conflict and had hoped that international arbitration would replace
war as a means of settling international disputes. McKinley did not want war,
but neither did he want to wreck his presidency. Aware of his growing reputation as a spineless leader and recognizing that Republican legislators would be
unwilling to go along with a new peace initiative, McKinley drafted a message
in early April that put the Cuban matter into the hands of the infamously bellicose Congress.[44]

After McKinley delivered his message on April 11, jingoes continued to
criticize him for his refusal to resoundingly cry for war. As one critic said,
everybody except "the bankers and the ladies felt a sense of shame in reading
the message of the President." Such calumny discouraged McKinley from
seeking a last-minute solution to the crisis. On April 19 Congress submitted a
resolution to the president authorizing him to intervene to end the war in
Cuba. McKinley felt he had no choice but to sign, although he knew the resolution would surely lead to war. Spain immediately severed diplomatic relations with the United States. On April 22 the United States imposed a naval
blockade of Cuba; on April 24 Spain declared war; and on April 25 McKinley
asked Congress to declare war. Congress did so eagerly, predating the start of
war to April 21.[45]

McKinley's scanty personal records mean that arguments about his motives (gender-based or otherwise) ultimately must be based on conjecture. But
even though McKinley did not record his rationale, the debate over his backbone shows that gendered ideas about leadership limited the range of politically viable options available to him. McKinley's backbone became a central
issue in the debate over war because political activists, whether Republicans,
Democrats, or Populists, believed that manly character mattered in politics.
Men from across the country agreed that the character of the nation's leaders

attested to the acceptability of their policies, and following the *Maine* disaster, increasing numbers of men demanded a militant leader. Aware of the links between manhood, military prowess, and political power (indeed, eager to take advantage of them in the campaign of 1896), McKinley reached the logical conclusion that war was politically imperative. His decision to join the jingoes was less a reflection of his courage or cowardice, strength or weakness, than an acknowledgment that the political system he operated in would not permit any other course of action.

5

....

The Spanish-American War and the Martial Ideal of Citizenship

The Spanish-American War was a popular war. The military had no trouble raising troops for what was generally seen as a righteous war to liberate the Cubans and redeem American honor. After President McKinley called for 125,000 volunteers, men flocked to enlist. According to Secretary of War Russell A. Alger, "Within twenty-four hours the nation was aflame. Tenders of service came by the hundreds of thousands. It is safe to say that a million men offered themselves." A second call, for 75,000 more volunteers, led eager men to again overwhelm the administration with offers to enlist. "It was the apotheosis of patriotism," concluded Alger.[1]

Women, too, hastened to support the war effort. After the declaration of war, women involved in patriotic, literary, and reform organizations regeared their activities to help the military. "Will the women of our state falter or fail when they are needed? No! a thousand times no!" proclaimed a circular that urged Massachusetts Woman's Relief Corps members to raise funds for hospital supplies and to give one afternoon or evening a week to preparing bandages or soliciting jellies and fruit for sick soldiers. Before the war ended, in Massachusetts alone more than 320 women's societies aided the military. Across the country, thousands of women's organizations provided for servicemen by raising money, sending supplies, and looking after the health and well-being of soldiers stationed in U.S. military camps. After the armistice, activist women declared that women's support for the war had been unparalleled in the nation's history.[2]

The brevity of the conflict and the magnitude of the American victory added to the popularity of the war. From Commodore George Dewey's stun-

[107]

ning defeat of the Spanish flotilla in Manila Bay on May 1 (a victory that won him a promotion to admiral) to the Spanish capitulation of Manila on August 14, the fighting lasted three and a half months. Besides Dewey's overwhelming victory (in which the only American death was from heat exhaustion), notable American triumphs included the defeat of Admiral Pascual Cervera's squadron off the coast of Santiago de Cuba on July 3 (in which 323 Spaniards and 1 American died), the negotiated capitulation of Santiago de Cuba on July 16, and the feebly contested Puerto Rico campaign, which lasted from July 25 until news of the armistice with Spain arrived on August 13. (More costly victories for the United States came at Las Guásimas on June 24 and at El Caney and San Juan Hill on July 1.)[3]

The magnitude of the American victory led those who had been concerned about American honor to rejoice. But to those who were committed to *Cuba libre*, the war had a bitter end. At the close of the Cuban campaign, it appeared that one of the casualties of war was the prospect of Cuban independence. Although American troops had collaborated with the Cuban insurgents early in the war, by the time the United States negotiated the surrender of Santiago de Cuba in July, relations with the Cuban revolutionaries had deteriorated to such a degree that U.S. troops kept Cuban soldiers from entering the city, on the grounds that the insurgents might attack unarmed Spanish soldiers, assault women, and loot. Later, the United States reinforced its garrison in Santiago, the result being, as Louis A. Pérez has noted, that there were "more American soldiers in Cuba after the peace than during the war." Rather than liberating Cuba in the summer of 1898, the United States occupied it until 1902.[4]

To explain this shift in U.S. policy, historians have cited changing perceptions of the Cubans. Whereas prior to the U.S. intervention, American press accounts often depicted Cuban revolutionaries, including even Afro-Cubans such as Gen. Antonio Maceo, in favorable terms, after the intervention, American soldiers and journalists drew more heavily on racial stereotypes to explain their increasingly negative assessments of the Cubans. In the spring and summer of 1898, images of distressed Cuban damsels and heroic Cuban soldiers gave way to images of cigar-smoking Cuban women and lazy and cowardly Cuban men. House Speaker Thomas B. Reed (R, Me.) expressed the prevailing disappointment with the Cuban army when he described it as an "armed rabble as unchivalrous as it was unsanitary," far different from the heroic knights of prewar descriptions.[5] Rather than countering negative racial beliefs, the new images of Cuban insurgents reinforced them.

Racial convictions certainly predisposed white Americans to regard the Cuban revolutionaries unfavorably, but they were not the only factor behind the shift in public opinion. After all, if race alone were sufficient to explain

American disdain for the Cubans, then Maceo and other Afro-Cubans never would have been lionized by the American press. To a large degree, the shift in public opinion can be explained by American men's disappointment with the martial capacities of the Cuban revolutionaries, regardless of their race or class status. Lacking familiarity with the guerrilla warfare that Cuban men had been waging, American soldiers concluded that the Cuban *insurrectos* were cowardly and dishonorable. Rep. Theodore E. Burton (R, Ohio) voiced the sentiments of many Americans when he said of the Cubans, "I am perfectly frank to say, we were a good deal disappointed in them. We found that instead of armies fighting there, ready to strike blows for liberty, they were much more numerous when the call was made for rations than when the call was for battle. We found some smoking cigarettes and taking their ease in the shade, when our soldiers were fighting for their liberty; that is, the liberty of the Cubans."[6] Like numerous other observers, Burton concluded that Cuban men lacked the manly character supposedly demonstrated by American soldiers. Racial prejudices undoubtedly contributed to such negative assessments, but these assessments implied that more than race explained the Cubans' governmental incapacity, that the Cubans, irrespective of race (or class for that matter), lacked character attributes seen as necessary for self-government.

Negative evaluations of the Cubans' martial capacities had significant implications for the cause of *Cuba libre* because the Spanish-American War strengthened martial ideals of citizenship in the United States. The rise of militant ideals affected not only the conduct of politics at home but also U.S. policymakers' attitudes toward Cuba. The increasingly imperial cast of U.S. policies toward the former Spanish colonies reflected this wider political context.

In the wake of the Spanish-American War, the jingoes who had hoped to recapture the manly ideal of politics viewed the recent conflict with satisfaction, for the war helped military valor gain ascendance over other theories of citizenship, including natural rights, stake in society, and moral virtue. The association between military service and citizenship was not new, but it had started to lose its force among younger men prior to the Spanish-American War because they never had experienced a major war. After 1898, the existence of another generation of celebrated veterans made martial ideals of citizenship seem more compelling to those who had no memories of the Civil War and even to those whose memories were fading. Along with revitalizing martial ideals of citizenship, the Spanish-American War slightly altered them: in contrast to the acclaim for Civil War veterans, the praise for Spanish-American War veterans focused less on their noble purposes and more on their martial feats. Late-nineteenth-century admirers still looked to soldiers as embodiments of civic virtue and a fraternal spirit, but after critical assessments of the Cuban patriots tarnished the chivalric veneer of the Spanish-American War, those who held up U.S. soldiers as model citizens placed a relatively greater emphasis on their physical capacity.

The invigorated conviction that citizens were quintessentially military heroes can be seen in the effusive praise of servicemen that filled newspapers, speeches, and letters of the time. Caught up in the enthusiastic effort to honor servicemen as model citizens, the men of Clay County, Texas, passed a resolution declaring the "gallant heroes" of the war honorary citizens of their county. In the celebratory aftermath of the war, such military heroes as Theodore Roosevelt, Leonard Wood, and George Dewey won recognition as representatives of "the highest type of the American citizen." Statements to the effect that "the American soldier and the American sailor is but the American citizen in uniform," showed that the war solidified the belief that citizens were those who could fight.[7]

In addition to strengthening the view that servicemen exemplified the highest ideals of citizenship, the Spanish-American War breathed new life into the belief that military men made the best leaders. Before the war, political commentators had predicted that the military heroes who rose to prominence in the war would reap political benefits. In support of this prognostication, an editorial in the *Atlanta Constitution* pointed out that American men always had expressed their appreciation for military heroes by electing them to office. It listed the examples of George Washington, Andrew Jackson, William Henry Harrison, Zachary Taylor, and Ulysses S. Grant and then concluded that Americans "have never engaged in a conflict of any magnitude without making a leading general of it their president." The editorial continued, "Who can doubt, if there should be another war, that history would repeat itself? Surely, some officer of the army or some officer of the navy, now comparatively unknown, would be a hero of it, and would for a time overshadow in public interest everybody else, however prominent in civil walks. A war with Spain now would be likely to end just about the right time to make the victorious chief a candidate for the presidency in 1900." Not all commentators viewed this prospect with so much enthusiasm. The reformer Henry B. Blackwell worried that the war would create "a new crop of political generals [and] politicians."[8] The *Atlanta Constitution*'s enthusiasm and Blackwell's distress were well-founded: at the close of the war, servicemen did win recognition for representing the overlapping virtues of ideal men, citizens, and political leaders.

One of the men who benefited from this line of thought was President McKinley, who no doubt was delighted to find that being commander in chief during a war restored his image as a capable leader. Following the victory in Cuba, favorable political cartoons put McKinley's reputation as a spineless

14. "Coming into port." *Philadelphia Press*, in *Cartoons of the War of 1898 with Spain* (Chicago, 1898). Courtesy of Harvard College Library.

coward to rest by depicting him as an authoritative captain of the ship of state (fig. 14). Articles on the greatest heroes of the war often included the commander in chief. "Above all," gushed one such story, in the *Rochester Democrat and Chronicle*, "we have had in William McKinley a heroic war president—a war president worthy to stand in line with Lincoln, a high principled, patriotic, patient and yet energetic executive, who has been in fact as well as in name the commander-in-chief of the army and navy during one of the most exciting and momentous years in American history."[9] McKinley's wartime leadership enabled his champions to credibly describe him in the election of 1900 as an "ideal man" and fearless leader. As a Republican campaign song said,

When the war with Spain awakened all our spirit, *not* our fear,
And there came a time for action to be done,
Then our Army and our Navy to the roll call answered, "Here!"
And McKinley was the Man Behind the Gun.[10]

After McKinley was assassinated in 1901, eulogies recalled the prewar charges that he was a "jelly-fish" but then cited his wartime leadership to show how ill-founded these aspersions had been. His bereaved votaries contended that he deserved a place alongside Washington and Lincoln in the pantheon of great American presidents. Like Washington, he was a military hero; like Lincoln, he had, as one partisan put it, "guided the nation through the perils of warfare and brought the Ship of State in safety to the harbor of peace."[11]

McKinley was not the only man to find his war record politically useful after the war. Foremost among the veterans who found that military service could be parlayed into political prominence was Theodore Roosevelt, who had given up his position as assistant secretary of the navy at the start of the war in hopes of seeing action with the 1st United States Volunteer Cavalry, popularly known as the Rough Riders. The Rough Riders did see action at Las Guásimas and again on Kettle Hill in the battle for San Juan Heights overlooking Santiago. Roosevelt proved at least as effective a self-promoter as a military campaigner, and he emerged as one of the best-known heroes of the war. In the fall of 1898, the New York political boss Sen. Thomas Collier Platt, acting on the widespread idea that a popular war hero would help the ticket, secured the Empire State's Republican gubernatorial nomination for the eager Roosevelt.[12]

Political cartoonists presented Roosevelt's campaign for the governor's chair as a continuation of his military campaigns (fig. 15). Editorials did likewise. One paper that highlighted Roosevelt's military experience was the *Chicago Tribune*, which wrote, "Colonel Roosevelt has opened his campaign Santiago fashion. He has made his first advance upon the enemy with all the dash, vigor, and magnificent alertness which characterized his onset at . . . San Juan, and here as there he has led the way." On the stump, Roosevelt, who traveled with an escort of Rough Riders, stressed his military experience: "In my regiment of Rough Riders I had men from the North, South, East, and West; men of money and men without money. I treated the Northerner as I treated the Southerner; I treated the poor Rough Rider as I treated the rich Rough Rider; and so shall it be if I am elected governor—every man shall be treated on his merits as a man." Although the New York Republican Party's record of corruption had made Roosevelt's prospects look doubtful at the start of the campaign, the men of New York elected the war hero.[13]

Two years later, Roosevelt's military record helped him win the vice pres-

15. **"The Rough Rider's Latest Charge."** *New York World.* **Theodore Roosevelt Collection, Harvard College Library.**

idential slot on the Republican ticket. At the Republican convention, speakers referred to Roosevelt, who appeared in his Rough Riders hat, as the "heroic fighter," the "fighter who has proved great as Governor," and the "fighting Republican." "His life to us is an embodiment of those qualities which appeal everywhere to American manhood," said one Massachusetts delegate. At the convention, Sen. Chauncey M. Depew (R, N.Y.) spoke at length on Roosevelt's military record, describing Roosevelt as a child of privilege who had manifested his toughness first as a cowboy and then as a soldier. He proclaimed that Roosevelt's experiences under fire had transformed him from an effeminate dude to a hero. Wrote one Republican about what ensued, "Depew and the Colonel of the Rough Riders were the center of a veritable cyclone of applause which whirled through the great convention hall until

15,000 people were drawn into it to cheer the name of the hero of San Juan Hill." The convention heartily nominated Roosevelt for vice president—the only opposing vote was his own.[14]

During the campaign of 1900, Roosevelt's war record continued to be useful to the ticket. Newspapers contrasted it to that of the Democratic presidential nominee, William Jennings Bryan, and asserted that the nation needed leaders who, as the *New York Sun* put it, "left office to be in the thick of the fight and not the other way around." For their part, Bryan's followers highlighted *his* commission as a colonel in the late war, but they struck a markedly defensive note when they insisted that he would have proven himself a greater hero if Republican maneuvering had not kept him in camp in the United States throughout the conflict. The McKinley-Roosevelt ticket won the election, and Roosevelt became president following the assassination of McKinley in 1901. When Roosevelt ran for the presidency in 1904, his war record continued to give him a boost.[15]

Roosevelt, though the most successful, was not the only serviceman to reap political profits from his military service—party activists and voters were eager to back other military heroes as well. After the former Confederate general Joseph Wheeler (D, Ala.) relinquished his seat in Congress to serve as a general in the Spanish-American War, he won even greater political popularity. A newspaper editor wrote to Wheeler in July 1898, "You are the popular idol and they [the voters in his district] love and worship their 'Fighting Joe Wheeler' as an ideal patriot and representative of the dear South." The editor went on to say that even Wheeler's political opponents had developed respect for Wheeler as a result of his war record. "There has been a complete change of sentiment in the whole district," he smugly noted. Other political commentators agreed that Wheeler had bolstered his political position by serving in the war. "The fact is, I do not believe there is a man in the world who could defeat you for Congress in your district, especially since you have so endeared yourself to all the people of the United States by the work you have done in the field," wrote a Montgomery district attorney to Wheeler.[16]

Recognizing the value of his military record, Wheeler's supporters milked it for all it was worth. They maintained that men should judge it a privilege to endorse his wartime achievements and manliness by voting for him in the congressional election of 1898. As one newspaper put it, "No officer who has served in this war deserves higher honor both as a soldier and a manly character, than Major General Joseph Wheeler. The State of Alabama, of which he has been so long a representative in Congress, has reason to be proud of him, and that his candidacy for re-election is practically unopposed, proves that the State is worthy of such a citizen. He ought to receive the unanimous vote of his District, every citizen deeming it a privilege that he has an opportunity to give that recognition of General Wheeler's gallant and brilliant service in the war, and his ability and magnanimity as a man." Wheeler the military hero proved so popular that, according to a New Orleans paper, Republicans and Populists "asked permission to vote at the Democratic primaries for the gallant old soldier in order to show their appreciation of his heroism and service in the Santiago campaign." In its coverage of the Alabama election, the Syracuse *Courier* concluded that his distinguished military record had made it "dead easy" for Wheeler to win office.[17]

After his nearly unanimous victory (no one dared oppose the popular war hero), Wheeler's promoters began to talk of higher office, including the Senate, governor's chair, and vice presidency. Part of Wheeler's political appeal can be attributed to the tendency to view him as a symbol of North-South reconciliation. But his champions typically paid more attention to his fighting spirit than to his political principles, thus suggesting that his martial image contributed a great deal to his appeal as a leader. Some of Wheeler's admirers maintained that if McKinley ran with one war hero, then the Democrats should pick Wheeler as their war hero. Others held that the general was such a hero that he could cross party lines and win a place next to McKinley on the Republican ticket. His most dedicated adherents had even higher aspirations for Wheeler—they declared that his war record could win the presidency for the Democrats. As one approving New York paper said, "Maj. Gen. Joseph Wheeler, patriot, soldier, statesman. The Democratic party will nominate him—the people will elect him."[18] These grand hopes were dashed when Wheeler left Congress to serve in the Philippines. But regardless of Wheeler's personal political fortunes, his story, like Dewey's, conveyed a point to the thousands of American men who read about his military exploits and political appeal: the nation was eager to honor its military heroes by choosing them as political leaders; military service and political authority were linked.

A northern counterpart to Joseph Wheeler was John Lind, a former Minnesota congressman who had lost a bid for governor on the Democrat/Populist ticket in 1896. At the start of the Spanish-American War, he won a political appointment as regimental quartermaster of the 12th Minnesota Volunteers. During the war, which he spent in camp in Chattanooga, he decided to run for governor again, and this time he positioned himself as a soldier-hero. He kept his military post while his Minnesota supporters campaigned for him at home. His continued military service led one friendly newspaper to comment, "He will depend on the people to fight his battles while he is fighting theirs." Favorable newspapers described Lind as a "gallant soldier" and predicted that the "Spaniard fighter" would win. They exaggerated the arduousness of his military service, saying that he was "in the field," "bravely" serving his country.[19]

In response to such efforts to portray Lind as a military hero, Republican papers questioned his military prowess. "It is nauseating to the extreme," commented one paper which pointed out that Lind had incurred little danger in his quartermaster post in Tennessee, "to observe the exultation of the Demopops as they refer to their candidate for governor as the 'soldier candidate.'" Another hostile paper belittled the candidate's military service by saying that the "woods are full of men good as John Lind who would go into the service at the rear end of a regiment and deal out hard tack and salt pork to the soldiers." Still another paper accused Lind of cynically seeking a commission in order to "work the young soldier argument." The questioning of Lind's military record reveals his opponents' conviction that it was, indeed, relevant to the election, that it was helping him win support. But the Republicans' criticisms failed to take hold. Lind the military hero won the governorship that Lind the civilian had been unable to win two years earlier. Running on the Democratic ticket, he took the highest office in the Republican stronghold of Minnesota.[20]

In addition to bolstering the political standing of politically active men, the tendency to view military prowess as a sign of the capacity to govern propelled even men with little or no political experience into the limelight. One of the war's most famous heroes, Lt. Richmond Pearson Hobson, the youthful commander of a well-publicized mission to block Santiago harbor by sinking a coal ship in the narrow channel, won a congressional seat shortly after the war. The greatest military hero of the war, Admiral Dewey, found that his feat had brought him from anonymity to the center of public attention. The admiral was inundated with letters and telegrams proposing that he run for the presidency. When the press started proclaiming Dewey's political appeal, the Republican loyalist Sen. Redfield Proctor (R, Vt.) ventured what appeared to be a joke in a letter to President McKinley: "We may run him [Dewey] against you for President. He would make a good one." To Dewey, Proctor wrote a more serious letter: "You are being mentioned for President by a good many papers. It is urged that several successful Generals have been honored in this way, but no naval commander; that we shall hereafter be much more of a naval power than ever before, and that it would be a fit recognition. I do not think that this is an improbable outcome, and I am sure it would be a fortunate one for the country." Proctor was not joking when he said that a good many papers were mentioning Dewey for president: a panoply of stories and political cartoons depicted him as an ideal candidate because of his illustrious military record (fig. 16).[21] The press devoted so much attention to Dewey's heroic character and so little to his principles that one excited New York Republican exclaimed, "Dewey could be elected President to-morrow, and nobody knows anything of his politics." Although Dewey finally ruined his politi-

16. "Let History Repeat Itself." *New York World,* in *Review of Reviews,* November 1899. Courtesy of Harvard College Library.

cal prospects by belittling the presidency (he described the office as "not such a very difficult one to fill"), the enthusiasm for his candidacy illustrates political activists' eagerness to place military heroes on the ballot, their assumption being that this would help their party at the polls.[22]

The postwar propensity to acclaim military heroes as prime candidates for office did not mean that all politically ambitious veterans won high office or that all high offices were filled by veterans in the postwar period. What it did mean was that the Spanish-American War had fostered a climate in which political capacity seemed even more closely connected to military prowess than it had been at the start of the war. Those who had worried that the veneration of military virtues was fading along with the Civil War generation breathed somewhat easier after the war. To the great satisfaction of the jingoes who had hoped to reinvigorate martial ideas of politics through war, the Spanish-American War gave new life to the martial strains in U.S. political culture by exposing a younger generation to war.

Although militarist thought particularly benefited politically ambitious ex-servicemen, it also enhanced the political standing of some men who did not serve. In the postwar period, men from different social groups worked to raise their political standing by citing the military service of men from their class, region, or race. Foremost among the groups that refurbished their political image during and after the war were "dudes." The dude was the stereotypically effeminate wealthy man, usually from the Northeast. Prior to the war, jingoes often depicted such men as symbols of the corrupting power of money. In the debate leading up to war, a number of jingoes accused wealthy men of holding the nation back because they feared to fight. They ridiculed elite men for being, as the *Chicago Tribune* put it, "non-combatant under any possible circumstances. They would take a slap in the face and leave it out to arbitration."[23] Wealthy dudes seemed to put comfort above national honor; their life of monied ease appeared to have debased their manly character. Detractors held that their lack of manly prowess indicated their unworthiness to wield political power.

Not only did the dude appear unmanly, but his detractors argued that he was antagonistic to manhood. Populists and Democrats had made the battle between money and manhood a staple political image even before the war debate, but during the debate they drew on this theme with great relish. In one heated speech, Rep. James A. Norton (D, Ohio) questioned, "Must we sacrifice our manhood to corporate greed and insatiate avarice?" Later, Rep. John J. Lentz (D, Ohio) exclaimed, "The money power shall not dictate the policy of American manhood." Rep. John W. Gaines (D, Tenn.) gave the money versus manhood theme a regional cast when he contrasted southern military manliness with northern commercial sloth. He promised that two million "Southrons" would muster in a week, "ready and shouting for the fray," while "their greedy countrymen in the land of trusts are gloating over fat jobs and growing rich off the Government and speculating in blood."[24] Charges that moneyed men from the Northeast cared more about their personal comfort and profits than about "American manhood" cast doubt on their worthiness to lead.

In hopes of lifting the dudes' political standing, elite men had called for them to develop the "manly virtues" in the years leading up to the Spanish-American War. In "The Manly Virtues and Practical Politics" (1894), Theodore Roosevelt exhorted middle-class men to enter the "battles of the political world," to go out into the "rough hurly-burly of the caucus, the primary, and the political meeting." Roosevelt admitted that it was pleasant to associate merely with cultivated, refined men, but he admonished his peers to mingle on equal terms with coarse men and to develop the "rougher, manlier virtues, and above all the virtue of personal courage, physical as well as moral," for he believed these were essential in politics. "We must be vigorous in mind and body, able to hold our own in rough conflict with our fellows, able to suffer punishment without flinching, and, at need, to repay it with full interest," he wrote.[25] To succeed in politics, concluded Roosevelt, men must demonstrate the hardy virtues of the soldier.

The Indiana lawyer and future senator Albert J. Beveridge also preached martial virtues to elite men. In a speech made in 1897, he told an audience of fraternity brothers that college men who did not participate in politics were civic failures. He continued, "In a republic the fittest will survive. If today the politician, rather than the scholar, is seated on the throne of power, it is because he ought to be there rather than the college men, who, in their studies and in their clubs, weakly lament the decadence of public virtue instead of entering politics like men." Beveridge proposed to resolve the problem of aloof college men by having them follow military models. Just as earlier members of Delta Kappa Epsilon had displayed their devotion to democratic government on the battlefield, the current generation of "Dekes" should fight to maintain what their fathers had created. "The mission of Delta Kappa Epsilon in politics today," he said, "is the same as Delta Kappa Epsilon believed its mission to be when the bayonets of war were flashing more than thirty years ago—active participation in the fray, the unsheathing of real swords rather than swords of lath, the firing of actual artillery, instead of the explosion of the ordinance of empty speech, and, instead of the vain notoriety of theorizing words, the immortality of doing and of deeds."[26]

Such exhortations may have inspired college men to try to attain greater political roles, but they also deepened college men's political frustrations. In peacetime it was difficult for genteel men to live up to militaristic admonitions to mingle with men from other classes, demonstrate their courage and physical prowess, and act like their martial fathers. Hence, to many middle- and upper-class men, the war against Spain appeared to be their long-awaited opportunity—a chance for them to validate themselves as men, citizens, and leaders, to dispel the notion that "mere intellectual struggles" had turned them into, as the sociologist Franklin Henry Giddings put it, "anaemic bookworms, unfit for the serious work of practical politics."[27] The task of rehabilitating the dude was not an easy one, however, for to prove the dude's manly character, his supporters first had to disprove charges that he feared war and shunned military service.

In the spring of 1898, Professor Charles Eliot Norton of Harvard appeared to confirm the belief that elite men were degenerate citizens, fearful of war and disdainful of service. Norton won national notoriety for his institution and class after describing the war as barbaric and suggesting that his students should not enlist. Ardent newspapers lambasted Norton and his students for being too refined to participate in the great issues of the day. "In other words," commented an article in the *New York Sun,* "the young men of [Norton's] class are to remain in placid contemplation of the grace of Greek sculpture and the beauties of medieval paintings while their fellow countrymen are putting themselves to the inconvenience of fighting at the front." Critics informed Norton that men of his type had no place in public life. "The country does not look to or listen to men of your stamp in shaping the destinies of the nation," wrote one. ". . . Go back to University Hall and your aesthetics and cease to weary the ears of heroes with the caterwaulings of the academy."[28]

The belief that elite men lacked the manly qualities that made for good citizens was exacerbated by charges that the wealthy young men who did volunteer sought easy commissioned jobs. Rep. Willis Brewer (D, Ala.) raised this issue in congressional debate when he charged that the military's supply and pay departments had been placed in the hands of "the inexperienced scions of certain wealthy and notorious families," who were "accorded soft yet responsible positions without regard to their qualifications, but simply because they stand as shadows of mighty names." Similarly, Sen. Richard F. Pettigrew (Silver R, S.D.) accused the McKinley administration of giving "worthless dudes" and "these scions of wealth and indolence" army commissions that they were not qualified to hold.[29]

The gravamen of these charges—that rich men were poor citizens because they lacked character and civic virtue, the combination of which led them to demand privileges they had not earned—was not new. What was new in 1898 was the military cast to these accusations and the opportunity to refute them. During the war, the "best men" responded vigorously to criticisms of elite men's lack of character. In answer to the Norton scandal, Harvard men defended their institution and class by listing their graduates who were in the military. (Their fellow Ivy Leaguers drew attention to the more patriotic example of E. Benjamin Andrews, president of Brown University, who stated a desire to enlist with his students and march with them to the front.)[30] In response to the preferment charges, the bourgeois press declared that dudes had spurned soft commissions and had enlisted as privates.

The idea of dudes enlisting as privates was such a novel one that it seemed to surprise even their advocates. Henry L. Higginson, a Union veteran and a fellow of the Harvard Corporation, was thrilled that the elite men of his club had volunteered, particularly because they had not sought soft officer positions. He wrote to Sen. Henry Cabot Lodge that some Harvard students he knew had enlisted as privates. "Had to! Couldn't help it! We of '61 got commissions and these boys go us one better and enlist! . . . Here I sit in the dude club—sports—loafers—athletes—dandies—raised in cotton wool . . . a little club and 40 men have already gone—11% of the club, which has *many* old men as well as young—20 seniors of Harvard college and many of the other schools are in the service—chiefly privates." His fellow Harvard graduate Theodore Roosevelt (who had been tagged with the epithet dude when he entered politics in the 1880s), also was pleased that college men enlisted in the ranks. Referring to those who enlisted in the Rough Riders, he exuberantly reported, "With hardly an exception they entered upon their duties as troopers in the spirit which they held to the end, merely endeavoring to show that no work could be too hard, too disagreeable, or too dangerous for them to perform, and neither asking nor receiving any reward in the way of promotion or consideration."[31]

To clinch their arguments on the manliness of dudes, middle- and upper-class men asserted that some of the greatest heroes of the war were dudes. Henry Watterson, in his *History of the Spanish-American War,* wrote that Hobson (the hero who had tried to trap the Spanish fleet in Santiago harbor), was "so careful of the conventions of dress, manner, and the little amenities of society, that he was esteemed a 'dude' among those with whom he enjoyed the relaxations of social life." But, continued Watterson, "like Dewey, also, the garb of the 'dude' covered the clear brain, the cool courage, the quiet heart, and the steel nerves of the dauntless American fighter." Watterson went on to describe Admiral Dewey, the greatest hero of the war, as "the dude of dudes." In a similar vein, one of Dewey's many biographers noted, "They might call him 'Dewey the Dude,' but he was not afraid of getting his clothes soiled at Manila."[32] Both of these authors used Dewey to help strip the word *dude* of opprobrium, to associate the dude with manly character.

Descriptions of valiant dudes helped elite men back up their contention that men of their class were not devoid of manly character, that they were "real men" who would take, without whimpering, "their doses of steel medicine on the battlefields of Cuba." The war had made it an offense to criticize the dude, crowed his thrilled supporters. These backers included Richard Harding Davis, a journalist who had been ridiculed as a fashionable dandy in his days as a cub reporter. Although he often reported on high society, Davis had managed to remake his dandified image, in part by writing about strenuous expeditions to Texas and South America. But Davis remained sensitive to slurs on dandyish elite men, especially because he had turned down a captaincy in the army at the start of the war, thus implicating himself in the charges that shirking dudes were not real men. Although he did not go to Cuba in a military capacity, Davis attached himself to the Rough Riders and went as a reporter. His dispatches criticized military strategy and the conduct of the war, but they contained such glowing praise for the elite men who were risking their lives in Cuba that Davis concluded, "Some of the comic paragraphers who wrote of the Knickerbocker Club dudes and the college swells of the Rough Riders organization, and of their imaginary valets and golf clubs, ought, in decency, since the fight at Guasimas, to go out and hang themselves with remorse."[33] Agreeing with these sentiments, a wartime ditty proclaimed that fighting had rehabilitated the dude:

> They laughed when we said we were going,
> They scoffed when we answered the call;
> We might do at tennis and rowing,
> But as warriors!—O, no—not at all!
> Ah, let them look there in the ditches,
> Blood-stained by the dudes in the van,
> And learn that a chap may have riches
> And still be a man![34]

According to Davis and other defenders of the wealthy, the dude had confirmed his manly character on the field of battle.

After insisting that the dude's military service should redeem his reputation as a man, the dude's supporters contended that it should redeem his reputation as a citizen, for the one followed the other. The point that dudes had evinced their citizenly worth in combat can be seen in *The Rescue of Cuba*, one of the chronicles of the war that was rushed to press as soon as the conflict was over. Its author, Andrew Draper, president of the University of Illinois, reported that "college men and the bronzed men of the plains, millionaires and negroes, all were standing upon the common level of American citizenship, true brothers in devotion to duty; and there were no differences in courage or manliness." On the floor of the Senate, Sen. William J. Sewell (R, N.J.) also applauded the dude's willingness to prove his citizenship by serving in the ranks: "The darling of the parlor, the athlete at Yale, Harvard, or Princeton, are lined to-day on the picket line before Santiago with the farmer and the mechanic, each equal, each claiming no more right as an American citizen, and each anxious and eager for the fray. It is the most sublime spectacle, I say to the Senate of the United States, that ever has been witnessed that our very best blood, our brightest young men, claim the right of citizenship to the extent that they go to the front line of battle and vie with anybody and everybody, no matter from what rank of society."[35] Sewell happily concluded that contrary to the stereotype, elite men did not shirk the harsh duties of citizenship by avoiding service or seeking privileged treatment. Instead, he maintained that their martial spirit testified to their political fitness.

Supporters did not stop at depicting the dude's equal capacity as a citizen-soldier—they moved on to affirm his natural superiority and leadership. This can be seen in Davis's story of a sergeant in the Rough Riders who had been a college and club man. Davis found that the dude's life of privilege did not prevent him from holding his ground among his rougher associates but neither did his hardy military pursuits obscure his good breeding. "There was not a mule-skinner or cow-puncher in the regiment that did not recognize in him something of himself and something finer and better than himself," wrote Davis. "The Dude," a poem published in the *Chicago Record*, also conveyed the point that the dude's natural superiority led other men to turn to him for leadership. It described a pampered youth who went to war with eyeglasses, fine silken underwear, pajamas, and a manicure set. As he departed for camp, his old companions spoke of "'Reggie Belligerent' as a capital joke."

> The girls who had known him at ball and rout
> Laughed when his act was noised about
> And each of them pictured with keen delight
> Reggie, the dude, involved in fight.

Upon his arrival in camp, Reggie was hazed by his fellow soldiers, who stole his manicure set and dipped his toothbrush in turpentine. Reggie surprised them all by beating up his lead tormenter, a Texan. Later, in battle, he proceeded to the head of the line, establishing his leadership and heroism beyond doubt when he called for the confused men to follow him. "That was the end of bewilderment; then / Ended confusion and men became men." Reggie perished in the battle, shot through the heart. His death was, perhaps, the strongest evidence of his manly fortitude, for his final words were to ask the Texan for boxing advice.[36]

According to his backers, the dude's prowess in war justified the authority he enjoyed in peacetime. Frank Edwards made this point in his history of the 6th Massachusetts Volunteers, which told the story of five men who, after a long march had left the troops exhausted and wet, volunteered to go for food. Of the five, four were graduates of Harvard, and the other was a graduate of the Massachusetts Institute of Technology. Said Edwards, "They were dudes." Their superior manhood, however, demonstrated by their service in camp, justified their power in civilian life. Edwards concluded his story of their patriotic labors by writing, "Whenever hereafter I hear a Socialist on Boston Common damning all wealthy persons, I shall feel like asking him what he was doing while so many of the American dudes were cleaning the guns, watering the mules, and eating hardtack in Porto Rico."[37] Although class distinctions without any underlying commonality could lead to an abdication of leadership, elite men thought it was safe to glorify "natural" class differentiations that arose from the shared experience of military service.

Bourgeois men like Edwards used the popular equation of military virtue and political authority to enhance the political reputations of wealthy educated men. Their efforts, though not universally persuasive, nonetheless help explain the growing acceptance of the political leadership of educated experts during the Progressive Era. In contrast to the lampooned mugwumps of the 1880s, reform-minded professional men won considerable political credibility in the early years of the twentieth century, in part because elite men seemed more closely allied with manliness after the Spanish-American War. Middle- and upper-class writers' persistent declarations that dudes should be welcomed in the male political brotherhood because they had demonstrated their worthiness in military service helped give dudes the credibility needed to lead.[38]

Just as dudes strove to enhance their political position by citing their military records, so did southern white men. Taking advantage of the association between martial prowess and citizenship, numerous southern commentators (including many of General Wheeler's supporters) announced that the Spanish-American War had reintegrated ex-Confederates into the Union. Gen. John B. Gordon conveyed this point in a speech before the United Confederate Veterans. After praising southern men for demonstrating their loyalty, heroism, and prowess in the war against Spain, he said that youthful southern soldiers had gone forth to represent the Confederate veterans who were too old to fight. The result of their service, he said, would be to completely obliterate all "sectional distrusts" and establish the "too long delayed brotherhood and unity of the American people."[39] The brotherhood he alluded to was one between white men who, earlier divided by war, could now be reunified because of war.

During and after the war, northern men joined with southern men such as Gordon to proclaim that the Spanish-American War had ended the divisions of the Civil War, supposedly recementing the sections into a Union "such as only comradeship in arms can make." The outpouring of nationalist enthusiasm can be seen in Roosevelt's remark: "The war with Spain was the most absolutely righteous foreign war in which any nation has engaged during the nineteenth century, and not the least of its many good features was the unity it brought about between the sons of the men who wore the blue and of those who wore the gray."[40] Northern political commentators like Roosevelt welcomed Confederate veterans and through them southern white men generally into the national political fold with great fanfare not because of any demonstrated civic virtue in the past thirty-three years, but because of military service. The much-touted national reconciliation brought about by the war reminded men of the theory that the basis of republicanism was a brotherhood in arms.

As acclaimed military heroes, dudes, and southern white men strove to enhance their political standing by citing their military capacities, they lent further credence to the conviction that military prowess should confer political authority. Significantly, those who held up Spanish-American War veterans as model citizens often paid at least as much attention to their physical capacities as to their noble objectives, fraternal spirit, and chivalric behavior. This glorification of physical attributes reflected a growing disillusionment with the idea of the war as a chivalric crusade. It also reflected wider cultural currents that applauded toughness, muscularity, and a fighting spirit in men, currents promoted by the war itself. The postwar eagerness to link martial capacity to political authority had implications not only for veterans' political standing, but also for U.S. political culture more generally. By highlighting the idea that military prowess had bearing on governmental capacity, promoters of the political-military nexus suggested that self-government was not an inherent right, but rather, one that rested on a specific kind of manly character. Not surprisingly, the militarist political thought that flourished in the aftermath of the Spanish-American War had exclusionary implications.

First of all, it hampered suffragists' efforts to carve out a greater political role for women. This was not from a lack of support for the war among women: the organized women who had been claiming that their housekeeping skills and nurturing qualities were needed in civic life shifted their energies during the war to aid the military. Women focused much of their energy on providing for soldiers' basic needs, including food. A sampling of aid efforts provides a sense of women's contributions. When men arrived at recruiting posts in New Mexico only to find that the military had made no provisions for them, women in Santa Fe, Albuquerque, Las Cruces, Las Vegas, and other towns quickly organized Soldiers' Aid Societies and raised funds to feed and care for the troops until they were mustered in. The Little Rock chapter of the DAR donated two days' rations for two thousand men headed to Camp at Chickamauga Park; the Brattleboro, Vermont, chapter fed lunch to a regiment of twelve hundred men and then sent nine hundred pounds of groceries to the regiment in camp. In several cities, WCTU members ran rest stations where soldiers on leave could wash, nap, read, write letters, or eat a good (presumably alcohol-free) meal without charge. Women who lived in the vicinity of military camps tried to boost morale by offering soldiers cookies, milk, sandwiches, and coffee.[41]

Women's organizations dispensed health care as well as supplies. In several towns, women looked after soldiers who were attempting to travel even though they had been weakened by tropical diseases picked up in Cuba. The need for such services was often dire. After some soldiers who had been discharged from a Long Island quarantine station passed out on sidewalks and ferryboats, the Red Cross opened a relief station by the railroad depot. It soon filled its one hundred cots with exhausted men and had to scramble to set up fifteen tents, enough to hold another ninety men. Halfway across the country, members of the St. Paul Red Cross Aid Society tended the ailing soldiers who stopped at their railroad booth. In five months, they helped more than eight hundred hungry and weakened soldiers. Besides helping enfeebled soldiers return home, Red Cross workers, many of them women, established "diet kitchens" in military camps. In these kitchens, they prepared special food for soldiers suffering from typhoid, dysentery, and other ailments who could not stomach regular camp fare. One such kitchen was directed by Junia McKinley at Camp Hobson, near Atlanta, Georgia. For the three weeks of its operation (at the end of which the camp disbanded), it served 3,242 meals. Women also established convalescent homes for returning volunteers, and some women even welcomed recuperating soldiers into their homes. These patriotic women included Mrs. A. Livingston Mason, president of a Rhode Island sanitary and relief association, who took in forty-nine men suffering from typhoid and other fevers. All recovered.[42]

Besides providing health care on a voluntary basis, women contributed to the war effort in an official capacity by serving as nurses. Army Surgeon-General George M. Sternberg authorized women to serve as nurses, first in base hospitals and later in army camps. When the government proved unable to process all the applications from potential nurses, he accepted the DAR's offer to screen female applicants. The DAR set to work under the leadership of Dr. Anita Newcomb McGee, whom Sternberg had appointed assistant surgeon-general, a position that conferred on her the rank of second lieutenant. Under McGee's direction, the DAR processed about 4,600 applications and furnished the military with more than 1,000 trained nurses.[43]

Whereas some women nurses served under military command, others tended sick and wounded troops under the auspices of the Red Cross. The most famous Red Cross volunteer was Clara Barton, president of the American Association of the Red Cross, who went to Cuba to provide relief for noncombatant Cubans and ended up aiding Cuban and American troops at Siboney, a landing spot outside of Santiago. When the American officers declined her initial offer of help, she set to work helping the Cuban forces. Only after American soldiers complained about the contrast between the well-run Cuban hospital and their own miserable conditions did the chief American surgeon request Barton's assistance. Barton found wounded American soldiers lying on the ground, uncovered even in the rain. Some had gone without food for three days because they were unable to eat the army rations of salt meat, hardtack, and coffee. Barton and her staff immediately set to work cooking gruels and soups for the wounded.[44]

Women's multifold contributions to the war effort did not go unnoticed by women's suffragists. At the close of the war, suffragists repeatedly cited women's contributions to justify their cause. The *Woman's Journal* ran an article that based its plea for suffrage on the point that women now "take an active part in all the great movements, both in peace and war, giving liberally of their money, and their personal service on the battle field."[45] The prosuffrage *Union Signal* followed its praise of one woman's wartime activism with the statement, "The full privileges of a citizen should at least be extended to her—to be exercised or not as she saw fit." In a similar vein, the suffragist Julia Ward Howe praised women for bringing "succor and comfort to the camp, hospital and battlefield" before pointedly questioning, "Should they not be counted among the citizens of the great Republic?"[46]

Finding that the press paid significantly more attention to servicemen's feats than to women's endeavors, suffragists cast a critical eye on men's conduct of the war. To show that women's energies were needed in all aspects of political life, they insisted that women never would have done some of the foolish things that military leaders had, such as setting up camp five miles from water or failing to outfit soldiers with water filters and vessels in which to boil their water. After observing that the military had benefited greatly from women's housekeeping skills during the war, the president of the Iowa Equal Suffrage Association concluded, "The experience of this war ought to have effectively destroyed the last trace of the mediaeval sentiment concerning the propriety of women mixing in the affairs of government, and also the last shadow of doubt as to the expediency of recognizing them as voters." With reports of men's military mismanagement in mind, a *Union Signal* article drew a similar lesson from the war: "Neither in peace nor in war does the government prove itself able, by man alone, to take care of the home side of its responsibilities."[47]

As suffragists cited the relevance of women's housekeeping skills to military operations, they tried to profit from the newly strengthened assumptions about military service and governance. Rather than refute the argument that military service underlay citizenship, they tried to broaden the definition of military service to encompass women. Ironically, by claiming political rights for women based on their military service, suffragists drew on the political theories that frequently were used against women. Suffragists' efforts to coopt militaristic ideas about citizenship reflected a recognition of the political context they operated in and a willingness to work within that context to win political rights.

Suffragists' militaristic line of argument came up against several obstacles, however. First, servicemen won substantially more acclaim than the women who mobilized to help the war effort. In magazines and newspapers of the time, stories glorifying soldiers and sailors are hard to miss. In contrast, stories covering women's wartime contributions are difficult to find. Soldiers and war correspondents routinely overlooked women's contributions in their accounts of the war. This omission led Barton to criticize the Rough Riders' self-aggrandizement. When the assistant surgeon of the Rough Riders testified before an investigating commission that the Rough Riders had fared so well because "we hustled for ourselves," Barton reminded the public that he had "hustled" his supplies from the Red Cross, which had provided him with food and equipment from its steamer anchored off of Siboney.[48]

The men who did acknowledge women's contributions typically refused to recognize them as comparable to servicemen's. Descriptions of women's wartime activities often portrayed women as best suited for supportive roles: they won recognition for helping or inspiring soldiers, who were thought to be the central figures of the war effort. The commentator who praised trained nurses for being "almost as important" as soldiers underlined the belief that women played only a secondary role in war. Susan B. Anthony painfully realized that men's combat experiences overshadowed women's wartime activities while viewing a victory parade in Chicago. After the event she wrote in her journal, "The streets were all decorated with arches and banners, but not on one of them nor in any of the speeches was there the name of a woman; all was for the glorification of man!"[49]

In contrast to the coverage of servicemen, much of the praise for women made no mention of their war work. "The Dewey Girl," a poem published by *Judge* magazine, serves as one example. It held that the nation's daughters should share credit for military victories along with the nation's sons, "since the power that always makes our arms victorious / Is the girls behind the men behind the guns." But rather than credit women for their war work, the poem, illustrated by a drawing of a fancily attired belle, patronizingly lauded them only for inspiring servicemen. The Dewey Girl of the title, it turns out, was a maiden who worshipfully admired the admiral. General Wheeler was equally patronizing. In between loud cheers by a New York crowd at a victory celebration, he credited the "God-directed influence of woman" for being the "power which has won all our victories."[50] At base, praising women for inspiring men buttressed the idea that women's political role was to influence men, not to engage in politics on their own accord. And praising women for honoring men merely magnified the greatness of the men thus honored.

To suffragists' despair, men who did acknowledge women's endeavors often refused to see them as having any bearing on women's roles as citizens. Instead, men frequently interpreted women's wartime service as a sign of their ability to stand above politics as extraworldly angels and to inspire men to acts of heroism. The praise won by Annie Wheeler, a volunteer nurse, illustrates this point: "Amid scenes of sorrow, agony, and blood, she stood as a ministering spirit; surrounded by the pandemonium of war, she walked as a sweet angel of peace; binding the brave soldier's wounds with tenderest touch, soothing with soft gentle hand, his burning brow . . . she never flinched or faltered in that divine mission of mercy and humanity, to which God Almighty had inspired her."[51] Whereas the military service of her father, General Wheeler, proved that he was a man, Annie Wheeler's service proved that she was more than a woman, she was an almost divine being. Whereas contemporaries regarded General Wheeler's service as proof that he was fit for the presidency, they regarded his daughter's as evidence that she was fit for sainthood. Such sentimentalized appraisals refused to connect women's wartime activism to their political position.

Political leaders' unwillingness to draw connections between women's wartime service and their positions as citizens is perhaps best demonstrated by the case of Clara Barton. The Senate officially thanked Barton for her services, but only after a debate over whether the resolution of thanks would give her the privileges of the Senate floor, as it had to men who had earlier been commended. Only after reluctant senators had been assured that Barton would not win floor privileges did the Senate pass the resolution. The debate over recognizing Barton was fraught with symbolic meaning. Lawmakers were willing to praise her services but not to admit her to their circles lest women be encouraged by her example to press for greater political rights. They had cause to be worried because Barton was an ardent suffrage supporter. Suffragists readily cited her plea to grateful soldiers: just as she had toiled for them when they were weak, they should toil for her and all other women by endorsing women's suffrage. "As I stood by you, I pray you stand by me and mine," she reportedly told the troops.[52] Senators felt they should acknowledge Barton's life-saving contributions to the military, but they shied away from acknowledging her as the full citizen she wanted to be.

The final problem with women's militaristic suffrage arguments was antisuffragists' belief that it was not just the patriotism or the self-sacrifice of military men that made them such good citizens, but rather their physical power. Antisuffragists cited the war against Spain to underscore their old premise that ballots represented male force. "Men would fain have *voted* freedom to Cuba and the islands of the sea," said one antisuffragist in a hearing on the issue, "but found that only his [sic] sword could win it. This is as true, though not as evident, of every law's enactment and every poll's decision. For this reason women cannot vote on equal terms with men."[53]

Antisuffragists argued that the war had shown that force was still a fundamental quality needed for full citizenship. Manhood suffrage, they reasoned, was necessary for the survival of American democracy "because the final arbiter [in politics] is manhood strength." Women's suffrage would undermine American government because women could cast only "blank-cartridge ballots"—that is, ballots with no force behind them.[54] Women's suffragists had called such assertions outdated in the years before the war, but they found it harder to do so afterward. In the shadow of the Spanish-American War, antisuffragists maintained that "in the civilized world the duty of defending the country in war falls on the male sex alone, and it would seem that there ought to be some connection between that duty and political power." They warned that "the transfer of power from the military to the unmilitary sex involves a change in the character of a nation. It involves, in short, national emasculation." The danger was clear. In an age of military struggles, the nation could not afford to consider women's suffrage lest that undermine its manly character and hence its international standing. With such militaristic arguments in mind, Alice Stone Blackwell glumly noted in the *Woman's Journal* that the war had "called out a fresh crop of assertions that women ought not to vote, because they cannot render military service."[55]

Suffragists could demand political rights based on women's contributions to the military, but they could not demand political rights based on women's physical power. The reinforced belief that "politics is pacific war," a form of combat in which, as one antisuffragist put it, "will sets itself against will in what is essentially a masculine encounter," hampered suffragists' efforts to win voting rights beyond the local level. The "doldrums"—the fourteen-year gap between 1896 and 1910 in which no states granted women full suffrage—can be explained in part by the strengthened conviction that full citizenship belonged only to those who could fight for their country.[56]

Women's suffragists were not alone in finding the military ideal of citizenship inimical to their political ambitions. African-American men, many of whom, like women's suffragists, hoped that military service would help them win political rights, also found their political prospects dimmed. At the end of the war, black men tried to join with dudes and southern white men to claim political authority on the basis of military service. They argued that black men's "gallantry" in the Spanish-American War testified to their political fitness and that discrimination and disfranchisement were unconscionable because of black soldiers' valor. Like women's suffragists, black men demanded voting rights as the return for military service. A few white observers agreed with these arguments. The war correspondent Stephen Bonsal, for example, thought that the "gallant behavior of the colored troops" had demonstrated the "justice of certain Constitutional amendments," meaning the Reconstruction amendments that had granted citizenship and voting rights to freedmen.[57]

Claims for political rights for black men based on military valor were stymied, however, by the widespread resistance among white men to seeing black men as military heroes. As one observer, John Bigelow, wrote in his account of the Spanish-American War, southern whites thought of blacks as slaves, servants, vagrants, criminals, and paupers, but not soldiers. "They could not believe that he [the black soldier] had any fight in him," he noted. These presuppositions undoubtedly affected General Wheeler's assessment of black soldiers. When asked to introduce a book on black men's service in the Spanish-American War, Wheeler wrote that the black soldiers who had served in the war reminded him of loyal old Negro slaves. He depicted them not as heroic men well-suited to govern, but as submissive dependents whose relative lack of militancy cast doubt on their governing capacity. Theodore Roosevelt was even less enthusiastic—in his history of the Rough Riders, he wrote that black soldiers were "peculiarly dependent upon their white officers" and that while no white troops showed signs of weakening in the battle for San Juan Hill, the colored infantrymen "began to get a little uneasy and to drift to the rear."[58] A number of observers, black and white, challenged this assessment, pointing out that black soldiers had contributed significantly to the American victory and that those who did head to the rear had been ordered to transport the wounded and bring more equipment. These critics were sorely disappointed to find that Roosevelt's racial preconceptions had skewed his interpretation of the battle.[59]

To the great dismay of those who hoped that black men's military service would prove their political capacity, Roosevelt was not alone in viewing the war as a demonstration of white men's superior military prowess. Influenced by tales like Roosevelt's, white men commonly imagined military manliness to be a characteristic of white men. The thought that heroism, though sometimes demonstrated by black men, was an essentially white characteristic, can be seen in a line of verse about a brave black soldier: "His face wuz black ez de chimbly-black, but de heart what he had wuz white!"[60] Rather than extending this man's heroism to all black men, the poet used it to glorify white men, who served as the poem's implicit standard for manhood. As a result of such convictions, black men found it difficult to press for greater political rights in the most effective rights language of the day—that of military capacity.

The same political trends that militated against American women's and African-American men's efforts to establish a greater political presence can help explain the declining fortunes of Cuban revolutionaries, who, regardless of race, also found themselves excluded from the military valor and political authority equation. To numerous American observers, they did not appear to demonstrate the martial character seen as necessary for self-government. House Speaker Reed's disdain for the Cuban soldiers' chivalry and Representative Burton's admission that he was greatly disappointed in the Cuban army were not idle remarks—they addressed the Cubans' capacity for self-government. Such assessments, by no means atypical, undercut the Cubans' earlier image as chivalrous heroes and, in so doing, countered the earlier tide of sympathy for *Cuba libre*.

This is not to say that martial strains of political thought were solely responsible for the shift in U.S. policy but that martial theories of citizenship worked in tandem with racial and class assumptions to justify U.S. control over Cuba and, indeed, over the other former Spanish colonies acquired in the war. In addition to affecting the character of U.S. political culture at the turn of the century, the martial theories of citizenship and political leadership promoted by the Spanish-American War helped lay the groundwork for empire.

6

....

The Problem of Male Degeneracy and the Allure of the Philippines

BEGUN AS A CHIVALROUS CRUSADE to redeem American honor and liberate the Cubans from Spanish oppression, the Spanish-American War ended as a self-aggrandizing war, a war that resulted not only in the temporary occupation of Cuba but also in the annexation of Puerto Rico and Guam. Most ironic of all, it ended in a bloody colonial war in the Philippines that involved over 126,000 American soldiers, more than 4,000 of whom lost their lives.[1] For years, historians have grappled with the question, Why did the United States finish one war, waged in the name of liberty, only to start another, waged in behalf of empire?

The United States initially became involved in the Philippines as part of the war effort against Spain. After Commodore Dewey sank the Spanish fleet in Manila Bay, President McKinley sent reinforcements, who took the city of Manila from the Spaniards in an attack on August 13, 1898. (During the hostilities the Filipino nationalists who ringed the city established a foothold in some of its suburbs.) The peace treaty with Spain, signed on December 10, ceded the Philippines along with Guam and Puerto Rico to the United States. The treaty, known as the Treaty of Paris, then went to the U.S. Senate for ratification. But the Filipinos who had been fighting for independence from Spain did not want to be ceded. On February 4, 1899, shortly before the Senate voted on the treaty, fighting broke out between Filipino troops and American soldiers when a private from Nebraska fired at Filipinos who refused to obey his command to halt. The Senate went ahead and narrowly ratified the treaty ending the war with Spain on February 6, leaving the nation to confront an even greater issue: whether to wage a war against the Filipino nationalists.[2]

Economic motives certainly played a significant role in the decision to fight for the control of the Philippines, which were located close to the hotly contested and potentially lucrative China market. Those who believed the nation needed strategic bases to secure its share of eastern profits regarded the Philippines as a stepping-stone. Yet a troubling question remains: What led Americans to set their democratic scruples aside and wage a trans-Pacific war of conquest? To answer this question, a number of historians have turned to the racial assumptions of the time. Imperialists generally thought the Filipinos unfit for self-government. They viewed them as even less adept than the Cubans, who at least had enjoyed a favorable image as heroic fighters prior to the Spanish-American War.[3]

Imperialists based their assertions that the Filipinos were unfit for independence on three stereotypes that gave meaning to racial prejudices by drawing on ideas about gender. All three presented the Filipinos as lacking the manly character seen as necessary for self-government. The first was that of uncivilized savages. This stereotype implied that the Filipinos were not manly as Americans understood the term. As one American reported from the Philippines, "They are not *men*. Honesty, truth, justice, pity—are either extinct among these people, or else still undeveloped." In addition to lacking moral character, the stereotyped savage lacked the self-control, work habits, and chivalrous restraint that supposedly characterized civilized men. He seemed to be driven by a crazed desire to fight. William Howard Taft, who served as military governor of the Philippines, conveyed this idea when he said of the Moro (meaning Muslim) Filipino, "Fighting is about as normal to him as peaceful life."[4]

Although imperialists tended to applaud the martial spirit as proof of manly character and governing capacity in white American men, they refused to consider the warlike Filipinos as manly. Instead, they argued that savage Filipinos fought from animalistic instincts. Rather than being rational in battle, they were frenzied. Rather than being honorable, they were cruel, revengeful, and merciless. Their seemingly insane desire for combat and their reported commitment to head-hunting as a means of proving their manliness and courage made them parodies of strenuous models of manhood.[5] Combat might serve as a wholesome remedy for "overcivilized" men but, in the eyes of smugly "civilized" observers, it made "savage" men resemble animals.

Descriptions of "savage" Filipino men had antecedents in negative depictions of Native-American men. They also paralleled the images of African-American men as bestial rapists that white supremacists were working so hard to disseminate in this period. Sen. John C. Spooner (R, Wis.) played on fears of dark-skinned rapists when he drew attention to the vulnerable European women living in Manila. "We cannot withdraw," he insisted, for that would "give over Manila to loot, pillage, and rape." Rep. George N. Southwick (R, N.Y.) painted a similarly dire picture of the havoc that would follow an American departure. The islands, he said, would be left to "general slaughter, pillage, rapine, and ruin."[6] In both the case of the stereotyped savage and that of the stereotyped black rapist, their lack of self-control over physical impulses and disregard of honorable behavior signaled their unworthiness for self-government. These stereotypes also helped justify the power of "civilized" white men, who theoretically would protect the weak and dispense justice.

Besides promising to end the bloodshed between Filipinos and protect white women and children, imperialists promised to civilize Filipino men. Although one thread of imperialist thought maintained that Filipinos would never become truly civilized because of racial limitations, another claimed that Americans would make men of the Filipino savages. They would start by teaching Filipino men self-discipline. After teaching them to work diligently and regularly, American imperialists would teach them to exercise paternalistic authority as heads of households. As Rep. William H. Douglas (R, N.Y.) proposed, Americans would "show to the Filipino men the necessity of taking on their shoulders a more active part in the domestic circle and support of the family." If teaching Filipino men to govern their families was one step toward instilling the rudiments of self-government, then teaching them military discipline was another. Imperialists contended that American soldiers would turn the bloodthirsty Filipino warriors into disciplined soldiers. (Given the duration of the war, there was a certain irony to this pledge.) They promised that American rule would, as Rep. James Albert Norton (D, S.C.) put it, "vitally effect a change of character and conditions of the Filipino people for their good."[7]

In addition to stereotyping the Filipinos as savages, imperialists cast them as children, the implication clearly being that they could not be left to their own devices. Sen. Albert J. Beveridge (R, Ind.) was one of many imperialists who cited the Filipinos' supposed childishness as proof of their incapacity for self-government. "We must never forget that in dealing with the Filipinos we deal with children," he said. Similarly, Sen. Henry Cabot Lodge (R, Mass.) thought the Filipinos were no more able to govern themselves than primary school children were able to administer public school systems. The assessment of Brig. Gen. Thomas Rosser was a little more generous—he found the Filipinos as "incapable of self government as college freshmen."[8] The stereotype of the childlike Filipino paralleled long-standing images of African Americans as children who were too immature to participate in government and of Native Americans as wards of the state. In all these cases, depicting a people as childlike implied that they lacked the manly character necessary to govern themselves.

17. "Recommended by Hoar. Hoar: 'Give the child over to the nurse, uncle, and it will stop crying.'" *Minneapolis Tribune*, in *Review of Reviews*, June 1899. Courtesy of Harvard College Library.

Building on the stereotype of childlike Filipinos, imperialists justified their policies by saying they intended to care for the Filipinos until they reached maturity. President McKinley, who referred to Filipinos as "these wards of the Nation," spoke of "our obligation as guardian." Representative Southwick pledged that the United States would supply the Filipinos "with a course in the kindergarten." Presenting the occupation of the Philippines in terms of tutelary duties toward children helped make imperialist policies seem to be an expression of American benevolence. A cartoon published in the Minneapolis *Tribune* helped convey the imperialists' point that the United States had a moral obligation to look after the Philippines. Depicting a paternalistic Uncle Sam cradling the Filipino infant, it suggested that if the United States turned the islands over to the unkempt nurse, Independence, they undoubtedly would suffer at her depraved hands (fig. 17).[9]

The imperialists' third stereotype was that of the feminized Filipino. As the *Tribune* cartoon shows, this sometimes meant depicting the islands as a hideous savage woman who lacked the delicacy associated with civilized women. It also meant rendering Filipino men as effeminate and Filipina women as highly feminine. To demonstrate Filipino men's effeminacy, imperialists portrayed them as occupying the dependent roles that Americans usually associated with women. This can be seen in the observations of the Philippine traveler and eager expansionist George Becker, who noted that "ordinarily a Filipino woman is brighter than her husband, and I know of no other country where women exert an equal amount of influence." Imperialists averred that besides having greater energy, intelligence, and assimilative powers, Filipinas were the most productive members of society. Filipino men, they stressed, did not "believe in work," and hence Filipinas had to assume responsibility for supporting their families. While they earned the family bread, "or rather, rice, their staple food," their husbands reportedly looked after the children and cooked dinner.[10] The apparent reversal of Western gender roles in such reports underscored the conviction that Filipino men lacked the manly character seen as necessary for self-government. It also seemed to indicate the need for U.S. intervention to put the Philippine gender order right.

If some accounts used Filipina women to discredit Filipino men, others used Filipinas to make the islands seem more attractive. These stereotyped Filipinas as alluring belles. Periodicals that published drawings and photographs of young Filipinas labeled "Typical Filipino Beauty," "Philippine Girls Bathing," and "dusky Venuses" pictured the islands as a land of sexually desirable, feminine women. "The Philippine woman," wrote one expansionist author, ". . . is by no means unattractive. . . . she makes a good wife, a respected mother, and, above all things she is a woman. . . . I always feel encouraged and thankful when I see a woman who is wholly feminine." Not only attractive, Filipina belles also appeared willing. Even a War Department report noted that Filipinas were eager to secure the attentions of American men. In some portrayals, the islands as a whole appeared to be awaiting a virile suitor. "The Philippines is a large and virgin territory awaiting the magic touch of American push and enterprise," noted a volume on opportunities in the colonies.[11]

Building on the romantic image of Filipina women, imperialists pictured the imperial relationship as a marriage. One imperial advocate observed that "God himself" had united the United States and Philippines and concluded, in ministerial tones, "Whom God hath joined together let no man dare to put asunder." The marriage metaphor suggested consent. It made the imperial relation appear to be a sacred one that should not be interfered with. Furthermore, because the marriage relation served as a prime example of "natural" differences in power, imperialists echoed Christian marriage vows to explain Philippine subordination. As an expansionist wrote in *Scribner's Magazine*, "For better for worse, for richer for poorer, the Philippines have become subject to the jurisdiction of the United States."[12] Finally, imperialists used the marriage metaphor to imply permanency. In contrast to savages, who could be civilized, or boys, who would eventually become men, women presumably would remain women. The marriage metaphor implied that the Filipinos would remain in a subordinate role.

Unlike the anti-imperialists, who drew on negative stereotypes of the Filipinos to argue that the United States should not admit the islands into the Republic, imperialists employed images of savage, childish, and feminine Filipinos to argue that the United States had humanitarian obligations in the Philippines. Claiming that the seemingly unmanly Filipinos were unfit to govern themselves, imperialists held that the United States had a duty to do it for them. Yet given the brutality of the war (an estimated sixteen to twenty thousand Filipino soldiers and two hundred thousand civilians died in the conflict) such humanitarian assertions seem more a justification of imperialist policies than a reflection of a guiding spirit of altruism.[13] But if assessments of the Filipinos served primarily to make U.S. policies seem more palatable, we are left with the original question: Why did the United States wage a lengthy war for control of the Philippines? What explains the imperialist impulse?

To more fully understand the imperialist impulse, meaning the desire to take and govern the Philippines, it is necessary to turn the spotlight from perceptions of the Filipinos to American self-perceptions. Imperialists' comments on American men and American democracy indicate that they wanted to govern the Philippines not only because they doubted the Filipinos' governing capacity, but, just as important, because they doubted their own. In addition to being motivated by markets (and the military bases that seemed necessary to secure them), imperialists were driven by another fundamentally self-interested motive: the conviction that holding colonies would keep American men and their political system from degenerating.[14]

Although a number of Americans believed that, by creating a new cohort of veterans, the Spanish-American War had ensured the well-being of the nation's political system for another generation, some men continued to be plagued by anxieties that an extended peace would lead to, as one author put it, "effeminate tendencies in young men," foremost among them the middle- and upper-class white men who enjoyed the many comforts of industrial society. Rather than easing their minds, the post-Spanish-American War valorization of the serviceman as the ideal citizen and political leader only underscored the question that had troubled them before the war: What would happen if the martial spirit dissipated in the United States? Theodore Roosevelt mentioned some of these concerns in 1901 in a letter to his English friend Cecil Arthur Spring Rice: "I do not wonder that you sometimes feel depressed over the future both of our race and of our civilization," he wrote. ". . . I should be a fool if I did not see grave cause for anxiety in some of the so-cial tendencies of the day: the growth of luxury throughout the English-speak-ing world; and especially the gradual diminishing birth rate; and certain other signs of like import are not pleasant to contemplate."[15] Fearful that the short Spanish-American War had not permanently rectified the softness wrought by industrialization, Roosevelt turned to empire as a more lasting remedy.

Imperialists like Roosevelt believed that holding colonies could prove to be a longer-term solution to modern civilization's seemingly dangerous ten-dency to make young, middle-class, and wealthy men soft, self-seeking, and materialistic. They thought that the experience of holding colonies would cre-ate the kind of martial character so valued in the nation's male citizens and po-litical leaders (especially in the aftermath of the Spanish-American War), and that, in so doing, it would prevent national and racial degeneracy. James C. Fernald, who in less militant moments worked on abridging the *Standard Dictionary*, conveyed this idea in his expansionist tract *The Imperial Republic*, published in 1898. Imperial pursuits, he wrote, would "provide adventurous occupation for a host of sturdy men," thereby preventing the United States from retrograding "toward Chinese immobility and decay." Fervent imperial-ists joined with Fernald to contend that American men must embrace rigor-ous overseas challenges lest they lose their privileged position in a Darwinian world. "The law of evolution is pitiless and he who gets in its way will be run over," wrote one expansionist to his senator. "There is no standing still, for-ward or backward we must go." Sen. Jonathan Ross (R, Vt.) drew on similar logic in a speech advocating retention of the Philippines: "Stagnation is decay and ultimate death. Honest struggle, endeavor, and discussion bring light, growth, development, and strength."[16] To such men, colonies held the key to character.

Imperialists wanted to build manly character not only because they were concerned about American men's standing relative to other races and nations but also because they were worried about American men's position vis-à-vis women. Fernald illustrates this point. Seven years before publishing *The Im-perial Republic*, he published a tract titled *The New Womanhood* that de-plored women who did not devote themselves to maternity and homemaking. In this tract, Fernald said that "for high manly health," boys needed "a certain roughness and severity of exercise," but that women would be destroyed by such strenuous endeavors. He was so committed to womanly delicacy that he deplored the style of dress that tried to give women the "high, square shoul-ders which are the beauty of the manly figure." He went on, "The tendency of man is toward authority, command, and penalty; of woman, toward tenderness, persuasion and reward" and concluded that women should be sheltered from the wider world for their moral well-being. From Fernald's point of view, women who ceased to devote themselves to men and instead competed with them, who preferred "manly" self-assertion to "womanly" self-sacrifice, threatened the health of the race. But just as worrisome was women's threat to traditional male prerogatives. Warning that softness in men and assertiveness in women indicated degeneracy, Fernald offered imperial policies as a solution.[17] He looked to overseas policies to solve domestic problems because he believed that the rigors of combat and challenges of establishing colonial control would test American men more thoroughly than domestic pursuits. Beyond that, they seemed certain to separate American men from effeminizing domestic influences.

The conviction that imperial policies would prevent degeneracy had three roots. The first was British imperialists' assertions to that effect. Spokesmen for British imperialism heralded manhood as one of the greatest benefits accruing to Britain from empire. As Sir G. S. Clarke told American readers of the *North American Review*, "To India we owe in great measure the training of our best manhood. India makes men." Lest anyone had missed his point, Clarke went on to say that imperial responsibilities fostered a "high ideal of manhood. . . . The empire, with all its anxieties and burdens, is now more than ever producing men." Echoing nineteenth-century intellectuals who maintained that war had beneficial social effects, late-nineteenth-century proponents of British imperialism avowed that empire was exceptionally conducive to character building; that, as the English author Sir Charles Dilke put it, colonial dependencies formed a "nursery of statesmen, of warriors."[18] These arguments appealed to American imperialists who respected the kind of manhood supposedly represented by British imperialists—the warrior type, who knew how to govern subordinates.

The second reason imperialists believed that expansion would build manly character came from their assessments of American history. Drawing on the idea that earlier generations of American men had developed their character in the Civil War and in continental expansion, some imperialists regarded the Philippines as a character-building challenge for upcoming generations of American men. Expansion would, they said, make modern American men more like their seemingly virile forefathers. Rep. Henry R. Gibson (R, Tenn.) cited anti-imperialists' reluctance to continue in their forefathers' expansionist footsteps as powerful proof of the need to expand: "In this day some of us Americans have become so effeminate, either through wealth, or through excess of civilization, or through the refinements of political or theological polemics, that they dread boarding a ship to go to the Philippine Islands, when their forefathers girded up their loins, saddled their horses, packed their mules, yoked their oxen to their own wagons, and took their wives and their children, traveling on foot 3,000 miles across plains and deserts, across mountains and valleys, across creeks and rivers, among Indians and wild beasts, in order to reach California; and they were not afraid." Imperialists like Gibson viewed expansion into the Philippines as a test of their generation's mettle. Agreeing with Frederick Jackson Turner's thesis that the challenges of the frontier had promoted democracy, they saw continued expansion as necessary for national and individual well-being.[19] Because the census of 1890 suggested that the nation's internal frontier line had disappeared, imperialists regarded the Philippines as a greatly needed opportunity to foster the forceful style of male character they considered essential to democratic government.

The third and perhaps most important reason imperialists looked to empire to build character among American men was that the Spanish-American War had seemed to bear out the jingoes' claims that martial endeavors would have this effect. Prior to the Spanish-American War, declarations that combat built character rested on fading memories of the Civil War, but afterward, their seeming truth was freshly imprinted on Americans' minds. Instead of souring the nation on military endeavors, the so-called "splendid little war" left the nation more receptive to them.[20] As it promoted the idea that military heroes were model citizens and leaders, it seemed to confirm the jingoist assertion that war built character among American men.

The magnitude of the nation's victory over Spain meant that even reports of army mismanagement failed to dim the glowing judgment that American men had proven their manly character to the watching world. The many histories of the war rushed to press at the end of the conflict conveyed the point that the Spanish-American War had been a glorious display of American manhood. In one such narrative, *The Story of our War with Spain,* Elbridge S. Brooks exulted that the war had "brought us a higher manhood" and "compelled admiration for American valor on land and on sea." John Henry Barrows, the president of Oberlin College, struck a similar chord in a speech at a Chicago peace jubilee. He proclaimed that the war had refuted Europeans' belief that Americans were a "fat" people. It had "shown that we are strong where we were thought to be weak. Our good fighters have done more to open the eyes of Europe than our good scholars. Dewey's victory in Manila, the heroism of Santiago, the splendid shooting and seamanship which destroyed the fleet of Cervera, have brought more to American prestige than our wealth, our schools, our libraries, and our prosperity had accomplished."[21] In the heady celebration of the victory, triumphant Americans crowed that the prowess demonstrated by U.S. soldiers in the war had placed American men beyond reproach.

Besides enabling American men to prove their physical prowess, the war supposedly had enabled them to refute the pre-war charges that they cared only for profits. At the end of the war, enthusiastic observers proclaimed that it had given young American men an opportunity to set aside commercial pursuits and prove their commitment to their fathers' lofty principles. Secretary of War Russell A. Alger trumpeted that the war had taught that "thirty-three years of peace had made no change in the American character. . . . The sons of those who fought under Grant and Lee showed that the soldierly and patriotic spirit of their sires had lost nothing in intensity by the lapse of years." The popular author Henry F. Keenan believed the war had "confirmed the assurance that our sons and brothers were of the same simple, self-confident fibre of the fathers. . . . Our apparent dedication to sordid ends . . . had not reached the moral marrow; our youths were still indoctrinated with the stirring old simplicities of manliness, zeal, courage."[22] Alger, Keenan, and numerous other commentators rejoiced that American men had proven their manliness in the war.

Enthusiastic observers also rejoiced in the apparent fraternity among American men brought about by the war. They were pleased by the reports that pronounced political, class, regional, and ethnic divisions irrelevant in camp. As one nationalistic commentator said, "Such terms as Republican, Democrat, and Populist were unknown and unheard" among soldiers, for partisanship took a back seat to fraternalism in the army. If men were distinguished at all within the military it was not by their political principles or social status but by their fundamental manhood.[23] Much of the fervor over war-induced fraternalism focused on the Rough Riders, whose extraordinary popularity owed a great deal to the vision they offered of a male community in which a common masculine character united men from different walks of life. Edward Marshall helped project this image in his history of the regiment. "All the officers expected clashes between the Eastern contingent and the Western men," he noted, "but the clashes did not come. The men mixed fraternally, and officers ceased to be surprised when they found that an Arizona bronco buster had chosen as his bunkie some Eastern college man." Tales of wartime military fraternity suggested that the war had strengthened American democracy by bringing men from different walks of life together in pursuit of common objectives. In an address in 1901, Theodore Roosevelt summed up the view that the fraternalism of the Spanish-American war had been beneficial to the nation. "It was a good thing," he said, for American men "to be brought together on such terms."[24]

As the nation celebrated its victory, some observers concluded that American men had done more than prove their manhood in war—they had improved it. Manhood, they opined, was the greatest legacy of the war. The newspaper editor Henry Watterson conveyed this idea in his *History of the Spanish-American War*. "Above all, it [the war] elevated, broadened, and vitalized the manhood of the rising generation of Americans," he wrote. Similarly, an article in *Century Magazine* held that "exhibitions of the finer and rarer qualities of manhood, added to the record of bravery made by white and black, regular and volunteer, all these are national possessions that can never be taken away from us, that can never work us injury; they are of more real value than any territorial possessions that the war has brought or may bring to these United States. For it remains forever true that it is the manhood, the nobility, the character of its people, and not the extent of its territory, that makes a country great." Such statements implied that the war had been, above all, a wonderful and ultimately successful opportunity for American men to "vitalize" their manhood and then flaunt it before everyone who had doubted it. This included American men themselves. In the Republican convention of 1900, Sen. Chauncey M. Depew (R, N.Y.) applauded the war's effects on American men's psyches. Thinking of charges such as those made by Theodore Roosevelt on the eve of the war that "shilly-shallying and half-measures at this time merely render us contemptible in the eyes of the world; and what is infinitely more important in our own eyes too," Depew declared, "There is not a man here who does not feel four hundred percent bigger in 1900 than he did in 1896. Bigger intellectually, bigger hopefully, bigger patriotically, bigger in the grasp of the fact that he is a citizen of a country which has become a world power."[25]

It was against this martial backdrop that the United States confronted the Philippine issue. The ascendant belief that martial endeavors were good for the nation because they vitalized American men made overseas colonies appear desirable not only for their economic and strategic benefits but also for their character-building potential. This assumption was particularly noticeable in the thought of the prominent imperialists Theodore Roosevelt, Albert Beveridge, and Henry Cabot Lodge, all of whom regarded manly character as the bedrock of American democracy.

In the period after the Spanish-American War, Roosevelt, in his capacities as candidate, governor, vice president, and president, often spoke on behalf of imperial policies and what he called the strenuous life. The two were related—imperialism was a means to attain the strenuous life, the strenuous life a justification for imperialism. Roosevelt called for the strenuous life because of his conviction that industrial society was weakening white, native-born, middle- and upper-class men, men such as himself. "The old iron days have gone," he lamented, "the days when the weakling died as the penalty of inability to hold his own in the rough warfare against his surroundings. We live in softer times. Let us see to it that, while we take advantage of every gentler and more humanizing tendency of the age, we yet preserve the iron quality which made our forefathers and predecessors fit to do the deeds they did."[26] Roosevelt fretted about the martial capacities of soft city men not only because of the possibility of external threats but also because he thought that iron character determined the health of American democracy. "Back of the laws, back of the administration, back of the system of government lies the man, lies the average manhood of our people," he said, "and in the long run we are going to go up or go down accordingly as the average standard of our citizenship does or does not wax in growth and grace."[27]

What was his solution for softness? His plan for preserving the iron quality? Strife. As a youth, the small, asthmatic Roosevelt had followed his father's admonitions to build his body by strenuous exercise. As an adult, the beefy, masterful Roosevelt firmly believed that men and nations could build themselves through strenuous endeavor. "Greatness means strife for nation and man alike," he said in 1898 in his run for governor of New York. "A soft, easy life is not worth living, if it impairs the fibre of brain and heart and muscle. We must dare to be great; and we must realize that greatness is the fruit of toil and sacrifice and high courage."[28]

Convinced that strife helped constitute manhood, Roosevelt advocated strenuosity as a guiding principle for all endeavors. But some endeavors, he felt, were inherently more strenuous than others. Most strenuous of all was war, and close behind lay empire. In his writings and speeches, Roosevelt praised the Civil War for having built character among American men. "No qualities called out by a purely peaceful life stand on a level with those stern and virile virtues which move the men of stout heart and strong hand who uphold the honor of their flag in battle," he wrote in 1897. In addition to extolling the Civil War's effects on American men, he applauded continental expansion for having fostered the qualities of "daring, endurance and far-sightedness, of eager desire for victory and stubborn refusal to accept defeat, which go to make up the essential manliness of the American character." There were no weaklings or cowards among the frontiersmen, he contended.[29]

Roosevelt's experiences in the Spanish-American War strengthened his belief that military endeavors built manhood. Roosevelt prized his military service as personally beneficial—"I am very glad the Spanish war came when it did," he wrote in February 1899, "for a little more of this sedentary life would render it hopeless for me ever to get back into active work, where I had to stand labor and hardship." The next month he again reflected on the war in a letter to a friend: "It was a great thing!" he wrote, "a great crisis and a great movement in which to take part, and we have both cause to feel profoundly satisfied that in the biggest thing since the civil war we did actually do our part, and had the luck to get into the fighting."[30] With his personal experiences in mind, Roosevelt looked to the Philippines to prevent individual men and the nation as a whole from slipping back into the "sedentary life."

Roosevelt's commitment to building strenuous character in American men shaped his arguments on behalf of imperial policies. In his remarks at the Republican convention in 1900, Roosevelt presented the Philippines as a crucible for American manhood. "We respect the man who goes out to do a man's work, to front difficulties and overcome them, and to train up his children to do likewise," he said. "So it is with the nation. To decline to do our duty is simply to sink as China has sunk." He went on to urge the nation to hold the Philippines, the clear implication being that this would build character and thereby prevent national decay. To be sure, Roosevelt also thought that imperial policies would increase the nation's trade. But riches were not his major motivation. He affirmed that to men and nations alike, more important than riches was the "memory of great deeds valiantly done." Perhaps influenced by the example of his dissolute brother Elliott (Eleanor Roosevelt's father), he argued that material prosperity was a curse, not a blessing, if unaccompanied by character.[31]

Roosevelt thought that the greatest benefit of imperial policies would be to improve the governmental capacity of American men. It was no accident, he maintained, that of the men whom he revered as the nation's three greatest presidents—Washington, Lincoln, and Grant—two were soldiers and one was a war president. Roosevelt's premise that military endeavors built the kind of manliness necessary to govern can explain his interest in the governor-generalship of the Philippines. Before becoming president, Roosevelt longed to become a colonial administrator no doubt because he believed that "the men who have made our national greatness are those who faced danger and overcame it, who met difficulties and surmounted them, not those whose lines were cast in such pleasant places that toil and dread were ever far from them."[32] The Philippines offered dangers and difficulties and, through them, an opportunity to forge individual and national greatness in the dawning century.

Sen. Albert Beveridge, whose commitment to expansion led one newspaper to comment that he "talks like a young Attila," also looked to imperial policies to build manhood. An Indianapolis lawyer, he won election to the U.S. Senate in 1898 at the age of thirty-six. There he secured a seat on the Philippines committee, a bittersweet appointment because he had hoped to chair it. He felt entitled to do so, despite his lack of seniority, because he had made an investigative trip to the Philippines in the spring of 1899. Upon his return, Beveridge counseled President McKinley on Philippine policy. Beveridge's outlook paralleled Roosevelt's in many respects. He believed that a major purpose of the government was to "manufacture manhood," and he looked upon imperial policies as an effective way to do so.[33]

Like Roosevelt, Beveridge had grown up in the aftermath of the Civil War, and, like Roosevelt, he had admired soldierly character since his youth. His earliest memory, he said, was that of soldiers marching home at the end of the war. These men included his father. Growing up in the shadow of the conflict, Beveridge dreamed of attending West Point, and when he did not get in, he ended up drilling with a cadet company at DePauw. In later years, Beveridge applauded the fraternalism between the men who had fought in the Civil War. Even northern and southern men, he said, had "learned on the field of battle the qualities of each others character and the purity of each others purposes."[34] Beveridge regarded soldiers as models of manhood in an age when, he thought, manhood could not be taken for granted.

Like Roosevelt, Beveridge had doubts about male character. These led him to call for a "strengthening of national *character*" and later to write a guidebook for young men. "Be a man," it exhorted,"—that is the first and last rule of the greatest success in life for the greatest success in life does not mean dollars heaped in bank-vaults, nor volumes written, nor railroads built, nor laws devised, nor armies led. No, the greatest success is none of these. The supreme success is character." Beveridge, who had labored as a harvester, railroad section hand, logger, and teamster before becoming a lawyer, admonished his readers to be firm and strong. "If you let luxury relax your nerves and soften your brain tissues and make your muscles mushy, a similar mental and moral condition will develop. And then, when you go out into real life, you will find some sturdy young barbarian, with a Spartan training and a merciless heart, elbowing you clear off the earth." Like many of his contemporaries, Beveridge believed that China showed the potential for degeneration: "There was a time when China was heroic, masterful, consolidated, militant, devotional," he noted, but too much complacency had led the Chinese to decline.[35] Colonies, he thought, would help the United States avoid a similar fate.

Beveridge's fear of degeneracy led him to conclude that Americans should feel "gratitude for a task worthy of our strength" in the Philippines. If, as Beveridge believed, struggle filled a Darwinian function, if it made men, races, and nations more fit, then men had to confront challenges in order to thrive. Seeing challenges as "opportunities to prove our worthiness," Beveridge argued that taking the Philippines would help American men develop the ability to compete with sturdy young barbarians. It would enable Americans to become the "master people of the world," the people with superlative character. Like Roosevelt, Beveridge expressed an interest in becoming a colonial administrator. "I would rather," he exclaimed during the Spanish-

American War, "take part in organizing our colonial system than to do anything else on this earth."[36]

Along with manhood, Beveridge also cared about markets, but to him, they were a means to an end and not the end itself. In his estimation, the ultimate purpose of commerce was to build character. Like Roosevelt, Beveridge deplored excessive wealth, for he believed that the children of the wealthy were often dissipated—lacking challenges, they became mentally, morally, and physically weak. For this reason, he counseled young men not to think of money "as the *real* reward for your life's work" and declared, "The work itself is your reward." Beveridge wanted to expand business opportunities to provide American men with an outlet for their energy. Set on this goal, he insisted that the European businessmen who resided in the Philippines led strenuous lives. "A finer body of physical manhood can not be gathered at random in America," he said.[37]

Sen. Henry Cabot Lodge, the chair of the Senate's Philippine committee, likewise looked to martial policies as a fount for manly character. Lodge's idea of character? He admired the man "who knew life was a battle, who did not fear blows and who never complained or whimpered over the chances of war;" the man who went down "into the arena of life to fight a good fight in the great world of men."[38] Like Roosevelt and Beveridge, Lodge, though too young to fight in the Civil War, was influenced profoundly by the conflict. During the war Lodge longed to enlist as a drummer. This dream thwarted by his upper-crust family, he drilled in a military company in school. As an adult, Lodge recalled the Civil War as an endeavor that had built a "noble spirit" among those who fought it; he commended Civil War veterans as model citizens and men. In his view, war deflected attention from "the spirit of commercialism and its base doctrines" and brought out the "nobler and heroic side" of men.[39]

In the three decades after the Civil War, two types of conflict reconfirmed Lodge's belief that martial endeavors built character. The first was British imperialism. Lodge admired Britain's imperial pursuits, saying they displayed "the true spirit of our race." During a trip to England in 1895 he noted, "I am more than ever impressed with the vast difference between the Englishman who has traveled and governed abroad and those who have not. The latter are insular and self-absorbed and stiff as a rule and the former are almost always agreeable and worth meeting." Just as he believed that imperial endeavors built character in English men, Lodge was certain that continental expansion had built it in American men. When his close friend Theodore Roosevelt dedicated his ode to expansion, *The Winning of the West*, to him, Lodge wrote Roosevelt, "Our philosophy of active life is here [in the book] and here are the principles we have tried to live up to and sought to preach. Whether anyone has been moved by our little sermon put forth in words and deeds I do not know but at least we can hope so and I am sure that our gospel is a manly and honest one."[40]

Lodge's appreciation of the "active life" undoubtedly was related to his concern that industrialization had undercut the character of the wealthy, white, native-born men who had profited most from the new economic trends. With these men in mind, Lodge worried that in the years since the Civil War, the "insidious gentleness of peace and prosperity had relaxed . . . the practice of some of the virtues called out by war." Above all, he looked on the super-rich as models of degeneracy who dissipated their energy on vulgar and frivolous amusements. To counter their example, he denounced "decrepit dilettantism" and exhorted college men to embrace "the spirit of action" and to "count in the battle of life." Lest his own sons fall prey to dissipation, he encouraged them to take up hunting and, arguing that deprivation built character, he kept them on a tight allowance.[41] But Lodge's commitment to developing manly character went beyond exhorting elite young men—he also supported martial policies. To him, the war against Spain was a blessing.

Lodge was a petite man, a bookish man, a man of aristocratic temperament who always had known the comforts of wealth. He was perceived as an effeminate dude by some of his political associates, as a man who, even as a senator, depended on his mother's financial largess to pay some of his bills. But Lodge had taken up riding, sparring, and hunting to develop his physique and courage; he said his "real education" as a youth had been physical—consisting of football, baseball, hockey, and "savage snowball fights" with scruffy lower-class boys.[42] Lodge never lost his youthful admiration for prizefighters, athletes, hunters, and adventurers; he spoke of the virtues of "vigorous outdoor life" and "rough-and-tumble games." In 1898, Lodge, like his close friend Roosevelt, longed to join in the fight. After the start of the Spanish-American War, he wrote his son, "I can understand your feeling about wanting to go to the front. I have it very strongly myself and it seems sometimes as if I could not stay here [in the Senate] any longer." He regarded the Spanish-American War as a much-needed challenge for American men, a challenge that he be-lieved they had met. At the end of the war, he toasted American servicemen as follows: "They have faced death in battle, wounds, hardship, disease and suffering, and have emerged triumphant. . . . We are proud, very proud, of our soldiers and our sailors, prouder than ever of our dear old flag."[43]

Lodge was particularly pleased with the prowess shown by American servicemen because he was convinced that men must possess a "character of force" to be competitive in the international struggle for survival. Even as Lodge professed admiration for the "spirit of our race," which, he believed, had led to past expansion, he feared that this spirit would deteriorate if not cultivated. The nation that "cowers in the presence of a new task approaches its decline," said Lodge. "That fatal hour may draw near on leaden feet, but weakness and timidity are sure signs that it is coming." To stay fit, to preserve character, men and nations must assume exacting responsibilities: "The athlete does not win his race by sitting habitually in an armchair. The pioneer does not open up new regions to his fellow-men by staying in warm shelter behind the city walls. A cloistered virtue is but a poor virtue after all. Men who have done great things are those men who have never shrunk from trial or adventure. If a man has the right qualities in him, responsibility sobers, strengthens, and develops him. The same is true of nations." Echoing an old speech in which he had prompted college men to "go down into the dust and heat and do something, even if you stumble and fall and rise again begrimed and scarred from the doing," Lodge pictured the war in the Philippines as a character-building enterprise: "We have always risen, bruised and grimed sometimes, yet still we have risen stronger and more erect than ever and the march has always been forward and onward."[44]

Manly character was not Lodge's only motive in the Philippines. He spoke also of the "great markets of the East" and "our share of the markets of the world." But to Lodge, wealth came second to character. "Material success with all that it implies is a great achievement," he wrote, "but it is as nothing to the courage and faith which make men ready to sacrifice all, even their lives, for an ideal or for a sentiment. The men who fell upon the decks of the *Constitution,* or who died at Gettysburg and Shiloh, represent the highest and noblest spirit of which a race is capable. Without that spirit of patriotism, courage, and self-sacrifice no nation can long exist, and the greatest material success in the hands of the cringing and timid will quickly turn to dust and ashes."[45] Valuing character above great wealth, Lodge wanted the Philippines as much for the challenges it seemed likely to pose as for the rich Asian markets it promised to help American manufacturers and merchants obtain. He was not so avaricious that he would have countenanced war for strictly commercial reasons. However, believing that war itself could confer benefits, he advocated imperial policies.

Roosevelt, Beveridge, and Lodge had plenty of company in glorifying imperial policies for their effects on character. Similar strains of thought can be seen in the statements made by many of their fellow imperialists, including even President McKinley. After resisting the pressures for war with Spain in the early months of 1898, McKinley caught a mild dose of war fever. "What a wonderful experience," he said of the Spanish-American War. The success of the war and his own increased status made McKinley more receptive to taking and holding the Philippines. Though never an ardent imperialist, McKinley went along with the affirmations put forth by such imperialists as Roosevelt, Beveridge, and Lodge. Echoing their assertions, he explained his decision to

take the Philippines by saying, "The progress of a nation can alone prevent degeneration. There must be new life or there will be weakness and decay."
McKinley proffered the Philippines as a challenge with great potential, as "the
mightiest test of American virtue and capacity." Like a number of other imperialists, he concluded that aggressive Philippine policies would build character
in American men. "We have not only been adding territory to the United
States," he declared in 1899, "but we have been adding character and prestige
to the American name (continued applause)."[46]

Driven by a desire to build character in American men, imperialists welcomed the Philippine War as a great challenge. Behind their noble-sounding
talk of U.S. obligations to the Filipinos lay a self-serving motive: the belief that
the Filipinos were opportunities as well as responsibilities. The imperialists'
calls to duty, calculated to appeal to Americans' sense of mission, masked the
less benevolent idea that conquering and governing the Philippines would
benefit American men. The stereotypes of the Filipinos discussed earlier can
reveal much about these self-interested concerns if they are interpreted with
their implications for American men foremost in mind.

The stereotype of the Filipino as savage set up the occupation of the
Philippines as a rigorous challenge for American men, who supposedly could
prove their stuff by subduing and then civilizing such barbaric foes. Imperialists deemed the task of civilizing the savage Filipinos a physically demanding
one, the summit of the strenuous life, for, however barbaric, the wild islanders
were fierce and hardy opponents. Indeed, descriptions of savage Filipino men
often mixed revulsion for their mindless barbarity with admiration for their
physiques. The author Albert G. Robinson found that members of one Philippine tribe were "remarkably fine specimens of developed physical manhood."
Dean C. Worcester, a zoologist turned Philippine expert, characterized the
physical development of the men of Mindanao, one of the archipelago's southern islands, as superb, and William Howard Taft (who overcame his initial
hesitancy and went to the Philippines only after Secretary of War Elihu Root
told him, "Here is something that will test you") conceded that the Mindanao
tribes included "some very fine physical specimens of manhood."[47]

Imperialists such as Roosevelt, Beveridge, and Lodge believed that warring against such physically powerful savages would build the "savage virtues"
in overcivilized men. If, on the one hand, imperialists considered too much
savagery a sign of unmanliness and governmental incapacity, on the other
hand, they thought that if civilized men lost all traces of savagery, they would
lose the power to govern. As Lodge once remarked, the "primary or 'savage'
virtues make states and nations possible and in their very nature are the foundations out of which other virtues have arisen. If they decay, the whole fabric
they support will totter and fall."[48] Fearful of this possibility, imperialists

turned to military struggles against "savage" Filipino men as a preventive measure.

Imperialists' desire to develop savage virtues emerged from their assumption, rooted in Darwinian thought, that, the advance of civilization notwithstanding, force was still important in international relations, especially in dealings with the so-called savage races. Representative Gibson expressed this view when he proclaimed, "Force rules the world, and all our rights are based on force." When the anti-imperialist congressman Edward Robb (D, Mo.) asked him if "justice and morals" would permit the United States to invade the Philippines, Gibson responded, "My friend and brother, nations do not go to Sunday school." Imperialists argued that rather than deny the relevance of brute force to world affairs, political leaders should accept this fact and support the imperial policies needed to build a powerful citizenry. Roosevelt sketched out this vision of citizenship in 1901 in a speech, "Manhood and Statehood": "We need then the iron qualities that must go with true manhood. We need the positive virtues of resolution, of courage, of indomitable will, of power to do without shirking the rough work that must always be done."[49] Those who accepted the premise that the international arena was marked by strife reasoned that fighting the savage Filipinos would let American men—above all, the nation's seemingly soft men of means—test themselves against embodiments of brute strength and better their ability to rule in a world based ultimately on force. They believed that taking and governing the Philippines would build up the "iron qualities" that Roosevelt prized. Ironically, the Filipinos' tenacious resistance to American onslaughts fueled the imperialists' conviction that American men needed strenuous challenges. According to this logic, if American men could not defeat the supposedly unmanly Filipinos, they must be in truly dire need of character-building struggles.

In spite of the military's difficulties in the Philippines, imperialists looked to American soldiers as embodiments of courage, patriotism, fraternal loyalty, and physical power; they envisioned the volunteer as, in the words of one imperialist author, a "free, glorious man, the real sinews of a republic in the days when too many of us are city bred." Not surprisingly, the soldiers of imperialist accounts often embodied the manly character that appeared endangered in the United States. Sen. Louis E. McComas (R, Md.) depicted the troops in the Philippines as almost superhuman examples of toughness and endurance. "Wherever they have gone, by night or by day, suffering from fever, going without food, without water to drink, marching on long expeditions, fighting here and there, bearing and enduring suffering always, scaling mountains, wading rivers, creeping out in jungles and over the swamps, whether they were suddenly attacked, or whether they were, when on pacific errands bent caught in ambush, promptly rallying, always the same brave, resourceful Americans everywhere." Beveridge, who visited the Philippines in May 1899, was equally thrilled with the servicemen he saw. He explained his decision to land on the island of Panay in the midst of a typhoon by saying, "I wished to see our boys holding the outposts in the Philippine thickets under those terrible conditions." He found what he was looking for: men who, he said, literally laughed with glee as they fought for the flag, men whose faces seemed to gleam with "virile life." Even after his wife died of dysentery contracted on their Philippine trip, Beveridge remained convinced that conquering and governing the Philippines would build "physical manhood."[50]

Lodge and Roosevelt regarded the U.S. soldiers in the Philippines with comparable esteem. Lodge described them as exemplars of "fine and manly character," and he did his utmost to defend them in a series of hearings on U.S. atrocities in the islands. Roosevelt referred to them as "gallant fellow Americans" and applauded them for their heroic endeavors and great success against an "elusive and treacherous foe vastly outnumbering them." In a speech commemorating President Grant, Roosevelt said he had but little respect for young men who did not hasten to serve in the Philippines. "Let us uphold these men who are fighting in the Philippines in everything," he said, before going on to say that they demonstrated "qualities that make us proud of our American citizenship." Such soldiers met the criteria set forth by Franklin Henry Giddings, a Columbia University sociologist and supporter of imperial policies, for the "perfect citizen"—"virile, a personal force, an organism overflowing with splendid power, alert, fearless, able to carry to perfect fulfillment any undertaking to which he may put his hand."[51] Such soldiers were proof that American men could compete in global struggles for mastery. They were the model citizens for the nation, in themselves a reason for expansion.

This is not to say that imperialists rejected more peaceable domestic attributes in men. Beveridge wrote a book about masculine domesticity, Roosevelt preached fatherhood and reveled in his brood, and Lodge, a father at age twenty-one, a grandfather at forty-four, and a great-grandfather at sixty-six, took pride in his family. But they qualified their support of male domesticity by insisting that it alone did not constitute manhood. "Study the Germans!" Beveridge admonished young men, for they were "domestic yet warlike." Roosevelt also entreated men to combine domestic and warlike attributes. He said that though he appreciated "amiable domesticity" and "the practice of home virtues" in men, he also thought that "if unsupported by something more virile, they may tend to evil rather than good."[52] Like other imperialists, Roosevelt believed that too much domesticity stifled men, that it bred effeminacy. "It is with the nation as with the individual," he wrote. "None of us respects the man whose aim in life is to avoid every difficulty and danger and stay in the shelter of his own home, there to bring up children unable to face the roughness of the world. We respect the man who goes out to do a man's work."[53] Imperialists like Roosevelt, Beveridge, and Lodge portrayed the Philippines as a place where American men, especially middle- and upper-class men, could build manly character by separating themselves from the domestic sphere, a double entendre meaning both their households and the United States. Their objective was not to make men less domestic but to enhance their capacity to govern. They were persuaded that establishing authority over the Filipinos would teach white American men not only to govern men of other nationalities and races, but also to be better heads of households and hence pillars of American democracy.

At the turn of the century, Lodge, Beveridge, and Roosevelt worried that American men were abdicating their domestic authority, thus causing women to become more active in public life. Like Fernald, the imperial publicist and exponent of domesticity for women, all three deplored women's growing political presence and insisted that electoral politics should remain a male preserve. They envisaged ideal women to be women like Anna Cabot Mills Lodge, Senator Lodge's wife. Anna Lodge was known for her dainty grace at the tea table, her devotion to her husband and children, and her love of poetry, art, music, and the beauty of nature. Though widely read, she self-effacingly deplored her ignorance; though versed in the pressing issues of the day, she avoided the public glare. As one friend noted at the time of her death, "Mrs. Lodge was not the leader of any 'cause.' Though she was interested in many philanthropic enterprises, she never had her name in the newspapers."[54]

Believing that the refinement and purity of such women as Anna Lodge depended on their distance from ugly political and commercial struggles, Henry Cabot Lodge and his like-minded allies on the imperial issue preached men's responsibility to shelter and protect women. Starting with his first vote against women's suffrage in the Massachusetts legislature in 1879, Lodge remained adamantly opposed to enfranchising women. Beveridge, too, objected to politically active women. In his guidebook for young men, he criticized women who mixed in politics. He voiced his admiration for women who made and kept homes but not for those who sought a more public life; indeed, Beveridge viewed the "propaganda that woman is the equal of man" as a sign of "decadence in our manhood." For his part, Roosevelt maintained that a healthy state relied on women's domesticity as well as men's heroism. "The woman must be the housewife, the helpmeet of the homemaker, the wise and fearless mother of many healthy children," he wrote in "The Strenuous Life." "When men fear work or fear righteous war, when women fear motherhood, they tremble on the brink of doom." Fearing that "race suicide" would enfeeble the nation, Roosevelt told his turn-of-the-century audiences that women's primary political role was to bear and raise children.[55]

Roosevelt, Beveridge, and Lodge wanted to build American men's governing capacity in part to counter women's increasing political activism. They believed that more authoritative men would dispel the pernicious "propaganda" of women's equality and cause women to return to domestic pursuits. These objectives contributed to their commitment to martial policies, for they assumed that by teaching American men to wield authority, such policies would teach them to govern their households with a firm, though benevolent, hand. Arduous struggles, they believed, would enable men to regain women's respect, devotion, and admiration. The same logic which held that an inability to govern household dependents served as evidence of Filipino men's political incapacity led Beveridge and other imperialists to think that shouldering responsibility for childlike or feminine colonial dependents would demonstrate American men's political fitness.

The imperialists' domestic objectives affected the meaning they attached to their stereotypes of childlike and feminine Filipinos. Drawing on the first of these stereotypes, they envisioned American men as fathers who would check each wayward step of their youthful charges in the Philippines. By assuming this role, American men would become accustomed to responsibility. As Rep. Jonathan P. Dolliver (R, Iowa) said in remarks on the Philippines, "I do not recognize that that is the highest type of manhood which simply takes care of itself." To the contrary, he conceived of the highest type of man as the one who took on responsibilities for others. "It is true of nations as it is true of individuals that no man liveth to himself alone," he said. The widespread belief that "a man becomes a man in the full sense only when he assumes the responsibilities of a man" lent credence to imperialists' claims that assuming responsibility for childlike dependents would serve to "strengthen and form" the nation. If men exhibited their best qualities when, as one imperial publicist wrote, "the inarticulate appeals of children touch their hearts, and, with irresistible eloquence, excite unselfish emotions," then nothing would improve the character of the nation as much as "responsibility for the weal or woe of dependent peoples."[56] Imperialists drew on the stereotype of the childish Filipinos to make the point that governing the Philippines would allow American men to develop paternalistic capacities.

The stereotype of the feminine Filipino contained a similar promise, for imperialists believed that marriage, too, built manly character. In addition to giving men a constructive outlet for their sexual energies, marriage, like fatherhood, promised to teach men to exercise authority. Lodge's conviction that this was so can be seen in his response to his son's elopement in 1900— Lodge took it well, expressing hope that marriage would "develop him." For

Beveridge, too, marriage was a character-building endeavor. He urged men to marry young, saying, "It has been races of marrying men that have made the heroic epochs in human history. The point is that the man who is not enough of a man to make a home, need not be counted." He went on to admonish young men, "If your arm is not strong enough to protect a wife, and your shoulders are not broad enough to carry aloft your children in a sort of grand gladness, you are really not worthwhile."[57] Fearful that men were failing to fulfill their obligations as heads of household and were thereby leading women to enter public life, Beveridge turned to the seemingly feminine Filipinos to develop American men's political capacity. His goal was twofold: to reclaim electoral politics as male terrain and to build the qualities in white, bourgeois American men that would permit them to maintain power relative to men from other races, classes, and nationalities.

Whether they imagined the Filipinos as savages, children, or feminine figures, imperialists regarded them a means for American men to develop their ability to govern. One adherent of imperialism summed up this belief when he averred that "the necessities involved in the unexpected annexation of strange dependencies will *call forth the governing faculty*."[58] The savage, childlike, and feminine stereotypes appealed to imperialists because they not only suggested the Filipinos' incapacity for self-government, but also enabled imperialists to cast themselves as civilizers and authoritative heads of household—that is, as men who wielded power. Heedful of British imperialists' claims that empire made men and interpreting colonial endeavors as unparalleled challenges, imperialists looked to the Philippines to turn white, middle- and upper-class American men into what they considered to be ideal citizens—physically powerful men who would govern unmanly subordinates with a firm hand, men accustomed to wielding authority, men who had overcome the threat of degeneracy.

7

....

The National Manhood Metaphor and the Fight over the Fathers in the Philippine Debate

IMPERIALISTS WHO WANTED to take and hold the Philippines to build American manhood faced a major problem: persuading their fellow citizens to go along with what promised to be an expensive and bloody scheme. To their consternation, their bellicose policies sparked considerable opposition. In November 1898, opponents of expansion organized an Anti-Imperialist League in Boston, the first of a number of leagues that mobilized public sentiment and lobbied against imperial policies. The grassroots anti-imperialist movement attracted a heterogeneous group of adherents, including a number of African Americans, Catholics, labor activists, and women, but it was dominated by a more politically powerful group: white, Protestant, professional men, whose commitment to reform, in many cases, could be traced back to the antislavery movement of the mid nineteenth century. These primarily northern, mugwumpish league leaders struck up an uneasy alliance with congressional antis, who tended to have very different backgrounds. Most congressional antis were Democrats and Populists from southern and western states. One notable exception was the Massachusetts Republican George Frisbie Hoar, the most prominent anti in the Senate.[1]

Although various parts of the anti-imperialist coalition raised different points in their arguments against imperial policies, there was a common core to anti-imperialism: the belief that taking and governing the Philippines was a shocking break from American democratic traditions. Antis from across the coalition contended that the new policies corrupted the political ideals that had guided the nation since its inception. As Senator Hoar put the matter, "The danger is that we are to be transformed from a republic founded on the

Declaration of Independence, guided by the counsels of Washington—the hope of the poor, the refuge of the oppressed—into a vulgar, commonplace empire founded upon physical force, controlling subject races and vassal states."[2] Claiming that imperial policies violated the nation's democratic principles, antis such as Hoar tried to associate themselves with the founding fathers. They invoked Washington and other Revolutionary leaders to show that imperial policies were inconsistent with the nation's democratic traditions and to suggest that those who slighted the fathers' strictures were unworthy to lead.

As they struggled to build support for their cause, imperialists had to confront this two-pronged assault on their policies and political authority. To understand why the nation pursued their belligerent, antidemocratic proposals at the turn of the century rather than the antis' more peaceable and democratic counsel, we need to take a closer look at the Philippine debate. With the prospect of empire hanging in the balance, imperialists turned to the assertive ideals of manhood that had served them so well in the past.

In response to the accusations that their Philippine policies violated the nation's deepest convictions, imperialists brandished a national manhood metaphor. The youthful republic had become an adult, they declared, and should assume the responsibilities of a mature man. Rather than dwelling on its childish past, the nation should manfully shoulder its new obligations. As the expansionist author William Levere said, it was "natural for a nation to grow, even as it is for a child. It must sometime put aside childish things and assume the functions of manhood. This means responsibilities. The man who shirks them is considered a weakling. So will history adjudge a nation." A writer in the *Yale Review* fleshed out the metaphor, emphasizing prerogatives more than responsibilities: "The big boy [the United States] who was hulking in the background, until the last few years, has changed his voice and come forward to claim his own. He proposes henceforth to have his full part in the game of *Weltpolitik,* and he will, by the right of the stronger."[3]

Through such statements, imperialists presented a dynamic model of American government, one in which the nation shouldered greater responsibilities as it matured. According to this line of thought, colonial obligations would have been too burdensome for the young nation, but now that it had grown strong, it was ready to take on the manly role of governing dependents. Arguing that it was, as Levere put it in an expansionist tract, "time for America to step out from the swaddling clothes of her childhood and become a World Power," imperialists implied that failing to assume responsibility for dependents would reveal an unwillingness to advance from childlike dependency to paternalistic power. In short, it would reveal a lack of manhood in the nation.[4] Asserting that the nation's greatest mission was to develop manhood, imperialists maintained that expansion was fully consistent with national tenets.

In addition to using the national manhood metaphor to argue that it was immaturity, not political principles, that had kept the nation from holding overseas colonies prior to 1898, imperialists used it to depict imperial policies as the inevitable result of manhood. The metaphor portrayed the annexation of overseas colonies as part of a natural growth process, the result of biological imperatives even more fundamental than legislative traditions. "There comes a time in the life of a nation, as in the life of an individual, when it must face great responsibilities, whether it will or no," said Theodore Roosevelt in a speech in 1898. "We have now reached that time." Senator Albert Beveridge agreed: "When a people reach its young manhood, as the American people has reached its young manhood," he said, "they naturally look beyond their boundaries for their energy and enterprise. The world becomes their field. . . . an expulsive energy sends them outward to the ends of the earth."[5]

In presenting the nation as a vigorous young man, imperialists cast assertive policies as unavoidable, for late-nineteenth-century understandings of youth suggested that forceful men could and should not be confined to the domestic sphere. To Americans of the time, it seemed self-evident that boys needed an outlet for their "superabundant vitality" and that they often found it in rough-and-tumble pursuits. The well-known psychologist G. Stanley Hall seemed to be stating the obvious when he advocated strenuous exercise for young men to keep their minds off of unwholesome sexual thoughts and to develop "muscular power." Noting that soldiering had "seasoned the bodies of youth" in ancient Greece and Rome and in modern Europe, Hall presented vigorous endeavors as the key to the proper development of young men. If boys suffered from too much self-restraint, he argued, they would lose their nervous force and fall prey to debilitating neurasthenia. To attain adult strength of character, boys had to follow their passionate instincts instead of repressing them. Although Hall did not advocate imperial policies, his theories of adolescent development lent credence to the imperialists' pronouncements that the youthful nation should not be restrained.[6]

Beyond reflecting contemporary theories of maturation, imperialists' use of the national manhood metaphor reflected their convictions about political power. They reasoned that in a strife-filled world, power was best wielded by the strongest members of society, and that, for many imperialists, meant robust young men. Through their national manhood metaphor, imperialists promoted the idea that the kind of character necessary for political power should be defined in opposition to old age as well as to womanhood, savagery, and childhood. To be truly manly was to be virile. This conviction was not unique to imperialists. It emerged from wider cultural currents that valorized the energy and physical prowess of youth. To many late-nineteenth-century men, the energy and exuberance of the young proved more appealing than the passivity, weakness, and staid decorum associated not only with women but also with old men. Because they were committed to the exercise of force, imperialists were particularly likely to view older men as diminished men.[7] To be manly, suggested imperialists, was to be vigorous and young as well as male.

With strenuous ideals of manhood in mind, imperialists urged the nation to demonstrate the vigor of a young man. As one of the foremost promoters of the national manhood metaphor, the freshman senator Beveridge said, "America is the young man of the nations. We are engaged in our great rivalry with the other powers of the world. And this is the destiny of every nation that achieves its manhood. According to Beveridge, the United States, the "young man of the nations," should be true to its nature and flex its powerful muscles overseas. Beveridge's ally on the imperial issue, Theodore Roosevelt, presented a similar image of the United States as a powerful young man. "Is America a weakling, to shrink from the world-work of the great world-powers?" he questioned. "No," he answered. "The young giant of the West stands on a continent and clasps the crest of an ocean in either hand. Our nation, glorious in youth and strength, looks into the future with eager eyes and rejoices as a strong man to run a race."[8]

If, on the one hand, the belief that powerful young giants should wield greater political power helped justify a more assertive role for the seemingly youthful United States, on the other hand, it helped justify the political power of assertive young men. Significantly, leading imperialists appeared to be younger than leading anti-imperialists. Many prominent antis—most evidently, those from New England—were elderly men who had been adults during the Civil War. The president of the Anti-Imperialist League, George S. Boutwell, was over eighty, a number of his colleagues were over seventy, and others were in their mid to late sixties. In contrast, the leading imperialists averaged about fifteen years younger. Even McKinley, aged fifty-five in 1898, was younger than many of the prominent league antis.[9]

The image of the young nation assuming a greater political role encapsulated the personal ambitions of the relatively youthful imperialists. Prominent imperialists like Theodore Roosevelt, Albert Beveridge, and Henry Cabot Lodge, aged forty, thirty-six, and forty-eight, respectively, in 1898, saw themselves as part of a rising generation of intrepid politicians who were struggling against older men for leadership. They felt, with good reason, that their generation had been overshadowed by the Civil War generation. A third of a century after the war, Civil War veterans still held many top political positions and continued to insist that they deserved special recognition because they had fought so valiantly in the 1860s.

The generational distinction became especially clear to Beveridge in his senatorial campaign of 1898, during which his rivals avowed that he was too young to deserve the office. When Beveridge beat out the Indiana "gray-beards" in the Republican primary, he received a flood of letters from young men across the country congratulating him on his victory. These young men viewed Beveridge's victory as a symbol of a generation's political coming-of-age. "Being a young man myself, it gives me especial satisfaction to see merit and fitness for these high places in our government recognized in the young men," wrote one supporter. "I can not help but feel that there are great things ahead for you. The young men can not be kept down," wrote another. "As a young man I rejoice in the success of young men" wrote a third.[10]

Although he won a Senate seat, Beveridge still felt overshadowed by older men. After hearing his father's tales of the Civil War, he longed for a comparable rite of passage for his generation. He was frustrated by the seniority system that kept him from chairing the committee on the Philippines. In his second Senate speech he was humiliated by senior colleagues who walked out on him as a warning that he was not sufficiently deferent to his elders in the chamber. (The seniority system held so much sway in the Senate that senators customarily made no floor speeches during their first year in office. Beveridge broke this tradition when he gave a lengthy speech on the Philippines shortly after taking his seat.) Fearful that he looked too young to have any credibility, Beveridge took pains to dress in a dignified fashion.[11] His desire to wrest political power from older men suggests that, when he spoke of reaching national manhood and exercising greater power, he spoke of his own aspirations. Beveridge and his relatively youthful fellow imperialists saw the Philippine debate as part of a larger generational struggle. Older imperialists joined with them in using generational imagery because generational struggle served as a powerful proexpansion metaphor.

As part of their effort to wrest political authority from an older generation of men, imperialists held that, rather than putting memories of bygone eras such as the Revolution and Civil War at the forefront of political discussion, the nation should look toward a new era that would be defined by the rising generation. "We of America," said Roosevelt, "we, the sons of a nation yet in the pride of its lusty youth . . . know that the future is ours if we have in us the manhood to grasp it, and we enter the new century girding our loins for the contest before us, rejoicing in the struggle, and resolute to bear ourselves that the nation's future shall even surpass her glorious past." Beveridge joined Roosevelt in predicting that manly young men would attain a glorious future for the nation. "The millions of young Americans with a virile manhood unequalled in the world will not admit or submit to the proposition that their flag is not to fly in the midst of the swiftly coming world events, so vast that all history have been but preparation for them," he said.[12] Their talk of "lusty youth," "virile manhood," and "loins" indicates that Roosevelt and Beveridge regarded the Philippine endeavor as an expression of young men's potency, the fruits of this endeavor being new territory for the American union.

Imperialists' emphasis on youthful virility helped them deflect attention from the antis' claims that their policies violated the strictures of the fathers. In response to such assertions, imperialists held that it was time to break away from the fathers and assert independence. "It is practical statesmanship with which America is concerned to-day," said Beveridge, "not academic debates on what Jefferson meant, or Hamilton meant, or anybody else meant, as to the problems of their day. Let us not fall into China's fatal error of paralysis through ancestor worship." Backed by the example of China, which was in the process of being carved up by foreign powers, Beveridge urged his colleagues not to slavishly venerate the fathers. "Great as our fathers were," he said in another speech, "the citizens of this Republic, on the whole, are greater still to-day, with broader education, loftier outlook. And if this were not so, we should not be worthy of our fathers, for, to do as well as they we must do better."[13]

Instead of relying on the fathers as the ultimate symbols of manly character, imperialists often stressed more contemporary models: American soldiers. Taking advantage of the post Spanish-American War tendency to honor soldiers as model men, citizens, and leaders, imperialists commonly opined that statesmen should follow soldiers' dictates rather than the reverse. "I do not know how others may vote," said Senator Lodge in one speech, "but I vote with the army that wears the uniform and carries the flag of my country." Similarly, Rep. Charles B. Landis (R, Ind.) called for a continued occupation of the Philippines by telling the story of a dying American soldier who pleaded not to relinquish them. In his final breaths, the soldier supposedly begged the nation to stay in the islands, saying, "We soldiers who served in the Philippines do not want to have it said in years to come that we followed a retreating flag." As they invoked American soldiers, imperialists employed a logic of fraternalism which held that if American soldiers had died to put up the flag, it would be disrespectful to lower it. "All shame to us if the statesmen flinch where the soldiers have borne themselves so well," said Roosevelt. "Shame, thrice shame, to us if we fail to uphold their hands," he said in another speech exhorting Americans to support expansionist policies.[14] To avoid the humiliation that would ensue from defeat at the hands of the seemingly unmanly Filipinos, imperialists called on American men to rally behind American troops.

As they cast themselves as the true allies of American soldiers in the Philippines, imperialists tried to associate themselves with soldiers' seemingly virile qualities. This, they anticipated, would help them win the support of their countrymen, above all that of militant young men. In a speech titled "The Young Men of America" made in 1900, Beveridge presented the Republican Party as the party of youthful militancy in hopes of winning adherents among men who would be voting for the first time:

> The question for the millions of young men, who in this campaign are going to enlist in one of those two great political parties is, where can they find their most congenial, most natural, most helpful and most hopeful comrades? In the ranks of which party can they, during the period of their active manhood, best advance the power and authority of the American people? In the ranks of which party can they help to carry the American flag farther and farther up the heights of glory? Our nation is young. Our country is young. Our flag is young. Our destiny is the destiny of the young among the nations. The question for the young men of this Republic to decide is whether they will enlist with the Republican party, which is harmonious with all those natural elements of youth, of progress and of power and whose foreign policy is the policy of American advance, or with the Democratic party, which is at war with every constructive development of our civilization and whose foreign policy is the policy of American retreat.[15]

In the speech, Beveridge implied that all truly virile young men should applaud a combative spirit and that Republican expansionists, including himself, were the best embodiments of this spirit.

To his great satisfaction, Beveridge's efforts to portray expansion as a manifestation of a contentious youthful spirit struck a chord among a number of men. One constituent, rejoicing that Beveridge was "in the position to assume the leadership of the young and aggressive element in the party," revealed his hopes that the young Republicans would become the "aggressive element in the great army of voters." A notary public from Indianapolis told Beveridge that it was a "great victory" for young Republicans to have a "young man in the United States Senate and especially one who will be aggressive and active." Another Indiana man interpreted the election as proof that voters wanted "young blood" to "give ginger to the older blood." Although imperialists counted older men among their numbers, their truculent policies helped them present themselves as youthful, bold, and energetic, as manlier than the anti-imperialists.[16]

In contrast to their self-image as vigorous, forward-looking men, imperialists painted the antis as elderly and backward-looking, devoid of the imperialists' vigor and out of keeping with the national manhood metaphor. Although the anti-imperialist movement included younger men, most notably William Jennings Bryan, imperialists nonetheless stereotyped the antis as old and out of touch with the new bellicose spirit, as a "lot of over-ripe and decayed citizens." "It is a misfortune that we have so many Rip Van Winkles in this country who can not be made to believe that time passes, progress advances, and trade and commerce increase while they sleep, unconscious of the change," said Rep. Cyrus A. Sulloway (R, N.H.), in reference to the antis. Depicting the antis as remnants of an earlier epoch (an image commonly used to depict men of color) implied that, like men of the so-called lesser races, the antis lacked the manly qualities necessary for leadership.[17]

The Senate's leading anti-imperialist, George Frisbie Hoar, age seventy-two in 1898, was a favorite target of imperialist attacks. Many of the letters written to Hoar in the wake of his Philippine speeches encouraged him, often indelicately, to resign because he seemed too old to exemplify the manly robustness expected in the nation's leaders. As a less than charitable minister from Rockford, Ohio, wrote Hoar, "It is the judgment of *men* everywhere that you have outlived your days of usefulness in the Senate. . . . Why, sir, you have blundered in your conception of the aggressiveness of this age and of the nation." A New Yorker who signed himself "Republican and Patriot" was equally vituperative: "What this country needs most at this time are patriotic Americans not a lot of old women and decrepit politicians in their dotage who pose as statesmen. . . . You are behind the times, the nation has outgrown you. Give yourself a rest in some old man's home and give the nation a chance to grow. You have outlived your usefulness. You are a back number." These sentiments were echoed in a letter that called Hoar a fossil and encouraged him to give up his place to "a young man who is progressive and who lives in the present and not in the musty past."[18]

By casting themselves as the more virile leaders in the imperial debate young imperialists could seize center stage from older, more experienced politicians. Acting on the advice of the expansionist writer Murat Halstead, who maintained that "life is too short for those who have superior knowledge of the current public questions to wait upon the proceedings of the elder members who have gotten up an idea that they keep school," Beveridge shocked the Senate by refusing to defer to Senator Hoar, a fellow Republican. Taking Halstead's advice to heart, Beveridge disagreed with Hoar on the floor of the Senate. Soon after, he received a letter praising him for his disregard of seniority. Uncle Sam had "outgrown his boyhood and has reached the vigor of manhood, and who shall say him nay?" it said. "Surely the voice of the waning generation as embodied in your antagonist on the floor will avail but little— he may hinder but never prevent doing our God given duty."[19]

Imperialists justified their assertiveness and that of their Philippine policies by maintaining that antis resembled overweening school marms or, as Rep. Henry R. Gibson (R, Tenn.) put it, "doting mothers" who did not want their "baby boys" to become men.[20] By posing as young men who were trying to break from women's confining grasp, they played on gendered and generational assumptions about the legitimate exercise of political power. Linking their struggle for political authority to the nation's struggle for colonial authority, imperialists reasoned that both were justifiable as a natural result of manhood.

Imperialists were not the only ones to draw on ideals of manhood in the Philippine debate. Anti-imperialists also turned arguments over political principles into clashes over which kind of manhood was most appropriate for political authority. But in contrast to imperialists, who asserted that the nation was just attaining its manhood and hence needed forceful young leaders, antis maintained that the nation was mature and hence needed thoughtful, experienced leaders who could keep the country loyal to the principles of the fathers. Whereas imperialists argued that the United States must prove its strength, antis responded that the strength of the United States was not in question. The nation, they said, "undoubtedly has the physical force to make the islands a desolation. . . . If it is a mere question of brute strength—of money and men and ships and guns—we can employ it without limit. We can kill and burn and destroy like Avengers of God. No one doubts that."[21] Antis said that rather than proving the nation's manhood, seizing colonial dependents would lessen the country's standing in the family of nations by undercutting its professions of virtue and benevolence. For some antis—especially the white southern antis who practiced a kind of internal colonialism over African Americans—protesting against brute force as an unmanly way to conduct international affairs was primarily a rhetorical device, adopted in part because it was a stock feature of the anti-imperialist arguments developed by northern reformers. For many of these northern reformers, however, this rhetoric emerged from a fundamental conviction: the true measure of the nation's greatness, like the true measure of a man's greatness, was not the ability to use force but rather moral standing.[22]

Whereas imperialists tended to draw their arguments about male and national character from the standards of bellicose manhood that were taking hold in the late nineteenth century, anti-imperialists tended to draw on older ideals of manhood that had flourished in the mid nineteenth century. Earlier standards of manliness, especially among the northern bourgeoisie, stressed moral maturity and self-control more than the physical power and belligerence that were valorized in the late nineteenth century. Influenced by the sentimental values and seemingly feminized religious precepts that were in vogue in the middle of the century, northern middle-class men who came of age before the Civil War did not emphasize untrammeled self-assertion or dominance as much as their youthful descendants. Of equal importance for the imperial issue, the generation of men who grew up after the Revolution and then experienced the Civil War as adults were inclined to place greater value on independence and liberty than did late-nineteenth-century men, who, accus-

tomed to greater class divisions among white men and a more corporate economy, formulated ideals of manhood that stressed hierarchy and authority.[23]

Senator Hoar serves as a revealing example of an anti-imperialist who adhered to mid-nineteenth-century standards of manhood. Hoar was a Unitarian who took his faith seriously, at times going to church twice on Sunday. Perhaps influenced by his close friend, the Reverend Edward Everett Hale, he
asserted that the most "perfect example of manhood" was the man who glorified God.[24] In contrast to leading imperialists who considered strength, toughness, and authority central to male character, Hoar defined character as "the
moral and spiritual side of man's nature." Unlike those who preached the
strenuous life as the most suitable philosophy for a world based on force, Hoar
affirmed that "the most important force in human history is that of which Darwin has nothing to say, and which science does not explain": "the spiritual side
of man."[25] To Hoar, manliness had a significant spiritual component.

In keeping with his religious values, Hoar believed that the only wars that
could test men's heroic qualities were righteous wars—that physical prowess
and courage meant nothing if not subordinated to a higher moral purpose. His
respect for soldiers was contingent on the moral purposes they fought for and
their willingness to lay down their swords when their purposes were accomplished. Unlike some of his bloodthirsty imperial opponents, Hoar refused to
glorify war. Although in his mind the Civil War was a righteous conflict, he
still recalled it with horror: "I know and dread the horrors of war," he wrote at
the start of the war against Spain, "of which the loss of life and health to soldiers and sailors is by no means the larger part. The corruption which always
follows a war, the piling up an enormous debt, the making other wars easier,
the arresting of the influence of the spirit among nations which tends to peace
—all these are most deplorable."[26]

Born in 1826, Hoar had been an adult during the Civil War, but he did
not serve in the military because, he said, his eyesight was too poor. Unlike
Roosevelt, Lodge, and Beveridge, who believed they had missed the defining
event of the century, Hoar did not seem troubled by having avoided military
service. When taunted on the subject in 1894, he calmly replied, "I do not
think anybody in Massachusetts, certainly no soldier in Massachusetts, thinks
that I failed to perform to the full extent of my power, physical or mental, in
any way the services of a good citizen during the rebellion. The whole war was
not fought out by the brigadiers general."[27] In Hoar's opinion, military service
was not necessarily the supreme test of civic virtue; intelligence and morality
were the qualities most relevant to governance.

Hoar sounded like his detractors in the imperial debate when he said he
believed that "the fate of the nation depends in last resort on individual character," but he understood character in less militant terms than they. His heroes

were not military men but men of conscience; the ideal citizen was not a warrior but "the man who loves his household and his neighbor best." What had made George Washington so remarkable, he thought, was not his capacity as a general but his "absolute goodness," his "prudence and patience and veracity." Washington's greatest virtues, in Hoar's judgment, were human virtues, "the virtues that you like to think of in your father and mother and sister and brother."[28]

When Hoar addressed college audiences on the issue of character, he applauded gentlemen and scholars, not athletes. In one paean to college education, Hoar praised colleges for teaching "refined taste manifesting itself in conduct and character." He went on to say that a good college provided an education "not merely of the intellect, but of the moral and religious nature." Another of his college addresses incurred him Roosevelt's ire: "We hear a good deal of late about the strenuous life," Hoar told Harvard students in 1900. "But your work in this world is to be done with your brains. The object of your education is not to fit you to hunt grizzly bears."[29] Hoar spoke more highly of minds and spirits than of muscles; he praised the scholar, not the Rough Rider. Like other antis, Hoar refused to deem the exercise of physical power essential to manliness.

Secure in his sense of self, the septuagenarian Hoar felt less of a need to distinguish himself from women than his younger opponents on the Philippine issue. A women's suffrage sympathizer, Hoar thought the highest character attributes were human ones, that model men had much in common with model women. He did not look upon heroism and patriotism as innately male traits, but rather, as desirable human ones. Neither did he think domesticity a particularly feminine virtue—domestic tasks, he believed, built character in boys as well as in girls. In his recollections of youth, he described building the household fire on freezing winter mornings as one of the most arduous aspects of his childhood. Whereas his adversaries on the imperial issue insisted that male domesticity must be accompanied by strenuous pursuits, Hoar seemed to think domesticity in itself a worthy aspiration for men. Above his mantel hung a Latin inscription that he translated as, "Rest I at home. What need I more? Here comfort is and Mrs. Hoar."[30]

Yet Hoar was no homebody. Not only was he a political figure of national stature, but he also had a passion for nature that grew out of his childhood walks with Henry David Thoreau in the woods around Concord. Unlike Theodore Roosevelt, known for his hunting exploits, Hoar did not regard his forays into nature as an opportunity to prove his mastery. To the contrary, in 1897 he led a Massachusetts campaign to stop the hunting of songbirds for their feathers. Tellingly, he presented his case from the birds' perspective: "Cruel boys destroy our nests and steal our eggs and our young ones. People with guns and snares lie in wait to kill us, as if the place for a bird were not in the sky, alive, but in a shop window or under a glass case." Hoar approached nature with an empathetic sensibility, rather than a desire to dominate or control it. According to a friend, he found in nature "that joyous uplifting of the soul which made him love God and man better."[31]

Hoar thought that the manliest endeavors were those aimed not at establishing authority but at promoting liberty. As a young man, convinced that slavery was wrong, he left the Whig Party for the Free Soil Party and later the Republican Party. As an older man, he predicted that the men who stood by the Declaration of Independence "shall live in the eternal memory of mankind; and the men who depart from it, however triumphant and successful in their little policies, shall perish and be forgotten, or shall be remembered only to be despised."[32] In place of what a fellow anti termed the "brute rule of blood and iron," Hoar, who did not enjoy the best of health at the turn of the century (he was, it turned out, in the last years of his life), advocated government based on reason and moral principles. In 1903, looking back at his long career in public office, he concluded that he had never acted from "emotion or [party] attachment or excitement," but only from "cool, calculating, sober, and deliberate reflection." So reserved that even his closest friends never called him by his given name, Hoar deplored boisterous political assemblies, preferring reasoned discussion to bellicose posturing.[33] And he abhorred belligerent international policies, favoring deliberation and peace.

Not surprisingly, the understanding of manliness that Hoar shared with other aged, northern antis affected his political principles and positions. Decrying imperial policies as unmanly, antis such as Hoar condemned them as demonstrations of "brute force"—exhibitions of animal passions rather than high principles. "This is the doctrine of purest ruffianism and tyranny," said Hoar in reference to the nation's Philippine policies. "There is nothing of the Declaration of Independence in it. There is nothing of the Constitution of the United States in it. There is nothing of the fathers in it. There is nothing of George Washington in it, or Thomas Jefferson."[34] Like many of his fellow anti-imperialists, Hoar thought that manliness consisted of more than the physical power wielded by young men: above all, it meant the moral maturity exemplified by older men.

With this vision of manliness in mind, antis ridiculed the imperialists as brash youths unsuited for wielding power. Senator Hoar derided the boastfulness and swagger demonstrated by the imperialists as suitable "to little nations and little men, and not to large ones. It belongs to a period of infancy." In another address, he lampooned the imperialists' rhetorical flourishes. "Nobody ever said anything to another baby more foolish," he commented. In this respect, his arguments paralleled those of his fellow antis who ridiculed the im-

perialists as childish or called them "infants kept in cradles and bibs" who
were suckled with McKinley's "expansion pap."[35] Speaking of the nation's imperial adventures, the Reverend J. T. Sunderland, a Unitarian minister, said
that those who endorsed expansion resembled small boys who were carried
away by the military's drums, brass bands, tinselry, and show. "The Roosevelt
view of life is essentially a boy's view, and if it were to become the permanent
basis of a national policy would make us the most turbulent people the world
has ever seen," said an article in *The Anti-Imperialist,* a periodical published
by Edward Atkinson, a Boston industrialist turned insistent reformer in his
old age. William James, a staunch opponent of imperial policies, also lampooned Roosevelt, describing him as "still mentally in the Sturm and Drang
period of early adolescence." Just as imperialists tried to stereotype the Filipinos as childish to deny them political power, antis portrayed the imperialists as childish to discredit them politically. Whereas imperialists declared that
young men were manlier than old ones, antis held that brash young men
lacked the intellectual and moral capacities that defined manhood. They
depicted the imperialists as essentially boyish both to negate their claims to
political authority within the United States and to counter their efforts to
tout themselves as paternal figures who would raise the childlike Filipinos to
adulthood.[36]

As they depicted the imperialists as childish, antis posed as comparative
models of maturity. The youthful Senator Beveridge proved an irresistible
foil. Sen. George Turner (Pop., Wash.), who was twelve years older than Beveridge, criticized him for attacking senators who "have been in public life for a
period longer than he has been in existence." Sen. Benjamin R. Tillman (D,
S.C.), fifteen years older than Beveridge, patronizingly commented that Beveridge knew nothing about war because he had been a baby during the Civil
War, and Senator Hoar, thirty-six years Beveridge's senior, condescendingly
called him "an enthusiastic youth" in the course of one speech. Also fixing attention on Beveridge's youth and on his own maturity, Sen. Henry M. Teller
(Silver R, Colo.), thirty-two years older than Beveridge, said that "perhaps
when he grew older" Beveridge would develop his capacity to think criti-
cally.[37]

Besides taking a paternalistic stance vis-à-vis the imperialists, antis furthered their image as senior statesmen by highlighting their own age and experience. After proclaiming that the antis "had proved their devotion to their
country" when Frederick Funston, a hero of the Philippine War and supporter of imperial policies, was "mewling and puking in his nurse's arms," Sen.
Edward W. Carmack (D, Tenn.) went on to call the antis "men whose white
hairs are a crown of glory." His fellow antis urged Republicans to listen to
those who were around when the party was formed (presumably because they

would stay true to its principles), namely, such anti-imperialists as George Boutwell, Carl Schurz, and Hoar. Hoar promoted a fatherly image of himself when he explained his opposition to the colonizing impulse as an effort to "save the Republican party, at whose cradle I stood."[38]

The image of the antis as senior statesmen caught on among their followers. One of Hoar's correspondents contrasted the "statesmen" who opposed imperialism to the "boys" who favored it. Another said he was glad to have "such cool headed men as yourself to quiet the impetuous, head-strong young men on such a serious and momentous occasion as now confronts us." Still another praised Senator Hoar as "one of the old Lincoln stamp" and said, "I only wish we had some more men in the halls of Congress left over from Lincoln's time, for they are the men with experience." "Let us be thankful that the race of American statesmen is not extinct," said a Boston newspaper that praised Senator Hoar for a speech that "recalled the best days and the loftiest ideals of the American Senate—the days of giants."[39]

In addition to posing as venerable solons who personified those who had stood for freedom at the time of the Civil War, antis tried to ally themselves with the founding fathers. As Senator Hoar said, "I am very confident I am in the company of the framers of the Constitution, the signers of the Declaration, the men of the Revolution, and the great statesmen and lovers of liberty of every generation until six months ago." In a later speech, he imagined a roll call of the nation's founding fathers on the imperial issue. Washington and his associates, he warranted, would have voted against imperial policies. Hoar tried to associate himself with the fathers because they served as powerful symbols of moral rectitude and democratic convictions. He also admired them as men. The fathers, he declared, were men who respected human rights, men who fought for liberty, men who believed in the "dignity of pure manhood." "If the United States forsake this doctrine of the fathers, who shall take it up?" he questioned. "Is there to be no place on the face of the earth hereafter where a man can stand up by virtue of his manhood and say, 'I am a man?'" Asserting that the antis stood for the "character" of the founding fathers as well as their "example and teachings," Hoar claimed an affinity with the fathers not only to underscore the antis' allegiance to the nation's principles but also to show that they embodied a truer manhood than the imperialists did.[40]

As a boy in Concord, Hoar had known Revolutionary War veterans, and in all likelihood, when he invoked the founding fathers, these elderly men came to mind. Over the course of the nineteenth century, older men had lost the venerated position they had enjoyed in the colonial period, but Hoar believed that older men still merited respect. "The vigour and enterprise of youth," he said, were best tempered by the "counsel, responsibility, trustworthiness, [and] matured experience of age."[41] Relying on his memories of elderly Revolutionary War veterans, Hoar presented the fathers as models of maturity who could temper the high spirits of his contemporaries. When, in the course of one debate, he appealed "from the clapping of hands and the stamping of feet and the brawling and the shouting to the quiet chamber where the fathers gathered in Philadelphia . . . from the Present, bloated with material prosperity, drunk with the lust of empire, to another and a better age," he intimated that his reckless contemporaries had much to learn from the fathers' mature example.[42]

An avid genealogist, Hoar also associated the fathers with his own ancestors, five of whom, he liked to recall, "stood in arms at Concord bridge in the morning of the revolution." Hoar was especially proud of his maternal grandfather, Roger Sherman, who had joined with John Adams, Thomas Jefferson, and Benjamin Franklin to present the Declaration of Independence to the Continental Congress. That was the "foremost action of human history," he averred. Regarding the nation's fathers as literal forebears, Hoar felt a deep sense of filial loyalty to them. (Hoar's respect for his own father illuminates his ideas about filial obligation: he once refused the presidency of the Harvard Alumni Association rather than be obliged to shake hands with a man who had insulted his father.) Hoping to benefit from principles of filial respect, Hoar worked to ally himself with the founding fathers.[43]

Just as Senator Hoar tried to enhance his authority in the Philippine debate by associating himself with the founding fathers, he and his fellow antis tried to prove the Filipinos' worthiness for self-government and the nobility of their cause by allying them with the fathers as well. The Filipino nationalists were, insisted Hoar, fighting for the "doctrines of our fathers." In a similar vein, Rep. John C. Bell (Pop., Colo.) maintained that the Filipinos considered their leader, Emilio Aguinaldo, the father of their country "as truly as the colonists of America regarded George Washington as the father of their country."[44] Like the *Cuba libre* backers who had compared the Cuban revolutionaries to the fathers to prove their capacity for self-government, anti-imperialists appealed to the fathers to show that imperial policies denied heroic Filipino fighters the political rights that belonged to all manly men.

As they proclaimed themselves and the Filipinos the modern embodiments of the fathers, the antis denounced imperialists for foolishly claiming to have outgrown the fathers' strictures, which they allegedly viewed as mere nursery rhymes for the Republic's infancy. "Have we indeed outgrown our much-boasted and often-praised Constitution?" rhetorically questioned Rep. Robert W. Miers (D, Ind.), who suggested that the imperialists wrongly judged the Constitution "a childish thing."[45] Rep. Edward W. Carmack (D,

Tenn.) excoriated the imperialists for wrongly discarding the founding fathers as relevant only to the period of national infancy:

> One of the champions of this new doctrine [of expansion] disposes of all the wisdom of the fathers of the Republic by saying that it was milk for babes, but that we must have meat for the full-grown man. Yea, let us have meat! And so our mighty Nimrod of the White House [McKinley] has gone forth into the wilderness to bring food fit for the proud stomach of this stalwart generation! Away with the counsels of Washington and of Jefferson! Away with these nursing bottles of our infancy! I may not have got beyond the tastes of infancy, but to me it seems that Washington's Farewell Address is yet proper food for full-grown American freemen.[46]

Deriding the imperialists for claiming to have "outgrown 'the swaddling clothes' made by Washington and Madison," the antis poked fun at their national manhood metaphor, sanguinary policies, and youthful pretensions. They hinted that if anyone lacked manhood, it was the imperialists, whose unrestrained bloodlust made them resemble not only youths but savages.

In contrast to the imperialists, who found a trace of savagery a positive attribute in "civilized" men, anti-imperialists generally saw savage attributes as antithetical to manhood. Savages, they argued, resembled immature youths—neither could control their "primitive passion." In making such statements, they had plenty of "scientific" evidence to back them up. According to the Darwinian theories of the time, races developed along the same lines as individuals. Civilized races had progressed from childhood to maturity; savage races had stopped at childhood. Adult savages thus resembled civilized youths: both were understood as being impulsive, emotional, disorderly, and irrational; both supposedly adhered to the principle of "might makes right."[47] Hence, in depicting the imperialists as reckless and unrestrained, antis suggested that they resembled both youths and savages, neither of whom appeared to possess the manly self-control needed to govern. In sum, they used the same logic against the imperialists that the imperialists used against the Filipinos.

To underscore their point that the imperialists resembled uncivilized adolescents, antis scolded them for casting aside their fathers' legacy in a misguided fit of generational rebellion. Said Senator Hoar, "When I hear attributed to men in high places, counselors of the President himself, that we have outgrown the principles . . . which were sufficient for our 13 States and our 3,000,000 of people in the time of their weakness, and by which they have grown to 75,000,000 and 45 States, in this hour of our strength, it seems to me these counselors would have this nation of ours like some prosperous thriving youth who reverses suddenly all the maxims and rules of living in which he has been educated and says to himself, 'I am too big for the Golden Rule.'" Representative Carmack also presented imperialism as a fit of adolescent rebelliousness when he described the imperialists as "those childish creatures who delight in novelty for its own sake . . . who are ready to renounce with disgust every established faith for no other reason than that their fathers believed it." Antis warned that spurning the fathers' wise and sober legacy would lead only to ill for the nation. It would, as Rep. Thomas Spight (D, Miss.) said, "call down upon our heads the curse of degeneracy," presumably reducing the entire nation to a condition of savagery.[48]

The antis' efforts to cast the imperialists as rebellious adolescents, disrespectful of both the founding fathers and the antis themselves, were more than just a rhetorical strategy. In the eyes of the senior antis, the imperialists really were brash upstarts. These antis were deeply shaken by their younger colleagues' aggressive demands for power, at home and abroad. As one of Hoar's correspondents sadly wrote, "Some of us, not born yesterday, who thought we knew and felt something of the old spirit of the American nation, were almost in despair, as we have rubbed our eyes, and tried to see of this war the United States of old, and wondered how it had come to pass that of a sudden we had become only old fogies, and unvenerated fossils, while the younger voices . . . shouted strange things and looked on us askance!"[49] Newcomers to public office should defer to those with seniority, reasoned Hoar, in whom the imperialists' brashness elicited equal dismay. Clearly troubled, he described the imperialists' exploits in terms that equated their disrespect for liberty with their disrespect for antis such as himself. "All we hear is boasts of the exploits of our nation," he said, "the young athlete which has struck down an old man of ninety."[50] Although the "old man of ninety" presumably referred to Spain, Hoar may have been thinking of himself, especially because Americans commonly characterized Spain as an old woman.

Antis who felt upstaged by the imperialists hoped that invoking the fathers would lead American men to demonstrate their filial loyalty and rally to their cause. "Have we no fathers? Did our fathers accomplish nothing for which we should have a manly pride?" questioned the anti-imperialist author John Clark Ridpath. Rep. Thomas J. Selby (D, Ill.) took up this refrain in the House of Representatives. "Let us be true to the principles of the Declaration of Independence, let us be true to the Constitution of this Republic, let us honor the memory of our fathers," he exclaimed.[51] As antis exhorted Americans to be true to the fathers, they spoke of fealty not only to past generations but also to themselves, the nation's experienced, mature leaders. Wrapping themselves in the mantle of the fathers, they joined with the imperialists in conflating democratic ideals with ideals of manhood.

Realizing that their image as immature upstarts who were assaulting the venerated fathers could subvert their political position among those who were not as enthralled as they with youthful qualities in their leaders, imperialists responded with an argument somewhat at odds with their national manhood metaphor and its valorization of youth: they tried to ally *themselves* with the fathers. They started by denying the antis' avowals that they and the Filipinos were the fathers' true heirs. Imperialists were so convinced that Filipinos should be seen as savages, children, or feminine figures that they dismissed their purported association with the fathers offhandedly. "There is no parallel whatever between Aguinaldo and George Washington," confidently asserted Maj. Gen. Joseph Wheeler. "We would suggest to the enthusiastic objectors who compare the guerrilla warrior of Luzon to the immortal Washington," said Sen. William M. Stewart (Silver R, Nev.), "that their language would be more accurate if they would compare Aguinaldo to Tecumseh, Sitting Bull, Old Cochise, or some other celebrated Indian warrior whose exploits in the recent past surpass in gallantry the wily little Filipino."[52]

It was not as easy to dismiss the antis' claims to the fathers' legacy, but imperialists tried to do so by dwelling on the idea that the antis lacked the fathers' virility. Unlike older antis like Hoar, younger imperialists had no first-hand memories of the fathers. Hence, instead of envisioning the fathers as elderly men, they imagined them as vigorous men in the prime of life, who were remarkable as much for their physical attributes as for their intellectual and moral ones. This can be seen in *Hero Tales,* a book co-written by Henry Cabot Lodge and Theodore Roosevelt. It described George Washington as "physically a striking figure" and "remarkably muscular and powerful." In later years, Roosevelt continued to expound on this theme, commenting in "The Strenuous Life," "Thank god for the iron in the blood of our fathers." In another address, Roosevelt applauded Washington and Lincoln's "moral and mental strength," noting that "the least touch of flabbiness, of unhealthy softness, in either would have meant ruin for this nation."[53]

With such images of physically powerful, steadfast fathers in mind, imperialists contended that their forceful policies embodied the fathers' spirit. Holding the Philippines, said the imperial publicist Levere, would put American men in accordance with Thomas Jefferson, expansionist par excellence and "father of the fathers." Parting with the islands, in contrast, would make American men "traitors to the spirit of the men of Valley Forge who marked the white snow red in their sacrifices for independence." It would show American men to be, as Roosevelt put it, "cravens and weaklings, unworthy of the sires from whose loins we sprang." Even President McKinley offered imperial policies as modern expressions of the fathers' spirit. Arguing that it would have been a "weak evasion of manly duty" to shirk the nation's responsibilities in the Philippines, he maintained that Americans had taken up arms "with the instinct of our forefathers."[54]

If expansion meant loyalty to the fathers and their ideals, then withdrawing from the Philippines meant a shocking rupture from their manly traditions. "We are undergoing the same ordeal as did our predecessors nearly a century ago," said President McKinley in his inaugural address in 1901. "We are following the course they blazed. They triumphed. Will their successors falter and plead organic impotency in the nation?" Roosevelt, too, cast the issue as a choice between the national, racial, and male power exemplified by earlier generations of men or humiliating decay: "If we are frightened at the task, above all, if we are cowed or disheartened by any check, or by the clamor of the sensation-monger, we shall show ourselves weaklings unfit to invoke the memories of the stalwart men who fought to a finish the great Civil War."[55] Imperialists cited earlier exemplars of manhood to show that expansion was more than a matter of policy, it was a test of character.

Building on their conviction that the Philippines was a test of character, imperialists argued that withdrawing from the islands before they were "pacified" (that is, conquered) would signal degeneracy in American men. Rep. Galusha A. Grow's (R, Penn.) admonishment not to shrink from a "manly discharge" of duty and Rep. Jonathan P. Dolliver's (R, Iowa) proclamation that the United States should "manfully" perform its duty by staying in the Philippines reveal their assumption that failing to take and hold the archipelago would indicate more than a lack of political commitment—it would show that American men had lost the heroic stuff of their forebears. Rep. James A. Tawney (R, Minn.) summed up what imperialists thought was at stake in the Pacific when he said that withdrawing from the islands before accomplishing what the United States had set out to do would be tantamount to a "confession of impotence on our part."[56]

As they argued that withdrawing from the Philippines would reveal a lack of manhood, imperialists often flip-flopped the old jeremiad of youthful declension and charged the older generation of losing touch with the fathers. Imperialists called their opponents "nerveless and debilitated," and they accused antis of having, as William McKinley put it, "lost the virility of the founders of the party which they profess to represent." They exploited anxieties about overcivilization by presenting the antis as degenerate neurasthenics, men whose soft and pampered lives had eroded their manly fiber, rendering them effeminate. Declaring that he believed in expansion, "because where I come from all those who are not women are men," Roosevelt suggested that the antis were all unmanly.[57]

According to the imperialists, the effeminate antis demonstrated neither the manly character of previous generations of American leaders nor, indeed, that of those who followed in their footsteps by implementing martial policies. Unlike real men, they failed to give force its proper due. The imperialists' disdain for the antis' manhood can be seen in a *Chicago Tribune* article on Senator Hoar. After Hoar remarked that imperial policies would transform the United States from a republic into a "vulgar commonplace empire, founded upon physical force," the proexpansion *Tribune* commented, "This republic was founded on physical force, with Washington at the head of the force." It continued in a more vituperative vein: "The American people, whose most precious liberties since the beginning of recorded time have been secured by physical force, are not wont to feel much respect for the dudish-like lisping mugwumps who weep over the 'brutal tendencies that will be encouraged by the recognition of force as the last appeal.' . . . Senator Hoar would find it hard to cite a single great civilizing, moralizing, Christianizing movement in history . . . that has not triumphed by 'vulgar physical force.'"[58] The article, like many others at the turn of the century, insinuated that those who lacked the militant character embodied either by soldiers or earlier generations of American men should have but little role in political life, for they lacked the forceful nature necessary to wield political authority.

By imperialist accounts, the antis deserved little credibility in political debate because they were effeminate, homebound critics, not bold men of action. In "The Strenuous Life," Roosevelt blamed the "silly, mock humanitarianism of the prattlers who sit at home in peace" for costing the lives of American men in the Philippines. The timid antis, he maintained, spoke of liberty and the consent of the governed merely to "excuse themselves for their unwillingness to play the part of men." Roosevelt continued this theme in another address: "We need display but scant patience with those who, sitting at ease in their own homes, delight to exercise a querulous and censorious spirit of judgment upon their brethren who, whatever their shortcomings, are doing strong men's work as they bring the light of civilization into the world's dark places."[59]

As imperialists derided the antis' manliness and presented themselves (and the soldiers they aligned themselves with) as the true heirs of the fathers' virile legacy, they found it easier to convince their listeners of their virility than of their resemblance to the fathers. On this latter issue, they found themselves at a disadvantage relative to the older antis, who could convincingly assert that their age and maturity made them the true spokesmen for the fathers. But, as the image of effeminate homebound antis suggests, the imperialists held the trump card: they undermined the antis' fatherly image by portraying them as womanly.

Though depicting men as boyish, decrepit, savage, or degenerate could undercut their political authority by casting doubt on their manhood, depicting men as women was the most effective way of showing they lacked the manly character necessary for political authority. In contrast to boys and old men, who were passing through different stages of male development, or savages and degenerates, who could demonstrate some male characteristics, women seemed to be a relatively fixed counterpoint to men. Hence, to weaken antis' pretensions to political authority, imperialists called them "old women with trousers on" and "squaw men." The antis, they said, were the "old lady element" in public affairs; they resembled a "nagging wife."[60] An Indiana postmaster made it doubly clear that he regarded the antis as womanly when he praised Beveridge for stirring up "the old fossils including old Granny Hoar" and then went on to ridicule the "aunties." A drawing in *Judge* that depicted Senator Hoar at the forefront of an anti-imperialist parade dressed in a long skirt, with a ribbon labeled "Auntie Hoar" in his bonnet (fig. 18) also enlisted the auntie pun to counter admiration for Hoar as an "archetype of true American manhood" and "Father of the Senate."[61]

In their efforts to discredit the antis, imperialists drew on the same images that interventionists had used in the debate over war against Spain. Just as jingoes had portrayed McKinley as a foolish old woman who tried to sweep back the sea, imperialists declared that the antis would be as efficacious as Mrs. Partington, a foolish Boston "dame" who supposedly had tried to sweep back the incoming tide with her broom. "The same failure will attend the efforts of these mugwumps, who ought to be in skirts, to resist the in rolling tide of manifest destiny," said the proexpansion *Chicago Tribune*. Echoing the jingoist pronouncements of the spring of 1898, imperialists belittled the antis' protestations as feminine "shrieking," and, playing on the supposition that women were especially subject to hysteria, they contended that the antis had assailed their policies "with a rancor almost hysterical in its impotent rage."[62] Not only did these arguments resonate with earlier cries for war, but the image of the antis as irrational old women also resonated with the image of them as soft and cowardly homebound critics who could not understand the fathers' vigorous principles.

As they struggled to stigmatize antis as womanly, imperialists benefited from the widespread tendency to construe opposition to war as a sign of cowardice, weakness, or other supposedly unmanly attributes. Especially in the frenzy of militarism that followed the Spanish-American War, militance seemed to indicate manly character, and a lack thereof, effeminacy. Imperialists also benefited from the composition of the anti-imperialist forces. Women were, indeed, important to the anti-imperialist cause. Although the Anti-Imperialist League had no women in its elected leadership, women were highly visible among the ranks. In the first mass meeting to protest imperialism, held in June 1898, half of the people in attendance were women. The

18. "The Anti-Expansion Ticket for 1900" *(detail)*. *Judge*, July 8, 1899. **Courtesy of Harvard College Library.**

antis' campaign to recall volunteer troops from the Philippines in the spring of 1899 relied heavily on the energies of women, who lobbied to have the troops returned. Women also helped sustain the anti-imperialist movement financially. In the second meeting of the New England Anti-Imperialist League, an officer reported that "noble-hearted ladies in Boston and New York" had contributed "ten or a dozen times each" to the league.[63]

Eager for allies and receptive to women's activism (though not their leadership) male antis encouraged women to help. Herbert Welsh, a Philadelphia anti, wrote to the WCTU to ask it to spread anti-imperialist tracts. Edward Atkinson estimated that he had sent one of his pamphlets to about nine hundred women's clubs, and he noted, "The organization of women is proceeding . . . throughout the country in a most extraordinary manner." In their speeches and addresses, antis acknowledged women's importance to their cause and stressed that they should be consulted on the imperial issue. "The question whether this war shall continue is a question for every man and every woman in this country to answer," said Moorfield Storey. Hoar also furthered the idea that women should be consulted on the imperial issue by insisting that it should be decided in the nation's churches, schools, colleges, and homes, not just in its political assemblies, and by declaring that every citizen should say "what he thinks is right or what she thinks is right."[64]

The male leadership of the anti-imperialist movement did not stop with encouraging women to protest imperial policies. They also tried to present their cause as one that had broad support among women. Anti-imperialist men acknowledged the women in their ranks when they praised the "patriotic men and women" who gathered for their speeches. They warned imperialists that if they did not end the fighting they would have to face the wrath of mothers. A failure to withdraw would "invite the execration of the mothers of our land," wrote one anti to President McKinley. Another, Sen. William E. Mason (R, Ill.), brought up the maternal threat in Congress: "When your ships come home laden from Manila with the putrid remains of our boys, and you take the coffin to the mother's door, you never will dry her tears, you never will soothe her heart by telling her that you have extended your commerce at the cost of her dead boy."[65]

Antis presented American mothers as staunch opponents of war because women's moral stature helped make their cause seem righteous. Furthermore, antis truly believed that women were less likely to approve of the Philippine War because of women's prewar support for international arbitration and peace and because an antiwar stance seemed consistent with late-nineteenth-century ideas of femininity. As Hannah J. Bailey, head of the WCTU's department of peace and international arbitration, said, "Many a man has not the moral courage to plead for peace, for fear he shall be accused of effeminacy or cowardice. Woman has no such fear; to be the advocate of peace is congenial to her character."[66] Along with other antis, Bailey hoped to promote the cause of peace by persuading women that they could resist war without appearing desexed; what she failed to grasp was that women's visibility in the anti-imperialist movement could be used to desex their male allies.

By depicting the antis as women, imperialists suggested that the elderly, peaceable, seemingly female (if not literally female) antis did not represent the fathers as much as themselves, for, although older, the antis lacked the fathers' manly character. Despite their relative youthfulness, imperialists could say that they resembled the manly fathers more than the womanly antis did. Because of the martial ideal of citizenship that flourished in the aftermath of the Spanish-American War and the more fundamental assumption that manhood mattered in politics, these claims significantly benefited imperialists. The valorization of manly character in late-nineteenth-century U.S. politics meant that the "aunties," as the "old lady element" in public affairs, appeared less qualified to judge whether American policies were consistent with American principles than the imperialists, who might have seemed boyish but always seemed male.

8

···

Imperial Degeneracy: The Dissolution of the Imperialist Impulse

GIVEN THE imperialists' compelling argument that their policies would strengthen American democracy by building masterful male citizens, the U.S. conquest of the Philippines is not as surprising as what followed: the United States retreated from its venture into overseas territorial annexation. After the militarist surge of the late nineteenth century, the United States did not embark on a concerted course of conquest in the early twentieth century. This was not from a lack of power to annex more territory or from an absence of opportunity (as later interventions in the Caribbean attest). Neither was it from a significant change in economic or strategic conditions. It was because colonial endeavors had lost much of their allure.[1]

During the course of the Philippine-American War, it began to appear that imperial policies were not, as the imperialists had pledged, building American manhood. To the contrary, a growing number of Americans began to believe that imperial policies were undermining the character of American men. As Sen. Charles A. Towne (D, Minn.) said, "This new policy is advocated by some men because, as they contend, we need the discipline of war. I deny it. I affirm, on the contrary . . . that war in and of itself is an awful and unmatched calamity, and in no respect more so than in its effect on the character and morals of men." The concerns about manhood that made such imperialists as Roosevelt, Beveridge, and Lodge embrace the prospect of empire so enthusiastically did not suddenly disappear, but the argument that the best way to address these concerns was through imperial policies became increasingly suspect as the war in the Philippines dragged on. How imperial policies came to seem antithetical, rather than conducive, to manhood may be found in the anti-imperialists' warnings of imperial degeneracy.[2] What they failed to accomplish by invoking the fathers, the antis eventually accomplished by invoking the sons, that is, the future generations of American men who, they maintained, would deteriorate if the nation continued on its imperial path.

Even before the start of the Philippine War, there was some question about white Americans' ability to live in the tropics without degenerating. The English writer Benjamin Kidd helped bring this issue to public attention in his book *The Control of the Tropics* (1898). Kidd declared that white men could never acclimatize themselves to torrid zones: "In climatic conditions which are a burden to him; in the midst of races in a different and lower stage of development; divorced from the influences which have produced him, from the moral and political environment from which he sprang, the white man does not in the end, in such circumstances, tend so much to raise the level of the races amongst whom he has made his unnatural home, as he tends himself to sink slowly to the level around him."[3] Kidd believed that the "English-speaking peoples" could (and should) govern the tropics in spite of these dangers, but anti-imperialists took the threat of degeneration more seriously.

To chill the hot passion for empire, antis drew on turn-of-the-century understandings of pathology and presented the tropics as a veritable breeding ground of pestilence. They referred to the Philippines as "this colony of lepers in the tropics" and "those distant and disease-ridden islands," and they argued that life in such a fever zone would make soldiers "invalids for life." Adding the risk of injury in combat to this scenario, antis inveighed against the "ghastly effects" of empire—"the wounded limbs, the fever-racked bodies, the loathsome diseases of tropical Asia." American men, they predicted, would return from the Philippines "gaunt and physically wrecked," if they returned at all. An anti-imperialist cartoon that depicted Uncle Sam before and after his wish for expansion graphically conveyed this point. Before his disastrous experiment with imperial policies, Uncle Sam stood erect, with the prosperity that spewed from his smokestacks testifying to his virile accomplishments. Afterward, he sat helplessly at home, a broken, unproductive man whose bandaged and missing limbs hinted at his postimperial impotence (fig. 19).[4]

Taking advantage of contemporary medical opinion on the harmful implications of a tropical climate for white settlers, antis argued that those who did not fall prey to disease or injury risked other, equally pernicious, perils— the indolence and sensuosity of the tropics. These, admonished the antis, would lead to mental and moral as well as physical degeneration. In contrast to the imperialists, who contended that colonial pursuits would counter the demoralizing influence of domestic ease and Gilded Age excesses, antis held that the Philippine climate and the spoils of empire would lead to even greater indolence and decadence. As the Supreme Court justice David J.

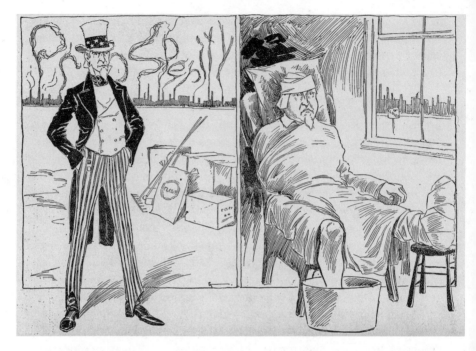

19. "Uncle Sam before and after his wish for expansion." "Expensive Expansion"
(Boston, 1900). Courtesy of Harvard College Library.

Brewer said in 1899, imperial pursuits would cast the "descending gloom of
luxury, decay and ruin" upon the nation. "However energetic men and women
may be, when they go to the tropics they degenerate as respects indolence,"
proclaimed Sen. Joseph L. Rawlins (D, Utah) in a hearing on the Philippines.
Like the abolitionists who had deplored slavery's pernicious effects on white
masters, anti-imperialists maintained that governing subject colonies would
degrade those who implemented the nation's policies. Imperial conditions
would not only foster indolence, but, in a perversely Darwinian fashion, reward it. Saying that "the dull sodden malarial heat of the tropics spares the in-
dolent longest," David Starr Jordan, the president of Stanford University, predicted that the weak, lazy, and cowardly men who had the greatest tolerance
for tropical conditions would propagate themselves disproportionately, to the
detriment of the race.[5]

   If tropical conditions were not bad enough, antis cautioned that the horrors of war posed an even greater threat to American manhood. Jordan responded to the imperialists' claims that war built manhood by arguing that if
this were so the nation should engage only in civil wars to keep the benefits

for itself. If war was so beneficial, why not schedule it on a regular basis? But that was unthinkable, he concluded, because war clearly resulted in waste and corruption. Jordan, a zoologist by training, stressed what he saw as the evolutionary perils posed by military policies. Citing the line "send forth the best ye breed" from Kipling's "The White Man's Burden," Jordan commented that such a policy would lead the nation to breed only "second-rate men." Rejecting the imperialists' view that the nerve-strains caused by overcivilization were leading to decadence, Jordan asserted that the true source of decadence lay in reproduction. "If a nation sends forth the best it breeds to destruction," he said, "the second best will take their vacant places. The weak, the vicious, the unthrifty will propagate and in default of better will have the land to themselves." The result? "The warlike nation of to-day is the decadent nation of to-morrow."[6]

In contrast to Jordan, who focused on long-term genetic degeneracy, many of his fellow antis thought the Philippine War would lead to immediate degeneracy by corrupting American men's character. War in general was brutalizing, they argued, but war against savages was extraordinarily so and would lead inevitably to the degradation of the civilized forces. George S. Boutwell, the Boston-based president of the Anti-Imperialist League, mapped the path of decay in one of his anti-imperialist speeches. American servicemen, he wrote, "have seen savage sights; they have eaten the food of savages; they have thought savage thoughts; the cries of savages are ringing in their brains. In all their surroundings there is not one single object to remind them that they belong to an era of civilization. Their lust for slaughter is reflected from the faces of those around them. They crave slaughter more than food and sleep." Surrounded by brutality, American soldiers could not help but lose their manly self-control and moral grounding as they degenerated into brutish killers. Because the Lamarckian theory of evolution popular at the time held that acquired traits could be passed from generation to generation, it appeared that the future of the nation was at risk.[7]

According to anti-imperialists, the great irony of imperial endeavors was that they were making American soldiers even more savage than the people they were sent to redeem. Sen. George L. Wellington (R, Md.) deplored this state of affairs when he said that the army had "step by step departed from the broad highway of honorable warfare—honorable modern warfare as recognized by civilized nations—and has adopted methods of barbarism and savagery such as the wild natives of the unconquered Philippine Islands themselves could not approach."[8] Though careful to profess their admiration for servicemen's patriotism (a failure to honor soldiers could be politically fatal, given the tendency to view them as ideal citizens in the aftermath of the Spanish-American War), antis nonetheless portrayed soldiers as victims of imperial policies, as men who were not made but unmade by imperial pursuits.

Imperialists responded to such assertions by insisting that, as William H. Taft, then governor of the Philippines, put it, "there never was a war conducted, whether against inferior races or not, in which there were more compassion and more restraint and more generosity." But antis found plenty of evidence from the field of battle to buttress their argument that the Philippine War was turning American soldiers into savages. After fighting a conventional war against the United States from February to November 1899, the outgunned Filipino nationalists adopted guerrilla tactics. Unable to distinguish hostile Filipinos from friendly ones, American forces instituted reconcentration policies similar to the vilified ones used by General Weyler in Cuba. They also torched crops and villages, executed prisoners, and resorted to torture, including the infamous water cure, which involved forcing water down captives' throats until they talked or, as sometimes happened, died.[9] Some of the best-publicized atrocity stories came from the island of Samar, where Brig. Gen. Jacob H. Smith commanded his subordinates to kill all Filipinos capable of bearing arms against the United States. When asked for clarification, he said that meant males over the age of ten. His subordinates, taking his orders to turn Samar into a "howling wilderness" to heart, executed Filipinos on suspicion of disloyalty. News of such tactics made it back to the United States in soldiers' letters, press accounts, court-martials, and, starting in January 1902, congressional hearings. Recognizing the horror that these stories elicited (even Senator Lodge expressed revulsion at one point), antis vigorously publicized American atrocities, some substantiated better than others, to underscore their point that imperial policies were debasing American men.[10]

News of American atrocities made it appear to many Americans that rather than fighting another "splendid little war" like the one in Cuba, replete with honorable deeds and noble acts of heroism, the United States was fighting a sordid war, one unworthy of American men. "This is not civilization. This is barbarism," said Rep. Joseph C. Sibley (R, Penn). ". . . We are taking the boys who left Christian homes, full of love of country, of patriotism, and of humanity, and brutalizing them." Senator Rawlins agreed. In reference to American atrocities, he counseled that "good men, men of the highest character can not do that which is interdicted in the providence of the Almighty without being degraded." According to the antis, the nation had come full circle. After protesting the brutal policies of the infamous Spanish general Weyler, the United States had adopted his methods. Rep. Thomas J. Selby (D, Ill.) was one anti who rued the great distance the nation had traveled from its earlier chivalrous intent toward Cuba. "What American," he questioned, "ever dreamed that within four years after our denunciation of Weylerism in Cuba our generals in the Philippines would be following the notable and brutal methods of that Spanish dictator?"[11]

Realizing that many of their countrymen could stomach the mistreatment of so-called savages who, it could be argued, had brought their fate upon themselves through their own barbarous cruelties, antis sometimes stepped back from their position that fighting a savage foe would render American soldiers even more savage. Instead, to magnify the horror of American atrocities, they depicted Filipinos as civilized Christians. Sen. Richard F. Pettigrew (Silver R, S.D.) tried to debunk the savage stereotype by saying that "all the people we are fighting are members of the Catholic church," and his colleague Senator Wellington did the same by pointing out that the University of Manila was founded before any college in the United States. In the House, Rep. Malcolm R. Patterson (D, Tenn.) glowingly described skilled Filipino physicians and learned Filipino lawyers, and Rep. David A. De Armond (D, Mo.) opined that Filipino lawyers, teachers, and businessmen would "compare favorably with the best of those classes in other countries." To further the image of the civilized Filipino, antis emphasized Filipinos' domestic attributes. Whereas imperialists depicted Filipino men as neglectful heads of household, antis found it helpful to maintain that Filipino men cherished the "virtue of their wives" and were devoted to their families. They called the Filipinos a "home-loving" people and interpreted Filipinas' attainments as evidence of their society's advancement rather than as evidence of Filipino men's abdication of domestic responsibilities. As Senator Hoar noted, "Among the Filipinos there are many cultured people who would ornament society anywhere in the world —ladies who have studied and traveled, men who have had a good education." Images of home-loving, educated, professional Filipinos made American brutalities seem completely inexcusable, for rather than civilizing savages, it appeared that the United States was savaging exemplars of civilization. Reports that American soldiers had desecrated Filipino churches and looted crucifixes, candlesticks, and even vestments underscored the antis' point that Americans were more savage than their foe.[12]

Even the antis who doubted the culture and refinement of the Filipinos (many antis did, indeed, hold that the United States should not let Filipinos into the Union because they were racially inferior) questioned the imperialists' stated commitment to civilizing them. Moorfield Storey, for one, denounced the imperialists' talk of civilizing the Filipinos for being only talk: "The purpose of our government will not be to develop the Filipino people, using their resources in trust for that purpose, but to develop mines and forests; not to make men, but to make dollars. That is to be the primary object of our policy. We may talk about educating them, civilizing them, elevating them; but these are general phrases by which we deceive ourselves and others." The greed for dollars, charged antis, would lead the United States to corrupt, not improve, the Filipinos. Accounts of the new American saloons that were tempting Filipino men provided particularly compelling evidence for this assertion. As Justice Brewer said, "To hear some talk you would think that all the influences going out from this Christian nation to the heathen have been Christian, purifying, elevating, but the fact is that even from Puritan New England there have gone more hogsheads of rum than missionaries, more gallons of whisky than Bibles."[13] According to the antis, instead of assuming the role of benevolent civilizer, the Americans in the Philippines were assuming the role of debaucher. The imperialists' noble declarations were a sham.

In making their case for the unchivalrous character of American deeds, opponents of expansion did not always describe the Filipinos as models of civilized refinement: they also employed the imperialists' stereotype of childlike Filipinos. But rather than applaud the nation's efforts to raise the supposedly childlike Filipinos to maturity, they chastised imperialists for glorying in their Philippine victories "as a full-grown man might in his ability to break every bone in the body of the street waif. The disparity is too glaring."[14] Antis warned that fighting a childlike foe would debase the nation's manly honor. "We are in the position of a strong man who has been attacked by a weak and puny child," said Sen. George Turner (Pop., Wash.). "What would be thought of such a man if he were to insist on continuing the fight until his assailant had been whipped into submission on the ground that his dignity would be injured and his prestige impaired by pursuing any other course?" The imperialists' claims to benevolence invited charges of hypocrisy, and Senator Turner was eager to level them. Parodying the imperialists, he exclaimed, "We love you [Filipinos] as a father loves his children; we yearn for your welfare with the bowels of compassion; but in the meantime let the slaughter and the burning go on." In the eyes of the antis, rather than reflecting fatherly nurturance, protection, and love, imperialism involved burning, killing, and destruction. Rather than teaching American men to be paternalistic father figures, it was turning them into tyrants.[15]

The imperialists' images of feminine Filipinos proved equally useful to the opposition. Rejecting the notion that imperialism should be seen as a marriage, antis suggested that rape was a more accurate characterization. An article in the *Journal of the Knights of Labor* pointed out that the Filipinos had not consented to U.S. advances: "We believe that expansion is like marriage, both sides ought to agree to it. We do not believe in expansion carried on with an army." Similarly, Carl Schurz, a longtime political activist and president of the National Civil Service Reform League, averred that the Filipinos had not "willingly consented" to the nation's proposal of marriage. Instead, the islands were struggling against the "treacherous embrace" of the United States. Sen.

Edward W. Carmack (D, Tenn.) was more blunt. Going straight to the point, he accused the United States of having raped the Philippines. In keeping with the idea of imperialism as a metaphorical rape, anti-imperialists presented the nation's Philippine endeavors as a manifestation of uncontrolled lust, the result of unrestrained passions. They spoke of the "lust of empire" and the "lechery of world conquest." The United States, they said, was "drunk with the lust of empire" and "delirious with the lust of conquest."[16] Picturing imperialism in these terms buttressed the antis' arguments that it brought out primitive qualities in formerly civilized men. These characterizations implied that men who participated in such a fundamentally corrupt endeavor could only debase their manhood—rather than becoming respected heads of household, the Americans who joined in the metaphorical rape of the Philippines literally would degenerate into rapists.

Citing letters from soldiers stationed in the Philippines, antis contended that army life had degraded American troops to such an extent that young girls could not walk out in the cool of the evening for fear of being assaulted. Some of these letters were quite explicit: "When President McKinley was elected I voiced the opinion of many soldiers when I said: 'The *people* of the United States want us to kill all the men, fuck all the women, and raise up a new race in these Islands.' You will excuse my vulgarity, please, as I am telling the truth. I did not act upon that but some apparently did. . . . In war time, men do not have time to seduce women with slippery tongue, &c., so they do it more after the matter of their calling—by force." Another soldier detailed some of the army's outrages in a letter to Senator Carmack. "Brutality began right off," he wrote. "At Malabon three women were raped by the soldiers. . . . Morals became awfully bad. Vino drinking, and whiskey guzzling got the upper hand of benevolent assimilation."[17]

Although exceptionally appalling, rape was not the only sign of sexual degeneracy in the Philippines. Antis also decried the prevalence of prostitution. John Foreman censured this evil in an anti-imperialist tract: "Brothels were absolutely prohibited under Spanish rule, but since the evacuation there has been a great influx of women of ill fame, whilst native women have been pursued by lustful tormentors." His fellow anti, William Lloyd Garrison (son of the abolitionist), drew on a similarly shocking picture of moral debasement. He noted that American troops had found few brothels in the Philippines upon their arrival. But this soon changed. "Immediately from all quarters came a great and sudden accession," he wrote. "From Vladivostock, Singapore, Yokohama, Hong Kong, Calcutta, and other treaty ports, abandoned women poured into the new and active market. . . . Three hundred were reported as arriving on one steamer. They found cordial welcome, and their houses were guarded by United States soldiers under orders to protect the traffic."

Shocked by the fact that the U.S. military regulated the sex trade (in hopes of reducing the incidence of venereal disease), antis excoriated the regulation of vice in the islands. As one anti-imperialist doctor grimly reported, the military had established "a system of nasty weekly medical inspection of hundreds of women by our army surgeons," so that "our officers and soldiers and sailors, and men and boys generally, might safely commit fornication and adultery, saving their bodies but destroying their souls."[18]

Hoping to fill out their picture of the Philippines as a den of sexual iniquity, antis tried to gather information on homosexual acts as well. At least one soldier came forward with stories of "sexual degeneracy, sodomy, etc.," among the troops, but such information proved much harder to come by than the widely circulated accounts of prostitution. Nonetheless, antis hinted obliquely at same sex relationships when they spoke of degeneracy, a word often used in reference to homosexuality. Morrison Swift hinted at homosexuality more directly in contending that "the professional soldier is an anachronism in civilization, the male prostitute, being among men what the abandoned woman is among her sex."[19] Swift's ostensible point was that soldiering was an immoral profession, but his reference to the "male prostitute" cast this immorality in specifically carnal terms.

With images of sexual profligacy in the Philippines as their backdrop, antis warranted that subjecting men to the debased temptations of barracks life, far from the uplifting influences of home, would inevitably lead to a deterioration of their moral fiber. "The life of soldiers is in every sense animal, and venereal pleasures are foremost among its relaxations," wrote Swift. "If an innocent fellow comes among them it is their chief delight to debauch him; to send a young man soldiering is to farm him out to the lowest vices—the average one of them might as well be made pimp to a house of ill fame without ado." But moral fiber was not all that was at risk. Numerous antis, Swift among them, insisted that despite the medical inspections, the soldiers' moral debasement often led to their physical decline. Emphasizing that soldiers who had "rotted themselves down with prostitution" were "ready victims of disease," Swift declared that U.S. soldiers would "carry and spread the venereal decay which they contract." In a more veiled reference to venereal disease (which was, after all, a taboo subject in polite company), George S. Boutwell painted a dire picture of syphilis-induced insanity: "Consider what has been done to our soldiery, the youth of America, that have been sent out to the Philippine islands. They have come home insane, diseased, without the power to serve their country or provide for themselves."[20]

Venereal disease occupied a prominent position in the antis' litany of imperial ailments because it suggested a loss of male virility and because it threatened to harm future generations. Late-nineteenth-century physicians were beginning to recognize that besides ruining men's health, venereal diseases caused deformity in children and sterility in women. This led them to deplore syphilis and gonorrhea as "family poison," and antis were quick to agree. "I do dread the corruption of the blood more than anything else," said Edward Atkinson of the nation's Philippine policies. Shortly thereafter he admonished President McKinley: "The greatest and most unavoidable danger to which these forces will be exposed will neither be fevers nor malaria, it will be venereal diseases in their worst and most malignant form. . . . It is no time to mince words or to forbear plain speech under a false sense of delicacy. These words must be spoken. This danger must be publicly named and these facts must be widely known and the exposure to the corruption of the young blood of the nation must be stopped." Sen. Henry M. Teller (Silver R, Colo.) echoed Atkinson's assertions that venereal disease contracted in the Philippines threatened the well-being of future generations. He warned that Americans would be "cursed in our physical and mental and moral manhood," and he spoke of the "curse of curses" that would contaminate American blood to an unprecedented extent. Claiming that the British population was suffering from an epidemic of syphilis contracted in the course of empire, antis predicted that a similarly dismal fate awaited the United States if it did not forswear imperial endeavors.[21]

Talk of contaminated blood struck a powerful chord because it resonated with the specter of miscegenation. White Americans typically believed that they were at the top of the evolutionary pyramid and that racial mixing would lead to debased bloodlines. Hence antis stressed the cross-racial nature of imperial liaisons to underscore their point that Philippine sexual encounters would have terrible devolutionary effects. Senator Pettigrew was one anti who played on fears of miscegenation. "The vigorous blood, the best blood, the young men of our land, will be drawn away to mix with inferior races," he prophesied. Swift, too, spoke disparagingly of cross-racial sexual liaisons in his tract *Imperialism and Liberty*: "The wives and daughters of the Filipino 'niggers' will be assimilated by the males of the higher race, as the wives and daughters of the colored race were by the planters during slavery. It will be in brothels and elsewhere, and this mixing of the blood will be called civilization." And such mixing would not stop in the Philippines: raising the specter of miscegenation within the United States, antis warned that "shovel[ling] Filipinos into the American household" would lead to racial deterioration at home.[22]

Unlike the imperialists, who aimed most of their arguments at men, antis stressed the prospect of sexual degeneracy in the Philippines in part to mobilize American women. Referring to the loose morals among American soldiers, Garrison remarked that "nothing should stir the indignation and purpose of women like this sin." As Atkinson circulated his pamphlet on venereal disease, he happily noted that "it appeals to women." Male antis expected these findings to appeal to women because righteous women had campaigned against men's sexual transgressions even before the Philippine War. Most notably, women organized in the WCTU made "social purity" a central issue in their multifaceted reform agenda. Besides agitating against prostitution in the United States, WCTU members joined with British women to condemn the official regulation of prostitution in India.[23]

After the start of the Philippine-American War, WCTU members shifted their attention to vice in the Philippines. One article in the *Union Signal*, the WCTU mouthpiece, described "home boys . . . untutored in world ways, untried, many of them almost untempted" being led to liquor and "impurity" far from their mothers' influence. "Is there a mother in a Christian land ready to consign her son to the demoralizing, brutalizing conditions of the camp and battlefield?" questioned another. "Mothers, if you have boys in the army, I am sure it would nearly break your hearts," said a third. "Our boys are being debauched. Mothers tell us that they go away from them in the very flush of ripe manhood and they come back to them disgraced, dishonored, diseased, and this American nation is to blame for it." The prosuffrage *Woman's Journal* joined with the *Union Signal* in raising the specter of male degeneracy in the Philippines. It denounced the "moral ruin wrought upon men by the terribly unnatural conditions of army and navy life" and speculated that the "ravages of drunkenness and immorality among our young men will be fearful. The labors of our temperance and purity organizations, largely composed of women, will be greatly augmented."[24]

Galvanized by reports of immorality in the Philippines, upright middle-class women lobbied to abolish military canteens and the regulation of prostitution on the islands. Members of a Wisconsin WCTU chapter were so troubled about moral conditions in the Philippines that they sent an agent to the islands to investigate. He returned with stories of American soldiers keeping Filipina mistresses and frequenting Filipina prostitutes. "The women who consent to live with Americans are, as a rule, ignorant, lazy, and filthy in their habits," he said, "generally afflicted with some loathsome cutaneous disease, and it is hard to comprehend that an educated American, decently brought up, can live among dirty, frowzy natives, who have not one redeeming quality." Although the agent highlighted the risks that sexual contact with Filipinas posed to American men, activist women often were more worried about the dangers of prostitution to women. Margaret Dye Ellis, a WCTU member, focused on Filipina women's plight when she accused American officials and soldiers of "dragging down hundreds of pure Filipina women into lives of shame and degradation." Other activists pointed out that disrespect for Filipinas boded ill for American women. Army canteens and brothels, argued the suffragist Rachel Aldrich Bailey, served as "a standing insult to every wife and mother who shared in the demanding sacrifice to furnish the sinews of war." Susan B. Anthony also represented imperial policies as a threat to American women when she said in reference to the regulation of prostitution in the Philippines, "To treat thus even degraded women lowers respect for all women."[25] The women who complained about male immorality in the Philippines did not always broaden their critiques to attack imperialism itself, but their condemnation of imperial sexual practices nonetheless weakened support for imperial policies.

Although many American women accepted the imperialists' arguments that taking and occupying the Philippines would benefit Filipinas by promoting civilized values (some American women even aided the imperial endeavor as schoolteachers, missionaries, nurses, spouses, and publicists), anti-imperialists' claims that American soldiers were mistreating Filipina women cast doubt on the imperialist promises to rescue them from abuse at the hands of savage Filipino men. In addition to deploring U.S. soldiers' sexual degradation of Filipinas, antis argued that U.S. troops did not spare women and children in their military campaigns. After winning applause from the women in the House galleries for saying he hoped American women would take an interest in Filipinas, Rep. John S. Williams (D, Miss.) went on to say, "When I hear of military glory, martial deeds, and national prestige in the Philippines, I somehow see another picture—the poor brown woman escaping from the flames of her bamboo hut . . . the brown woman with her baby at her breast!"[26] Besides telling of American soldiers who burned down huts, leaving women and infants to die of starvation and exposure, antis told of American soldiers who tortured women to elicit information. They deflated accounts of American chivalry by asserting that U.S. troops destroyed even the meager belongings of crippled women and did not hesitate to attack the women who dared defend their homes. When Gen. Elwell S. Otis captured Aguinaldo's wife and baby, one anti sarcastically reported that "the surrender was unconditional" and that the spoils of war had included "a bottle of perfumery, a box of hairpins, two dozen safety pins and a considerable number of square pieces of muslin drying on the grass, which constituted an essential part of the infant's wardrobe."[27] Rather than proving themselves chivalric rescuers of benighted Filipinas, the soldiers of such accounts proved themselves cowardly villains who shamefully waged war on women.

Antis even cast doubt on American women's ability to elevate their Filipina "sisters" by questioning whether white women could live in the tropics without succumbing to disease or regressing to a more primitive state. "There is not a [white] woman on that island who has been there any length of time who has a blush in her cheek, not one who has a rose in her face, not one who does not look jaded, pale, debilitated, and sick," said Rep. John W. Gaines (D, Tenn.). "With individual deterioration goes social decay," wrote David Starr Jordan. "Man becomes less careful of his dress, his social observances, his duties to others. Woman loses her regard for conventionalities, for her reputation, and for her character. The little efforts that hold society together are abandoned one by one. The spread of the 'Mother Hubbard,' [a loosely fitting dress worn without corsets] crowding out more elaborate forms of dress, indicates a general failure of social conventionalities. . . . where it is too warm or too malarial to be conventional, it is too much trouble to be decent." Jordan made it clear that men's morals were not the only ones at risk, that the decay sure to ensue from imperial endeavors would be at least as fatal for women, who would lose their position as moral arbiters as they succumbed to dissolute habits. What made these pronouncements especially convincing was that imperialists commonly agreed that American women (meaning, presumably, white American women) would deteriorate in the tropics, with harmful results for society as a whole.[28]

Even the women who stayed home would not be safe, warned the antis, for the "brutalizing effect" of war would, as Senator Pettigrew put it, have a "reflex action upon the mass of the people, brutalizing the sentiment of the whole nation." Tales of previously genteel citizens "gloating over telegraphic reports of carnage," of children giving free rein to their barbaric instincts as they played at war, and of prizefights attracting greater audiences suggested that demoralization already was setting in. Drawing on the belief that women were more refined and vulnerable than men, antis pictured this apparent retreat from genteel values as singularly threatening to women. An article on militarism and public morals published in Scribner's Magazine made this clear. The "degradation of character due to militarism" would weigh most heavily on women, it explained, for they would suffer most from the "callousness and cruelty" and "moral laxity" caused by war.[29]

Just as threatening to women as the prospect of increasing male brutality was that of weakening marriage ties, something that the antis avowed would surely follow from the nation's new relations with the polygamous Muslims who lived on some of the Philippine islands. Specifically, antis warned that an arrangement struck with the sultan of Sulu (referred to as "that foul, polygamous beast" by one anti-imperialist senator) would strip the "sacred names of wife and mother . . . of every ennobling quality" and make them "synonymous with shame." Citing the government's tolerance of polygamy, antis intimated that instead of exporting their values to the Philippines, Americans might end up importing Filipino values. As the suffragist Henry B. Blackwell cautioned, "Civilization is annexing the Orient with its harem and zenana and licensed prostitution. India, China, and Japan are two thousand years behind us in the relations of men and women. Either we must raise them to our level, or they will drag us back to theirs. Women must either advance or retrograde. To stand still is impossible."[30] Doubtful that the United States would be able to civilize the Filipinos through force of arms, Blackwell foresaw retrogression for American women.

The antis' gripping stories of degeneration show that gender convictions did not always benefit imperialists. As the Philippine-American War dragged on, the antis managed to turn the language of degeneracy to their own advantage. The U.S. army's difficulty in securing victory indicated that imperial challenges had not, as imperialists promised, turned American men into supermen. With well-publicized accounts of disease, atrocities, lustfulness, intemperance, and other signs of degeneracy to back them up, antis contended that imperial pursuits were causing American men to follow in the footsteps of the British, who, they said, had been so debased by their imperial activities that they were too "weak and impotent" to defeat the Boers, and the Spaniards, whose impotence, they averred, had been demonstrated thoroughly in Cuba. To make things worse, debauched American men would drag American women down with them. The antis' warnings of degeneration fueled a popular push to bring the volunteers home and, beyond that, a growing sense of dissatisfaction with the nation's Philippine pursuits.[31] These alarms discredited imperialists' claims that military policies were the best remedy for concerns about manhood. But to turn the nation from its imperial path, anti-imperialists still had to address the root of the imperialist impulse, the conviction that the nation needed to build militant manhood to shore up American democracy.

With the growing dissatisfaction with the war in the Philippines to spur them on, antis returned to the questions that had undergirded the arbitration issue and the nation's subsequent path into war: What kind of character was most relevant to citizenship? What was the best way to foster it? In the late nineteenth century, the martial ideals expounded by jingoes and imperialists had proven most persuasive in debates over the international arbitration treaty, the war against Spain, and the U.S. occupation of the Philippines. As the Philippine War took its toll on American men, however, the more peaceable ideals expressed by the antis (particularly the mugwumpish league antis) began to hold their own.

Whereas imperialists often reasoned that the nation needed to build martial virtues in American men because government rested ultimately on force, anti-imperialists stressed that the nation needed to foster intelligence and civic virtue because governments rested on those qualities. Drawing on a men and nations analogy, Moorfield Storey said that "the true greatness of a nation, as of a man, depends upon its character, its sense of justice, its self-restraint, its magnanimity, in a word upon its possession of those qualities which distinguish George Washington from the prize-fighter, the highest type of man from the highest type of beast." Jordan also urged the nation to place greater stock in moral and intellectual attributes than in physical ones: "We have drawn more strength from Harvard College than from a thousand men-of-war," he said. ". . . It is our moral and material force, our brains and character and ingenuity and wealth that make America a power among the nations."[32]

Building on their assumption that intelligence and morality were the foremost qualities needed in the nation's citizens, antis often maintained that ideal citizens emerged from homes, not military camps. As Rep. Claude A. Swanson (D, Va.) said, "Let us continue to boast, as did our fathers, that the glory of our country does not consist in vast colonies, in great armies or navies, in the pomp or luxury of rulers, but that it consists of myriads of happy homes dotting the fair bosom of our land, whose inmates, possessed of plenty and blessed with the refining influence of education and Christianity, surround government with a strength greater than that derived from armies or from navies and more enduring than fortresses." Swanson's statement resembled those made by activist women, including the suffragist Anna Howard Shaw, who insisted that world power status should be determined not by a nation's military strength, but by its homes, schools, and churches.[33] Like the men and women who had supported international arbitration in the 1890s, anti-imperialists often argued that the elevated qualities associated with women were needed in public life. Although not all antis supported women's suffrage, this vision of citizenship resonated with suffragists' arguments.

Frustrated that their claims to political rights based on their activities during the Spanish-American War had made them little headway, many suffragists changed tack during the Philippine-American War. They returned to their prewar declarations that militarism was a manifestation of brutish male values that boded only ill for women. To be sure, some suffragists supported U.S. military activities in the Philippines. Elizabeth Cady Stanton, Julia Ward Howe, and others believed that the United States had a responsibility to "civilize" the Filipinos and could best do so by exercising political and military control over the islands. As the Philippine-American War wore on, however, suffragists increasingly cited militaristic ideals of citizenship to explain their political defeats. In 1900, the National American Woman Suffrage Association published a pamphlet rebutting arguments against women's suffrage—foremost among them that women should not vote because they did not fight. Agreeing with the pamphlet, the suffragist Alice D. Le Plongeon blamed women's disfranchisement on men's acceptance of "the rule of the more dominant," and Alice Stone Blackwell lamented that the war had "called out a fresh crop of assertions that women ought not to vote, because they cannot render military service." In her address as president of the National American Woman Suffrage Association in 1901, Carrie Chapman Catt also stressed this point. "The complete emancipation of women will never come until militarism is no more," she said, for "militarism is the oldest and has been the most unyielding enemy of woman."[34]

The conviction that militarism was hampering women's suffrage efforts led a number of suffragists to redouble their efforts to promote nonmilitary ideals of citizenship. They were joined in this endeavor by other activist women who, despite varying commitments to suffrage, agreed that women's advancement depended on the valorization of what Ellen Martin Henrotin, president of the General Federation of Women's Clubs, called the "peaceful arts and the principles of conciliation." Asserting that militarism was inimical to the feminine values that underlay civilized progress, even women in such conservative groups as the Congress of Mothers and the Woman's Relief Corps (a Grand Army of the Republic auxiliary) rejected the military ideals of citizenship that had been strengthened by the Spanish-American War.[35] The activist women who deplored male brutality often concluded that there was only one remedy for it—extending women's influence.

In contrast to the activist women who cast a suspicious eye on all men, anti-imperialist men were more specific—rather than blaming martial policies on men per se, they blamed them on strenuous ideals of manhood that glorified force. Referring to Roosevelt's admonitions on the strenuous life, Representative Williams exclaimed, "I do not want my children taught that the real strenuous life—the life, therefore, to be lived—is that of the professional fighter—regardless of the cause for which he fights." Likewise, the *Nation* denounced the "strenuous life" as "the gospel of war for the sake of war, of fighting, not merely or necessarily for a just and righteous and inevitable cause, but for the effect upon your own virility. Whatever you do, you must fight."[36]

Antis objected to Roosevelt's vision because they thought not only that it honored the fight more than the reason for fighting, but also that too much of an emphasis on force would undercut American democracy. "Any form or degree of domination has a like tendency," argued Swift. "It fosters the degrading sense of superiority, contempt, arrogance, aloofness, the domineering spirit, all of which canker the superior man's nature. It prevents the growth of brotherliness—the highest idea of civilization; of equality—the basis of Democratic evolution." With reports of degraded citizenship in mind, the anti-imperialist Garrison warned that "it is not the armed savagery of the Philippines that threatens America, but the savagery that Theodore Roosevelt represents."[37] In the preceding years international arbitration supporters and those who opposed war with Spain had made similar protests to little avail, but the troubling war in the Philippines gave them a newfound weight.

Building on the growing skepticism of the martial virtues, anti-imperialists castigated imperial policies for fostering them. They admonished that rather than create better citizens, imperial policies would turn American men into poor ones, "degraded and debased by the military scourge." Above all, they would sap American men's traditional commitment to independence. In an article entitled "The Military Idea of Manliness" published in the highbrow *Independent* in 1901, the pacifist and social reformer Ernest Howard Crosby criticized military policies for developing a "new manliness," defined by "absolute obedience" and "readiness to obey orders to do anything." Crosby and other antis argued that imperialism would breed a massive pool of unthinking soldiers. This distrust of the military ethos also can be seen in his poem, "Thinking and Obeying," printed in an anti-imperialist tract:

> "Captain, what do you think," I asked,
> "Of the part your soldiers play?"
> The captain answered, "I do not think—
> I do not think—I obey." . . .
> "Then if this is your soldier code," I cried,
> "You're a mean, unmanly crew,
> And with all your feathers and gilt and braid
> I am more a man than you.
> For whatever my lot on earth may be,
> And whether I swim or sink
> I can say with pride, 'I do *not* obey—
> I do *not* obey—I think!' "[38]

According to the antis, militarism would subvert the "manly freedom of opinion" that was so important to American democracy; it would turn American men into "civic cowards." "No wonder that war has always proved so dangerous to the vitality of democracies; for a democracy needs to keep alive above all things the civic virtues, which war so easily demoralizes," commented Carl Schurz.[39]

If war was dangerous, imperial policies were doubly so, for they would turn American men into tyrants. "The more successful we are in making the Filipinos our subjects by force of arms," said Schurz, "the more will our triumph corrupt our morals, tarnish our honor and undermine our free institutions of government." Rejecting the imperialists' premise that military policies would foster manhood, antis contended that democracy made men. Jordan, as president of Stanford, a coeducational liberal arts college, was exceptionally

committed to cultivating nonmilitary ideals of citizenship. "For more than a
century our nation has stood for something higher and nobler than success in
war," he wrote. ". . . We have stood for civic ideals, and the greatest of these,
that government should make men by giving them freedom to make themselves. The glory of the American Republic is that it is the embodiment of
American manhood. It was the dream of the fathers that this should always be
so,—that American government and republican manhood should be co-
extensive, that the nation shall not go where freedom cannot go." Convinced
that the function of democracy was not to make government good but to make
men strong, Jordan denounced imperial policies for interfering with the development of self-governing manhood.[40] Through the struggle to make
democracy work, men attained the character needed to make it work. For evidence of this proposition, Americans need only look at the Philippines.

In contrast to the imperialists, whose position was that the occupation of
the Philippines would eventually teach the Filipinos to govern themselves,
antis argued that independence was the best way for the Filipinos to develop
self-governing manhood. The irony of trying to turn the Filipinos into free
men by, as the historian Charles Francis Adams said, "pounding out of them,
in the first place, every manly aspiration they might possibly have had," was
not lost on the antis, who pointed out the impossibility of teaching men self-
government by denying their desire to practice it. Insisting that "no people
ever learned self-government under a tutor," Senator Carmack predicted that
rather than elevating the Filipinos, American rule would "degrade the character of the people" and would "utterly unfit them for self-government." Antis
regarded self-government as preferable even to good government because
only by self-government could manliness prosper. "Good government means
that the governmental machine runs well; but self-government produces the
best men," observed an anti-imperialist pamphlet. "Self-government is the
best *man-factory.*"[41]

If self-government was "the best man-factory," then imperialism was note-
worthy for unmanning subject peoples. Hoping to discredit the nation's Philippine policies, Adams said that when the Romans occupied Britain they rendered the people of England "emasculated and incapable of self-government."
The Roman occupation had, he continued, "crushed all local vigor" so thoroughly that it took eight hundred years to get it back. Other antis drew on
more recent British examples to prove their point that imperialism degraded
the character of subject peoples. Senator Hoar went so far as to state that
there had never been a tropical colony that did not degrade the "citizenship"
and "manhood" of its subjects. Even Jacob Gould Schurman, sent by President McKinley to the Philippines as president of the first Philippine commission, warned that if the United States did not grant the Filipinos greater

governing power, U.S. policies would tend "to discourage and emasculate them."[42]

If self-government made men, antis went on to say, it did not follow that imperial responsibilities made supermen. In response to the imperialists' arguments to this effect, antis echoed the antislavery contention that governing subject races had a pernicious effect on the master class. They maintained that the ordinary workings of democracy developed the highest ideals of character. The recent war with Spain, their rationale went, had shown that democracy prepared men for whatever emergencies a nation might face. Antis reminded their audiences that despite a generation of peace, the Spanish-American War had shown "no defect of courage." The American army was the greatest in the world, asserted J. Laurence Laughlin in an anti-imperialist tract. "Such examples as those of Roosevelt and many others at San Juan and Caney, and Funston at the Rio Grande, are splendid evidences that the strenuous life of a republic in times of peace abundantly well provides, for the emergencies of war, the best fighting material in the world." Jordan emphatically agreed: "It is the business of the Republic to make a nation of heroes," he said.[43]

Finding domestic pursuits more conducive to manhood than imperial endeavors, antis proposed that those who had misgivings about American manhood should work to strengthen democracy at home. As Jordan said in response to those who called for new political challenges "worthy of our national bigness," "I have not patience with such talk as this. The greatest political problems the world has ever known are ours to-day, and still unsolved—the problems of free men in freedom. Because these are hard and trying we would shirk them in order to meddle with the affairs of our weak-minded neighbors. So we are tired of the labor problem, the race problem, the corporation problem, the problem of coinage and of municipal government. Then let us turn to the politics of Guam and Mindanao, and let our own difficulties settle themselves!" Jordan had a firm reply to such claims: "Shame on our cowardice!"[44] If imperialists truly wanted to build the kind of manhood best suited for democracy, they should turn their energies to the challenges posed by democracy.

The tales of degeneracy that emerged from the Philippines made Jordan's stance ever more convincing. Whereas in the late 1890s seemingly feminine strains in U.S. political culture had given rise to martial ones, in the early 1900s, the excesses of the martial spirit strengthened the hands of those who advocated peace. Domestic pursuits began to appear a more promising way to build manhood than overseas conflicts, in large part because of the antis' persistent chiseling away at the links between martial policies and manly character. The antis' arguments that militarism made bad citizens undercut the imperialist impulse; their argument that democracy made good ones helped them deflect what was left of it to domestic reform.

By 1902, the year Theodore Roosevelt declared the Philippine "insurrection" over (somewhat prematurely, for U.S. forces fought skirmishes against the Moros for more than a decade afterward), the imperialist impulse was on the decline. Although policymakers found it difficult to extricate the United States from the Philippines, which it held until Japan took the islands during World War II, after the turn of the century the Philippines no longer seemed, to most Americans, a glorious opportunity to build manhood. Some diehard imperialists did continue to consider colonial policies a way to build male character, but the antis had managed to cast substantial doubt on the idea that imperialism would strengthen American democracy by building more virile citizens.[45]

During his presidency, Roosevelt continued to fret about the "general softening of fibre" and the need to encourage the "fighting qualities" in American men. He took the Panama Canal Zone and sent troops to Cuba. But he faced considerable skepticism on the desirability of assertive overseas policies. In 1906, prior to intervening in Cuba, he worried about marshaling public opinion. Somewhat ruefully, he noted that before the Spanish-American War Americans had been "spoiling for a fight" but afterward they no longer desired one. Unable to build greater public support for bellicose schemes and fairly satisfied with the martial qualities inculcated by the Spanish-American and Philippine-American wars, Roosevelt and his associates muted their clamor for belligerent international policies. In their quest to, as Roosevelt put it, "make men better," they shifted their energies to the character-building challenges of domestic reform.[46]

The United States did not wholly forswear imperial policies in the early twentieth century—but martial endeavors no longer seemed so desirable for their own sake. Prior to the Spanish-American War, jingoes had clamored for war, any war, and at the start of the Philippine-American War imperialists had touted the benefits of colonial endeavors for American men's character. But in later years, concerns about manhood no longer drove U.S. policies. Early-twentieth-century U.S. interventions in the Caribbean resulted more from economic and strategic appraisals than from a burning desire for combat or colonial adventures.[47] And these interventions were more the exception than the rule, for the United States pursued an informal, economic empire more energetically than it sought military intervention and political control. Confronted with the specter of male degeneracy, the militant strain of the imperialist impulse had dissipated, an ironic casualty of the Philippine-American War.

··

Conclusion: Engendering War

HAVING reconsidered the Spanish-American and Philippine-American wars with gender in mind, it is worth returning to our starting question: How does adding gender to the picture affect our understanding of these conflicts? The preceding chapters argue that domestic concerns traditionally not considered relevant to international relations—namely, concerns about gender roles—significantly affected militant U.S. policies at the turn of the century. This is not to say that gender issues can fully explain the Spanish-American and Philippine-American wars. Just as it would be myopic to attribute these conflicts strictly to economic, strategic, or partisan motives, it would be foolishly reductive to say that the United States went to war against Spain and later fought to take the Philippines strictly for reasons of gender. The point of this book is not to comprehensively explain the two wars but to explore a neglected aspect of their cultural origins. Earlier studies of the conflicts have shown that racial beliefs influenced U.S. actions, but these convictions were only part of the cultural framework that undergirded U.S. policies. Gender beliefs, often working in tandem with racial beliefs, also affected the rise and fall of the nation's imperialist impulse.

Adding gender to the historical picture helps explain why the United States went to war at the turn of the century by illuminating two important issues: jingoes' motivations and the methods they used in political debate to build support for their aggressive policies. To start with motives, jingoes looked to martial policies to address their anxieties about manhood. These concerns can be traced, in part, to the urbanization, industrialization, and corporate consolidation of the late nineteenth century. The middle- and upper-class men who held supposedly soft white-collar jobs and could afford the comforts of modern life were particularly worried about the seeming dangers of "overcivilization." They feared that a decline in manly character would impair their ability to maintain not only their class, racial, and national privileges, but also their status relative to women, especially when assertive New Women scoffed at submissive ideals of womanhood. The aging of the Civil War generation and the closing of the frontier focused further attention on male character, for it seemed that modern young men, lacking their own epic challenges, would not be able to live up to their forefathers. Darwinian convictions made the stakes of the gender order appear to be survival itself.

It may seem strange that jingoes looked to governmental policies to address their anxieties about manhood, but jingoes, like other Americans of the time, regarded gender as an issue of national importance. Believing that the well-being of American democracy rested on a specific gender order, jingoes looked to foreign policy to shore up that order. Their search for a political solution also reflected their conviction that the nation had a political problem: that American politics was losing its fraternal character and was no longer guided by high standards of manly honor. Women's encroachments into electoral politics posed a further threat to the manly ideal of politics that jingoes held so dear. Convinced that the nation had a political problem, jingoes sought a political solution. Fearing for the future of their nation, jingoes resolved to shore up the manly character of electoral politics by forging a new generation of martial heroes.

If it seems strange that jingoes looked to governmental policies to build character in American men, it seems even stranger that they considered war the best way to do so. But there were several reasons why, as they cast about for character-building challenges, jingoes embraced the prospect of war. The first was that war seemed to offer what they wanted most: a significant departure from everyday conditions. Jingoes imagined war as the most rigorous challenge possible, the most effective means to develop the characteristics such as courage and physical strength that they thought were sorely lacking in modern men. They also regarded war as the best way to foster fraternalism and a regard for high ideals among men and to highlight distinctions between men and women.

That jingoes saw war as a character-building endeavor had much to do with romanticized memories of the Civil War. Jingoes were seduced by more than thirty years of claims that Civil War veterans were model citizens and men. But the legacy of the Civil War was not the only reason jingoes regarded war favorably: they also were captivated by British imperialists' claims that empire made men and by the idea that frontier challenges had built manly character in American pioneers. Assertions that martial challenges built char-

acter seemed borne out by the Spanish-American War, which led to enthusiastic declarations that the greatest legacy of the war was manhood itself. With
such claims to buck them up, imperialists argued that taking and governing
the Philippines would solve the problem of degeneracy in American men.
Those who embraced martial endeavors as an end in themselves did so less
from some kind of turn-of-the-century original sin than because their inherited culture encouraged them to do so.

To turn from motive to method, jingoes built support for assertive Cuban
policies by drawing on chivalric gender ideals. Taking advantage of the popular images of Cuba as either an imperiled maiden or a courageous hero and
Spain as a bestial villain or an effeminate aristocrat, jingoes argued that intervening in the Spanish-Cuban War would enable American men to assume the
role of chivalric rescuer or fraternal ally. In either case, intervention would enable American men to bolster chivalry and honor in the United States. The
Maine disaster seemed to underscore their point that American chivalry was
on the line. After the disaster, jingoes built support for their martial policies
by presenting themselves as the manly defenders of the nation's honor and
their opponents as weak and spineless cowards. Later, in debates over whether
to take and hold the Philippines, imperialists also laid claim to assertive ideals
of manhood. Drawing on a national manhood metaphor, they portrayed themselves as virile young men, well-suited to lead a virile young nation, and anti-
imperialists as carping old women who had no place in the nation's political
life.

For their part, anti-interventionists and anti-imperialists struggled to present themselves as manly by stressing their supposed maturity, self-restraint,
and resemblance to the nation's fathers. Like their bellicose political opponents, they tried to associate themselves and their policies with manhood because they realized that it served as a prerequisite for political authority, that
men who did not appear manly risked becoming as politically liminal as
women. Although the meaning of manhood was hotly contested in foreign
policy debates, the common belief that it mattered added to the strength of
the standard: because political activists from different walks of life agreed that
manhood was relevant to wielding political authority, a failure to appear manly
seemed certain to erode men's political standing. Realizing that their claims to
power were at stake, political leaders took the issue of manhood seriously.

That interventionists and anti-interventionists alike struggled to depict
themselves as manly does not mean the playing field was level. The militant
ideals of manhood that were in the ascendance in the late nineteenth century
meant that those who advocated assertive policies were able to manipulate
the language of manhood more effectively in the 1898 debate over war. The
Spanish-American War underscored these martial ideals, thereby helping im-

perialists associate themselves and their policies with manhood in the early years of the Philippine-American War. But when the Philippine war resulted in more stories of atrocities than of chivalric feats, more casualties than supermen, imperialists' claims that empire would build manhood lost credibility. As the war in the Philippines dragged on, anti-imperialists were able to argue more convincingly that imperial policies would undermine, rather than build, American manhood. Faced with growing suspicion of their militant stand, many of those who continued to fret about American men's manly character focused on domestic reform as a more viable solution.

By showing how gender angst affected the United States's turn-of-the-century martial policies, this book contributes to the growing field of scholarship which maintains that gender is relevant to understanding international relations. Historians long have recognized the relevance of gender to understanding women's peace activism, yet when I embarked on this project, only a few international relations scholars had paid attention to gender in other international relations issues, the underlying assumption being that gender refers specifically to women and that, with the exception of women's peace activism, international relations has involved mostly men. In recent years, however, both of these assumptions have been called into question. Historians of gender have pointed out that men, too, have been held to gendered codes of conduct.[1] And international relations scholars have begun to study how gender can illuminate issues besides women's peace activism.

Although the increasing attention paid to men's gender roles and beliefs is laying the groundwork for a much wider variety of gender-sensitive international relations studies, much of the scholarship on gender and international relations continues to focus on women. Because women have been underrepresented in international security positions, one approach followed by those who wish to consider their role in international relations has been to bypass security issues and broach such topics as nongovernmental contacts between people from different nations, including contacts fostered by missionaries, international organizations, and tourism. A related approach has been to broaden the definition of national security to include not only military issues but also topics like economic and environmental well-being.[2]

This book takes a third approach. It uses gender to illuminate a traditional security issue, war. Given that men had a monopoly on international relations policymaking positions at the time of the Spanish-American and Philippine-American wars, they occupy center stage in this account. But casting the same actors has not meant telling the same tale. Even though this book focuses on the male political leaders who are the stock characters of most diplomatic histories, its emphasis on gender means that it tells a new story, one in which late-nineteenth-century political leaders were motivated by concerns about their status as men, including their position relative to women. Political historians have shown how gender has affected the inclusiveness, language, and rituals of politics; this book illuminates some ways in which gender also affected the formulation of policy. It shows that politically powerful men drew on their understandings of appropriate male conduct when deciding how the nation should act. By considering how political leaders' identities as men affected their political convictions and positions, this book shows that "personal" identity issues usually not thought relevant to international relations had the power to affect the conduct of foreign affairs.[3]

Its focus on male political leaders notwithstanding, this book finds that women were an integral part of the story. This is not to say that activist women were able to determine the shape of U.S. foreign policy. Women were highly visible in the international arbitration movement of the 1890s and later in the anti-imperialist movement, but their lack of political power meant that their peaceable proposals were often more significant for the antagonistic responses they generated than for their direct effect on the conduct of foreign relations. By challenging men's monopoly on political power, activist women exacerbated men's uneasiness about their status as men, thereby leading some to regard military endeavors more favorably. Jingoes did little to encourage women who agreed with them to speak out; to the contrary, their reliance on militant standards of honor and the language of fraternalism made like-minded women hesitate to clamor for war lest they be seen as unsexed. In turn, women's relative silence on the jingoist side of foreign policy debates helped jingoes present themselves and their policies as manly. Women who opposed militant international policies lent a certain moral authority to the anti-imperialist cause during the Philippine debate, but their visibility also helped discredit anti-imperialist policies among those who were steadfastly committed to the manly ideal of politics.

Considering how the wider cultural context affected policymakers' decisions not only broadens the cast of characters but also complicates the issue of national security. For years, historians have debated whether U.S. policies toward Cuba and the Philippines reflected rational assessments of national interest or irrational desires. This book proposes that U.S. policies cannot be categorized so neatly. From a later perspective, much of the impassioned talk about manhood may seem irrational, but for many late-nineteenth-century policymakers and other political activists, manhood *was* a national security issue. These policymakers believed that the nation had a responsibility to inculcate manhood in its male citizens because the nation could not long survive if it failed to do so.

Besides shedding new light on the origins of the Spanish-American and Philippine-American wars, this study has ramifications for the way we view international relations more generally. In an essay titled "Culture and Power: International Relations as Intercultural Relations" (1979), Akira Iriye argued that international relations should be seen as "interactions among cultural systems." To better understand international relations, wrote Iriye, historians must examine domestic cultural arrangements, including the customs that help maintain social order.[4] Because gender has been of great importance in allocating social roles and shaping ideas about power in more countries than just the United States and in time periods other than the late nineteenth century, it stands to reason that gender should be recognized as a cultural arrangement with significant implications for the conduct of international relations in a range of different contexts.

Studies of British imperial history bear out this premise by showing that gendered motivations and justifications for empire were not unique to the United States. The suspicion that growing luxury and idleness were leading to a decline in virility and good citizenship was common in late-nineteenth-century Britain as well as in the United States. Just as assertive New Women aggravated forebodings about manhood in the United States, they caused unease across the Atlantic. Oscar Wilde's sensational trial for homosexuality in 1895 fostered even greater doubts about British manhood. Fears of "declining virility" led to the creation of militaristic British youth groups and, beyond that, to widespread support for imperial policies among the British public. Like their American imitators, late-nineteenth-century British imperialists appear to have viewed military adventures as a means of turning British men into heroes and perpetuating the traditional male prerogatives that seemed in doubt to a number of British men. That supporters of empire regarded their policies as a way to promote conservative gender roles for women can be seen in their calls for a new generation of imperial mothers who would focus their energies on raising a strong "imperial race."[5]

In addition to illuminating how British imperialists thought that empire would reshape their society, gender analysis can elucidate their visions of the wider world. Late-nineteenth-century British literature presented Britons as manly and their imperial subjects as childlike and effeminate. This way of conceptualizing the players on the imperial stage led to the conclusion that the British had both the right and the obligation to rule. Viewing subject men or the entire Orient as feminine was not the only line of gendered thought to shape imperial policies; so did reports on the status of women overseas: to justify their "civilizing" policies, British imperialists readily cited what they saw as the degraded status of African and Asian women. The British example demonstrates that the United States was not exceptional, that gender can help explain the impulse behind empire and the ways empire was conceived and legitimized in the leading imperial power of the time.[6]

If we step back from late-nineteenth-century imperial pursuits, it appears that gender beliefs have had some bearing on the pursuit of martial policies in other periods. Although historians are only beginning to methodically investigate the connections between gender beliefs and foreign policy developments, they have uncovered plenty of evidence suggesting that gender beliefs have affected the appeal of militant and peaceful policies at different points in history. A few scattered examples, taken primarily from U.S. history, illustrate this point. On the eve of the War of 1812, some Jeffersonian Republicans looked to another war with Britain to foster character in the seemingly degenerate sons of the founding fathers. Saying that honor was at stake, they clamored for a fight. Roughly a century later, in the years preceding World War I, those who valorized male aggression and toughness reached the dangerous conclusion that war was, as Michael C. C. Adams has put it, a "valuable human endeavor." In the U.S. debate over entering the war, militant interventionists promised that war would counter the effeminizing tendencies of peace. Said Rep. Augustus P. Gardner, Henry Cabot Lodge's son-in-law and a Spanish-American War veteran, "Today we leave the seat of ease and we enter the arena of blood and lust, where true men are to be found." In the 1930s and 1940s, gender assertions added to the appeal of fascism. Hitler mobilized his followers by promising a new social order, the keystones of which were racial "purity" and traditional gender roles. Fascist literature presented softness as a loathsome feminine attribute that had to be expurgated by hard male warriors.[7]

If, on the one hand, historians have uncovered some of the links between assertive ideals of masculinity and war, on the other, they have highlighted the relevance of gender to understanding women's peace advocacy. Many of the women who swelled the ranks of the U.S. peace movement in the twentieth century agreed with the turn-of-the-century American women who asserted that aggressive international policies reflected male values. Furthermore, like the turn-of-the-century suffragists who denounced military policies as inimical to their cause, later twentieth-century women peace activists also condemned military policies as an obstacle to women's advancement. As one suffragist argued in the fall of 1914, it was "the spirit of militarism, the glorification of brute force, and this alone, that has kept woman in political, legal and economic bondage throughout the ages." Believing that women have had distinctive perspectives on peace issues (whether because of culture or biology) and distinctive reasons to advocate peace, a number of twentieth-century American women joined groups like the Women's International League for Peace and Freedom, the Woman's Peace Party, and Women Strike for Peace to protest what they regarded as male militarist policies.[8]

Along with affecting attitudes toward military policies, gender beliefs have affected self-perceptions and perceptions of the wider world in various periods. Much as *Cuba libre* supporters claimed that the manly character of the Cuban revolutionaries showed that they were better fitted for self-government than their seemingly effete Spanish rulers, American revolutionaries employed gendered thought to justify their cause. By casting themselves as embodiments of manly republican virtue and the British as idle, luxury-loving, effeminate tyrants, revolutionary patriots refuted the view that theirs was a patricidal uprising against the rightful patriarchal power of the king. Instead, they characterized their actions as a highly commendable effort to escape illicit feminine power. Claiming that England was, in the words of Alexander Hamilton, an "old, wrinkled, withered, worn-out hag," rather than a benevolent father, the revolutionaries utilized gendered beliefs about the rightful exercise of power to show the righteousness of their cause. A similar predisposition to associate manly character and the right to wield political power surfaced in debates over U.S. continental expansion. Like the late-nineteenth-century imperialists who depicted Filipinos as lacking manly character to justify American rule, earlier proponents of continental expansion depicted Native-American and Mexican men as devoid of manly character and therefore unfit to govern themselves.[9]

Just as gender beliefs affected Americans' self-perceptions and perceptions of other people and nations prior to the late nineteenth century, they had some bearing on earlier efforts to claim political power in foreign policy debates. Late-nineteenth-century jingoes' efforts to cite manhood as a justification for war had precedents in 1861 as well as in 1812. Like the war hawks of 1812, southern secessionists claimed to be fighting for the defense of their manly honor. To build support for their policies, they called southern unionists unmanly cowards, a tactic that no doubt influenced their descendants in 1898. Even in the aftermath of women's suffrage, militant ideals of manhood continued to have some (albeit considerably weaker) coercive power in political debate, something recognized by President Lyndon Johnson, who hesitated to withdraw U.S. troops from Vietnam lest he be seen as "an unmanly man. . . . A man without a spine."[10] These examples indicate that the gendered rhetoric of late-nineteenth-century imperial debate was not a great aberration, that gender has helped justify policies and set the bounds of the politically permissible in a variety of situations.

That gender beliefs have been brought to bear in different conflicts leads to questions about their causal significance. If gender concerns have been present in a number of political contexts, should they then be deemed a historical constant and hence not really important as a causal factor at any given moment? The answer, I believe, is no. Gender beliefs have changed over time, and even at any given moment they have been contested. At the turn of the century, one set of gender convictions led jingoes to regard war as an end in itself, another fostered opposition to war. In 1898, the jingoist vision won out in political debate, but this was only a temporary victory, for by 1902, growing doubts about the implications of belligerent policies for American manhood had undercut the imperialist impulse. Reifying gender roles does not help us understand why nations have been more aggressive in some periods than in others. Neither can a rigid dichotomy between warlike men and peaceful women explain why men have disagreed over foreign policy issues or why some women have wholeheartedly supported martial policies. History shows that men are not inherently and immutably warlike nor women inherently and immutably peaceable.[11]

The preceding chapters conclude that a convergence of historically specific factors gave concerns about gender unusual weight in late-nineteenth-century debates over war and empire, but placing late-nineteenth-century imperialism in a larger context requires systematic investigation of the ways in which gender beliefs affected other conflicts. The apparent reverberations from one time period to another point to the need to study not only the ways in which gender beliefs have been brought to bear in specific policy debates, but also the process of transmitting ideas about gender and war from one generation to the next.

If the Spanish-American and Philippine-American wars are intriguing because gender beliefs appear to have played an exceptionally powerful and traceable role in shaping martial policies, they are important because they were not unique. Situating the two wars in a larger historical context suggests that, like the locusts that lie dormant for years before emerging en masse to ravish the landscape, belligerent ideals of manhood have surfaced and scattered in cyclical fashion. Yet persistent though they may be in leading successive generations to embrace aggressive policies, militant ideals of manhood are not inevitable—to the contrary, they must be learned and willfully repeated. However difficult, what has been learned can be unlearned; what has been taught can be rethought. To foster a more peaceable world, we must address the gender convictions that have proven so conducive to war.

Notes

Introduction

1. "Guinea" and "In Memory of Fred Douglass," *New Orleans Picayune*, Feb. 25, 1895; "Foreign Affairs" and "Mrs. Katherine Stevenson," *Baltimore Sun*, Feb. 25, 1895; "Last Shot is Fatal," *Chicago Tribune*, Feb. 25, 1895.

2. Earlier uprisings included the Ten Years War, or La Guerra Grande (1868–78) and La Guerra Chiquita (1879–80), Pérez, *Cuba Between Empires*, xv. "The Trouble Thought to Be Slight," *Baltimore Sun*, Feb. 27, 1895; "A Revolution in Cuba," *New Orleans Picayune*, Feb. 27, 1895. Although the initial rebellion collapsed, the revolutionaries Maceo, Gómez, and Martí continued the struggle, Smith, *The Spanish-American War*, 8.

3. Two studies of political culture that cover rhetoric and political style are Rodgers, *Contested Truths* and McGerr, "Political Style and Women's Power."

4. Baker, "The Domestication of Politics," 628; Baker, *The Moral Frameworks of Public Life*, 24–40; Scott, "Gender: A Useful Category," 1067, 1069–73. See also Brown, *Manhood and Politics*, Di Stefano, *Configurations of Masculinity*; Kann, *On the Man Question*.

5. A note on nomenclature: I use the name *Spanish-American War* rather than *Spanish-Cuban-American War* for three reasons: the first is brevity, the second is that the longer appellation discounts the Philippine theater, and the third is familiarity.

The United States was implicated from the start of the Spanish-Cuban War, for the Cubans were economically dependent on the United States, their largest market. The Wilson-Gorman Tariff Act (1894) imposed a new 40 percent duty on sugar, thereby causing an economic crisis on the cane-growing island. The Spanish government failed to negotiate a lower tariff, and its protectionist countermove threatened to exacerbate the island's commercial woes. Distressed Cubans focused a more critical eye on Spanish rule and local inequalities, Pérez, *Cuba Between Empires*, 30–34, 54–55, 144–45, 395; Pérez, *Cuba: Between Reform and Revolution*, 149–51, 167.

6. Pérez, *Cuba Between Empires*, 141, 197–98; Pérez, *Cuba and the United States*, 84; Foner, *Spanish-Cuban-American War* 1:218.

7. Foner, *The Spanish-Cuban-American War* 2:388.

8. On the navy's war plans, see Grenville, "American Naval Preparations for War with Spain," 34, 36; Smith, *The Spanish-American War,* 181. On treatment of Cubans, see Offner, *An Unwanted War,* 222; on the course of the war, see Dierks, *A Leap to Arms;* Cosmas, *An Army for Empire;* Trask, *The War with Spain in 1898.*

9. Alger, *The Spanish-American War,* 453–54; on praise for manhood, see Brooks, *The Story of Our War With Spain,* 336.

10. Smith, *The Spanish-American War,* 200; Offner, "Treaty of Paris," 547.

11. Musicant, *The Banana Wars,* 52–63.

12. Smith, *The Spanish-American War,* 225; Sarkesian, "Philippine War," 424–28; Gates, *Schoolbooks and Krags,* 233; Agoncillo and Alfonso find that after 1902, Filipino resistance did not endanger American rule, *History of the Filipino People,* 269, 273, 298.

13. Linn, "The Struggle for Samar," *Crucible of Empire,* 166; May, *Battle for Batangas,* 242.

14. One strand of the economic argument holds that the Spanish-American War resulted from a desire for markets, intensified by the depression of 1893–97. Williams argues that Americans believed, in dogmatic fashion, that national prosperity depended upon "sustained, ever-increasing overseas economic expansion," *The Tragedy of American Diplomacy,* 15, 31–32, 45. He attributes the aggressive policies of the late nineteenth century to agrarians who demanded that the government help them expand their markets, *The Roots of the Modern American Empire,* 23, 25, 409. LaFeber agrees that a generalized desire for markets drove policy, but he emphasizes businessmen's search for markets, *The New Empire,* 91, 155, 326, 370, 379, 403–04. Late-nineteenth-century farmers and businessmen undoubtedly did agitate to expand their markets, but commercial ambition alone does not explain why the United States entered the Spanish-Cuban War. To begin with, war-torn and impoverished Cuba was not a particularly promising market. Before the punitive Wilson-Gorman Tariff of 1894 sent the Cuban economy into a tailspin, slightly less than half of American exports to Central and South America went to Cuba. This was only a small part of American trade, for 75–80 percent of American exports went to Europe in the late nineteenth century. As for the argument that American policymakers viewed Cuba as a stepping-stone to greater markets, it is not clear why a generalized thrust for markets embedded the United States in such a thorny local conflict. Other markets were less troublesome and other measures, including lower tariffs, customs unions, reciprocity treaties, a trained consular service, and government subsidies to American merchant ships, were less complicated ways to access them. Yet policymakers did not feel compelled to pursue these peaceable options in a concerted fashion, perhaps because American traders and investors had been increasing their overseas presence with tremendous success ever since the Civil War. On exports, see Pletcher, "Rhetoric and Results," 98; for a critique of the economic explanation for American expansion, see Holbo, "Economics, Emotion, and Expansion," 204–12. On the lack of a trained consular service, see De Santis, "The Imperialist Impulse and American Innocence," 82; on commercial expansion, see Field, "American Imperialism," 659, 661. The markets explanation also leaves questions about timing. By 1898, the nation had emerged from its depression, and Cuba's symbolic role—as the elusive market (or path to markets) that could prevent future depressions—was no longer so important to increasingly prosperous farmers and businessmen. If markets drove U.S. policy, why did the United States not act during the depths

of the 1893–97 depression? Holbo notes that the hard times of 1882–86 did not result in expansionist policies, "Economics, Emotion, and Expansion," 204.

A variation of the economic explanation is that investments prompted U.S. intervention in the Spanish-Cuban War. According to this line of thought, Americans with property in Cuba clamored for intervention to protect their holdings. They had two goals: first, to stop the destruction on the island, and second, to incorporate Cuba within the American tariff wall. In 1898, when it appeared that the Cubans were close to attaining independence, these property owners increased their lobbying efforts, thereby helping to lead the nation into war. This explanation might prove persuasive to the conspiracy-minded, but investors were by no means unanimous for war. Some investors feared Spanish reprisals in the event of war, others, including those who had put their money into sugar beet farms in the United States, considered the possibility of closer ties to Cuba inimical to their interests. It stretches credulity to think that a handful of anxious investors could persuade a nation of seventy-five million citizens to go enthusiastically to war on behalf of their Cuban sugar plantations, mines, and ranches. On property holders, see Francisco and Fast, *Conspiracy for Empire*, 137, 150–51; on fear of reprisals, see Offner, *An Unwanted War*, 229. Holbo notes that congressmen discounted pleas and petitions from those who had a financial interest in legislation, "Economics, Emotion, and Expansion," 211.

A third variation on the economic argument is that business leaders advocated war to end the uncertainty caused by the prospect of war. According to this line of thought, influential businessmen advocated getting the seemingly inevitable conflict over with. They believed, as Massachusetts Senator Henry Cabot Lodge put it, that "one shock and then an end was better than a succession of spasms such as we must have if this war in Cuba went on." These businessmen supposedly persuaded President McKinley to intervene in order to end the political and economic uncertainty caused by the Cuban conflict. Lodge's assertions notwithstanding, many businessmen preferred minor "spasms" to the expense, risk, and destruction of war. Boards of trade and chambers of commerce passed resolutions against intervention, citing its economic consequences. When McKinley sought the counsel of businessmen, he heard pleas for both intervention and neutrality. There is no clear evidence that businessmen influenced him one way or the other. On getting the conflict over with and persuading McKinley to intervene, see LaFeber, *The New Empire*, 25, 400–05; Lodge cited in Williams, *The Tragedy of American Diplomacy*, 44. On the hostility of big business to war, see Hofstadter, "Cuba, the Philippines, and Manifest Destiny," 158; Wisan, *The Cuban Crisis*, 455; Pratt, *Expansionists of 1898*, 42; Faulkner, *Politics, Reform, and Expansion*, 228; May, *Imperial Democracy*, 118–20; Morgan, *America's Road to Empire*, 14; Linderman, *The Mirror of War*, 6–8. On McKinley, see Gould, *The Spanish-American War*, 52; Damiani, *Advocates of Empire*, 3.

A second explanation for the Spanish-American War centers on annexationist ambitions. Foner argues that, by 1898, the McKinley administration believed that Cuba was on the verge of winning independence. Rather than lose the opportunity to control the island, the United States intervened. If the surface motive was to bring good government to the war-torn island, the deeper cause was economic—"the rise of monopoly capitalism and its drive for markets," *The Spanish-Cuban-American War* 1:310. Pérez also discusses annexationist ambitions, but he places greater emphasis on a sense of historical destiny than on markets. Over time, he argues, the annexation of Cuba began to appear as part of the nation's manifest destiny. In 1898, the conviction that Cuban revolutionaries were close to victory led the United States to intervene lest it forever lose the island, *Cuba Between Empires,* 59, 64–65, 141, 170, 178; Pérez, *Cuba and the United States,* 40, 94.

Like the economic explanations, the annexationist argument illuminates part of the impetus for war. But it is important not to exaggerate Cuba's hold on American policymakers. Enthusiastic expansionists also called for the annexation of Canada and Mexico, and these proclamations did not determine U.S. policy. The annexationist explanation downplays the considerable opposition to annexation, much of it based on racial prejudice, and it fails to explain how a small group of annexationists persuaded the public that Cuba was worth the terrible costs of war. Given the nation's reluctance to peacefully annex Hawaii (attempts to incorporate the Hawaiian islands into the United States failed in 1893 and 1897), why was the nation willing to fight to obtain Cuba? On calling for the annexation of Canada and Mexico, see Rystad, *Ambiguous Imperialism,* 28. McKinley's failure to recognize Cuban independence may suggest acquisitive ambitions, but a more benign interpretation is that McKinley hesitated to provoke Spain by recognizing Cuba. After the United States entered the Spanish-Cuban War, McKinley still refused to recognize Cuban independence because he did not want U.S. troops to have to serve under Cuban commanders while on Cuban soil, Offner, *An Unwanted War,* 181–82, 227. On Bellamyites and single-taxers who wanted the nation to focus on domestic reform before annexing more territory, see Holbo, "Economics, Emotion, and Expansion," 204; De Santis, "The Imperialist Impulse," 82; on racist arguments against annexing dark-skinned people, see Weston, *Racism in U.S. Imperialism,* xiii; on Hawaiian annexation, see Osborne, "Empire Can Wait."

In addition to attributing the Spanish-American War to economic and annexationist ambitions, historians have attributed it to yet another national-self-interest explanation: geostrategic concerns. According to the geostrategic line of thought, there was a sea change in late-nineteenth-century American foreign policy. If earlier American policies could be characterized as spasmodic responses to exterior threats, late-nineteenth-century policies became more systematic defenses of more clearly defined interests. As advances in transportation and communication created a more interdependent world, Americans started to conceptualize their interests in global terms, to eye the balance of power. Supported by a strong current of public opinion, naval strategists urged the nation to acquire coaling stations and establish a stronghold near the site of a possible canal across the Isthmus of Panama. Strategists who feared British and German encroachments in the New World regarded war-torn Cuba as particularly vulnerable. They thus urged policymakers to intervene in Cuba as a preemptive measure. On naval strategist Alfred T. Mahan and his followers, see Campbell, *The Transformation of American Foreign Relations,* 151–59. Healy argues that U.S. imperialism was prescriptive—that fears of European encroachment in the New World (brought to a head in 1895 in a dispute with Great Britain over the Venezuela/British Guiana boundary) convinced strategists that the United States should seize desirable areas preemptively, *U.S. Expansionism,* 22–28; Beisner argues that the late-nineteenth-century interest in strategic issues reflected a sea change in American foreign policy, *From the Old Diplomacy to the New,* 78–94; on the naval buildup of 1882–93 and the popular support for navalism, see Shulman, *Navalism,* 1, 7, 47, 57, 151–56.

The geostrategic explanation helps explain why the United States went to war in 1898, but, like the economic and annexationist theories, it has some shortcomings. James A. Field, Jr., points these out in "American Imperialism: The Worst Chapter in Almost Any Book." Geostrategic thinkers were, he argues, "few in number and of doubtful leverage." Although a Venezuela boundary crisis did prompt fears of further British intervention in the Americas, no powers seemed likely to take Cuba from Spain, and even the Venezuela crisis was settled to the satisfaction of the United States. To clinch his argument against the geostrategic explanation, Field notes that very little came out of proposals to establish coaling stations and Pacific bases, Field, "American Imperialism," 647, 649, 652–54, 667. Indeed, policymakers' failure to beef up the army along with the navy in the 1880s and 1890s undercuts the argument that they intended to occupy strategic islands, see Smith, *The Spanish-American War*, 60.

The core of the political explanation is that a desire for partisan advantage led to war, that Democrats and Republicans alike thought that supporting war would help their parties win future elections. Added to this ambition was the hope that war would quell domestic unrest and unite the country after the divisive presidential election of 1896. These explanations illuminate jingoist policymakers' objectives, but they do not fully explain why leaders from both parties viewed war as an opportunity for partisan gain, social harmony, and national unity. Given that eighteen years later Woodrow Wilson won reelection with the platform "He Kept Us Out of War," why was there not a political premium on avoiding war? On partisan motivations, see May, *Imperial Democracy*, 147; Morgan, *America's Road to Empire*, 55; Offner, *An Unwanted War*, 180–81, 193; Karp, *The Politics of War*, 74. Williams argues that Americans believed that economic expansion was necessary for the health of American democracy because it helped avert domestic unrest, *The Tragedy of American Diplomacy*, 32; Faulkner argues that Americans regarded war as an opportunity to end partisan strife and unite the country, *Politics, Reform and Expansion*, 228.

Whereas some historians who have stressed the political causes of the Spanish-American War have highlighted political leaders' desire for war, others have argued that widespread humanitarian sympathy for the Cubans pushed policymakers into supporting bellicose policies. Spanish atrocities no doubt did develop a sense of hostility toward Spain and a desire to end its abuses. But why did Americans feel that it was their responsibility to interfere in a foreign dispute, and, even more curiously, to do so on the side of the mixed-race Cubans? Given white Americans' history of "removing" Native Americans to ever-smaller plots of land and their ability to stomach the disfranchisement and lynchings of African Americans, why did they feel compelled to promote democracy and end the suffering in Cuba? On humanitarian sentiment, see Pratt, *America's Colonial Experiment*, 41–42; on the desire to free Cuba, see Gould, *The Spanish-American War*, 53; Offner, *An Unwanted War*, 38, 228; Morgan, *America's Road to Empire*, 8; Hofstadter, "Cuba, the Philippines, and Manifest Destiny," 149. Pérez notes that many Americans viewed the racial and social heterogeneity of the Cuban army with dismay, *Cuba Between Empires*, 67.

A final variation on the political argument is that the sinking of the *Maine* provoked an overwhelming public demand for revenge. Goaded on by the yellow press, the American public clamored for war. But, as Richard Hofstadter has pointed out, not all naval incidents have led to war. (The sinking of the *Lusitania* in 1915 comes to mind.) Evidently, the *Maine* disaster ignited a powder keg of martial sentiments. On the yellow press, see Wisan, *The Cuban Crisis as Reflected in the New York Press*, 455; Wilkerson, *Public Opinion and the Spanish-American War*, 61, 121; Millis, *The Martial Spirit*, 108–09; Hofstadter, "Cuba, the Philippines, and Manifest Destiny," 149. "The press could not have created war sentiment out of nothing," writes Faulkner, ". . . The country was in a receptive mood," *Politics, Reform, and Expansion*, 228.

Hofstadter tries to explain this restless mood by arguing that a psychic crisis made war seem desirable for its own sake. According to Hofstadter, "Americans seemed to want not merely the freedom of Cuba but a war for the freedom of Cuba." Hofstadter explained the causes of this psychic crisis more carefully than he defined its nature, which remains somewhat elusive. According to Hofstadter, the depression of 1893 sparked the crisis. It was exacerbated by the specter of social convulsion (brought to mind by the Populist movement, free-silver agitation, and the heated election of 1896), the sense that there were fewer business opportunities for aspiring entrepreneurs (caused by corporate bureaucratization, the establishment of a solid industrial infrastructure, and the development of trusts), and by the apparent disappearance of the frontier line and filling up of the continent. Taken together, these developments gave rise to a "restless aggressiveness, a desire to be assured that the power and vitality of the nation were not waning." War served as the outlet for this restless mood. The major problem with Hofstadter's "psychic crisis" is that it is a nebulous explanation. What did these disparate developments have in common? How did the psychic crisis manifest itself? Hofstadter, "Cuba, the Philippines, and Manifest Destiny," 150–57. On Darwinian anxieties, see Pratt, *Expansionists of 1898*, 3–9; Healy, *U.S. Expansionism*, 101; on racial thought, see Weston, *Racism in U.S. Imperialism*, 11–12, 22; Hunt, *Ideology and U.S. Foreign Policy*, 80; Pérez, *Cuba Between Empires*, 61.

15. The word *jingo* was first associated with a bellicose spirit in a British music hall song of 1878. By the 1890s the martial spirit and the term had taken hold in the United States as well, *Oxford English Dictionary*, 2d ed., on line.

16. Mahan, *The Interest of America in Sea Power*, 26, 95, 193, 232, 268; on the nation's shift to an offensive defense, see Shulman, *Navalism*, 116.

17. On seeing Cuba as feminine and the United States as a chivalric rescuer, see Hunt, *Ideology and U.S. Foreign Policy*, 61; Kaplan, "Romancing the Empire," 661, 663, 666–67, 674; on viewing Cuban soldiers as analogous to the revolutionary heroes of 1776, see Pérez, *Cuba Between Empires*, 197.

18. Silber discusses Populists' concerns about their loss of manly independence in *The Romance of Reunion*, 99–100; on money and manhood rhetoric, see Palmer, "Man Over Money," 111; on "overcivilization," see Roberts, "The Strenuous Life," 98–139; Filene, *Him/ Her/Self*, 73; Lutz, *American Nervousness*, 28; Rotundo, "Body and Soul," 32; Gorn, *The Manly Art*, 187, 192–93; Kimmel, "The Contemporary 'Crisis' of Masculinity," 138–43; Wilkinson, *American Tough*, 147; Lears, *No Place of Grace*, 98–139; Bederman, *Manliness and Civilization*, 86–88.

19. Mallan, "The Warrior Critique of the Business Civilization," 216–18; Healy, *U.S. Expansionism*, 101, 115–19. Lears discusses elite men's hopes that embracing militarism would help them maintain their power in the face of what they considered to be a Darwinian class struggle, *No Place of Grace*, 102. Men's historians have found that bellicose ideals of masculinity were in the ascendence in the late nineteenth century. Although they have focused on explaining how men's roles and ideas about manhood have changed over time, these historians have made suggestive observations about the foreign policy implications of these martial ideals, Higham, "The Reorientation of American Culture in the 1890s," 83, 86; Filene, *Him/Her/Self*, 71; Dubbert, *A Man's Place*, 76; Wilkinson, *American Tough*, 106; Rotundo, *American Manhood*, 225–27, 232–36; Bederman, *Manliness and Civilization*, 171, 187, 190; Takaki, *Iron Cages*, 269–71; Roberts, "The Strenuous Life," 4–5. On vice, see Chauncey, *Gay New York*, 39, 44; Greenberg, *The Construction of Homosexuality*, 400,

413; Gay, *The Cultivation of Hatred*, 114–15; on memories of the Civil War, see Pettegrew, "'The Soldier's Faith'," 51, 58.

20. On the Philippine issue, see Smith, "William McKinley's Enduring Legacy," 205–49; Healy, *U.S. Expansionism*, 65–66; Rystad, *Ambiguous Imperialism*, 162–63. On hopes of capturing the China market, see McCormick, *China Market*, 107–08. Damiani argues that expansionist senators believed that assertive policies in the Philippines would have partisan benefits, *Advocates of Empire*, 43, 135; on businessmen's and evangelical Protestants' interest in the Philippines, see Miller, "Benevolent Assimilation," 17; on racial ideology, see Hunt, *Ideology and U.S. Foreign Policy*, 57–62; Rystad, *Ambiguous Imperialism*, 162–63.

Chapter 1. The Manly Ideal of Politics and the Jingoist Desire for War

1. On harbingers of peace, see "The New Year" and Benjamin Trueblood, "The Coming of Peace," both in *The Advocate of Peace*, 59, Jan. 1897, 5, 18. International arbitration was not a new idea—the Jay's Treaty of 1794 committed the United States and Great Britain to arbitrate several conflicts, and, more recently, the two nations had turned to arbitration to settle shipping disputes from the Civil War. What made the treaty of 1897 seem so auspicious was that it would make arbitration a matter of principle rather than convenience, Davis, "Arbitration, Mediation, and Conciliation," 34–35, 37; on crowning glory, see James Keith, cited in *Proceedings of the American Conference on International Arbitration*, 156; on future treaties and hopes for peace, see Russell of Killowen, "International Law and Arbitration," *Forum* 22, Oct. 1896, 192–216, 208; Mary Jewett Telford, "Militarism versus Patriotism," *Union Signal* 22, Dec. 24, 1896, 3.

2. The enthusiasm was particularly noticeable among peace society members, church leaders, Anglophiles, professionals, business groups, college students, and social reformers, Blake, "The Olney-Pauncefote Treaty of 1897," 230–37; Carl Schurz, "The Arbitration Treaty in Danger," *Harper's Weekly* 41, Jan. 30, 1897, 99.

3. On honor in the Chilean episode, see May, *Imperial Democracy*, 10. On HONOR, see Resolutions adopted by the Junior Order of United American Mechanics, Butte City, Montana, Dec. 23, 1895; Foreign Relations Committee, 54th Congress; Records of the U.S. Senate, record group 46, NA; on honor and integrity, see Sen. Henry M. Teller, *CR* 28, pt. 1, Dec. 19, 1895, 247; on true men, see Thomas J. Gurgun [signature semilegible] to Richard Olney, Dec. 27, 1895, reel 15, Richard Olney Papers, LC. Sen. William M. Stewart, *CR* 28, pt. 1, Dec. 19, 1895, 259.

4. Blake, "The Olney-Pauncefote Treaty," 232, 237; Patterson, *Toward a Warless World*, 42–45; DeBenedetti, *The Peace Reform*, 67–69.

5. "Address of Samuel Gompers," *The Advocate of Peace* 59, April 1897, 87; Blake, "The Olney-Pauncefote Treaty," 237. On refined values, see John Fiske, "The Arbitration Treaty," *Atlantic Monthly* 79, March 1897, 399–408, 404; "Nearing Ratification," *NYT*, March 23, 1897; "The Treaty," *NYT*, Feb. 10, 1897. Margaret Bradshaw to George F. Hoar, March 13, 1896, George F. Hoar Papers, MHS. By the late nineteenth century, more middle- and upper-class men boxed, but arbitrationists harked back to the middle of the century when boxing was primarily a working-class sport, Gorn, *The Manly Art*, 129–47, 198–99.

6. "The Old Stone Age Senators," *NYT*, Jan. 21, 1897; S. T. Willis, "Reasons for an Anglo-American Supreme Court of Peace," *Godey's Magazine* 132, June 1896, 613–16, 615.

7. "Against War," *Union Signal* 22, Jan. 9, 1896, 10; Bordin, *Woman and Temperance*, 109–10; Robbins, ed., *History and Minutes of the National Council of Women*, 241; Croly, *The History of the Woman's Club Movement*, 185, 307–08, 533; Avery, ed., *Proceedings of the Twenty-Eighth Annual Convention*, 89, 96; "Arbitration Conference," *Woman's Tribune* 13, May 2, 1896, 45; Craig, "Lucia True Ames Mead," 69; Ellen M. Henrotin, "Address," 1896, folder: speeches 1896/05, Presidents' Papers (Record Group 2), GFWC; Wisconsin Federation of Women's Clubs Petition, *CR* 30, pt. 1, March 16, 1897, 34; Women's Club of River Forest, Illinois, *CR* 30, pt. 1, March 23, 1897, 154; *Proceedings of the American Conference on International Arbitration*, 147–48; *Report of the First Annual Meeting of the Lake Mohonk Conference*, 69, 84. On vital interest to women, see Petition of the Heptorean Club, March 1897; Committee on Foreign Relations, 53d Congress, Records of the U.S. Senate, record group 46, NA.

8. On Union veterans and military training, see Dearing, *Veterans in Politics*, 476; on true glory, see Alice May Douglas, "All Can Help," *Union Signal* 21, Sept. 5, 1895, 3; Willard cited in Pivar, *Purity Crusade*, 182.

9. Merrill E. Gates, cited in *Report of the First Annual Meeting of the Lake Mohonk Conference*, 60; "Civilization Demands Arbitration and Peace," *Judge* 32, Feb. 20, 1897, cover.

10. Philip S. Moxom, cited in *Report of the Third Annual Meeting of the Lake Mohonk Conference*, 91.

11. Benjamin F. Trueblood, "The United States, Great Britain and International Arbitration," *New England Magazine* 14, March 1896, 21–27, 26; Rev. Dr. Crane, cited in "The Treaty of Peace Before War," May 8, 1896, *Evening Post*, clipping in Scrapbook, 1895–97, box 241, John Basset Moore Papers, LC.

12. E. P. Powell, "Should War be Abolished," *Arena* 12, May 1895, 353–57, 357; Henry Childs Merwin, "On Being Civilized too Much," *Atlantic Monthly* 79, June 1897, 838–46, 839; Sen. John T. Morgan, *CR* 30, pt. 2, May 29, 1897, 1347.

13. On the amendment, made in late March, see Blake, "The Olney-Pauncefote Treaty," 237. On pusillanimity, see *New York Sun* editorial quoted in the *Literary Digest* 13, May 2, 1896, 5; on deluded gentlemen, see "A Humbug Disposed Of," *Washington Post*, May 7, 1897.

14. Theodore Roosevelt to Henry Cabot Lodge, April 29, 1896, *Selections from the Correspondence of Theodore Roosevelt and Henry Cabot Lodge* 1:218.

15. Sen. George F. Hoar, *CR* 29, pt. 2, Feb. 6, 1897, 1615.

16. Foner, *Reconstruction*, 276, 472, 590–92; DuBois, *Feminism and Suffrage*, 96; Kousser, *The Shaping of Southern Politics*, 29; Kleppner, *Who Voted?*, 8.

17. Baker, "The Domestication of Politics," 628; Baker, *The Moral Frameworks of Public Life*, 24–29. On fraternal organizations, see Carnes, *Secret Ritual and Manhood;* Clawson, "Nineteenth-Century Women's Auxiliaries," 40–61; Clawson, *Constructing Brotherhood*.

18. On Anna Dickinson, see Flexner, *Century of Struggle*, 108. Although women did not wield much direct power in political affairs, they did turn out for rallies and other political events, see Varon, "Tippecanoe and the Ladies, Too," 498, 501. On women in public ceremonies, see Ryan, *Women in Public*, 52–54; on inculcating virtue, see Kraditor, *The Ideas of the Woman Suffrage Movement*, 2; on grand position, see O. B. Frothingham, "The Real Case of the 'Remonstrants' Against Woman Suffrage," *Arena*, July 1890, 175–81, 177.

19. Elihu Root, "Address Delivered before the New York State Constitutional Convention on Aug. 15, 1894," "Pamphlet Published by the New York State Association Opposed to Woman Suffrage," folder 211, antisuffrage pamphlets, reel D43, Maud Wood Park Papers, SL; Finley Peter Dunne quoted in Keller, *Affairs of State*, 539.

20. On politicians as specimens of manhood, see Morgan, *From Hayes to McKinley*, 143; Baker, *The Moral Frameworks of Public Life*, xiii; for antecedents to this, see Etcheson, "Manliness and the Political Culture of the Old Northwest," 59–77. Rep. Henry R. Gibson, *CR* 29, pt. 1, Dec. 22, 1896, 410.

21. On she-men see Goldberg, "'An Army of Women,'" 268; on Populism as a womanly movement, see Ostler, *Prairie Populism*, 129; on mugwumps, see Josephson, *The Politicos*, 356, 384; Marcus, *Grand Old Party*, 15; Blodgett, "The Mugwump Reputation," 883; Hofstadter, *Anti-intellectualism*, 186, 188.

22. Wyatt-Brown, *Southern Honor*, 4, 14, 34; Wyatt-Brown, *Yankee Saints*, 185–87; Greenberg, *Honor and Slavery*, 7, 88, 131. See also Ayers, *Vengeance and Justice*, 29. On honor in the eighteenth century, see Wood, *The Radicalism of the American Revolution*, 39. On male honor in late-nineteenth-century Europe, see Mosse, *The Image of Man*, 21; McAleer, *Dueling*, 59, 83, 109; Nye, *Masculinity and Male Codes of Honor*, vii, 153; Girouard, *The Return to Camelot*, 199–260. Clinton, "'Southern Dishonor,'" 58.

23. On dignity, see Wyatt-Brown, *Yankee Saints*, 191; on the decline in honor in the North and northern admiration for southern chivalry, see Silber, *Romance of Reunion*, 20, 175; Stevens, *Pistols at Ten Paces*, 92, 245. On the assumption that Civil War soldiers were honorable, see Linderman, *Embattled Courage*, 11–12; on the Civil War's role in popularizing chivalric ideals, see Fraser, *America and the Patterns of Chivalry*, 26; on chivalry in romance novels, see Kaplan, "Romancing the Empire," 659, 661, 666; Blight, "'For Something Beyond the Battlefield,'" 1167; on chivalry and gender roles, see Girouard, *The Return to Camelot*, 199; Nye, *Masculinity and Male Codes of Honor*, vii. That chivalric ideals appealed to working-class men can be seen in the name Knights of Labor, Fink, *Workingmen's Democracy*, 13. On working-class men and honor, see also Gorn, *The Manly Art*, 143.

24. On Confederate veterans, see Foster, *Ghosts of the Confederacy*, 25–26; on the legacy of manhood, see Pettegrew, "'The Soldier's Faith,'" 51–57. Even before the Civil War, military heroes played a prominent role in American politics. Presidents Washington, Monroe, Jackson, Harrison, Taylor, and Pierce had notable military records, Cunliffe, *Soldiers and Civilians*, 70, 73. On war as the "master image" of Democratic politics prior to the Civil War, see Baker, *Affairs of Party*, 287–88. The Civil War energized the long-standing connection between manhood, military service, and politics by infusing a large pool of veterans into public life. In the aftermath of the Civil War, both leading parties competed for veterans' votes by nominating soldiers, Dearing, *Veterans in Politics*, vii, 65, 72, 127–28, 148, 159, 186, 252; Ayers, *The Promise of the New South*, 48; Jensen, *The Winning of the Midwest*, 23–25; Foner, *Reconstruction*, 572. Stoddard, *As I Knew Them*, 51.

25. On torchlights, Baker, *Affairs of Party*, 290; on uniforms, see McGerr, *The Decline of Popular Politics*, 24–25; on fights, see Dearing, *Veterans in Politics*, 181; on lieutenants and fighters, see C. D. Sheldon to Chase S. Osborn, May 28, 1898, Correspondence, 1898–99, box 5, Chase S. Osborn Papers, UMBL; on the voting booth, see "The Close of the Campaign," *NYT*, Nov. 1, 1896; on military language and images in general, see Jensen, *The Winning of the Midwest*, 11, 164–65; Baker, *The Moral Frameworks of Public Life*, 28–29.

26. On brave-hearted heroes, see Rep. Michael Griffen, *CR* 28, pt. 1, Jan. 16, 1896, 743; these record-citing veterans included African-American men, who reminded their northern supporters that they had fought for the Union, Cullen, "'I's a Man Now,'" 81.

27. J. Newton Fiero, "Paper at Anti-Suffrage Meeting," May 11, 1894, *Pamphlets Printed and Distributed by the Women's Anti-Suffrage Association*, n.p.

28. On elitist political trends, see Sproat, *"The Best Men,"* 270–71; McFarland, *Mugwumps, Morals and Politics,* 49–50; Keller, *Affairs of State,* 272. On the "abandonment of the army style of campaigning," after 1888, see Jensen, *The Winning of the Midwest,* 33, 166, 306. McGerr argues that in the election of 1892, "education displaced demonstrative partisanship as the dominant political style of the North," *The Decline of Popular Politics,* 106. On a "partial feminization of male political style," see McGerr, "Political Style and Women's Power," 864–65, 870. On women's efforts to influence government from outside electoral channels, see Baker, "The Domestication of Politics," 621.

29. On exhorting men of the better class, see "A Hinderance to Reform," *LW* 80, Jan. 10, 1895, 18. Kleppner, *Who Voted?,* 8–10, 60. Kousser notes that, motivated by economic concerns and partisanship, southern white Democratic leaders in black belt districts worked to disfranchise the poor whites of white counties, *The Shaping of Southern Politics,* 7, 52–53. That white men tried to disfranchise black men legally does not mean that they forsook violence, Gilmore, *Gender and Jim Crow,* chap. 4. The elitism of the disfranchisement movement could cut across racial lines in surprising ways: a few wealthy African-American men supported limiting government to the wealthy, Painter, *Standing at Armageddon,* 9.

30. Painter, *Standing at Armageddon,* 60, 70, 98; Kleppner, *The Third Electoral System,* 288; Keller, *Affairs of State,* 571; Ostler, *Prairie Populism,* 1.

31. Painter, *Standing at Armageddon,* 137–39; Keller, *Affairs of State,* 559, 584; Marcus, *Grand Old Party,* 248–49; Jensen, *The Winning of the Midwest,* 305; "War Upon Property," *LW* 83, Sept. 10, 1896, 162; on class against class, see "A Degenerate Candidate," *LW* 83, Oct. 15, 1896, 242.

32. On the army as a leveling force, see McConnell, *Glorious Contentment,* 19; Grover Cleveland, "Address at Princeton University," Oct. 22, 1896, reel 157, Grover Cleveland Papers, LC.

33. On ex-Confederates, see Wilson, *Baptized in Blood,* 8; Foster, *Ghosts of the Confederacy,* 142; on northerners, see "Some Gotham Patriots," *Boston Globe,* April 22, 1897; on private ambitions, see James A. Tawney, Memorial Day speech, 1895, folder: speeches, undated, box 6, James A. Tawney Papers, MNHS; on pension complaint, see Skocpol, *Protecting Soldiers and Mothers,* 2; Kemble, *The Image of the Army Officer,* 128.

34. On wealthy reformers' complaints, see Sproat, *"The Best Men,"* 68; John Jay Chapman, "The Capture of the Government by Commercialism," *Atlantic Monthly* 81, Feb. 1898, 145–58, 146. McKinley cited in Smith, *McKinley's Speeches in September,* 260.

35. Rep. John Sharp Williams, *CR* 30, pt. 2, May 20, 1897, 1197; on critiquing materialism, see Painter, *Standing at Armageddon,* 69, 136; Goldman, *Rendevous with Destiny,* 49.

36. "Woman's Growing Influence in Public Affairs," *ROR* 12, Dec. 1895, 649. For a discussion of men's concerns about women's influence, see Roberts, "The Strenuous Life," 161, 164–65; Testi, "The Gender of Reform Politics," 1511–12. Lebsock has called the period from 1880 to 1920 "a great age for women in politics," "Women and American Politics," 35; Edwards finds that women's partisan activities accelerated from the 1880s through 1896, "Gender in American Politics," 11, chaps. 2–6.

37. Stewart, *The Philanthropic Work of Josephine Shaw Lowell*, 416, 480; Waugh, "Unsentimental Reformer," 506–07; Monoson, "The Lady and the Tiger," 100; "Woman's Growing Influence in Public Affairs," *ROR* 12, Dec. 1895, 649; "The Lady or the Tiger," *Chicago Tribune*, Oct. 19, 1895; Lillian W. Betts, "Women and Public Affairs," *Outlook* 53, Feb. 29, 1896, 396–97, 396; Davis, *American Heroine*, 122; Wheeler, *New Women of the New South*, 67; on matinee, see "Women Cheer for Mr. Low," *NYT*, Oct. 28, 1897; see also "Women Have a Big Rally," *New York Tribune*, Nov. 3, 1894.

38. On prohibitionist women, see Jensen, *The Winning of the Midwest*, 94; on Populist women, see Ostler, *Prairie Populism*, 128; "A Local 'Jeanne d' Arc' in Maryland," *ROR* 12, Dec. 1895, 650–51; "Women and Politics," *New York Tribune*, Oct. 25, 1896; on women officeholders, see "Women Won the School Elections," *New York Journal*, Aug. 6, 1897; Laura M. Johns, "Woman Mayor in Kansas," *WJ* 26, April 20, 1895, 124; ASB, "Kansas Women Officers," *WJ* 27, April 18, 1896, 124; "Women Office-Holders in Colorado and Wyoming," *WJ* 26, Jan. 12, 1895, 10; "First Woman Juror in Colorado," *WJ* 27, May 16, 1898, 154; FMA, "The Woman Juror in Colorado," *WJ* 27, June 6, 1896, 180. On women officeholders in Utah and Colorado, see "Woman Suffrage in the West," *Literary Digest* 14, Jan. 9, 1897, 294. "It's Coming," *Judge* 29, Aug. 31, 1895, 138. On parades, see "Women as Lawmakers," *Chautauquan* 21, May 1895, 233; on Spring Hill, see Gehring, "Women Officeholders in Kansas," 54; see also "Woman's Onward March," *Atlanta Constitution*, Dec. 15, 1897.

39. On conventions, see "Women at St. Louis," *WJ* 27, June 27, 1896, 205; "Women in the Democratic Party," *WJ* 27, July 11, 1896, 220; "Woman's Share in the Populist Convention," *WJ* 27, Aug. 1, 1896, 244; on women in Canton, see "Republican Women," *Woman's Standard* 9, Aug. 1896; "The Flag and M'Kinley," *NYT*, Nov. 1, 1896; "The Political Campaign," *Chautauquan* 24, Nov. 1896, 219; Smith, *McKinley's Speeches in September*, 288, 290; on Bryan's speeches, see "Bryan to the Women," *The People's Party Paper*, Oct. 16, 1896, 1; Bryan, *The First Battle*, 547, 589; on campaign literature, see HBB, "New York Women in Politics," *WJ* 27, Sept. 5, 1896, 284; on debates and pamphlets, see HBB, "Women in American Politics," *WJ* 27, Oct. 17, 1896, 332; on Foster and Gougar, see Mary A. Fanton, "Women Workers in the Present Political Campaign," *LW* 83, Oct. 1, 1896, 218. Addie M. Billings, Speech, 1896, folder 7, box 1, Addie M. Billings Papers, SL.

40. "Women in the Recent Campaign," *Chautauquan* 24, Jan. 1897, 483; "Women Who Hope to Be Elected" and "Three Queer Election Results," *New York Journal*, Nov. 1 and Nov. 15, 1896. "Not Coming, But Arrived," *Judge* 31, Dec. 5, 1896, 354; on emancipator, see "Say 'No' in Leap Year," *Chicago Tribune*, Feb. 9, 1896.

41. On busybodies, see "The American Woman," *LW* 85, Oct. 14, 1897, 242. Wheeler, *New Women*, 117–18; "Women at St. Louis," *WJ* 27, June 27, 1896, 205; Catharine Waugh McCullouch, "Suffrage Hearing Before the Democratic Platform Committee," *WJ* 27, July 18, 1896, 229. The territory of Wyoming granted women suffrage in 1869 and became the first full women's suffrage state in 1890. In 1870 the territory of Utah enfranchised women. Congress disfranchised Utah women in 1883, but in 1896 the state of Utah granted women suffrage again. In 1893, Colorado enfranchised women; Idaho did so in 1896, Buechler, *The Transformation of the Woman Suffrage Movement*, 13. Women in Arizona, Connecticut, Illinois, Kansas, Kentucky, Massachusetts, Michigan, Minnesota, Montana, Nebraska, New Hampshire, New Jersey, New York, North Dakota, Ohio, Oregon, South Dakota, Vermont, Washington, and Wisconsin had school board suffrage. Kansas permitted women's suffrage in municipal elections starting in 1887 and Montana permitted tax-paying women greater

suffrage rights the same year. In 1894, Iowa allowed women to vote on bonds. See "Fifty Years Ago," *WJ* 26, Jan. 26, 1895, 1; "Souvenir Program for the Massachusetts Woman Suffrage Bazaar," Dec. 7–11, 1897, folder 150, printed suffrage matter, 1870–1914, reel D40, Maud Wood Park Papers, SL; Alice Stone Blackwell, "Gains in Equal Suffrage," reel B8, Mary Hillard Loines Papers, Women's Studies Manuscript Collections, SL; Anthony and Harper, eds., *History of Woman Suffrage* 4:977, 988; Kraditor, *The Ideas of the Woman Suffrage Movement*, 4.

42. On women's desire to change the political system, see Baker, *The Moral Frameworks of Public Life*, 72; DuBois, "Outgrowing the Compact of the Fathers," 851; on suffragists' shift from justice to expediency arguments, see Kraditor, *The Ideas of the Woman Suffrage Movement*, 52; Rev. Ida Hultin cited in Anthony and Harper, eds., *History of Woman Suffrage* 4:285; Sarah Grand, "The New Aspect of the Woman Question," *NAR* 158, March 1894, 270–76, 273; Sarah Grand, "Response," *NAR* 158, May 1894, 620–27, 625; on selfishness, see Mrs. M. A. Corley, "Why Southern Women Desire the Ballot," *WJ* 26, Jan. 16, 1895, 27.

43. On women's moral authority see Epstein, *The Politics of Domesticity*, 90; Pascoe, *Relations of Rescue*, xx; Bordin, *Woman and Temperance*, 8; Goldberg, "'An Army of Women,'" 144, 170; Klotter, "Sex, Scandal, and Suffrage in the Gilded Age," 225–43; Fuller, "An Early Venture of Kentucky Women in Politics," 224–42; Pivar, *Purity Crusade*, 210–11. The belief that women represented moral virtue led some women to oppose women's suffrage, for fear that voting would rob women of their moral stature, Thurner, "'Better Citizens Without the Ballot,'" 41. Elizabeth Cady Stanton cited in Anthony and Harper, eds., *History of Woman Suffrage* 4:269; on criminals, see M. A. Wadell Rodger, "How to Teach Citizenship," *Woman's Tribune* 14, March 20, 1897, 21.

44. On no fight, see Mrs. Edward Q. Norton, "Dual Suffrage," *Arena* 16, Oct. 1896, 751; Margaret Noble Lee, "Bishop Doane and Woman Suffrage," *Arena* 15, March 1896, 642–53, 652–53; on imagery, see Edwards, "Gender in American Politics," 11, 70, 125.

45. Anna Garlin Spencer cited in Anthony and Harper, eds., *History of Woman Suffrage* 4:308; see also Hoar, "Woman in the State," 3; Hannah J. Bailey cited in Davis, *The United States and the First Hague Peace Conference*, 12.

46. Rev. William Croswell Doane, "Why Women do not Want the Ballot," *NAR* 161, Sept. 1895, 257–67, 266.

47. Mallan, "The Warrior Critique," 218; Roberts, "The Strenuous Life," 18, 20, 161, 164; Filene, *Him/Her/Self*, 73; Lutz, *American Nervousness*, 28; Rotundo, "Body and Soul," 32; Gorn, *The Manly Art*, 187, 192–93; Kimmel, "The Contemporary 'Crisis' of Masculinity," 138–43; Wilkinson, *American Tough*, 147; Kern, *Anatomy and Destiny*, 103–04; Lears, *No Place of Grace*, 98–139; Macleod, *Building Character*, 46; Williamson, *The Crucible of Race*, 111; Bederman, *Manliness and Civilization*, 30, 88; Bederman, "'Civilization,' the Decline of Middle-Class Manliness," 8; Greenberg, *The Construction of Homosexuality*, 413; Chauncey, *Gay New York*, 39, 44; Mumford, "'Lost Manhood' Found," 75–77; Higham, "The Reorientation of American Culture," 92; Blanchard, "The Soldier and the Aesthete," 25–46.

48. Slotkin, *Gunfighter Nation*, 11–12, 61, 81; on frontier anxiety, see Wrobel, *The End of American Exceptionalism*, 3, 36. On the New Woman and male backlash, see Filene, *Him/Her/Self*, 93.

49. On women of either sex, see "Corsets in Kansas," *NYT*, Jan. 9, 1897; on efforts to

reform men's morals, see Ownby, *Subduing Satan*, 170–77; on concerns about effeminizing boys, see Macleod, *Building Character*, 48; Max O'Rell, "Petticoat Government," *NAR* 163, July 1896, 101–09, 104.

50. On government of force, see Francis M. Scott, "Address of June 14, 1894," *Pamphlets Printed and Distributed by the Women's Anti-Suffrage Association*, n.p.; on the Civil War, see Rossiter Johnson, "A Blank Cartridge Ballot," *Remonstrance*, 1895, 4; on antisuffragists' beliefs about force more generally, see Kraditor, *The Ideas of the Woman Suffrage Movement*, 28. On physical power in international affairs, see William Ludlow, "The Military Systems of Europe and America," *NAR* 160, Jan. 1895, 72–84, 83.

51. On danger, see A. T. Mahan to Herbert Welsh, February 13, 1896, folder: Correspondence L-W, 1896, box: International Arbitration Correspondence, Herbert Welsh Collection, HSP. *The Influence of Sea Power* went through fifteen editions by 1898, Takaki, *Iron Cages*, 266, 273–75; Taylor, *The Life of Admiral Mahan*, 302.

52. Rep. Vespasian Warner, *CR* 31, pt. 3, March 8, 1898, 2619; Rep. Albert S. Berry, *CR* 31, pt. 1, Jan. 19, 1898, 774–75.

53. Mahan cited in Taylor, *The Life of Admiral Mahan*, 303–04, 333–35.

54. On compensations, see Charles W. Buckley, quoted in the *Journal of the Thirty-First National Encampment of the Grand Army of the Republic*, 69; on British assertions, see Morris, *Pax Britannica*, 140. On Civil War memories, see Lodge, "The Blue and the Gray" (1887), *Speeches and Addresses*, 27; on spirit, see Lodge, "Our Duty Toward Hawaii," *Speeches and Addresses*, 167.

55. On empire over self, see Henry C. Lodge, "Shut Gates: Lodge on Perils of Immigration," clipping from March 1896, *Immigration Clippings, 8–13 April, 1895–Jan. 1897*, Widener Library, Harvard; on building character and noncommercial concerns, see Lodge, "The Restriction of Immigration" (1896), "Speech before the Republican State Convention of Massachusetts" (1896), both in *Speeches and Addresses*, 251, 285; on Harvard address, see Lodge, "Speech at the Alumni Dinner" (1896), *Speeches and Addresses*, 293.

56. Henry C. Lodge to Frank L. Sanford, Dec. 20, 1895, Henry Cabot Lodge Letterbook 31, Henry Cabot Lodge Papers, MHS.

57. Capt. H. C. Taylor, "The Study of War," *NAR* 162, Feb. 1896, 181–89, 183; Sen. Roger Q. Mills, *CR* 29, pt. 1, Jan. 11, 1897, 655–56.

58. On lifting Americans from materialism, see Carl Schurz cited in *Proceedings of the American Conference on International Arbitration*, 37; on abominable idea, see Schurz, "The Venezuelan Question" (1896), *Speeches*, Bancroft, ed., 5:250.

59. On social solidarity, see HMA, "The Warlike Spirit," *Harper's Weekly* 90, Aug. 28, 1897, 858; on trial of strength, see Rev. John S. Lindsay, "Was the War Worth All it Cost?" *Boston Globe*, May 30, 1897; see also Blight, "'For Something Beyond the Battlefield,'" 1162–63, 1167. Sen. Marion Butler, *CR* 28, part 1, Jan. 14, 1896, 660.

60. On men of Bunker Hill, see Roosevelt, "The Monroe Doctrine" (1896), *American Ideals*, 168–81, 184; on richer, see Theodore Roosevelt, "American Ideals" (1895), *American Ideals*, 4; on welcoming war, see Beale, *Theodore Roosevelt*, 37; Theodore Roosevelt to Henry Cabot Lodge, Dec. 27, 1895, *Selections from the Correspondence of Theodore Roosevelt and Henry Cabot Lodge* 1:204.

61. Sen. William M. Stewart, *CR* 28, pt. 1, Dec. 20, 1895, 259; Rep. James B. Clark, *CR* 31, pt. 1, Jan. 20, 1898, 794; Rep. Joseph Wheeler, *CR* 28, pt. 7, April 4, 1896, 453.

62. Law, *The Parties and the Men or Political Issues of 1896*, 258; on the naval buildup,

see LaFeber, *The New Empire,* 59. On Venezuela crisis demands, see *New York Tribune* article quoted in "War-Talk and Territorial Expansion," *Literary Digest* 12, Nov. 30, 1895, 123.

63. "Folly of the International Arbitration Scheme," *Chicago Tribune,* April 24, 1896; on hurrah for war, see Blake, "The Olney-Pauncefote Treaty," 238.

64. Anglophobes included a number of Irish Americans and silverites (who opposed a treaty with a gold standard nation). Supporters of a U.S. controlled isthmian canal feared that a treaty would hinder the government, and some senators feared that a standing treaty would undercut their power to ratify specific agreements, Davis, *The United States and the First Hague Peace Conference,* 32–34; Blake, "The Olney-Pauncefote Treaty," 235, 239–43; May, *Imperial Democracy,* 63; Patterson, *Toward a Warless World,* 40, 45. Kann comments on men's unwillingness to admit women to foreign-policy making circles: "It was one thing to recognize women's right to do some moralizing and municipal housekeeping but quite another to admit women into the manly discourse on foreign policy, national defense, imperialism, and war," *On the Man Question,* 293.

65. On Senate amendments, see Patterson, *Toward a Warless World,* 40, 45. Some supporters voted for these amendments in hopes of saving the treaty. On glorious privilege, see Senator Hawley, cited in "Hawley on Arbitration," Jan. 18, 1897, *Evening Post,* clipping in Scrapbook, 1895–97, box 241, John Basset Moore Papers, LC.

66. Blake, "The Olney-Pauncefote Treaty," 240; "The Fate of the Arbitration Treaty," *ROR* 15, June 1897, 652.

Chapter 2. Cuba and the Restoration of American Chivalry

1. On widespread sympathy, see McNulty, "The Cuban Crisis," 74, 80, 121; on funds and petitions, see Foner, *The Spanish-Cuban-American War* 1:167–68, 170, 175–76; on prayer societies, see *Judge* 33, July 10, 1897, 1; on demonstrations, see May, *Imperial Democracy,* 73; on New York gathering, see "Voices Raised for Cuba," *NYT,* Nov. 28, 1896; on platforms, see Morgan, *America's Road to Empire,* 16.

2. In April 1896, the two houses of Congress passed a concurrent resolution recognizing Cuban belligerency. Several months earlier, Senate Foreign Relations Committee member Sen. Don Cameron had presented a resolution calling for recognition of Cuban independence, Pérez, *Cuba Between Empires,* 66; Foner, *The Spanish-Cuban-American War* 1:179, 185–87. On military companies, see "Ready to Fight for Cuba," *NYT,* Dec. 17, 1896; "Charleston Feels for Cuba," *Atlanta Constitution,* Jan. 19, 1897.

3. Foner, *The Spanish-Cuban-American War* 1:169; Pratt, *America's Colonial Experiment,* 41–42; Morgan, *America's Road to Empire,* 4, 8. On the tenement poor, see clipping, "Public Ownership Review," June-July 1898, Doc. Records of the Hour, War Time, 1898, 2:5, Charles Eliot Norton Papers, HL.

4. Sen. Orville H. Platt to Isaac H. Bromley, Dec. 18, 1895, in Coolidge, *An Old-Fashioned Senator,* 266; newspapers hostile to the Cubans claimed that they were not white, Doyle, *Irish Americans,* 154. Hostile Spanish papers also tried to characterize the independence movement as black, Helg, *Our Rightful Share,* 80–81. Sympathetic press accounts often "whitened" the Cubans, but many white people praised Cuban leaders who were consistently identified as black or mulatto, chief among them General Antonio Maceo. On whitening the Cubans, see Linderman, *Mirror of War,* 131.

5. Hunt, *Ideology and U.S. Foreign Policy,* 60–62; Kaplan, "Romancing the Empire,"

666–72. Jacobson notes that U.S. coverage of the Cuban revolution was marked "by a rhetoric and iconography of sexual melodrama," *Special Sorrows*, 161. On the positive gender and class images of the black "Best Man" outweighing negative racial ones during Reconstruction, see Gilmore, *Gender and Jim Crow*, 63.

6. George F. Talbot, "The Political Rights and Duties of Women," *Popular Science Monthly* 49, May 1896, 80–97, 97; Johnson, *Woman and the Republic*, 298.

7. On the growth of chivalry after the Civil War, see Fraser, *America and the Patterns of Chivalry*, 8, 26. Fraser attributes northern interest in chivalry to elites' efforts to preserve class distinctions. As the many references to chivalric values in the *New York Journal* suggest, however, this standard also appealed to working-class and immigrant Americans. Silber has argued that concerns about chivalry led late-nineteenth-century northern men to admire southern men's apparent preservation of the standard, *Romance of Reunion*, 175. But even southern men worried about declining chivalry in the late nineteenth century. On reformist women, see Sarah Grand, "Response," *NAR* 158, March 1894, 620–27, 620; on suffragists, see Emily Richards, "Hearing of the NAWSA," Jan. 28, 1896, Committee on the Judiciary, House of Representatives, 15; on waving adieux, see Lida Calvert Obenchain, "Why Democratic Women Want the Ballot," *Woman's Tribune* 12, Oct. 12, 1898, 135.

8. On home-bodies and chaste spouses, see Cabrera, *Cuba and the Cubans*, 264–65; on the most feminine women, see Halstead, *The Story of Cuba*, 271. "Beautiful Cuba," *New York Tribune*, Dec. 27, 1896. In keeping with this assessment, when the Cuban revolutionary José Martí visited New York City in 1880, he deplored the emancipated behavior of the women he encountered, Turton, *José Martí*, 74.

9. On accounts of atrocities against Cuban women, see McNulty, "The Cuban Crisis," 145, 214, 302. Anneta Andalusia Marie y Estrada to Sen. Joseph B. Foraker, March 29, 1898, Box 13, folder A-C, Joseph Benson Foraker Papers, CHS.

10. Green, *Story of Spain and Cuba*, 197; Halstead, *The Story of Cuba*, 147, 327.

11. Rep. John S. Williams, *CR* 30, pt. 2, May 20, 1897, 1194.

12. On late-nineteenth-century fears of degeneration and the growing interest in male body-building, see Kern, *Anatomy and Destiny*, 103–04; Pick, *Faces of Degeneration*, 21, 23, 24. "A Campaign of Wonders in Cuba," *Chautauquan* 22, Feb. 1896, 614. May argues that those who thought that Americans had deteriorated since the Civil War looked to Cuban men as exemplars of heroism and honor in an age of self-interest, *Imperial Democracy*, 71–72.

13. On mementos, see Quesada and Northrop, *America's Battle for Cuba's Freedom*, 537–38; on sacred persons, see Rep. Charles F. Cochran, *CR* 31, pt. 1, Jan. 20, 1898, 806; on gallantry to women, see "Insurgents' Daring Deed," *New York Tribune*, Jan. 22, 1897.

14. Davis, *Cuba in War Time*, 65; on proud Castilian, see Anna H. Thorne, "The Insurgent," *Spanish-American War Songs*, Witherbee, ed., 862.

15. Rep. John S. Little, *CR* 31, pt. 1, Jan. 10, 1898, 490; Sen. William Mason, *CR* 31, pt. 2, Feb. 10, 1898, 1580; "Cuba's Patriot Leaders," *New York Sun*, April 5, 1895; Royal Daniel, "General Antonio Maceo: Hero of Cuba's War" and "Maceo and Liberty," both in the *Atlanta Constitution*, Dec. 13, 1896.

16. On Bloomington resolution, see "Hearts Beat for Cuba," *Chicago Tribune*, Nov. 1, 1895; on roughing it in the field, see "Stories of Maceo," *New York Tribune*, Dec. 20, 1896; on material age, see *New York Sun* article cited in *Chautauquan* 21, July 1895, 486; on rights of men, see "Cuban Independence," *Chautauquan* 22, Jan. 1896, 480.

17. Bonsal, *The Real Condition of Cuba*, 73; Davis, *Cuba in War Time*, 55; on the "black legend" of Spanish tyranny, see Hunt, *Ideology and U.S. Foreign Policy*, 101.

18. On license, see Quesada and Northrop, *The War in Cuba*, 93. Clark, *Cuba and the Fight for Freedom*, 298–99; Green, *Story of Spain and Cuba*, 234, 241; see also Simundson, "The Yellow Press on the Prairie," 218. On images of the black rapist, see Williamson, *The Crucible of Race*, 111; Frederickson, *The Black Image*, 275; Takaki, "The Black Child-Savage," 35.

19. Sen. William Allen, *CR* 29, pt. 3, Feb. 25, 1897, 2226; Rep. Alexander Hardy, *CR* 29, pt. 2, Jan. 29, 1897, 1336; testimony of Frederick W. Lawrence, "Conditions of Affairs in Cuba, Hearing before a Subcommittee of the Committee on Foreign Relations," Feb. 21, 1897, in John Tyler Morgan Papers, reel 10, LC.

20. Stephen Bonsal, "The Real Condition of Cuba To-Day," *ROR* 15, May 1897, 562–76, 564; Crittenden Marriott, "General Weyler's Campaign," *Arena* 18, Sept. 1897, 374–85, 377; Davis, *Cuba in War Time*, 72.

21. On trickery, see "Sympathy for Cuba," *Atlanta Constitution*, Dec. 15, 1896; Resolutions from a mass meeting of citizens of Lincoln, Nebraska, Dec. 1896; Foreign Affairs Committee, 54th Congress; Records of the U.S. House, record group 233, NA; on buying off insurgents, see "Spanish Methods in Cuba," *New York Tribune*, Nov. 25, 1897; on war on women, see "The News of Cuba," *New York Tribune*, Jan. 21, 1897. Rep. Alexander M. Hardy, *CR* 29, pt. 2, Jan. 29, 1897, 1336.

22. Flint, *Marching with Gomez*, 128.

23. "Free Cuba in Yiddish," *New York World*, Jan. 10, 1897; "Peace—But Quit That," *New York World*, in *ROR* 17, April 1898, 414; on Queen of the Antilles, see Quesada and Northrop, *The War in Cuba*, 17.

24. Rep. James M. Robinson, *CR* 31, pt. 1, Jan. 20, 1898, 804; "Secretary Sherman Talks to the Boy-King," *Twinkles* supplement to the *New York Tribune*, May 15, 1897, cover; "She is Getting too Feeble to Hold Them," *Judge* 40, Nov. 18, 1896, cover.

25. On smirks, see Sen. John T. Morgan, *CR* 30, pt. 1, April 8, 1898, 661; on most effete, see "No Entangling Alliances," *Nation* 65, July 22, 1897, 64–65, 65; on boudoirs, see "Cosas Españas," *New York Tribune*, Nov. 14, 1897.

26. Resolutions passed by a mass meeting in Kansas City, Nov. 30, 1895; Committee on Foreign Relations, 54th Congress; Records of the U.S. Senate, record group 46, NA; Rep. Charles W. Woodman, *CR* 28, pt. 7, March 2, 1896, 219.

27. On working-class and farming men, see Hofstadter, "Cuba, the Philippines, and Manifest Destiny," 158; on African Americans, see Gatewood, *Black Americans and the White Man's Burden*, 17; on Irish Americans, see Doyle, *Irish Americans*, 157; on Irish, Polish, and Jewish immigrants, see Jacobson, *Special Sorrows*, 136, 142, 144; on ex-Confederates, see Linderman, *Mirror of War*, 129; Clark, *Cuba and the Fight for Freedom*, 171; William Eleroy Curtis, "Cuba and Her People," *Chautauquan* 27, May 1898, 187; on northern reformers, see "Spain's Last Effort," *NYT*, Nov. 13, 1896; "Spanish Experts in Election Frauds," *LW* 82, April 30, 1896, 291.

28. Veterans' posts frequently petitioned Congress in favor of recognizing Cuban belligerency. See petition of Newburg, N.Y., GAR Post, *CR* 29, pt. 1, Dec. 19, 1896, 321; petition of Tennessee and Auburn, Maine, GAR posts, *CR* 29, pt. 1, Dec. 21, 1896, 323; *CR* 29, pt. 1, Dec. 21, 1896, 393; Dearing, *Veterans in Politics*, 488. On champion, see Rep. Amos J.

Cummings, *CR* 29, pt. 1, Jan. 16, 1897, 855; on knight, see Rep. John L. McLaurin, *CR* 29, pt. 1, Jan. 16, 1897, 864.

29. Normond B. Harris to President Cleveland, June 10, 1896, reel 94, Grover Cleveland Papers, LC.

30. "The Non-Interveners," *New York World*, March 19, 1898; on the shadow, see "The Martyrdom of Evangelina Cisneros," *New York Journal*, Aug. 19, 1897; see also Rep. John Avery, *CR* 28, pt. 4, April 4, 1896, 3597.

31. On outcry after searches, see Millis, *The Martial Spirit*, 67; Wilkerson, *Public Opinion and the Spanish-American War*, 44; Rep. David A. De Armond, *CR* 29, pt. 2, Feb. 13, 1897, 1809; Sen. William V. Allen, *CR* 29, pt. 3, Feb. 25, 1897, 2227; Davis, *Cuba in War Time*, 127; Brown, *The Correspondents' War*, 81.

32. Mary B. Lane to George F. Hoar, April 16, 1898, George F. Hoar Papers, MHS. On temperance and purity, see Bordin, *Woman and Temperance*, 7; Pivar, *Purity Crusade;* Epstein, *The Politics of Domesticity*.

33. On DAR members, see "Fiery Words for Cuba," *Boston Globe*, Feb. 26, 1897; on women's presence in the galleries during debates over Cuba, see also Foraker, *I Would Live it Again*, 219. On the Relief Fund, see "J. Ellen Foster Here," *New York Tribune*, June 10, 1897. Members included the wives of Senators Barrows, Morgan, Lindsey, Cullom, Fry, Gallinger, and Thurston. This last member, Martha P. Thurston, wife of Nebraska Sen. John M. Thurston, accompanied her husband on an investigative trip to Cuba, and the U.S. press reported her pro-Cuban comments, see "In Memoriam," *Woman's Tribune* 15, March 19, 1898, 23; on social functions, see Rubens, *Liberty*, 107.

34. "The Passing of Maceo," *American Home Magazine* 1, Jan. 1897, 3. On cowardly policy, see Helen Gougar, "Cuba and the Cubans," in Kriebel, *Where the Saints Have Trod*, 168; Margaret H. Alden, "Cuba," *Spanish-American War Songs*, Witherbee, ed., 46.

35. Sen. William E. Mason, *CR* 30, pt. 2, May 18, 1897, 1135; Rep. Alston G. Dayton, *CR* 31, pt. 4, March 24, 1898, 3192.

36. On African hell, see Marion Kendrick, "The Cuban Girl Martyr," *New York Journal*, Aug. 17, 1897; on dishonor, see "The Martyrdom of Evangelina Cisneros," *New York Journal*, Aug. 19, 1897. See also "Spanish Methods of War," *Union Signal* 23, Aug. 26, 1897; "A Crowning Indignity," *Atlanta Constitution*, Aug. 21, 1897; Cisneros, *The Story of Evangelina Cisneros*, 31; Musgrave, *Under Three Flags*, 94–99. This story followed on the heels of several similar ones; see "Escaped from Spanish Prison," *Atlanta Constitution*, Jan. 26, 1897; "War on Young Girls," *Atlanta Constitution*, Feb. 8, 1897; "Persecutes Women," *New York World*, Feb. 8, 1897.

37. On Cisneros as representative, see "The Voice of America," *New York Journal*, Oct. 17, 1897; on creatures, see "The Crime Against Evangelina Cisneros," *New York Journal*, Aug. 24, 1897.

38. Julian Hawthorne, "Introduction," in Cisneros, *The Story of Evangelina Cisneros*, 18–19; on sales, see Swanberg, *Citizen Hearst*, 122.

39. On telegrams, see Creelman, *On the Great Highway*, 181; Abbot, *Watching the World*, 215; Brown, *The Correspondents' War*, 97; "American Women Unite to Save Miss Cisneros," *New York Journal*, Aug. 22, 1897; "'Mother' M'Kinley Lends Her Voice," *New York Journal*, Aug. 24, 1897; Julia Ward Howe, letter, *New York Journal*, Aug. 19, 1897; on women's organizations, see "Relief Work for Cuba," *Woman's Tribune* 14, Sept. 4, 1897, 70; "Spanish Methods of War," *Union Signal* 23, Aug. 26, 1897, 2.

40. "Rejoices in Women's Uprising," *New York Journal*, Aug. 25, 1897. The *New York World* had cast a similar slight on American manhood in 1896 when it ran a story on the reporter Nellie Bly's proposal to raise a regiment and fight for Cuba. It highlighted her claims that "women have more courage than men and would make better officers," Kroeger, *Nellie Bly*, 288–89.

41. Swanberg, *Citizen Hearst*, 124; Abbot, *Watching the World*, 215–16.

42. On fairy princess, see Julian Hawthorne, "Introduction," in Cisneros, *The Story of Evangelina Cisneros*, 17–19, 26–27; on her praise, see "Evangelina Cisneros Reaches the Land of Liberty," *New York Journal*, Oct. 14, 1897. Although the *Journal* reported that she donned male dress to escape detection by the Spanish authorities, it emphasized that she eagerly returned to her feminine persona once safe at sea.

43. Hawthorne, "Introduction," in Cisneros, *The Story of Evangelina Cisneros*, 19.

44. On knights of old, see Mary Nevans Gannon, "As Chivalrous as the Knights of Old," *New York Journal*, Oct. 17, 1897; on undiminished flame, see "Enthusiastic Women Give Vent to Joy," *New York Journal*, Oct. 14, 1897.

45. "New York's Welcome to Miss Cisneros," *New York Journal*, Oct. 14, 1897.

46. Kaplan, "Romancing the Empire," 673–74.

47. "You've Earned Your Independence," *New York World*, in *ROR* 17, April 1898, 414.

48. *Atlanta Constitution* cited in "The Cuban Question Again," *Literary Digest* 11, Oct. 5, 1895, 663; Sen. Wilkinson Call, *CR* 29, pt. 1, Jan. 6, 1897, 487; on dignity, see E. J. Helber to President Cleveland, March 2, 1896, reel 93, Grover Cleveland Papers, LC.

49. Sen. William V. Allen, *CR* 31, pt. 1, Dec. 8, 1897, 40; Matthews, "The Cuban Patriots' Cause," 16.

50. Offner, *An Unwanted War*, 23–24; on impunity, see Ex-Attache, "America's Flag Abroad," *New York Tribune*, Feb. 28, 1897.

51. "Fitzhugh Lee's Position," *Atlanta Constitution*, Feb. 25, 1897.

52. Rep. James B. Clark, *CR* 31, pt. 1, Jan. 20, 1898, 794; "Our Weak Foreign Policy," *Judge* 29, Aug. 24, 1895.

53. Resolutions adopted by the Order of United American Mechanics, Lebanon, Pennsylvania, Dec. 9, 1896; Committee on Foreign Affairs, 54th Congress; Records of the U.S. House of Representatives, record group 233, NA; Rep. William H. King, *CR* 31, pt. 8, Jan. 20, 1898, 234; "Cuba Must be Free," *Chicago Tribune*, Nov. 12, 1895.

54. Sen. Wilkinson Call, *CR* 28, pt. 4, March 20, 1896, 3018.

55. Davis, *Cuba in War Time*, 66–67.

56. Clarence King, "Shall Cuba Be Free?" *Forum* 20, Sept. 1895, 50–65, 65.

57. Summers, ed., *The Cabinet Diary of William L. Wilson*, 188; Sen. George L. Wellington, *CR* 30, pt. 2, May 18, 1897, 1132; Rep. Charles A. Boutelle, *CR* 28, pt. 4, April 3, 1896, 3549.

58. Hoar, "Orderly and Decorous Conduct," 4–5; David B. Hill cited in *Official Proceedings of the Democratic National Convention*, 211.

Chapter 3. "Honor Comes First": The Congressional Debate over War

1. Sen. Charles W. Fairbanks, *CR* 31, pt. 4, April 14, 1898, 3845. In 1976 an American research team concluded that the *Maine* explosion had been caused by a spontaneous fire in the coal bunker, which was located next to the powder supply, Rickover, *How the Bat-*

tleship Maine *Was Destroyed.* A more recent study that relies heavily on testimony from 1898 and on an investigation of 1911 rejects this conclusion in favor of the older theory that an external mine precipitated the explosion that sunk the ship, Samuels and Samuels, *Remembering the Maine.* But even if an external mine sank the *Maine* (which, I believe, is by no means certain), the perpetrator and motive remain a mystery.

2. On Spain's refusal to apologize, see Lodge, *The War With Spain,* 30. Sen. Richard R. Kenney, *CR* 31, pt. 4, April 5, 1898, 3547.

3. Rep. John F. Fitzgerald, *CR* 31, pt. 3, March 8, 1898, 2606; Rep. Stephen A. Northway, *CR* 31, pt. 3, March 8, 1898, 2604. On the appropriation, see "Leave it to the President," *NYT,* March 10, 1898; Foster mentions that southern men focused on honor after the sinking of the *Maine* (*Ghosts of the Confederacy,* 146), but they were not alone in drawing attention to the nation's honor—men from all parts of the country did so. On "honor" in the secession debate of 1861, see Wyatt-Brown, *Yankee Saints,* 183–213.

4. Rep. William Sulzer, *CR* 31, pt. 4, April 7, 1898, 3673; Rep. David B. Henderson, *CR* 31, pt. 4, April 13, 1898, 3813; Sen. George Turner, *CR* 31, pt. 4, April 14, 1898, 3829. Following a naval incident in 1873 in which Spain executed crew members of an American steamer, the *Virginius,* for piracy, militant U.S. newspapers declared that American honor should be vindicated. But instead of going to war, the United States settled for an indemnity. It appears that there was not as much of a war spirit in 1873 as there was twenty-five years later because memories of the Civil War were too raw and American men were not as sensitive about their manhood. On honor and the *Virginius* affair, see Gibson, "Attitudes in North Carolina," 50, 52, 65; on the relative lack of concern about manhood in Cuban debates in the 1870s, see the *Congressional Globe,* 2d session, 41st Congress, part 7, appendix, 458, 492, 495–96, 500, 506, 541; *Congressional Record* 4, pt. 1, Dec. 7, 1875, 177.

5. Rep. James A. Norton, *CR* 31, pt. 5, April 28, 1898, 4370; Rep. Mahlon Pitney, *CR* 31, pt. 3, March 8, 1898, 2605.

6. Whitney, ed., *Century Dictionary* 4:2874; Rep. John J. Lentz, *CR* 31, pt. 4, March 31, 1898, 3444; Rep. John J. Lentz, *CR* 31, pt. 5, April 27, 1898, 4331.

7. George F. Hoar, pamphlet "Quality of our Honor," 1898, Pamphlet box 49, George F. Hoar Papers, MHS; Rep. James R. Mann, *CR* 31, pt. 5, April 28, 1898, 4362.

8. On late-nineteenth-century manhood, see Rotundo, *American Manhood,* 5–6; Rotundo, "Body and Soul," 26–28; Roberts, "The Strenuous Life," 5, 18–20; Gorn, *The Manly Art,* 187; Kimmel, *Manhood in America,* 120; Bederman, *Manliness and Civilization,* 18. Bederman draws a distinction between *manliness,* which implied moral qualities, and *masculinity,* which referred to inherent male qualities. I found that late-nineteenth-century men often conflated these meanings in the word *manliness,* and since they used that word much more than *masculinity,* I have used *manliness* and its variations too. On epithets, see Higham, *Writing American History,* 79; on cure for white-livered men, see "The Way to Win a Woman," *Boston Journal,* March 5, 1898. Amos J. Cummings, "A Manly Fighter is He," *Washington Post,* February 20, 1898; "The Value of War Oratory," *Rochester Democrat and Chronicle,* April 1, 1898.

9. Rep. Lorenzo Danford, *CR* 31, pt. 8, April 28, 1898, 313; Wiebe argues that political leaders in the early Republic believed that the standards of honor and shame that applied to individual men should apply to the nation, *The Opening of American Society,* 16; Kammen notes that analogies between individuals and the nation were pervasive in political talk at the turn of the century, *A Season of Youth,* 196; Field finds a parallel tendency among the British, *Toward a Programme of Imperial Life,* 24.

10. Rep. William Sulzer, *CR* 31, pt. 4, April 7, 1898, 3673; Rep. Joseph W. Bailey, *CR* 31, pt. 3, March 8, 1898, 2616; Rep. Joseph W. Bailey, *CR* 31, pt. 4, April 15, 1898, 3907.

11. Rep. William C. Arnold, *CR* 31, pt. 4, March 24, 1898, 3193; Sen. George C. Perkins, *CR* 31, pt. 4, April 4, 1898, 3498; Rep. James A. Norton, *CR* 31, pt. 3, March 16, 1898, 2879.

12. Rep. James H. Lewis, *CR* 31, pt. 3, March 8, 1898, 2610; Sen. Hernando de Soto Money, *CR* 31, pt. 4, March 28, 1898, 3280–82.

13. Rep. Mason S. Peters, *CR* 31, pt. 3, March 8, 1898, 2613; Rep. Reese C. De Graffenreid, *CR* 31, pt. 3, March 7, 1898, 2615. On wealthy and poor men, see Rep. Charles H. Grosvenor, *CR* 31, pt. 5, April 28, 1898, 4416.

14. Rep. Joseph Wheeler, *CR* 31, pt. 3, March 8, 1898, 2607.

15. "Which War does Mason Mean?" *Washington Post,* March 16, 1898. On American men as cowards, see "Bluster," *NYT,* April 17, 1898; on men of commerce, see "If War Should Come," *Atlanta Constitution,* March 9, 1898; Rep. John J. Lentz, *CR* 31, pt. 3, March 8, 1898, 2613.

16. Rep. Levin Handy, *CR* 31, pt. 3, March 4, 1898, 2503; Rep. Ferdinand Bruckner, *CR* 31, pt. 3, March 8, 1898, 2613; Sen. Lee Mantle, *CR* 31, pt. 4, April 4, 1898, 3499.

17. Blake, *Sulzer's Short Speeches,* 18; "James Hamilton Lewis," *National Cyclopaedia* 28:38; Senator Fairbanks also tendered his services, Smith, *Life and Speeches of Hon. Charles Warren Fairbanks,* 131. Rep. Henry U. Johnson, *CR* 31, pt. 4, March 31, 1898, 3434.

18. "Joseph Wheeler," *National Cyclopaedia* 9:19.

19. Henry Cabot Lodge to Henry Lee Higginson, July 3, 1898, in Perry, *Life and Letters of Henry Lee Higginson,* 427; Walters, *Joseph Benson Foraker,* 151.

20. "Blows Averted in the House," *NYT,* April 14, 1898; on hisses, see clipping, April 13, 1898, Scrapbook of Emily Carow, Theodore Roosevelt Collection, HL.

21. "Blows Averted in the House," *NYT,* April 14, 1898; see also "Startling Episode," *Boston Journal,* April 14, 1898. This fight fit into a larger pattern of political violence. During the Populist convention of 1896, a fight broke out among the delegates, leading some to draw their revolvers, McMath, *American Populism,* 204; according to the *Springfield Republican,* Sen. Henry Cabot Lodge made a threatening rush toward Sen. Henry M. Teller during a debate on the Philippines, cited in Schirmer, *Republic or Empire,* 235–36. In 1902, Sen. Joseph W. Bailey assaulted Sen. Albert J. Beveridge, Braeman, *Albert J. Beveridge,* 58. On earlier instances of violence in Congress, see Buel, *Securing the Revolution,* 153–54; Wiebe, *Self-Rule,* 63; Gay, *The Cultivation of Hatred,* 112. Not surprisingly, women's suffragists cited political leaders' violence to support their argument that women would elevate politics, Kraditor, *The Ideas of the Woman Suffrage Movement,* 108.

22. Henry B. Blackwell, "The War with Spain," *WJ* 29, April 16, 1898, 124; Alice Stone Blackwell, "Mr. Garrison on Women and War," *WJ* 29, April 30, 1898, 140.

23. Papachristou, "American Women and Foreign Policy," 495, 498, 501.

24. On standing "as one man," see Rep. Romulus Z. Linney, *CR* 31, pt. 3, March 7, 1898, 2613; Rep. William D. Vincent, *CR* 31, pt. 8, April 18, 1898, 304; Rep. George Spalding, *CR* 31, pt. 3, March 8, 1898, 2616. Wyatt-Brown finds that in the secession debate in 1861, southern men were afraid that deliberation would appear cowardly, *Yankee Saints,* 205–07.

25. Rep. David A. De Armond, *CR* 31, pt. 3, March 8, 1898, 2610; Rep. William

Sulzer, *CR* 31, pt. 4, April 7, 1898, 3669; Rep. Samuel B. Cooper, *CR* 31, pt. 3, March 8, 1898, 2606; *Cincinnati Post* cartoon printed in *ROR* 17, May 1898, 548; *Chicago Chronicle* cartoon printed in *Literary Digest* 16, March 12, 1898, 303; on nervous old ladies, see "The Horrors of War," *Rochester Democrat and Chronicle*, March 14, 1898.

26. Among the militant women were the members of a New York City art class who sent President McKinley a telegram saying, "To h— with diplomacy!" cited in Leffler, "From the Shadows into the Sun," 24. On the honor of Cuban women, see "Women and Cuba," *WJ* 29, April 16, 1898, 124; on good men, see John Coit Spooner to O. A. Ellis, April 27, 1898, Letterbook, April 9–May 5, 1898, box 135, John C. Spooner Papers, LC; on brotherhood, see Sen. Henry C. Lodge, *CR* 31, pt. 4, April 13, 1898, 3784. Rep. Harry Skinner, *CR* 31, pt. 4, March 24, 1898, 3211.

27. Darwin, *Second Report*, 45.

28. Sen. Joseph B. Foraker, *CR* 31, pt. 4, April 13, 1898, 3781; Sen. William V. Allen, *CR* 31, pt. 4, March 31, 1898, 3412; Sen. William B. Bate, *CR* 31, pt. 4, April 16, 1898, 3966.

29. Rep. John J. Lentz, *CR* 31, pt. 4, April 12, 1898, 3766; John Bergen to Joseph Benson Foraker, April 6, 1898, folder 1, box 13, Joseph Benson Foraker Papers, CHS.

30. Rep. James T. McCleary, *CR* 31, pt. 3, March 8, 1898, 2614; Rep. John F. Fitzgerald, *CR* 31, pt. 3, March 8, 1898, 2606; Rep. Albert S. Berry, *CR* 31, pt. 3, March 8, 1898, 2610; Rep. Samuel S. Barney, *CR* 31, pt. 3, March 8, 1898, 2612; Rep. James G. Maguire, *CR* 31, pt. 3, March 8, 1898, 2619.

31. Rep. George Foss, *CR* 31, pt. 3, March 8, 1898, 2614; Rep. Alexander Dockery, *CR* 31, pt. 3, March 8, 1898, 2603; African-American men shared this concern for the nation's honor, Gatewood, *Black Americans and the White Man's Burden*, 23.

32. Rep. Thomas McRae, *CR* 31, pt. 1, March 8, 1898, 2604.

33. Sen. William E. Mason, *CR* 31, pt. 4, March 29, 1898, 3295; Rep. Samuel J. Barrows, *CR* 31, pt. 4, April 7, 1898, 3688; Sen. Henry C. Lodge, *CR* 31, pt. 4, April 13, 1898, 3784.

34. Sen. Joseph B. Foraker, *CR* 31, pt. 4, April 13, 1898, 3781; Rep. William Sulzer, *CR* 31, pt. 4, April 7, 1898, 3669, 3672.

35. Sen. Edward O. Wolcott, *CR* 31, pt. 4, April 15, 1898, 3892; Sen. George Turner, *CR* 31, pt. 4, April 5, 1898, 3547.

36. Rep. James H. Lewis, *CR* 31, pt. 3, March 8, 1898, 2610; Field argues that late-nineteenth-century Britons believed that without individual "character" the nation could not survive, *Toward a Programme of Imperial Life*, 231. Even prior to the crisis, Darwinian theorists warned that nations which lost "the instinct of pugnacity" would perish, see Henry Childs Merwin, "On Being Civilized too Much," *Atlantic Monthly*, June 1897, 838–46, 840.

37. Rep. Leonidas F. Livingston, *CR* 31, pt. 3, March 8, 1898, 2603–04; Sen. George F. Hoar, *CR* 31, pt. 4, April 14, 1898, 3835.

38. On the House vote, see "Declaration of War," *Boston Transcript*, April 25, 1898; on both votes, see *CR* 31, pt. 5, April 25, 1898, 4244, 4252.

39. Rep. Albert J. Hopkins, *CR* 31, pt. 3, March 8, 1898, 2605; Orville Platt to Rev. William B. Carey, March 23, 1898, in Coolidge, *An Old-Fashioned Senator*, 270.

40. "Not Choice, But the Right," *Boston Journal*, March 11, 1898; Carl Schurz, "National Honor" (1898), in *Speeches* 5:452; J. J. Russell, "Against War with Spain," *NYT*, March 29, 1898.

41. Sewall cited in Patterson, *Toward a Warless World*, 49; Elizabeth Stuart Phelps

Ward to President McKinley, March 18, 1898, Microfilm Series 1, reel 3, William McKinley Papers, LC.

42. On the argument that no honor could be won by fighting a nation as weak as Spain, see Sen. Stephen M. White, *CR* 31, pt. 4, April 16, 1898, 3960, 3962. Sen. George L. Wellington, *CR* 31, pt. 4, April 16, 1898, 3953. "Deliberation," *Nation* 66, April 7, 1898, 258; on revealing the nation as a bully, see Rep. Albert J. Hopkins, *CR* 31, pt. 3, March 8, 1898, 2605; "Trust the President," *Washington Post*, March 24, 1898.

43. Samuel Essmond Shipp, "Spain an Unworthy Foe," *NYT*, Feb. 24, 1898.

Chapter 4. McKinley's Backbone: The Coercive Power of Gender in Political Debate

1. For a review of McKinley's historical image, see Fry, "William McKinley and the Coming of the Spanish-American War," 77–97. Fry writes that from the 1930s to the 1960s, historians depicted McKinley as spineless. Ernest May, for example, wrote that McKinley was "not a brave man." From the 1960s to 1979 (the year Fry's article was published), scholars reevaluated McKinley's role, concluding, in Fry's words, that he was "more courageous and capable than previously portrayed." William Appleman Williams praised McKinley's "presidential nerve," and Robert Beisner concluded that McKinley was not "spineless." After Fry published his review article, Gould argued that McKinley's conduct after the *Maine* disaster revealed "simple courage," *The Spanish-American War*, 52. Dobson portrayed McKinley as an administrator who delayed a decision on the war issue "simply by the force of his own character much longer than almost any other man could have," *Reticent Expansionism*, 4–5, 26. Beisner wittily depicted the essence of the debate over McKinley's leadership as "Chocolate Eclair or Clever Statesman?" in his response to "American Imperialism: The Worst Chapter in Almost Any Book," 673.

2. The specific policy objectives that may have influenced McKinley include extending capitalism (Gould, *The Spanish-American War*, 10); preventing a Cuban revolutionary victory (Foner, *The Spanish-Cuban-American War* 1:229, 310); reducing political and economic insecurity (LaFeber, *The New Empire*, 400); and ending the suffering in Cuba (Morgan, *America's Road to Empire*, 61; Offner, *An Unwanted War*, 38). McKinley may have wanted these things, but I believe that they alone did not lead him to support war—that McKinley did not assume an aggressive stance after the *Maine* incident because he hoped to avoid war; that political pressures, more than a ruthless pursuit of particular policy objectives, explain his eventual support for war. On the paramountcy of partisan considerations in shaping McKinley's decision to go to war, see Dobson, *Reticent Expansionism*, 65, 26; Offner, *An Unwanted War*, 193; Gould, *The Spanish-American War*, 47; May, *Imperial Democracy*, 268. McKinley's contemporaries devoted a considerable amount of effort to evaluating his character because they regarded it as relevant to his capacity as a leader. On the relevance of appearing manly to establishing political credibility, see Kimmel, *Manhood in America*, 38; Baker, "The Domestication of Politics," 628–29; Baker, *The Moral Frameworks of Public Life*, xiii, 24–40; Dubbert, *A Man's Place*, 34. On manhood and Western political theory, see Brown, *Manhood and Politics*; Kann, *On the Man Question*.

3. "De Lôme on the President, Spanish Minister Alleged to Have Insulted Mr. McKinley," *NYT*, Feb. 9, 1898; Rubens, *Liberty*, 287; Gould, *The Spanish-American War*, 34.

4. Morgan, *William McKinley and His America*, 356; "De Lôme on the President, Spanish Minister Alleged to Have Insulted Mr. McKinley," *NYT*, Feb. 9, 1898; "Insults for M'Kinley," *Chicago Tribune*, Feb. 9, 1898; Rep. John J. Lentz, *CR* 31, pt. 4, March 31, 1898, 3444; Rep. Charles H. Martin, *CR* 31, pt. 8, April 28, 1898, 314.

5. President McKinley, "Message to the Senate," *CR* 31, pt. 4, March 28, 1898, 3278; Gould, *The Spanish-American War*, 41; Stewart Woodford to W. R. Day, March 30, 1898, *Papers Relating to the Foreign Relations of the United States, 1898*, 721–22; Morgan, *William McKinley*, 368; Morgan, *America's Road to Empire*, 52; Offner, *An Unwanted War*, 143–46.

6. Morgan, *William McKinley*, 71; Offner, *An Unwanted War*, 156.

7. "Too Much Goody-Goody," *Atlanta Constitution*, March 14, 1898; "Wanted—A Man, an American," *Atlanta Constitution*, April 1, 1898; "The Duty of the United States," *Atlanta Constitution*, April 13, 1898. Claims that the president was indifferent to the people's demands were surely related to suspicions that he was conspiring to prevent war with holders of the Cuban bonds issued by the Spanish government. The bond conspiracy theory helped McKinley's opponents draw a distinction between money and manhood in the Cuban debate. On suspicions of a bond conspiracy, see Holbo, "The Convergence of Moods," 60–61, 70.

8. "Dollars versus Democracy," *New York Journal*, March 8, 1898; "Jackson's Way and Another Way," *New York World*, March 31, 1898; "What is President McKinley's Policy?" *Chicago Tribune*, March 26, 1898; Sioux Falls *Daily Press*, cited in Simundson, "The Yellow Press on the Prairie," 217. Simundson also notes that anti-administration papers in South Dakota "delighted in exposing what they considered to be McKinley's weak and even cowardly Cuban policy," 215. The *New Orleans Picayune* called the president a "timid man," "Will There be War?" March 30, 1898. On working-class standards of manhood, see Gorn, *The Manly Art*, 141–45, 252; on the moral component of manliness, see Bederman, *Manliness and Civilzation*, 18.

9. On verdict, see E. C. Kirkwood to William E. Chandler, April 4, 1898, Letterbook 120, Correspondence, Feb. 26–April 9, 1898, William Eaton Chandler Papers, LC. Sen. John W. Daniel, *CR* 31, pt. 4, April 15, 1898, 3881; Sen. George Turner, *CR* 31, pt. 4, April 14, 1898, 3827; Rep. William Sulzer, *CR* 31, pt. 4, April 7, 1898, 3673.

10. Roosevelt cited in Morris, *The Rise of Theodore Roosevelt*, 610; John Schuette to John C. Spooner, April 2, 1898, folder: April, 1898, box 20, John C. Spooner Papers, LC. The term *backbone* came to imply character traits like firmness and strength in the mid nineteenth century, *Oxford English Dictionary* 1:863. These qualities were ones that unusual women could demonstrate but that all true men were expected to demonstrate.

11. Samuel T. Dougherty to William E. Chandler, April 6, 1898, Letterbook 120, Correspondence, Feb. 26–April 9, 1898, William Eaton Chandler Papers, LC; *New Orleans Times-Democrat* article cited in Musicant, *The Banana Wars*, 13.

12. *Chicago Chronicle* cartoon in *Cartoons of the War of 1898*, n.p.; on changing ideals of manhood, see Rotundo, *American Manhood*, 3–6; Rotundo, "Body and Soul," 23–38; Carnes, *Secret Ritual and Manhood*, 138–43; Gorn, *The Manly Art*, 187; Kimmel, *Manhood in America*, 100, 111–12; Kern, *Anatomy and Destiny*, 103; Bederman discusses the late-nineteenth-century shift from valuing "manly" character, which had a strong moral dimension, to valuing "masculinity," which was devoid of moral meaning, *Manliness and Civilization*, 18. I agree with Bederman's depiction of this shift in emphasis but find that

turn-of-the-century political activists rarely used the word *masculinity*. Instead, they continued to use the word *manly* to refer to their new masculine ideal.

13. William McKinley, "Address to the Officers and Students of the University of Pennsylvania, Feb. 22, 1898," *Speeches and Addresses of William McKinley*, 77; "George Washington—A Fighter," *New York Journal*, February 22, 1898.

14. "Jackson's Way and Another Way," *New York World*, March 31, 1898; "Old Hickory's Way," *New York World*, April 1, 1898. Similarly, the South Dakota *Yankton Press and Dakotan* claimed that McKinley's post-*Maine* message lacked the fervor that Jackson would have put into the message, Simundson, "The Yellow Press on the Prairie," 225. The *Chicago Tribune* was also blunt in its appraisal, describing Jackson as "a man of action" who avenged affronts to his country and to American citizens. "But this was some time ago," it noted, "in the days of Americans who believed in resenting outrage and insult by striking back and doing the talking afterward. The breed seems to have deteriorated in Americanism since those days," "What Jackson would Have Done," *Chicago Tribune*, March 19, 1898.

15. Anonymous Chicago resident to John Davis Long, March 2, 1898, box 39, John Davis Long Papers, MHS; William Allen Swain to William E. Chandler, March 31, 1898, Letterbook 120, Correspondence, Feb. 26–April 9, 1898, William Eaton Chandler Papers, LC; Rep. William Sulzer, *CR* 31, pt. 4, April 7, 1898, 3667, 3673. On the military style of politics, see McGerr, *The Decline of Popular Politics*, 106.

16. R. Leeson to John Davis Long, March 31, 1898, box 39, John Davis Long Papers, MHS.

17. "The President's Stamina," *Los Angeles Times*, April 10, 1898; on firmness, see "Keeping Cool," *Baltimore Sun*, March 1, 1898; on courage, see "Moral Courage," *Baltimore Sun*, March 5, 1898; Leopold Minster, Letter to the Editor, "The Printing of 'Extras,'" *NYT*, April 5, 1898.

18. On waiting, see Rep. Joseph V. Graff, *CR* 31, pt. 3, March 8, 1898, 2614. On being hysterical, see Henry Cabot Lodge to Mr. Hayes, Feb. 25, 1898; on time to condemn, see Henry Cabot Lodge to Charles B. Mason, Feb. 25, 1898, both in Letterbook 37, Henry Cabot Lodge Papers, MHS; on repudiation, see "Patriotism Coincides with Party Policy," *Washington Post*, March 20, 1898.

19. On firmness, see "Keeping Cool," *Baltimore Sun*, March 1, 1898; on dignity, firmness, and statesmanlike behavior, see John C. Spooner to John G. Gregory, March 14, 1898, Letterbook 39, Feb. 23, 1898–April 9, 1898, box 134, John C. Spooner Papers, LC. On manly and just, see Edwin D. Mead to George F. Hoar, April 2, 1898, George F. Hoar Papers, MHS.

20. See Rotundo, *American Manhood*, 5–6. Sen. Edward O. Wolcott, *CR* 31, pt. 4, April 15, 1898, 3892; Rep. Charles H. Grosvenor, *CR* 31, pt. 3, March 8, 1898, 2608; "The President's Defamers," *Rochester Democrat and Chronicle*, March 9, 1898.

21. *Sacramento Bee* cited in "The True American Spirit," *Los Angeles Times*, March 5, 1898; "Steady in the Center," *Los Angeles Times*, April 8, 1898.

22. Jensen notes that McKinley relied heavily on military analogies in his speeches before 1892, *The Winning of the Midwest*, 171; on comrades, see Smith, "McKinley's Speeches in August," 95; on great thing, see Smith, *McKinley's Speeches in September*, 205.

23. Smith, "McKinley's Speeches in August," 81, 82, 84, 86, 90, 93, 95; Halstead, *Life and Distinguished Services of Hon. Wm. McKinley*, 18, 44. On McKinley's war record as an asset, see Glad, *McKinley, Bryan, and the People*, 15; on boy soldier, see Porter, *Life of*

William McKinley, 88; on gallantry, see Russell, *The Lives of William McKinley*, 59, 65, 329; Knight Templar photo in Porter, *Life of William McKinley*, plate following page 261; on warlike things, see Flood, "William McKinley and the Presidency," 3.

24. On Bryan's age, see Law, *The Parties and the Men*, 504; on boy orator, see Coletta, *William Jennings Bryan*, 180. "The Deadly Parallel," cartoon in *Harper's Weekly*, August 29, 1896, reprinted in Morgan, *William McKinley*, plate following page 116. Depew, *Four Days at the National Republican Convention*, 73.

25. Law, *The Parties and the Men*, 499; Ogilvie, ed., *Life and Speeches of William J. Bryan*, 15–16. Such statements seemed geared to show that Bryan did not suffer from neurasthenia. On that malady, see Lutz, *American Nervousnes*, 2.

26. On Bryan as a fighter, see "Mr. Bryan and Dignity," *New York Journal*, Sept. 18, 1896; on vigorous manhood, see Prescott, *The Great Campaign*, 18.

27. Joseph B. Foraker cited in Flood, "William McKinley," 16; Theodore E. Burton, "Extract from Speech of Hon. Theodore E. Burton, 13th Ward Republican Headquarters," Oct. 12, 1896, reel 94, Theodore E. Burton Papers, WRHS.

28. If, on the one hand, McKinley's military record heightened his fraternal appeal to working-class men, on the other hand, it heightened his law-and-order appeal to wealthier men. The "firm" character that McKinley had demonstrated in the 1860s indicated that he could be relied on to take a firm stance in times of domestic unrest. For example, in his biography (1896), Robert P. Porter pointed out that McKinley had not hesitated to use military force to quell labor strife during his term as governor of Ohio. McKinley "has had abundant opportunity of proving to the country what a tower of strength a courageous executive may be," wrote Porter. According to Porter, McKinley had faced more crises than any Ohio governor since the Civil War, and he had responded with a strong hand. In 1894 alone, he called upon the state government for military aid fifteen times. Local authorities supposedly had confidence in McKinley's leadership, for they "knew that all necessary aid would be forthcoming—there would be no faltering," Porter, *Life of William McKinley*, 400–01. In sum, McKinley's military record helped him reach out to both working-class and wealthier men. Despite their diverging interests on specific policies, men from different walks of life had a common appreciation of military experience; regardless of class or region, they viewed it as a sign of manly character.

29. On phalanx, see Smith, "McKinley's Speeches in August," 88; "Marching With McKinley to Victory," in Silber, *Songs America Voted By*, 175.

30. On Republican privates, see Smith, "McKinley's Speeches in August," 101; on military trappings, see Smith, *McKinley's Speeches in September*, 188, 193, 203, 229, 277; on the "battle field" and enlisting for the war, see "McKinley's Speeches in August," 106, 155. On the domestication of late-nineteenth-century politics, see McGerr, *The Decline of Popular Politics*, 106; Baker, "The Domestication of Politics," 641–42; Edwards, "Gender in American Politics," 11. On *Judge*'s Republican ties, see Mott, *A History of American Magazines* 3:553–54; "Judge Did It: The triumphant return of the victorious Republican army," *Judge* 3, Nov. 21, 1896, 328–29.

31. "A President and an 'Ex.' Talk," *New York Journal*, Feb. 23, 1898.

32. On McKinley and public opinion, see Leech, *In the Days of McKinley*, 70.

33. Theodore Roosevelt to "Bye," June 20, 1896, in Roosevelt, *Letters from Theodore Roosevelt to Anna Roosevelt Cowles*, 182; Morgan, *William McKinley*, 89, 319.

34. On real boy, see Russell, *The Lives of William McKinley*, 57; on strength and lung

capacity, see Porter, *Life of William McKinley*, 190. "Thomas Jefferson's Birthday," *New York Journal*, April 13, 1898; on old folks' home, see Leech, *In the Days of McKinley*, 110; on prime, see Halstead, *Life and Distinguished Services*, 119.

35. On joke, see "A Little Story About the Speaker," *NYT*, April 7, 1898. Rep. William Sulzer, *CR* 31, pt. 4, April 7, 1898, 3673; on McKinley's bankruptcy, see Leech, *In the Days of McKinley*, 58. McKinley's bankruptcy may have helped him win favor among voters fed up with dishonest politicians who profited from their offices and among voters who had suffered from the 1893 depression, but McKinley and his friends were greatly concerned about his bankruptcy's effects on his image, Morgan, *William McKinley*, 171, 176; Russell, *The Lives of William McKinley*, 270.

36. On mother's boy, see Leech, *In the Days of McKinley*, 19, 113. The supporters who called him a mother's boy meant it in a positive sense, but to those who adhered to rougher standards of masculinity, the term had a cutting edge. On queenly grace, see De Steel, *The New Napoleon*, lines 201–06. Serving coffee was the first of the two great acts of heroism cited in his biographies. His later act was braving fire to tell a unit it could retreat.

37. On white feather, see "Trying to Hypnotize and Fool Mr. M'Kinley," *Chicago Tribune*, March 13, 1898; "We Must Wait for an American President," *New York Journal*, March 29, 1898.

38. Every day McKinley looked at about five or six New York papers, the morning and evening Washington papers, one or two Chicago papers, and six others from large cities. He also had his friends summarize the news for him, and his secretary summarized his incoming letters, Ida Tarbell, "President McKinley in War Times," *McClure's Magazine* 11, July 1898, 208–24, 213. Rep. Joseph Wheeler, *CR* 31, pt. 4, April 16, 1898, 3994; Rep. David H. Mercer, *CR* 31, pt. 3, March 8, 1898, 2617.

39. By late March, an increasing number of letters to the president advocated war. See transcript of Cortelyou diary, March 18 and 27, 1898, Diary, 1898, box 52, George B. Cortelyou Collection, LC. On newspapers, see "American Freemen," *Los Angeles Times*, March 13, 1898.

40. *New York Journal* cartoon reprinted in *ROR* 17, May 1898, 546.

41. Morgan argues that McKinley could not count on congressional support for a peace policy, *America's Road to Empire*, 19; Gould argues that if McKinley had pressed for peace he would have encountered a rebellion in Congress, *The Spanish-American War*, 47; Linderman argues that forty to fifty members of the Republican caucus urged McKinley to make war, *The Mirror of War*, 34; Offner writes that McKinley restrained Congress until late March, but after that, Republican congressmen urged him to turn the issue over to them, *An Unwanted War*, 142, 180–81. "White House Conferences," *Washington Post*, March 29, 1898; "Congress Impatient," *Washington Post*, March 30, 1898; Joseph B. Foraker to A. S. Bushnell, April 4, 1898, Folder 6, Box 27, Joseph Benson Foraker Papers, CHS; Sen. Marion Butler, *CR* 31, pt. 4, April 12, 1898, 3732.

42. John C. Spooner to Willet Spooner, April 9, 1898, Letterbook 40, April 9 to May 5, 1898, box 135, John C. Spooner Papers, LC; see also Dobson, *Reticent Expansionism*, 63; on Republican concerns for the party, see May, *Imperial Democracy*, 147; Offner, *An Unwanted War*, 180–81.

43. Leech, *In the Days of McKinley*, 36. On friends' assessments, see John H. Flagg to Orville H. Platt, April 23, 1898, folder: correspondence, 1898–1899, box 1, Orville H. Platt Papers, CSL; Lyman Abott to Charles Eliot Norton, August 19, 1898, document 41, Letters

to Charles Eliot Norton, HL; Rubens, *Liberty*, 326–27, 336; Pérez, *Cuba Between Empires*, 178; Cullom, *Fifty Years of Public Service*, 283; Grosvenor, *William McKinley*, 14; Dawes, *A Journal of the McKinley Years*, 145, 149. Linderman notes that McKinley never claimed responsibility for the war, indeed, that in the fall of 1900, he said he had not wanted to fight in 1898, *The Mirror of War*, 35. Cosmas notes that he did not give the army or navy clear instructions prior to the declaration of war. This seems to suggest that he thought war could be avoided, *Army for Empire*, 75. William E. Chandler to Paul Dana, March 29, 1898, William Chandler Papers, Letterbook 120, Correspondence Feb. 26–April 9, 1898, LC; on rising temper, see William E. Chandler to Paul Dana, March 31, 1898, William Chandler Papers, Letterbook, 120, Correspondence Feb. 26–April 9, 1898, LC. Sen. Orville H. Platt wrote that the president believed that if he could not settle the Cuba issue by negotiations, then the people would insist that he should do so by force, Orville Platt to H. Wales Lines, March 25, 1898, in Coolidge, *An Old-Fashioned Senator*, 271.

44. On tears, see Leech, *In the Days of McKinley*, 182; on McKinley's abhorrence of war, see Linderman, *The Mirror of War*, 28–29; Trask, *The War with Spain*, 581. On arbitration, see William McKinley, "Inaugural Address, March 4, 1897," *Speeches and Addresses of William McKinley*, 12; on Republican legislators' unwillingness to support a peace initiative, see Offner, *An Unwanted War*, 178–81.

45. Jas. T. Whittaker to Sen. Joseph Benson Foraker, April 12, 1898, Folder T-Y, Box 13, Joseph Benson Foraker Papers, CHS; Gould, *The Spanish-American War*, 51.

Chapter 5. The Spanish-American War and the Martial Ideal of Citizenship

1. Alger, *The Spanish-American War*, 6; see also Jacobson, *Special Sorrows*, 144; Schellings, "The Advent of the Spanish-American War in Florida," 328. Leffler questions the extent of jingoist sensibilities prior to the war but notes that "the war, when it was eventually declared, was unquestionably popular," "From the Shadows into the Sun," 25, 121–22.

2. Headquarters, Massachusetts Woman's Relief Corps, "General Orders no. 6," May 16, 1898, vol. 3, circulars, 1895–1898, box 1, Woman's Relief Corps, SL; "Women's Work in the War," *WJ* 30, Jan. 7, 1899, 4; Davies, *Patriotism on Parade*, 331; *Second Report of the National Society*, 193; Hoganson, "The 'Manly' Ideal of Politics," chap. 5; Hewitt, "Varieties of Voluntarism," 72.

3. Smith, *The Spanish-American War*, 125, 149; John K. Mahon, "Santiago Campaign," *The War of 1898*, Beede, ed., 496; Cosmas, *An Army for Empire*, 213; Trask, *The War with Spain*, 364–65.

4. Pérez, *Cuba and the United States*, 97; Pérez, *Cuba Between Empires*, 217, 221, 227; the United States withdrew only after the Cubans added clauses to their constitution deeding a base to the United States at Guantánamo and authorizing the United States to intervene to protect U.S. interests on the island, Foner, *The Spanish-Cuban-American War* 2:340–55, 368, 575, 625, 666.

5. Reed cited in Pérez, *Cuba Between Empires*, 221; see also Helg, *Our Rightful Share*, 92; Linderman, *The Mirror of War*, 137; Pérez, *Cuba Between Empires*, 199; Kaplan, "Black and Blue," 225; Smith, *The Spanish-American War*, 128.

6. Healy, *The United States in Cuba*, 30, 32; Maj. Gen. Leonard Wood, "The Existing Conditions and Needs in Cuba," *NAR* 168, May 1899, 593–601; Foner, *The Spanish-*

Cuban-American War 2:356–60, 389; Theodore E. Burton, "Speech at Chagrin Falls, Ohio," Sept. 12, 1900, reel 94, cont. 29, fol. 451, Theodore E. Burton Papers, WRHS.

7. Resolution by citizens of Clay County, Texas, July 4, 1898, folder 7, Political, July 1–9, 1898, box 97, Wheeler Family Papers, ADAH; on Roosevelt and Wood, see Draper, *The Rescue of Cuba*, 161; on Dewey, see John D. Long, cited in *Patriotic Eloquence*, Fulton and Trueblood, eds., 211; on citizen in uniform, see Alger, *The Spanish-American War*, 466. In his study of Irish, Polish, and Jewish immigrant men, Jacobson notes that "in the festival of masculinism which accompanied war fever, 'manliness' became a litmus for political legitimacy," *Special Sorrows*, 163. On praise for citizen-soldiers, see also Leffler, "From the Shadows into the Sun," 118–20.

8. "Editorial Comment," *Atlanta Constitution*, April 4, 1898; Henry B. Blackwell to Ellen, April 9, 1898, folder 136, correspondence by HBB, 1897–1909, box 9, Blackwell Family Papers, SL.

9. *Philadelphia Press* cartoon in *Cartoons of the War of 1898*, n.p.; "Many Heroes," *Rochester Democrat and Chronicle*, May 25, 1899.

10. On ideal man, see Senator Foraker, cited in Curtis, *The Republican Party*, 401; on Man Behind the Gun, see "The Full Dinner Pail," Silber, *Songs America Voted By*, 177; McKinley was deeply involved in strategy decisions, and he closely followed the course of the war on the maps he pinned up in a makeshift White House war room, Cosmas, *An Army for Empire*, 102.

11. Benedict, *William McKinley*, 12, 15.

12. On the nomination, see Burton, *Theodore Roosevelt*, 58; on Roosevelt's skill as a self-promoter, see Ricard, "War and Myth," 63–64; on Guásimas and Kettle Hill, see Dierks, *A Leap to Arms*, 90–92, 106–08.

13. *New York World* cartoon in Emily Carow Scrapbook, vol. 2, Theodore Roosevelt Collection, HL; "Roosevelt Opens the Campaign," *Chicago Tribune*, Oct. 7, 1898; Roosevelt, "The Interest of Labor" (1898), *Campaigns and Controversies*, 307; Morris, *The Rise of Theodore Roosevelt*, 680, 683.

14. Curtis, *The Republican Party*, 405–06; on Roosevelt's hat, see Rystad, *Ambiguous Imperialism*, 201; on dude and cyclone, see Busbey et al., *The Battle of 1900*, 257; on nomination, see Morris, *The Rise of Theodore Roosevelt*, 729.

15. *New York Sun*, Sept. 24, 1900, cited in Miller, *"Benevolent Assimilation,"* 145; Coletta, *William Jennings Bryan*, 281; Foster, *William McKinley and the G.O.P.*, 233.

16. W. M. Bunting to Joseph Wheeler, folder 8, Political, July 10–31, 1898, box 97; J. M. Falkner to Joseph Wheeler, Aug. 2, 1898, folder 1, Political, Aug. 1–12, 1898, box 98, both in Wheeler Family Papers, ADAH.

17. "One of the Finest Characters of the War," *Sun*, Sept. 4, 1898, folder 7, political, Sept. 3–5, 1898, box 99; Clipping, *New Orleans States*, Sept. 20, 1898, scrapbook, 1898–99, box 173; Clipping, *Syracuse Courier*, Nov. 14, 1898, scrapbook 1898–99, box 173, all in Wheeler Family Papers, ADAH.

18. On higher office, see W. M. Bunting to Joseph Wheeler, folder 8, Political, July 10–31, 1898, box 97; S.E.V.H., "Governor Wheeler," *Decatur Weekly News*, June 16, 1899, folder 3, Military: Poems about JW, box 144, both in Wheeler Family Papers, ADAH. Wheeler got 99.9 percent of the vote, Moore, ed., *Congressional Quarterly's Guide*, 1080. On Wheeler as the Democrats' war hero, see Clipping, *Gurley Herald*, March 13, 1899, scrapbook, 1898–99, box 173; on winning a place next to McKinley, see T. C. De Leon,

Joseph Wheeler, The Man, The Statesman, The Soldier (Atlanta: Byrd Printing Co., 1899), in folder 4, Personal/Family: Printed Material, box 12; on patriot, soldier, see Clipping, "Town Topics," Oct. 20, 1898, scrapbook 1898–99, box 173; see also clipping, *St. Louis Mirror,* Oct. 27, 1898, scrapbook, 1898–99, box 173, all in Wheeler Family Papers, ADAH.

19. On service, see "Etc.," *Fairfield Democrat,* July 29, 1898, folder: newspaper clippings, June-July 1898; box 5; on battles, see Clipping, *Owatunna Press,* Aug. 5, 1898, folder: newspaper clippings, Aug. 2–11, 1898, box 5, both in John Lind Papers, MNHS; on Lind as a gallant soldier, see "Lind Accepts," *Willmar Tribune,* July 27, 1898; on Lind as a Spaniard fighter, see clipping, *Alexandria Citizen,* July 28, 1898; on the field, see "John Lind Accepts," *Fergus Falls Globe,* July 30, 1898, all three clippings in folder: newspaper clippings, June-July, 1898, box 5, John Lind Papers, MNHS.

20. On nauseating, see Clipping, *Fairfax Standard,* Sept. 1, 1898, folder: newspaper clippings, Sept.-Nov. 1898; on woods, see Clipping, *Caledonia Tribune,* Aug. 2, 1898, folder: newspaper clippings, Aug. 2–11, 1898; "John Lind's Parole," *Fairfax Standard,* July 28, 1898, folder: newspaper clippings, June-July, 1898, all in box 5, John Lind Papers, MNHS; on Minnesota's Republicanism, see Dunn, *From Harrison to Harding,* 270. Lind was the state's first non-Republican governor since 1865, Moore, ed., *Congressional Quarterly's Guide,* 689.

21. Richard W. Turk, "Introduction," Hobson, *The Sinking of the "Merrimac,"* xx-xxi; Dunn attributes Hobson's political success to his naval exploit, *From Harrison to Harding,* 273. Hobson had no prior political experience, "Lieutenant Richmond Pearson Hobson," *National Cyclopaedia* 9:10. Captain Chanler won election to Congress from New York, General Gobin became the lieutenant governor of Pennsylvania, and Colonel Hawkins became a Pennsylvania state senator, "Heroes of the Spanish War Elected to Public Office," *Philadelphia Press,* Nov. 10, 1898, scrapbook, 1898–99, box 173, Wheeler Family Papers, ADAH. Charles Dick, who volunteered for duty with his Ohio National Guard regiment and fought at Santiago, won election to Congress in 1898, *National Cyclopaedia* 13:445. Newspapers also presented Gen. Leonard Wood (who started the war as colonel of the Rough Riders) as a likely presidential or vice presidential candidate, Hagedorn, *Leonard Wood,* 257. Gen. Nelson A. Miles, who led the invasion of Puerto Rico, enjoyed a political boom that died down after he was implicated in a scandal over the army's beef supply, Cosmas, *An Army for Empire,* 292–93. After General Funston became a hero in the Philippines, the press bandied about the possibility of a Roosevelt-Funston ticket, Miller, "Benevolent Assimilation," 235–36; on proposals that Dewey run, see Spector, *Admiral of the New Empire,* 110; Barrett, *Admiral George Dewey,* 48; on good one, see Sen. Redfield Proctor to William McKinley, May 2, 1898; on fit recognition, see Sen. Redfield Proctor to Admiral Dewey, May 14, 1898, both in Box 8, vol. 39, Redfield Proctor Papers, PFL; "Let History Repeat Itself," *New York World* cartoon in *ROR* 20, Nov. 1899, 542.

22. On elected to-morrow, see Herbert B. Turner to Sen. John C. Spooner, May 10, 1898, folder: May 1898, box 21, John C. Spooner Papers, LC; Spector, *Admiral of the New Empire,* 113, 116.

23. "Jack Rabbits, Mugwumps, and Jingoes," *Chicago Tribune,* Feb. 28, 1898.

24. Rep. James A. Norton, *CR* 31, pt. 3, March 16, 1898, 2877; Rep. John J. Lentz, *CR* 31, pt. 4, March 31, 1898, 3444; Rep. John W. Gaines, *CR* 31, pt. 8, April 29, 1898, 320. On the Cuban-bond conspiracy that no doubt fueled the money versus manhood rhetoric, see Holbo, "The Convergence of Moods," 60–61, 70.

25. Theodore Roosevelt, "The Manly Virtues and Practical Politics," *Forum* 17, July 1894, 551–57.

26. Albert J. Beveridge, "The College Man in Politics," Nov. 1897, folder, 1897, box 297, Albert Jeremiah Beveridge Papers, LC.

27. Franklin H. Giddings, "Imperialism?" *Political Science Quarterly* 13, Dec. 1898, 585–605, 587.

28. Vanderbilt, *Charles Eliot Norton,* 141; "Wrong Advice from a Professor," *New York Sun,* April 27, 1898; on caterwaulings, see EJM, "Professor Norton's Insults," letter to the editor of the *Sun,* Aug. 26, 1898; on Norton as "sterile" and "anaemic," see "Disloyalty at Harvard," *New York Sun,* April 30, 1898; "Prigs Prate of Patriotism," *Commercial Tribune,* all clippings in Records of the Hour scrapbook, Charles Eliot Norton Papers, HL; see also "C. E. Norton and Maximo Gómez," *NYT,* May 1, 1898.

29. Rep. Willis Brewer, *CR* 31, pt. 8, June 9, 1898, 525; Richard F. Pettigrew to Jonas H. Lien, May 20, 1898, and Richard F. Pettigrew to F. M. Gee, May 20, 1898, both on reel 21, Richard F. Pettigrew Papers, PM.

30. G. C. Mead, letter to the editor, "Criticizes Prof. Norton," *NYT,* May 4, 1898; "Harvard Loyal as Ever," *Boston Journal,* and "A Real American at Brown," clippings from Records of the Hour scrapbook, Charles Eliot Norton Papers, HL.

31. H. L. Higginson to Henry C. Lodge, July 1, 1898, Henry Cabot Lodge Papers, MHS; Roosevelt, *The Rough Riders,* 9; on Roosevelt as a dude, see Watterson, *History of the Spanish-American War,* 108; Sullivan, *Our Times* 2:217; Filene, "Between a Rock and a Soft Place," 345; Fraser, *America and the Patterns of Chivalry,* 119–20; Ricard, "War and Myth," 62.

32. Watterson, *History of the Spanish-American War,* 89, 108; Young, *Life and Heroic Deeds of Admiral Dewey,* 63.

33. On steel medicine, see Marshall, *The Story of the Rough Riders,* 33; Richard Harding Davis, "The Rocking-Chair Period of the War," *Scribner's Magazine* 24, August 1898, 267; Staudacher, "Richard Harding Davis," 82.

34. "Dudes Before Santiago," from the *Cleveland Leader,* in *Spanish-American War Songs,* Witherbee, ed., 31.

35. Draper, *The Rescue of Cuba,* 96; Sen. William J. Sewell, *CR* 31, pt. 7, June 29, 1898, 6450. See also Jacob A. Riis, "Roosevelt and His Men," *Outlook* 60, Oct. 1, 1898, 287–93, 288.

36. Davis, *The Cuban and Porto Rican Campaigns,* 286–88; Clipping, "The Dude," *Chicago Record,* folder: Howard S. Greene, 1898, 12th Pa. Vl. Inf., N.J.C.O. #16, box: Pennsylvania Infantry, 12th Regiment, Spanish-American War Survey, MHRI. Slotkin argues that Roosevelt's military service developed his belief that the preservation of American democracy was "paradoxically dependent on the power and virtue of a heroic elite class," *Gunfighter Nation,* 57–58, 102.

37. Edwards, *The '98 Campaign,* 143.

38. These claims undoubtedly buttressed their self-confidence and sense of entitlement, too. Historians have credited Roosevelt with winning credibility for experts, but the regendering of elite men brought about by the war also contributed to his political ascent, Fraser, *America and the Patterns of Chivalry,* 128; Hofstadter, *Anti-Intellectualism in American Life,* 196.

39. John B. Gordon cited in *Minutes of the Eighth Annual Meeting,* 26–27. On the

Spanish-American War and sectional reconciliation, see Foster, *Ghosts of the Confederacy*, 145–59; on redefining southern men as patriotic after the war, see Silber, *Romance of Reunion*, 178–80.

40. On comradeship in arms, see Dewey, *The Life and Letters of Admiral Dewey*, 397; Roosevelt, "Fellow-Feeling as a Political Factor" (1900), *American Ideals*, 355–68, 356.

41. On suffragists' housekeeping arguments, see Kraditor, *The Ideas of the Woman Suffrage Movement*, 73; on aid, see Anthony and Harper, eds., *The History of Woman Suffrage* 4:838; *Second Report of the National Society*, 106; Florence M. Adkinson, "The Mother Element," *Woman's Column*, Sept. 10, 1898, 3; Hewitt, "Varieties of Voluntarism," 72; Will to Mother, May 11, 1898, folder: correspondence, May 1898, and Will to Mother, June 13, 1898, folder: correspondence, June 1898, box 2, Frederick Family Papers, UMBL. Groups that contributed to the Red Cross included a colored women's auxiliary in Kansas City, Kansas, the Council of Jewish Women in Montgomery, Alabama, the Woman's War Relief Association of Oneida County, New York, the Ladies' Relief Committee of Winchester, New Hampshire, and the Young Ladies' Mission Circle of the Reformed Church in North Branch, New Jersey. Across the nation groups such as the WCTU, the Needlework Guild of America, the Young Women's Christian Association, the Ladies' Union Veteran Legion, and the Legion of Loyal Women also provided supplies, *American National Red Cross Relief Committee Reports*, 163, 208, 279, 283, 285–86, 306–07, 311; Records, 1898, 3:2–61, St. Paul Red Cross Aid Society Papers, MNHS.

42. *American National Red Cross Relief Committee Reports*, 22, 255; Barton, *The Red Cross in Peace and War*, 403, 422, 424, 430; Records, 1898, 3:159–62, St. Paul Red Cross Aid Society Papers, MNHS; William Howe Tolman, "Some Volunteer War Relief Associations," *ROR* 19, Feb. 1899, 189–92, 190. Southern women also cared for traveling troops, see "Cut the Blood Red Tape to Tatters," *Woman's Standard*, Oct. 1898, 2. These diet kitchens were modeled after the ones developed by women during the Civil War, Leonard, *Yankee Women*, 87–89. On Mason, see *Second Report of the National Society*, 189.

43. The National Society of the Colonial Dames also offered their services to the surgeon-general, Lamar, *A History of the National Society*, 102; Lewenson, *Taking Charge*, 88; on the number of nurses, see *Third Report of the National Society*, 50; on the number of applications, see *Second Report of the National Society*, 51.

44. Barton, *The Red Cross in Peace and War*, 616, 645–46; Pryor, *Clara Barton*, 309–10.

45. "A Nation Without a Woman," *WJ* 31, Jan. 13, 1900, 15. The *Journal* optimistically declared that women's contributions to the war effort had strengthened sentiment on behalf of granting women full citizenship, "After the War—Woman Suffrage," *WJ* 29, Sept. 17, 1898, 298; see also "Women's Work in the War," *WJ* 30, Jan. 7, 1899, 4.

46. Untitled, *Union Signal*, 24, Sept. 1, 1898, 1; Howe, *Reminiscences*, 379; the *Woman's Journal* chimed in with a story on military mismanagement that euphemistically claimed the war had proven the need for women to "share in the general housekeeping," "The Lesson of 'Algerism,'" *WJ* 29, Sept. 24, 1898, 312.

47. On mediaeval sentiment, see Evelyn H. Belden quoted in *The History of Woman Suffrage*, Anthony and Harper, eds., 4:339–40; Harriet B. Kells, "Unexpected Victories in the Hispano-American War," *Union Signal* 24, Sept. 1, 1898, 5. See also Lida Calvert Obenchain, "The Philippine War," *WJ* 30, June 3, 1899, 169; Harper, *The Life and Work of Susan B. Anthony* 3:1121.

48. Barton, *The Red Cross in Peace and War,* 618.

49. On almost as important, see Clipping "Nurses Ready for War," *New York Mail and Express,* April 15, 1898, reel 112, Clara Barton Papers, LC; Anthony quoted in Harper, *The Life and Work of Susan B. Anthony* 3:1120; this finding is consonant with Higonnet and Higonnet's argument that although women have entered new occupations in wartime, men have preserved their privileged positions because warring nations have reserved their highest honor for soldiers, "The Double Helix," 35.

50. "The Dewey Girl," *Judge* 37, Sept. 30, 1899, 7; "Crowds Cheer Gen. Wheeler," *Chicago Tribune,* Oct. 1, 1898.

51. E. M. Robinson, "Miss Annie Wheeler," May 30, 1899, folder, Personal/Family, 1899, box 9, Wheeler Family Papers, ADAH.

52. On the debate over recognizing Barton and the Red Cross, see *CR* 32, pt. 1, Jan. 12, 1899, 600; on Barton's plea, see "Mrs. Laura Colgrove's Address," *Woman's Standard,* Dec. 1898, 4; "Clara Barton for Woman Suffrage," *WJ* 29, Aug. 20, 1898, 265; Lida Calvert Obenchain, "Women's Attitude Towards War," *WJ* 29, Aug. 13, 1898, 257; Carrie Chapman Catt, "Reading for Suffrage Clubs," *National Suffrage Bulletin,* Sept. 1898, 2.

53. Address read by Mrs. Arthur M. Dodge and written by Mrs. Rossiter Johnson and Mrs. Winfield Moody, "Address to the Judiciary Committees of the Senate and Assembly of the State of New York," Feb. 22, 1899, in *Why Women do not Want the Ballot,* 1903 ed., n.p.

54. Mrs. Rossiter Johnson, "The Blank-Cartridge Ballot," in *Why Women do not Want the Ballot,* Johnson, ed., 1904 ed., 7. The irony of this argument is that modern weaponry was enabling women to fire real bullets as easily as men.

55. Goldwin Smith, "Woman Suffrage" (1898), *Pamphlets Printed and Distributed by the Women's Anti-Suffrage Association,* 204–05; see also "Conditions of Suffrage," *Outlook* 64, Feb. 24, 1900, 434–36, 435; A.S.B. [Alice Stone Blackwell], *WJ* 29, June 18, 1898, 193. As the antisuffrage *Remonstrance* maintained, women's suffrage would render the nation powerless and unable to maintain its stature among nations, "An Impractical Substitution," *Remonstrance,* 1902, 2.

56. Lyman Abbott, "Why Women do Not Wish the Suffrage," *Atlantic Monthly,* Oct. 1903, 1–8, 5. On the antisuffragists' view of force as the ultimate basis of government, see Kraditor, *The Ideas of the Woman Suffrage Movement,* 28; Flexner called the years from 1896 to 1910 the "doldrums" in *Century of Struggle,* 262. In contrast to World War I, following which the Nineteenth Amendment granted women in all states equal suffrage, the Spanish-American War was conceptualized only briefly as part of a struggle to promote democratic ideals. After initial statements about freeing Cuba from Spanish tyranny, the rhetoric of democracy quickly faded from wartime discourse. Instead, war-related rhetoric focused on the primacy of force in international affairs and its relevance to self-government. The result was a political climate more hostile to women's suffrage than that of the post-World War I period.

57. At the start of the war, some black newspaper editors, including Edward E. Cooper of the Washington, D.C., *Colored American,* argued that military service would help black men improve their political position in the face of growing disfranchisement and Jim Crow legislation. With this goal in mind, thousands of black men volunteered, Gatewood, *Black Americans and the White Man's Burden,* 39, 62–63. On gallantry, see Coston, *The Spanish-American War Volunteer,* 9; on discrimination and disfranchisement, see Johnson, *History of Negro Soldiers,* 124. Bonsal, *The Fight for Santiago,* 229–30.

58. Bigelow, *Reminiscences of the Santiago Campaign*, 36–37; Joseph Wheeler, "Introduction," *Under Fire*, Cashin et al., xiv–xv; Roosevelt, *The Rough Riders*, 93; Gatewood, *Black Americans and the White Man's Burden*, 201.

59. Given the prevailing racial assumptions, it is not surprising that white officers hampered black soldiers' efforts to become military heroes by preventing them from fighting. States with black volunteer units generally refused to muster them into federal service. Only one black volunteer company, Company L of the Sixth Massachusetts Regiment, saw action. Furthermore, the white press did not present black men as leaders, in part because they did not hold high military positions. In 1898, the only black commissioned officers in the regular army were a few chaplains and a military science instructor at Wilberforce University. By the end of the war, three black volunteer regiments had black officers, but most black soldiers served under white commanders, Gatewood, *"Smoked Yankees,"* 7. The tendency of the white press to slight black soldiers except for a brief period of favorable press coverage at the end of the war made it easier for white audiences to associate military valor and whiteness, Dyer, *Theodore Roosevelt and the Idea of Race*, 100; Gatewood, *Black Americans and the White Man's Burden*, 7, 10, 63, 103, 105, 202; Fletcher, *The Black Soldier*, 45–46; Johnson, *History of Negro Soldiers*, 27–28, 45, 94; Kaplan, "Black and Blue," 219–36. When the white press recognized black soldiers, it was often for their work as nurses to fever patients, not as combat heroes, see Oliver O. Howard, "The Future of our Army and Navy," *Outlook* 60, Nov. 12, 1898, 659–62, 661.

60. At the end of the war, white Alabama soldiers won praise for demonstrating the "magnificent manhood of imperial Alabama," Koenigsberg, *Southern Martyrs*, 147, 205. By saying that the white troops represented "manhood" instead of "white manhood," Koenigsberg suggested that the only men capable of representing manhood were white, that the only manhood worth honoring was white manhood, that manliness was intertwined with whiteness. Dixon described the black volunteers as a "source of riot and disorder wherever they appeared," *The Leopard's Spots*, 409; see also Gilmore, *Gender and Jim Crow*, 81. On wuz white, see Frank L. Stanton, "With the Colored Regiment Band," *Century Magazine* 58, June 1899, 328.

Chapter 6. The Problem of Male Degeneracy and the Allure of the Philippines

1. Smith, *The Spanish-American War*, 225; Bain, *Sitting in Darkness*, 4.

2. Cosmas, *An Army for Empire*, 240–42; Trask, *The War with Spain*, 382, 481–82; Smith, *The Spanish-American War*, 200; Bain, *Sitting in Darkness*, 78.

3. On economic grounds for taking the Philippines, see McCormick, *China Market*, 107; LaFeber, *The New Empire*, 411; Rystad, *Ambiguous Imperialism*, 34–35; on businessmen's lack of interest in a formal empire, see Miller, *"Benevolent Assimilation,"* 6. Miller attributes U.S. policies to "military reasoning," 14. Yet it seems that if the United States did not have economic or other ambitions there would have been less reason to establish a military foothold in the area. Political calculations may have affected some policymakers' support for expansion, for Republican senators who favored expansion argued that the public wanted the United States to "keep" the islands, Damiani, *Advocates of Empire*, 43. On racism, see Weston, *Racism in U.S. Imperialism*, xiii, 11–12, 90 (Weston also argues that racism can explain the lack of tenacity in U.S. imperial policies, xiii); Williams, "United

States Indian Policy and the Debate over Philippine Annexation," 820; Drinnon, *Facing West*, 286. Doty argues that Americans represented the Filipinos as needing U.S. authority and control, *Imperial Encounters*, 36–39.

4. On honesty and truth, see H. P. Howard to Howard Townsend, Jan. 12, 1901, folder: Misc. Mss., Howard Townsend Collection, NYHS. William Howard Taft, "The People of the Philippine Islands," *Independent* 54, May 1, 1902, 1019–20, 1019. See also "Character of the Luzon Savages," *Rochester Democrat and Chronicle*, March 10, 1899; Schurman et al., *Report of the Philippine Commission* 3:374. The variations between Filipino tribes and the prejudices of ethnologists led to a range of ethnological assessments. Authors often drew on more than one stereotype depending on which Filipinos they were discussing. Furthermore, as Hunt has noted in *Ideology and U.S. Foreign Policy*, Americans selected images to fit their arguments or concerns, 60–62, 69, 81. On expanding our understanding of gender beyond simple male/female dichotomies, see Baron, "Questions of Gender," 178–99. Sinha notes that the British cited Indian men's supposed lack of manly character to justify imperial authority over Indian men, *Colonial Masculinity*, 41; on the moral dimension to late-nineteenth-century understandings of manliness, see Bederman, *Manliness and Civilization*, 18.

5. "Character of the Filipinos," *Rochester Democrat and Chronicle*, March 26, 1899; Rep. Charles F. Cochran, *CR* 35, pt. 1, Jan. 23, 1902, 937; F. F. Hilder, "The Philippine Islands," *National Geographic Magazine* 9, June 1898, 257–84, 280; Stickney, *Admiral Dewey*, 251; on head-hunting, see Foreman, *The Philippine Islands*, 132, 160.

6. On pillage and rape, see John C. Spooner to C. K. Adams, Feb. 24, 1899, letter-book 47, John C. Spooner Papers, LC; on European women in Manila, see Sen. John C. Spooner, *CR* 33, pt. 7, May 22, 1900, 5845; Rep. George N. Southwick, *CR* 35, pt. 8, June 26, 1902, 7464. On the stereotype of the bestial negro, see Frederickson, *The Black Image*, 275; Takaki, "The Black Child-Savage," 35; Williamson, *The Crucible of Race*, 111.

7. On making men of the Filipinos, see White, *Our New Possessions*, 221. Rep. William H. Douglas, *CR* 35, pt. 7, June 24, 1902, 350; Rep. James A. Norton, *CR* 35, pt. 4, March 27, 1902, 3354.

8. Sen. Albert J. Beveridge, *CR* 33, pt. 1, Jan. 9, 1900, 708–09; Lodge cited in "The Commonwealth in the Senate," *Dor. Beacon*, Jan. 11, 1899, Personal Scrapbook 24, George F. Hoar Papers, MHS; Thomas L. Rosser to William McKinley, Feb. 28, 1899, folder Feb. 21–28, 1899, box 71, George B. Cortelyou Papers, LC. On viewing Filipinos as childlike, see Healy, *U.S. Expansionism*, 15; Hunt, *Ideology and U.S. Foreign Policy*, 81. On the stereotype of African Americans as children, see Frederickson, *The Black Image*, 287–88; Takaki, "The Black Child-Savage," 32. On Indians as children, see Rogin, "Liberal Society and the Indian Question," 138, 151, 161. On Indians as wards and the relevance of that image to the Philippine debate, see Williams, "United States Indian Policy," 811–13, 825. On U.S. paternalism, see also Slotkin, "Buffalo Bill's 'Wild West,'" 211.

9. On wards, see William McKinley, Draft of letter to Henry Cabot Lodge, accepting the Republican nomination, Sept. 11, 1900, Reel 84, William McKinley Papers, LC; on the United States as a guardian, see William McKinley, "President's Message," *CR* 34, pt. 1, Dec. 3, 1900, 11. Rep. George N. Southwick, *CR* 35, pt. 8, June 26, 1902, 7468; Minneapolis *Tribune* cartoon in *ROR* 19, June 1899, 670.

10. Becker, "Conditions Requisite to our Success in the Philippine Islands," 5; Church, *Picturesque Cuba*, 117; on family rice, see "Philippine Customs," *New York Tribune*, Aug. 7,

1898; this story was based on Lucy M. J. Garnett, "The Philippine Islanders," *Fortnightly Review* 70, July 1, 1898, 72–87, 77. Phelps Whitmarsh claimed that Filipinas did all the work "while the men stalk about with spears in their hands," "Among the Wild Igorrotes," *Outlook* 65, May 26, 1900, 213–18, 213. McClintock notes that the English used images of domestic degeneracy to discredit the Irish and other groups, *Imperial Leather,* 53.

11. On beauties and bathing, see *Philippine Monthly Magazine* 1, April 1899, and 1, May-June 1899, n.p.; on dusky Venuses, see Foreman, *The Philippine Islands,* 413; on wholly feminine women, see Phelps Whitmarsh, "In Pampanga Province," *Outlook* 64, Feb. 17, 1900, 395–401, 399. Division of Insular Affairs of the War Department, "The People of the Philippines," Feb. 15, 1901, Senate Document #218, 56th Congress, 2nd Session, 22; on virgin territory, see M. E. Beall et al., *Opportunities in the Colonies,* 6. Viewing the Filipinos as feminine was related to viewing them as children because Victorians believed that adult women resembled children both mentally and physically, Russett, *Sexual Science,* 28; Stepan, "Race and Gender," 263. Like children and men of the so-called lower races, women of all races commonly were seen as unfit for political power.

12. On asunder, see William R. Moore to Edward Atkinson, Nov. 23, 1898, Edward Atkinson Papers, MHS. George F. Becker, "Are the Philippines Worth Having?" *Scribner's Magazine* 27, June 1900, 739–52, 739. Even descriptions of Filipino men could promote the idea of imperialism as a marriage. Halstead found the Filipino leader Emilio Aguinaldo "unexpectedly small," weighing only a little over one hundred pounds. He described him as "dressed in pure white" with a "modesty of bearing [that] would have become a maiden." The small, pure, maidenly Aguinaldo of this account seemed a suitable bride for Uncle Sam, *The Story of the Philippines,* 54. Similar arguments about expansion as marriage had been made in the debate over Hawaiian annexation (see Sen. George F. Hoar, *CR* 31, pt. 7, July 5, 1898, 6661) and in the 1840s during the Mexican-American War (see Horsman, *Race and Manifest Destiny,* 233–34). McCurry discusses how southern white men used the marriage metaphor to explain slavery, "The Two Faces of Republicanism," 1252, 1254; Silber discusses the tendency to view sectional reunion as a marriage between a seemingly masculine North and feminine South, *The Romance of Reunion,* 6–7. She notes that the marriage metaphor served to "depoliticize the sectional relationship" and yet suggest hierarchy in that relationship, 10, 38, 116.

13. On anti-imperialists, see Lasch, "The Anti-Imperialists," 319–29; Weston, *Racism in U.S. Imperialism,* xiii, 46, 90; on mortality figures, see Smith, *The Spanish-American War,* 225.

14. This argument puts a new twist on Thomson, Stanley, and Perry's claim that hopes of dispelling domestic anxieties drove American expansionism in the 1890s, *Sentimental Imperialists,* 105.

15. On effeminate tendencies, see Maurice Thompson, "Vigorous Men, A Vigorous Nation," *Independent* 50, Sept. 1, 1898, 609–11, 610–11. Theodore Roosevelt to Cecil Arthur Spring Rice, March 16, 1901, *Letters of Theodore Roosevelt* 3:15; on warnings of decay, see Brooks Adams, *The Law of Civilization and Decay;* Healy, *U.S. Expansionism,* 102; on British fears of male decay, see MacDonald, *Sons of the Empire,* 8; on fears of degeneracy, see Pick, *Faces of Degeneration,* 8, 21, 23–24, 39, 73. Higham has argued that concerns about native-born, middle-class men's ability to stand up to immigrant, working-class men contributed both to nativism and imperialism, *Strangers in the Land,* 76, 144. Northern native-born men's anxieties about immigrant men had a southern analogue in

white men's anxieties about their status relative to African-American men, anxieties that often culminated in lynchings.

16. Fernald, *The Imperial Republic*, 64; on law of evolution, see Samuel Kirkman to John Tyler Morgan, June 3, 1902, reel 5, John Tyler Morgan Papers, LC. Sen. Jonathan Ross, *CR* 33, pt. 2, Jan. 23, 1900, 1062. On concerns about the implications of a luxury economy for the nation's military well-being, see Mallan, "The Warrior Critique," 218–21; on nineteenth-century theorists who viewed war as a "rigorous tonic against the softening effects of effete civilization," see Russett, *Darwin in America*, 90. One reason southern whites did not support overseas imperial policies as enthusiastically as northern whites appears to be their belief that establishing white supremacy at home offered enough of a character-building challenge, see Williamson, *The Crucible of Race*, 297. Healy mentions the desire to "preserve the American character" in *U.S. Expansionism*, 109, but he does not consider the gender dimension of this issue.

17. Fernald, *The New Womanhood*, 20–21, 23–25, 43, 77, 214.

18. Sir G. S. Clarke, "Imperial Responsibilities a National Gain," *NAR* 168, Feb. 1899, 129–41, 137–38; Dilke cited in Healy, *U.S. Expansionism*, 105. Writers who argued that war was beneficial for its own sake included Carl von Clausewitz, Pierre Proudhon, John Ruskin, and Heinrich von Treitschke, see Pick, *War Machine*, 5, 15, 31, 46, 69–70, 84–85; Ely, *The Road to Armageddon*, 1–2.

19. Rep. Henry R. Gibson, *CR* 33, pt. 2, Feb. 6, 1900, 1566; Turner, *Rereading Frederick Jackson Turner*, 73–74; see also Bederman, *Manliness and Civilization*, 183.

20. On Civil War era claims that combat built manhood, see Fredrickson, *The Inner Civil War*, 155, 164, 188. John Hay called the conflict a "splendid little war" in a letter to Theodore Roosevelt, Freidel, *The Splendid Little War*, 3.

21. Brooks, *The Story of our War with Spain*, 336. On army administration scandals, see Cosmas, *An Army for Empire*, 262, 277, 303; on redeemed honor, see "America and Spain," *Living Age* 19, Aug. 6, 1898, 406. John Henry Barrows cited in Fulton and Trueblood, eds., *Patriotic Eloquence*, 14.

22. Alger, *The Spanish-American War*, 6; Keenan, *The Conflict with Spain*, 177.

23. Watterson, *History of the Spanish-American War*, 35.

24. Marshall, *The Story of the Rough Riders*, 35; Roosevelt, "Brotherhood and the Heroic Virtues" (1901), *American Ideals*, 466.

25. Watterson, *History of the Spanish-American War*, viii; "Sidneys of Our Day," *Century Magazine* 57, Dec. 1898, 315; Theodore Roosevelt to William Sheffield Cowles, March 30, 1898, *The Letters of Theodore Roosevelt* 2:803; Depew cited in Curtis, *The Republican Party*, 406.

26. Beale, *Theodore Roosevelt*, 77; Lutz, *American Nervousness*, 81; Bederman, *Manliness and Civilization*, 185–86; Healy, *U.S. Expansionism*, 115–16; on softer times, see Roosevelt, "Manhood and Statehood" (1901), *American Ideals*, 456.

27. On soft city men, see Theodore Roosevelt to Hermann Speck von Sternberg, Nov. 9, 1901, *Letters of Theodore Roosevelt* 3:192. On growth and grace, see Roosevelt, "Address at Symphony Hall" (1902), *Presidential Addresses and State Papers* 1:108.

28. Roosevelt, "The Duties of a Great Nation" (1898), *Campaigns and Controversies*, 291; on his father's exhortations, see McCullough, *Mornings on Horseback*, 112.

29. On virile virtues, see Roosevelt, "Captain Mahan's 'Life of Nelson'" (1897), *Literary Essays*, 284; see also Linderman, *Mirror of War*, 92; on essential manliness, see Roo-

sevelt, "National Duties" (1901); on frontiersmen, see Roosevelt, "Manhood and Statehood" (1901), both in *American Ideals,* 455, 469–70; see also Bederman, *Manliness and Civilization,* 183.

30. Theodore Roosevelt to Walter Gordon-Cumming, Feb. 18, 1899; Theodore Roosevelt to Winthrop Chanler, March 23, 1899, both in *Letters of Theodore Roosevelt* 2:949, 969.

31. On fronting difficulties, see Roosevelt, "The Administration of William McKinley" (1900), *Campaigns and Controversies,* 359; on memory of deeds, see Roosevelt cited in Beale, *Theodore Roosevelt,* 77. On expanding trade, see Roosevelt, "The Administration of the Island Possessions" (1902), *American Problems,* 278; Roosevelt, "First Annual Message" (1901), *State Papers,* 113. Hofstadter notes that the "personal goals and standards" of elite imperialists such as Roosevelt "were non-commercial," "Cuba, the Philippines, and Manifest Destiny," 158; on primacy of character over wealth, see Roosevelt, "Captain Mahan's 'Life of Nelson'" (1897), *Literary Essays,* 283; Healy, *U.S. Expansionism,* 119; Mallan, "The Warrior Critique," 218; Dalton, "Theodore Roosevelt, Knickerbocker Aristocrat," 50–52; on Elliott, see Saveth, "Theodore Roosevelt," 47–48.

32. Roosevelt, "Grant" (1900), *American Ideals,* 430–41, 431.

33. On young Attila, see Braeman, *Albert J. Beveridge,* 29, 46; on meetings with McKinley, see Bowers, *Beveridge,* 112–13, 116; on manufacturing manhood, see Beveridge, *The Young Man and the World,* 338.

34. Braeman, *Albert J. Beveridge,* 7; Bowers, *Beveridge,* 2, 4, 11, 15; Albert Beveridge, "Speech at a Republican mass meeting at Louisville, Kentucky," Oct. 20, 1900, folder 1900, box 297, Albert Jeremiah Beveridge Papers, LC.

35. On national character, see Beveridge, "Forefathers Day," *The Meaning of the Times,* 22, 27; on being a man and luxury, see Beveridge, *The Young Man and the World,* 12, 96; on Beveridge's employments, see Braeman, *Albert J. Beveridge,* 8; on China, see Beveridge, *The Russian Advance,* 176–77.

36. On gratitude, see Beveridge, "Our Philippine Policy," *The Meaning of the Times,* 59; on proving worthiness, see Beveridge, *Work and Habits,* 90; on proving worthiness and struggle, see Beveridge, "The Young Men of America," speech at a Republican mass meeting at Tomilson Hall, Indianapolis, Oct. 18, 1900, folder 1900, box 297, Albert Beveridge Papers, LC; on Beveridge's Darwinian convictions and desire to take part in organizing a U.S. colonial system, see Braeman, *Albert J. Beveridge,* 24, 26.

37. On work itself as reward, see Beveridge, *Work and Habits,* 30–31, 75; on physical manhood, see Beveridge, "Our Philippine Policy," *The Meaning of the Times,* 59.

38. Widenor argues that Lodge wanted to foster conditions that would "call forth 'the best' in the American people," *Henry Cabot Lodge,* 26. On Lodge's chairmanship, see Garraty, *Henry Cabot Lodge,* 205; on life as a battle, see Henry Cabot Lodge, "Funeral oration upon the death of Senator Davis," box 116, and Henry Cabot Lodge, funeral oration for Roger Wolcott, box 119, Henry Cabot Lodge Papers, MHS.

39. Widenor, *Henry Cabot Lodge,* 20; Lodge, *Early Memories,* 118; Lodge, "A Liberal Education" (1894), *Certain Accepted Heroes,* 170; Lodge, "Good Citizenship," *A Frontier Town,* 36–37; on nobler side, see Henry Cabot Lodge, notes for a speech on the war, box 116, Henry Cabot Lodge Papers, MHS.

40. On spirit of race, see Lodge, "Our Duty Toward Hawaii" (1895), *Speeches and Addresses,* 167; on Englishmen, see Lodge cited in Garraty, *Henry Cabot Lodge,* 157. Henry

Cabot Lodge to Theodore Roosevelt, Oct. 26, 1897, Henry Cabot Lodge III Papers, MHS.

41. On insidious gentleness, see Lodge cited in Widenor, *Henry Cabot Lodge*, 26; on amusements, see Garraty, *Henry Cabot Lodge*, 226; on dilettantism, see Widenor, *Henry Cabot Lodge*, 24; on remarks to students, see Lodge, "A Liberal Education," *Certain Accepted Heroes*, 177, 181; on his sons, see Garraty, *Henry Cabot Lodge*, 192.

42. On Lodge's image as a dude, see Schriftgiesser, *Gentleman from Massachusetts*, 97; on his mother's subventions, see Henry Cabot Lodge to Mother, Dec. 10, 1899, box 94, Henry Cabot Lodge Papers, MHS; Garraty, *Henry Cabot Lodge*, 133; on Lodge's strenuous activities, see Groves, *Henry Cabot Lodge*, 7; on real education, see Lodge, *Early Memories*, 84, 86.

43. Lodge, *Early Memories*, 58, 87; Henry Cabot Lodge to George, July 1, 1898, Letterbook 39, Henry Cabot Lodge Papers, MHS; Henry Cabot Lodge, toast in honor of the President, Box 118, Henry Cabot Lodge Papers, MHS. A similar pride in martial capacity surfaces in Lodge's description of his own role in imperial debate: "Our political foes make the Philippines the center of attack and as chairman of the committee I have to be on the fighting line every morning to watch over my charge and repel assaults," Henry Cabot Lodge to Mother, Feb. 4, 1900, box 94, Henry Cabot Lodge Papers, MHS.

44. On the character of force, see Widenor, *Henry Cabot Lodge*, 81; on the spirit of the race, see Busbey et al., *The Battle of 1900*, 191; on cowering and athlete, see Sen. Henry C. Lodge, *CR* 33, pt. 3, March 7, 1900, 2628; on begrimed, see Lodge, "Party Allegiance," address to Harvard students, March 8, 1892, in *Historical and Political Essays*, 212; on grimed, see Henry Cabot Lodge, Speech on the Philippines, box 118 (Undated Writings, Speeches, etc.), Henry Cabot Lodge Papers, MHS.

45. On markets, see Lodge, "Address by Henry Cabot Lodge . . . Under the Auspices of the Union League," 23; on dust and ashes, see Lodge, *A Fighting Frigate*, 21.

46. On wonderful experience, see McKinley, "Address at the Trans-Mississippi Exposition at Omaha" (1898), *Life of William McKinley*, Fallows, ed., 276; on decay, see McKinley, "Speech at the Citizens' Banquet, Chicago" (1898), *Speeches and Addresses of William McKinley*, 135; on mightiest test, see McKinley cited in March, *The History and Conquest of the Philippines*, 227; on character and prestige, see William McKinley, Speech, Oct. 14, 1899, series 4, reel 83, William McKinley Papers, LC. Smith reviews the debate over whether McKinley was a confident imperialist in "William McKinley's Enduring Legacy," 205–49. He sides with the confident school (205) but notes that McKinley displayed "caution, indecision, and even misgivings on the Philippines," 230. The historians who have presented McKinley as a dedicated expansionist include Gould, *The Spanish-American War and President McKinley*, 104, 111; those who have presented him as an unenthusiastic expansionist include Damiani, *Advocates of Empire*, 8.

47. Albert G. Robinson, "The Savages of the Philippines," *Independent* 52, Nov. 8, 1900, 2677–81, 2679; Worcester, *The Philippine Islands and their People*, 154; Root cited in Stanley, *A Nation in the Making*, 62; William H. Taft, "The People of the Philippine Islands," *Independent* 54, May 1, 1902, 1019–20, 1020. Kimmel notes that native-born white men saw black men and immigrants as simultaneously less and more manly, *Manhood in America*, 93.

48. Lodge, "A Fighting Frigate" (1897), *A Fighting Frigate*, 21. These virtues also seemed to underlie individual men's standing. As Giddings wrote, "Most men . . . still have

need of force and courage. . . . It is doubtful if the transition from chronic warfare to a busy industrial civilization materially diminishes the demand for primitive virtues," *Democracy and Empire*, 317. On the valuation of "primitive masculinity" in the late nineteenth century, see Rotundo, *American Manhood*, 227–30; Bederman, *Manliness and Civilization*, 73–74.

49. Rep. Henry R. Gibson, *CR* 33, pt. 2, Feb. 6, 1900, 1568; Roosevelt, "Manhood and Statehood" (1901), *American Ideals*, 457. Ninkovich notes that Roosevelt believed that the spread of civilization would lead to international order, "Theodore Roosevelt: Civilization as Ideology," 231. But in spite of his hope for international pacification, Roosevelt valorized the ability to wield force.

50. On real sinews, see Frederick Palmer, "White Man and Brown Man in the Philippines," *Scribner's Magazine* 27, Jan. 1900, 76–86, 85. Sen. Louis E. McComas, *CR* 35, pt. 8, July 1, 1902, 7747; Albert Beveridge, "Speech at a Republican mass meeting at Louisville, Kentucky," Oct. 20, 1900, folder 1900, box 297, Albert Jeremiah Beveridge Papers, LC. On Beveridge's Philippine visit and his wife, see Braeman, *Albert J. Beveridge*, 42, 49, 51; on virile life, see Bowers, *Beveridge*, 106.

51. On fine and manly character, see Henry Cabot Lodge to Mrs. Prescott, May 9, 1902, Letterbook 51, Henry Cabot Lodge Papers, MHS; on hearings, see Schriftgiesser, *The Gentleman from Massachusetts*, 203; on gallant fellow Americans, see Roosevelt, "The Administration of the Island Possessions" (1902), *American Problems*, 275; on qualities that make us proud, see Theodore Roosevelt, "At the Tomb of Grant" (1899), *Campaigns and Controversies*, 330. Giddings, *Democracy and Empire*, 307.

52. Lawrence, *Henry Cabot Lodge*, 24; Beveridge, *The Young Man and the World*, 13; Theodore Roosevelt to Edward Sanford Martin, Nov. 26, 1900, *Letters of Theodore Roosevelt* 2:1443.

53. Roosevelt, "The Administration of William McKinley" (1900), *Campaigns and Controversies*, 359; likewise, Sir G. S. Clarke wrote in the *North American Review*, "Domesticity is one of the virtues; but the man whose whole interests and responsibilities are limited to his home circle, lives at best a maimed and stunted life," "Imperial Responsibilities a National Gain," *NAR* 168, Feb. 1899, 129–41, 136; see also Bederman, *Manliness and Civilization*, 188.

54. Corrinne Roosevelt Robinson cited in Lodge, *Anna Cabot Mills Lodge*, 18–19, 47, 50, 59.

55. Schriftgiesser, *The Gentleman from Massachusetts*, 62; Beveridge, *The Young Man and the World*, 2, 177, 184; Roosevelt, "The Strenuous Life," *American Ideals*, 320–21; Gordon, *Woman's Body*, 138–39.

56. Rep. Jonathan P. Dolliver, *CR* 32, pt. 1, Jan. 25, 1899, 1032; on checking wayward steps, see Sen. Porter J. McCumber, *CR* 33, pt. 6, May 18, 1900, 5682; on assuming the responsibilities of a man, see Phelps Whitmarsh, "The Men Behind the Plow," *Outlook* 66, Dec. 15, 1900, 932–35, 934; on appeals and responsibility, see George F. Becker, "Are the Philippines Worth Having?" *Scribner's Magazine* 27, June 1900, 739–52, 752. As McCurry has noted in her study of the antebellum South, "Dependence was the stuff of which independence—and manhood—were made," *Masters of Small Worlds*, 72.

57. Henry Cabot Lodge to Theodore Roosevelt, Aug. 30, 1900, Henry Cabot Lodge III Papers, MHS; Beveridge, *The Young Man and the World*, 156; see also Beveridge, *Work and Habits*, 29. Roosevelt, too, believed that assuming responsibility for a wife and children

helped build manly character, see "The Administration of the Island Possessions" (1902), *American Problems*, 270.

58. Egleston, "Is a Limited Policy of Imperialism Justified?" 15.

Chapter 7: The National Manhood Metaphor and the Fight over the Fathers in the Philippine Debate

1. Legaspi, "The Rhetoric of the Anti-Imperialist Movement," 101–20; Harrington, "The Anti-Imperialist Movement," 211–30, 213; Tompkins, "The Old Guard," 366–88; Beisner, *Twelve Against Empire,* 5; Schirmer, *Republic or Empire,* 15–18, 26, 75, 159; McKee, "Samuel Gompers, the A.F. of L., and Imperialism," 194; Gatewood, *Black Americans and the White Man's Burden,* 199, 221; Doyle, *Irish Americans,* 263; Welch, "Organized Religion and the Philippine-American War," 185–90; Smith, "Southerners on Empire," 89–107; Zimmerman finds that many Chicago antis were Democrats, "Who Were the Anti-Imperialists?" 596; Cherny finds that anti-imperialists in South Dakota, Nebraska, and Kansas came from the free silver coalition, "Anti-Imperialism on the Middle Border," 27, 30.

2. White anti-imperialists often objected to admitting what they regarded as racially inferior people into the United States, Lasch, "The Anti-Imperialists, the Philippines, and the Inequality of Man," 319; Weston, *Racism in U.S. Imperialism,* xiii; Tompkins, *Anti-Imperialism,* 108–09, 112, 147, 205. Black anti-imperialists often objected to what they regarded as an effort to subordinate, if not exterminate, the colored peoples of the Philippines, Gatewood, *Black Americans and the White Man's Burden,* 199, 221. Labor activists feared that Filipino workers would undercut American wages and that costly imperial policies would benefit only trusts, McKee, "Samuel Gompers," 197–99. The women's suffragists who opposed imperialism often argued that anti-imperialism was analogous to their own cause, Hoganson, "The 'Manly' Ideal," chap. 7. Catholics worried that Protestant missionaries aimed to convert Catholic Filipinos, Welch, "Organized Religion and the Philippine-American War," 185–90. Irish-American anti-imperialists equated U.S. policies with British imperialism, Tompkins, *Anti-Imperialism,* 147. Parents of volunteer troops, mostly from the western states, strove to bring their sons back home, Schirmer, *Republic or Empire,* 156. Southern anti-imperialists were wary of a policy that they believed resembled the carpetbag governments of the Reconstruction period, Smith, "Southerners on Empire," 102. League members argued that imperialism would embroil the United States in international rivalries, that it violated the Constitution, and that it would lead to military despotism, Miller, *"Benevolent Assimilation,"* 27; Tompkins, *Anti-Imperialism,* 2, 48; George F. Hoar cited in "Against Imperialism," clipping from the *New York Evening Post,* Nov. 2, 1898, scrapbook, The Philippines, 1898–1899, box 244, John Basset Moore Papers, LC. On breaking from earlier ideals, see Pratt, *America's Colonial Experiment,* 69; Hofstadter, "Manifest Destiny and the Philippines," 173; on earlier anxiety about departing from the Revolutionary fathers, see Watts, *The Republic Reborn,* 76, 168–69. This chapter focuses on members of Congress, but it also considers publicists and political activists who were in dialogue with political leaders on issues of generation, gender, and political legitimacy.

3. Levere, *Imperial America,* 21; Simeon E. Baldwin, "The Entry of the United States into World Politics as One of the Great Powers," *Yale Review,* Feb. 1901, 399–418, 399.

4. As Rep. Benjamin F. Marsh argued, the Republic now had "responsibilities that did not rest upon it in its youthful days," *CR* 33, pt. 4, March 27, 1900, 3394; Levere, *Imperial America*, 11, 67.

5. Roosevelt, "The Duties of a Great Nation" (1898), *Campaigns and Controversies*, 290; Beveridge, "The Young Men of America," Oct. 18, 1900, folder 1900, box 297, Albert J. Beveridge Papers, LC. The national manhood metaphor can be traced back to the Jeffersonians, who conceptualized the nation as a young man entering the world, Watts, *The Republic Reborn*, 164.

6. On vitality, see Rev. John W. Dodge, "Boys and Civilization," *Pennsylvania School Journal* 20, Dec. 1871, 176–77; G. Stanley Hall, "Universities and the Training of Professors," *Forum* 17, May 1894, 297–309, 305. See also William H. Burnham, "Suggestions from the Psychology of Adolescence," *School Review* 5, Dec. 1897, 652–65, 659; Bederman, *Manliness and Civilization*, 89, 92, 112.

7. On valorizing youth, see Kett, *Rites of Passage*, 168, 173, 176; Rotundo, *American Manhood*, 256; Fischer, *Growing Old*, 101, 104.

8. Albert J. Beveridge, "The Young Men of America," address of Oct. 18, 1900, folder, 1900, box 297, Albert J. Beveridge Papers, LC; Roosevelt cited in Curtis, *The Republican Party*, 402.

9. Beisner observes that the leading mugwump anti-imperialists of the late 1890s were an older group, including Thomas Wentworth Higginson, who turned seventy-five in 1898; William Endicott, seventy-two; Charles Eliot Norton and Edward Atkinson, seventy-one; James Burrill Angel, Charles Codman, and Carl Schurz, sixty-nine; E. L. Godkin and Gamaliel Bradford, sixty-seven; Horace White and Charles W. Eliot, sixty-four, *Twelve Against Empire*, 9–10, 136–37; on the fifteen-year age gap, see Miller, *"Benevolent Assimilation,"* 117. See also Harrington, "The Anti-Imperialist Movement in the United States," 218; Tompkins, "The Old Guard," 386–87. Schirmer suggests that the rank and file of the anti-imperialist leagues may have reflected the age difference, too, *Republic or Empire*, 75. Zimmerman, however, finds that vocal anti-imperialists in Chicago were younger than expansionists, "Who Were the Anti-Imperialists?" 592–93; Jim Zwick also disputes the idea that the antis were significantly older than the imperialists, personal communication, Nov. 1997.

10. On Beveridge's campaign and graybeards, see Bowers, *Beveridge and the Progressive Era*, 79, 85–86. On especial satisfaction, see O. W. Christie to Albert J. Beveridge, Jan. 11, 1899, folder B, box 122; on great things, see W. A. Barron to Albert J. Beveridge, Feb. 7, 1899, folder B, box 122; on rejoicing, see A. L. Lawshe to Albert J. Beveridge, Jan. 11, 1899, folder L, box 123, all in Albert J. Beveridge Papers, LC.

11. On seniority, see Bowers, *Beveridge and the Progressive Era*, 115, 127; seniority also thwarted Senator Lodge's ambitions to chair the Committee on Foreign Relations, Schriftgiesser, *The Gentleman from Massachusetts*, 166; on dressing, see Braeman, *Albert J. Beveridge*, 34.

12. Roosevelt, "At the Founders' Day Banquet of the Union League" (1902), *Presidential Addresses* 1:220; Albert J. Beveridge, Speech in Indianapolis, n.d., folder 1900, box 297, Albert J. Beveridge Papers, LC.

13. On practical statesmanship, see Albert J. Beveridge, "The American Situation," speech of April 27, 1901, folder 1901, box 297, Albert J. Beveridge Papers, LC; on doing better, see Beveridge, "The Command of the Pacific" (1902), *The Meaning of the Times*, 196; on China, see Spence, *The Search for Modern China*, 230.

14. Senator Lodge, "Retain the Philippines" (1899), *Patriotic Eloquence,* Fulton and Trueblood, eds., 202; Rep. Charles B. Landis, *CR* 35, pt. 7, June 24, 1902, 7309; on shame to us, see Roosevelt, "The Treaty with Spain" (1899), *Campaigns and Controversies,* 311; on thrice shame, see Theodore Roosevelt, "The Philippine Problem," *World's Work* 4, July 1902, 2344–48. On the flag and self-respect, see Sen. William M. Stewart, *CR* 35, pt. 6, May 13, 1902, 5351.

15. Albert J. Beveridge, "The Young Men of America," address of Oct. 18, 1900, folder, 1900, box 297, Albert J. Beveridge Papers, LC.

16. R. E. Mansfield to Albert J. Beveridge, Jan. 15, 1899, folder M, box 123; Edward S. R. Seguin to Albert J. Beveridge, Jan. 11, 1899, folder S, box 124; Frederick A. Miller to Albert J. Beveridge, Jan. 12, 1899, folder M, box 123, all in Albert J. Beveridge Papers, LC; two of the older imperialists in Congress were Senators Orville H. Platt (R, Conn.) and William M. Stewart (Silver R, Nev.), both age seventy-one in 1898.

17. On decayed citizens, see "The American Flag in the East," *Rochester Democrat and Chronicle,* July 2, 1899. Rep. Cyrus A. Sulloway, *CR* 32, pt. 2, Jan. 26, 1899, 1116; on the Chinese, see Hunt, *Ideology and U.S. Foreign Policy,* 69–70; on the lack of manhood among "lesser races," see Russett, *Sexual Science,* 11, 14; Stepan, "Race and Gender," 263.

18. On judgment, see J. Williams to George F. Hoar, Feb. 7, 1899; on decrepit politicians, see "Republican and Patriot" to George F. Hoar, Feb. 7, 1899; on fossil, see Arthur C. Sadler to George F. Hoar, Feb. 8, 1899, all in George F. Hoar Papers, MHS.

19. Murat Halstead to Albert J. Beveridge, Jan. 5, 1900; G. D. Fellows to Albert J. Beveridge, Jan. 10, 1900, both letters in folder, Response to Philippine Speech, 1900, box 127, Albert J. Beveridge Papers, LC.

20. Rep. Henry R. Gibson, *CR* 34, pt. 4, March 1, 1901, 3377.

21. See Carl Schurz, "American Imperialism," January 4, 1899, folder, Printed Matter: Pamphlets on Philippines and Anti-Imperialism; box 18, William A. Croffut Papers, LC; Rep. James R. Williams, *CR* 33, pt. 8, June 5, 1900, 6722; on avengers, see "Why We Cannot Conquer the Filipinos," *Nation* 69, Aug. 24, 1899, 144. Similarly, William J. Bryan insisted that the United States long had been a world power, "America's Mission" (1899), *Speeches of William Jennings Bryan* 2:14.

22. On undercutting professions of virtue, see Schurz, "The Issue of Imperialism" (1899), *Speeches* 6:26. Southern antis, mostly Democrats, had not only party motivations for opposing imperial policies, but also fewer reasons to worry about overcivilization. As residents of a more rural, less industrialized and poorer region marked by struggles over asserting "white supremacy," they, like western men, had fewer reasons than their northern peers to seek out overseas character-building challenges.

23. On sentimental values, see Douglas, *The Feminization of American Culture,* 10–11; on older and newer standards of manhood, see Rotundo, *American Manhood,* 5, 223, 231, 233, 253; Vance, *The Sinews of the Spirit,* 10; Lutz, *American Nervousness,* 35; Kimmel, *Manhood in America,* 45; Townsend, *Manhood at Harvard,* 17. At the turn of the century, men increasingly regarded masculinity, meaning, as Bederman has pointed out, such apparently inherent biological attributes as physical power and virility, as more desirable than manliness, which had a significant moral component, *Manliness and Civilization,* 18. Although imperialists rarely used the new word in political debate, they nonetheless tended to adhere to the precepts of masculinity. In contrast, antis tended to remain com-

mitted to manliness. On independence in the Jacksonian era, see Pugh, *Sons of Liberty*, xvii; on the antis' great concern for independence, see Rotundo, *American Manhood*, 236.

24. Gillett, *George Frisbie Hoar*, 12, 295; Hoar, "Love of Country," *Book of Patriotism*, xiv; on Hale, see Gillett, *George Frisbie Hoar*, 90; Hoar, *Autobiography* 2:441.

25. Hoar, "American Citizenship," 31, 32.

26. Hoar, remarks in *Celebration of the . . . Naming of Worcester*, 59; Hoar, "Oration at the Celebration of the Founding of the Northwest," 35; on horrors of war, see Gillett, *George Frisbie Hoar*, 203.

27. Hoar cited in Gillett, *George Frisbie Hoar*, 232. Welch attributes Hoar's avoidance of military service to his professional and family obligations, *George Frisbie Hoar*, 14.

28. On character and household, see Hoar, "American Citizenship," 13, 35; on Washington, see Hoar, *The Character of Washington*, 29.

29. On refined taste, see Hoar, "An Address Delivered . . . at Amherst College," 11, 23; on strenuous life, see Hoar, *Conditions of Success*, 5. Later Hoar made amends to Roosevelt, who took the speech as a personal affront, George F. Hoar to Theodore Roosevelt, Dec. 11, 1900, George F. Hoar Autograph collection, MHS.

30. On heroism and patriotism, see Hoar, "Love of Country," *Book of Patriotism*, xvii. On Hoar's support of women's suffrage, see Welch, *George Frisbie Hoar*, 29–30. Rotundo notes that as the nineteenth century wore on, New Englanders became more obsessed with gender than they had been earlier, *American Manhood*, 10. On fire-building, see Hoar, *A Boy Sixty Years Ago*, 8; on inscription, see Gillett, *George Frisbie Hoar*, 91.

31. On walks, see Hoar, *A Boy Sixty Years Ago*, 33; on petition, see Gillett, *George Frisbie Hoar*, 171; on soul, see Rogers, "Characteristics of Senator Hoar," 608.

32. On party affiliations, see "Death of Senator George F. Hoar," 155. The greatest events, said Hoar, were not the heroic achievements of war but the advancement of liberty through such documents as the Declaration of Independence, the Constitution, and the Emancipation Proclamation, Hoar, "Oration at the Celebration . . . of the Founding of the Northwest," 6; on eternal memory, see Hoar, "The Lust of Empire," 21.

33. On brute rule, see Edward Atkinson to Mr. Youmans, Sept. 6, 1898, Letterbook, April 26–Sept. 8, 1898, Edward Atkinson Papers, MHS; on Hoar's health, see Hoar, "The Lust of Empire," 3; Hoar, *Autobiography* 2:231. Hoar died in 1904. On deliberate reflection, see Hoar, *Autobiography* 1:196; on Hoar's reserve, see Gillett, *George Frisbie Hoar*, 90; on his preference for sober discussion, see Hoar, "Justice and Humanity," 3.

34. Hoar, "The Lust of Empire," Senate speech of April 17, 1900, 133.

35. On period of infancy, see George F. Hoar, speech, folder: "Twentieth Century Club, Dec. 20, 1901," George F. Hoar Papers, MHS; on baby, see Hoar, "The Lust of Empire," 132; on fellow antis, see Schurz, "The Policy of Imperialism" (1899), *Speeches* 6:108; Swift, *Imperialism and Liberty*, 324.

36. J. T. Sunderland, "How to Make our Country Great and Glorious," Feb. 1899, folder: A Pacific Coast Pulpit, 1899, box 30, Jabez T. Sunderland Papers, UMBL; "Civilization vs. Barbarism," *The Anti-Imperialist* 1, July 4, 1899, 45; James, "Governor Roosevelt's Oration" (1899), *Essays, Comments, and Reviews*, 163. Townsend notes that Roosevelt had been James's student at Harvard, *Manhood at Harvard*, 244. On older, more disdainful views of boyhood, see Rotundo, *American Manhood*, 20–22.

37. Sen. George Turner, *CR* 33, pt. 2, Jan. 23, 1900, 1054; Sen. Benjamin R. Tillman,

CR 33, pt. 2, Jan. 29, 1900, 1261; Sen. George F. Hoar, *CR* 35, pt. 2, Feb. 11, 1902, 1586; Sen. Henry M. Teller, *CR* 33, pt. 7, June 4, 1900, 6510.

38. Sen. Edward W. Carmack, *CR* 35, pt. 5, April 25, 1902, 4673; Lincoln Republican Booklet no. 1, "To the Soldiers of our Civil War," 1900, folder, Printed Matter: Pamphlets on Philippines and Anti-Imperialism, box 18, William A. Croffut Papers, LC; George F. Hoar, untitled speech of March 7, 1902, George F. Hoar Papers, MHS.

39. On statesmen, see John W. Hoyt to George F. Hoar, Nov. 2, 1898; on cool headed, see A. H. Hodgson to George F. Hoar, April 16, 1898; on Lincoln stamp, see Paul Kefer to George F. Hoar, Jan. 9, 1899, all in George F. Hoar Papers, MHS; "Senator Hoar's Warning," clipping from *The Republic,* Boston, Jan. 14, 1899, scrapbook 24, Personal, 1897–1902, George F. Hoar Papers, MHS.

40. On lovers of liberty and doctrine of fathers, see Sen. George F. Hoar, *CR* 32, pt. 1, Jan. 9, 1899, 494; on roll call, see Hoar, "The Lust of Empire," 137; on pure manhood, see George F. Hoar, Senate Speech of Jan. 9, 1899, "On the Constitutionality," George F. Hoar Papers, MHS; on character and example, see George F. Hoar, "Our Duty to the Philippines," 17–18. That antis regarded the fathers as model men can be seen in another anti's appeal to the fathers to "restore your weakened descendants to pristine manhood!" Swift, *Imperialism and Liberty,* 281. As part of their effort to ally themselves with the fathers, the leaders of the Anti-Imperialist League appointed committees of correspondence, Erving Winslow, "The Anti-Imperialist League," *American Anti-Imperialism,* Markowitz, ed., 29. Other antis regarded themselves as the heirs of a more recent group of fathers, the mid-nineteenth-century abolitionists, see Edward Atkinson to Rev. Samuel May, May 3, 1899, Letterbook Jan. 10, 1899–May 18, 1899, Edward Atkinson Papers, MHS; Brown, *George Sewall Boutwell,* 113.

41. Hoar, *A Boy Sixty Years Ago,* 17; Fischer, *Growing Old,* 30, 78, 91; Hoar, *Old Age,* 9.

42. Hoar, "The Lust of Empire," 139.

43. Hoar, "A Question of Conscience," 10; on ancestors and insult to his father, see Hoar, *Autobiography* 1:7–9, 360.

44. On doctrines of fathers, see Hoar, "Letter from the Hon. George F. Hoar," 13. See also Sen. William E. Mason, *CR* 32, pt. 1, Jan. 10, 1899, 528; John H. Marble, "The United States and the Philippines," *Arena* 22, Nov. 1899, 554–70, 566. Rep. John C. Bell, *CR* 32, pt. 2, Feb. 20, 1899, 2114.

45. On nursery rhymes, see Schurz, "The Issue of Imperialism" (1899), *Speeches* 6:30; Rep. Robert W. Miers, *CR* 34, pt. 3, Feb. 9, 1901, 2217. When imperialists insisted that they were following the fathers, antis sometimes accused them of following false fathers, "the fathers of trusts and the kings of monarchical political machines," Swift, *Imperialism and Liberty,* 196; Sen. George F. Hoar, *CR* 32, pt. 1, Jan. 9, 1899, 494.

46. Rep. Edward W. Carmack, *CR* 32, pt. 1, Jan. 12, 1899, 612.

47. On views of adolescents, see Kett, *Rites of Passage,* 173; on primitive passion, see Smith, *Commonwealth or Empire,* 33; on racial thought, see Russett, *Sexual Science,* 50–54; G. Stanley Hall, "Universities and the Training of Professors," *Forum* 17, May 1894, 297–309; John W. Dodge, "Boys and Civilization," *Pennsylvania School Journal* 20, Dec. 1871, 176–77, 176. On might makes right, see Rep. James A. Norton, *CR* 35, pt. 4, March 27, 1902, 3349. See also Rotundo, *American Manhood,* 31, 256.

48. Sen. George F. Hoar, *CR* 32, pt. 1, Jan. 9, 1899, 494; Rep. Edward W. Carmack, *CR* 32, pt. 1, Jan. 12, 1899, 612. Even younger anti-imperialists adopted these age-based ar-

guments. William Jennings Bryan said that a young man upon reaching his majority could disregard his parents' teachings. But eventually he would pay for his misdeeds. "And so with the nation," he said, hoping to portray imperial policies as a kind of adolescent transgression, "Imperialism," speech of Aug. 8, 1900, folder, Printed Matter, box 18, William A. Croffut Papers, LC. Rep. Thomas Spight, CR 33, pt. 3, Feb. 22, 1900, 2105.

49. L. C. Manchester to George F. Hoar, Nov. 3, 1898, George F. Hoar Papers, MHS. Antis excoriated the imperialists for dismissing both them and the founding fathers as "old fogies." On imperialists viewing the fathers as old fogies, see Sen. Benjamin R. Tillman, CR 33, pt. 2, Jan. 29, 1900, 1256; on imperialists viewing the antis as old fogies, see Rep. James Cooney, CR 33, pt. 2, Jan. 31, 1900, 1351.

50. On Hoar's belief that newcomers should keep silent, see Hoar, Autobiography 1:205; on old man of ninety, see George F. Hoar to George S. Boutwell, May 1, 1899, George F. Hoar Autograph collection, MHS.

51. John Clark Ridpath, "The Republic and the Empire," Arena 20, Sept. 1898, 344–63, 358. See also Storey, "Is It Right?" 13; Rep. Thomas J. Selby, CR 35, pt. 1, Jan. 22, 1902, 885.

52. Joseph Wheeler, "Tranquilizing the Philippines," Independent 52, Dec. 20, 1900, 3043–44, 3044; Sen. William M. Stewart, CR 33, pt. 7, June 2, 1900, 6470.

53. Lodge and Roosevelt, Hero Tales, 12. In another article, Roosevelt praised Andrew Jackson's "physical prowess and hot courage," noting that they "rendered him a most redoubtable foe," Roosevelt, "Andrew Jackson" (1891), The Rough Riders, 196. Roosevelt, "The Strenuous Life" (1899), American Ideals, 321. On flabbiness, see Roosevelt, "Manhood and Statehood" (1901), American Ideals, 458.

54. Levere, Imperial America, 4, 50–51; Roosevelt, "The Philippine Problem," World's Work 4, July 1902, 2344–48, 2346; William McKinley, "The North West and the Middle West in Foreign Trade," speech, April 17, 1901, reel 85, William McKinley Papers, LC.

55. William McKinley, Inaugural Address, March 4, 1901, reel 84, William McKinley Papers, LC. "Has the republic lost any of its virility?" questioned McKinley in part of a speech in favor of keeping the Philippines, "Speech at the Citizens' Banquet, Chicago" (1899), Speeches and Addresses, 245. Roosevelt, "Grant" (1900), American Ideals, 430–41, 440. "Will you say by your vote that American ability to govern has decayed?" questioned Beveridge, "The March of the Flag" (1898), The Meaning of the Times, 49; on the revolutionary generation worrying about degenerate sons, see Watts, The Republic Reborn, 164, 168–69.

56. Rep. Galusha A. Grow, CR 33, pt. 1, Dec. 19, 1899, 588; Rep. Jonathan P. Dolliver, CR 33, pt. 3, Feb. 27, 1900, 2350; James A. Tawney, speech of July 1900, folder: speeches, April 1900–1901, box 6, James A. Tawney Papers, MNHS.

57. On nerveless, see Rep. Jonathan P. Dolliver, CR 32, pt. 1, Jan. 25, 1899, 1030; on founders, see William McKinley to Henry Cabot Lodge, Sept. 8, 1900, folder "McKinley's Acceptance of Nomination for President, 1900," box 16, Henry Cabot Lodge Papers, MHS. See also Roosevelt, "The Strenuous Life" (1899), American Ideals, 323; on neurasthenia, see Lutz, American Nervousness, 2, 6, 35. Roosevelt cited in Rystad, Ambiguous Imperialism, 56.

58. "Senator Hoar Goes Astray on the Philippine Question," Chicago Tribune, Nov. 4, 1898.

59. Roosevelt, "The Strenuous Life" (1899), American Ideals, 328–29; Roosevelt,

"Address at the Centennial Meeting of the Board of Home Missions of the Presbyterian Church" (1902), *Presidential Addresses,* 46.

60. On old women with trousers, see Spencer Borden to William McKinley, Jan. 3, 1899, reel 5, William McKinley Papers, LC; on squaw men, see George F. Hoar, "Our Duty to the Philippines," *Independent,* Nov. 9, 1899, pamphlets, George F. Hoar Papers, MHS; on the old lady element, see John F. Simmons to John Davis Long, August 1, 1898, Box 44, John Davis Long Papers, MHS; on nagging wife, see Taft, "Letters Regarding McKinley's War," 7; on women as the sharpest counterpoint to men, see Rotundo, *American Manhood,* 22.

61. On Granny Hoar, see John Zimmerman to Albert J. Beveridge, Jan. 11, 1900, folder, Response to Philippine Speech, 1900, box 127, Albert J. Beveridge Papers, LC; *Judge* 37, July 8, 1899, 108; on archetype, see "A Friend" to George F. Hoar, April 18, 1900, George F. Hoar Papers, MHS; on father of the Senate, see clipping from the *Philadelphia Public Ledger,* Jan. 11, 1899, Personal scrapbook 24, p. 20, George F. Hoar Papers, MHS.

62. "The Boston Mugwumps Exercised," *Chicago Tribune,* Nov. 21, 1898; on shrieking, see Theodore Roosevelt to Henry Cabot Lodge, Oct. 20, 1899, box 3, Henry Cabot Lodge III Papers, MHS; Henry Cabot Lodge to Samuel L. Parrish, Nov. 20, 1899, Letterbook 42, Henry Cabot Lodge Papers, MHS; on hysterical rancor, see Sen. Jonathan P. Dolliver, *CR* 35, pt. 6, May 19, 1902, 5622; on women as especially prone to hysteria, see G. T. W. Patrick, "The Psychology of Woman," *ROR* 12, July 1895, 83.

63. On women and anti-imperialism, see Papachristou, "American Women and Foreign Policy," 499–501; Schirmer, *Republic or Empire,* 18, 75, 149. Wrote one mother to McKinley, "We who are the mothers of the South Dakota boys, feel that we have a right to be heard for the sons we love. . . . My boy is the light of my life . . . and I can't know him liable to be shot down by savages—or killed by disease thousands of miles from home, when I feel in my heart—he is fully entitled to be at home," Antoinette Smith to William McKinley, June 15, 1898, reel 7, William McKinley Papers, LC; on noble-hearted ladies, see Haskins, "Report of the Second Annual Meeting of the New England Anti-Imperialist League," n.p.

64. Herbert Welsh to Isabella Beecher Hooker, November 6, 1899, letterbook June 1899–Feb. 1900, Herbert Welsh Collection, HSP; Edward Atkinson to William Fowler, Jan. 10, 1899, Letterbook Jan. 10, 1899–May 18, 1899, Edward Atkinson Papers, MHS; Clipping "The Speech of Moorfield Storey," Aug. 17, 1899, scrapbook, vol. 2, 1896–99, box 6, Moorfield Storey Papers, LC; on homes, see George F. Hoar, "Senator Hoar's Speech," *World's Work* 4, July 1902, 2348–50, 2348. Schirmer notes that the Anti-Imperialist League had no elected women leaders, *Republic or Empire,* 18. The antis' argument that imperial decisions should be made in the home was not tantamount to supporting women's suffrage. Some vocal antis, including William Jennings Bryan, Thomas Reed, James R. Mann, George F. Hoar, and Edward Atkinson, did support women's suffrage. But other leading antis like Carl Schurz, David Starr Jordan, Benjamin Tillman, and Moorfield Storey opposed it, Benjamin, *A History of the Anti-Suffrage Movement,* 61, 63. The point is not so much one of attitudes toward women's suffrage but rather, the more fundamental issue: should women participate in this political debate? On citizens, see Hoar, "Letter from the Hon. George F. Hoar," 9.

65. On patriotic men and women, see Herron, "American Imperialism: An Address," 1; on execration, see Edward Atkinson, "The Hell of War and its Penalties," *The Anti-Imperialist* 1, June 3, 1899, 18–19; Edward Atkinson to President McKinley, Nov. 14, 1898, Letterbook

Sept. 8, 1898–Jan. 10, 1899, Edward Atkinson Papers, MHS. Rep. William E. Mason, *CR* 32, pt. 1, Jan. 10, 1899, 533.

66. Hannah J. Bailey, "Gleanings," undated pamphlet, reel 69.2, Hannah Johnston Bailey Collection, SCPC.

Chapter 8. Imperial Degeneracy: The Dissolution of the Imperialist Impulse

1. As May argues, "Not only did the American government make no efforts after 1900 to acquire new islands in the Caribbean or Pacific, it deliberately spurned opportunities to do so. Theodore Roosevelt rebuffed Haitians and Dominicans who dropped proannexation hints, and during nearly eight years as President he acquired only one piece of real estate—the ten-mile wide Canal Zone in Panama. Though one may cite the Platt Amendment, as applied to Cuba, the acquisition of the Canal Zone, and the Roosevelt Corollary to the Monroe Doctrine as evidence that the United States still had a mild case of imperialism, the nation's expansion as a colonial power effectively came to an end as of 1899 or 1900," *American Imperialism*, 14. This is not to deny the importance of the nation's informal empire in the early twentieth century but to say that conquest no longer seemed desirable as an end in itself. Weston attributes the lack of tenacity in American imperialism, in large part, to racism, *Racism in U.S. Imperialism*, xiii. This chapter argues that concerns about American men were just as important as perceptions of the Filipinos in undercutting the imperialist impulse.

2. Sen. Charles A. Towne, *CR* 34, pt. 2, Jan. 28, 1901, 1555. Anderson finds that the initial concerns about tropical degeneracy had declined by 1914, "'Where Every Prospect Pleases,'" 83, 91, 95. For this chapter, I looked at the speeches and writings of anti-imperialists who were in Congress and of those whose activism and arguments seem likely to have come to political leaders' attention. In using the term *anti-imperialists*, I do not mean to suggest that all had exactly the same views on empire, but I do think they followed certain patterns in their manipulation of gender in the Philippine debate.

3. Kidd, *The Control of the Tropics*, 50.

4. On turn-of-the-century medical understandings of tropical diseases, see Anderson, "'Where Every Prospect Pleases,'" 86, 89. On colony of lepers, see Richard F. Pettigrew to Mr. Jonas H. Lien, July 4, 1898, Richard F. Pettigrew Papers, reel 21, PM; on disease-ridden islands, see Sen. William B. Bate, *CR* 32, pt. 3, Feb. 27, 1899, 2439; on invalids, see Boyd, ed., *Men and Issues of 1900*, 218. U.S. soldiers did, in fact, contract a variety of diseases, Linn, *The U.S. Army and Counterinsurgency*, 129; on the cholera epidemic of 1902 that U.S. troops helped spread, see Ileto, "Cholera and the Origins of the American Sanitary Order," 53–54; on ghastly effects, see Leonidas, *Private Smith*, 215; on wrecked, see Rev. Henry C. Potter, cited in "The Moral and Religious Aspects of the So-Called Imperial Policy," n.p. "Uncle Sam Before and After his Wish for Expansion," "Expensive Expansion," n.p.

5. Brewer, "The Spanish War," 33; Rawlins cited in *Affairs in the Philippine Islands* 1:343; Jordan, "The Question of the Philippines," 24. On abolitionists, see Walters, *The Antislavery Appeal*, 64–66; Hoganson, "Garrisonian Abolitionists," 582–85; on medical opinion on the implications of a tropical climate for white people, see Anderson, "'Where Every Prospect Pleases,'" 86–89; on early-twentieth-century fears of neurasthenia, see Kennedy "The Perils of the Midday Sun," 121–24; Anderson, "The Trespass Speaks," 1343–55.

6. Jordan, *The Blood of the Nation*, 11, 18, 21, 49, 62, 80. On Jordan's training, see Jordan, *The Days of a Man* 1:101.

7. George S. Boutwell, "A Slaveholder's Title and its Enforcement by the Administration and the Army," speech, ca. 1900, George S. Boutwell II Papers, MHS. Said Sen. George F. Hoar, "If you try to deprive even a savage or a barbarian of his just rights you can never do it without becoming a savage or a barbarian yourself," *CR* 35, pt. 6, May 22, 1902, 5791; on Lamarckian thought, see Russett, *Darwin in America*, 10, 92.

8. Sen. George L. Wellington, *CR* 35, pt. 6, May 21, 1902, 5723.

9. Taft cited in *Affairs in the Philippine Islands* 1:77–78; on Aguinaldo, see Sarkesian, *America's Forgotten Wars*, 37, 51, 168; Gates, *Schoolbooks and Krags*, 96; on American atrocities, see Brands, *Bound to Empire*, 57; Gates, *Schoolbooks and Krags*, 188, 259; Linn, *The U.S. Army and Counterinsurgency*, 27, 60, 114, 145, 154; Linn, "The Struggle for Samar," 166; May, *Battle for Batangas*, 147, 149, 242; *Affairs in the Philippine Islands* 1:75, 2:903, 1529, 3:1975, 2577–80, 2586, 2753; Herbert Welsh, "An Address to the People of the United States, Relative to the Use of Torture and Uncivilized Methods of Warfare in the Persecution of the Philippine Campaign," folder, Philippines, box 1892–1902, Herbert Welsh Collection, HSP; [Storey], "'Marked Severities,'" 65.

10. Linn, "The Struggle for Samar," 172; Miller, *"Benevolent Assimilation,"* 88, 129, 212, 220, 222, 228, 232, 236; Schott, *The Ordeal of Samar*, 136, 141; Gates, *Schoolbooks and Krags*, 254–55; Schirmer, *Republic or Empire*, 232, 236.

11. Rep. Joseph C. Sibley, *CR* 35, pt. 5, April 28, 1902, 4770; Sen. Joseph L. Rawlins, *CR* 35, pt. 5, May 5, 1902, 5051; Rep. Thomas J. Selby, *CR* 35, pt. 1, Jan. 22, 1902, 881.

12. Pettigrew, *The Course of Empire*, 297; Sen. George L. Wellington, *CR* 35, pt. 2, Feb. 18, 1902, 1856; Rep. Malcolm R. Patterson, *CR* 35, pt. 7, June 23, 1902, 7118; Rep. David A. De Armond, *CR* 35, pt. 7, June 23, 1902, 7242. On virtue of wives, see Rep. Malcolm R. Patterson, *CR* 35, pt. 6, May 27, 1902, 5956; on home-loving people, see Albert G. Robinson, "Roosevelt and the Filipinos," *The Anti-Imperialist* 1, Oct. 1, 1900, 35. Sen. George F. Hoar, *CR* 35, pt. 1, Jan. 14, 1902, 649; on church desecrations, see Wolff, *Little Brown Brother*, 254.

13. Storey, "What Shall We Do with our Dependencies?" 19; Brewer, "The Spanish War," 21; on saloons, see also A.G.R., "Dull Days in Manila," *Evening Post*, Sept. 21, 1899, in scrapbook, The Philippines, 1899, box 246, John Basset Moore Papers, LC.

14. "Why We Cannot Conquer the Filipinos," *Nation* 69, Aug. 24, 1899, 144. "Where is the glory when a great stalwart giant kicks a helpless child into the gutter?" questioned Rep. George W. Faris, *CR* 32, pt. 3, Feb. 27, 1899, 2500.

15. On puny child, see Sen. George Turner, *CR* 33, pt. 2, Jan. 23, 1900, 1056; on bowels, see Sen. George Turner, *CR* 35, pt. 5, May 6, 1902, 5083; on tyranny, see Sen. John L. McLaurin, *CR* 35, pt. 6, May 16, 1902, 5542.

16. "Expansion and Imperialism," *Journal of the Knights of Labor*, Oct. 1900; Schurz, "For American Principles," n.p.; Sen. Edward W. Carmack, *CR* 35, pt. 5, April 25, 1902, 4669; see also Sen. Donelson Caffery, *CR* 33, pt. 2, Feb. 6, 1900, 1537. If, on the one hand, antis argued that the supposed "marriage" was an act of violence against feminine Filipinos, on the other, they maintained that even Filipina consent did not justify such a bad match. "If we have rescued those unfortunate daughters of Spain, the colonies, from the tyranny of their cruel father, I deny that we are therefore in honor bound to marry any one of the girls, or to take them all into our household, where they may disturb and demoralize our whole

family," wrote Carl Schurz, "The Issue of Imperialism" (1899), *Speeches* 6:32. On lust of empire, see Sen. John C. Spooner, *CR* 33, pt. 7, May 22, 1900, 5844; on the lechery of world conquest, see "A Friend" to George F. Hoar, April 18, 1900, George F. Hoar Papers, MHS; on drunk with the lust of empire, see Sen. George F. Hoar, *CR* 33, pt. 5, April 17, 1900, 4306; on delirious with the lust of conquest, see Sen. George F. Hoar, *CR* 35, pt. 6, May 22, 1902, 5789.

17. On young girls, see Thomas J. Patterson cited in "Mass Meetings of Protest Against the Suppression of Truth about the Philippines"; see also Miller, *"Benevolent Assimilation,"* 200. On raising up a new race, see Robert E. Austill to Herbert Welsh, June 17, 1902, correspondence, box A, Herbert Welsh Collection, HSP. Peter MacQueen to Edward Carmack, May 6, 1902, folder May-June 1902, box 2, Edward Ward Carmack Papers, Southern Historical Collection, UNC. For an account of gang rape, see "Statement of Fred F. Newell," folder Philippines, 1899, box 1892–1902, Herbert Welsh Collection, HSP.

18. Foreman, "Will the United States Withdraw?" 9; William Lloyd Garrison, "Indictment by Mr. Garrison," *The Anti-Imperialist* 1, Oct. 1, 1900, 37; Dr. Arthur L. Parker, statement ca. 1902, folder, Philippines, 1900, box 1892–1902, Herbert Welsh Collection, HSP. On inspections, see *Affairs in the Philippine Islands* 1:403, 514–15, 2:1747–48, 1854, 1859–61, 1869; Gates, *Schoolbooks and Krags*, 58. Sexton writes that right after the U.S. occupation of the Philippines, 25 percent of the men on sick report suffered from venereal disease, *Soldiers in the Sun*, 57.

19. On sodomy, see "Statement of Fred F. Newell," folder, Philippines, box 1892–1902, Herbert Welsh Collection, HSP; on describing homosexuals as "degenerate," see Rotundo, *American Manhood*, 275; on the male prostitute, see Swift, *Imperialism and Liberty*, 208–09.

20. Swift, *Imperialism and Liberty*, 207–08; George S. Boutwell speech, Oct. 24, 1902, George S. Boutwell II Papers, MHS. On syphilis-induced insanity, see Brandt, *No Magic Bullet*, 9.

21. On family poison, see Brandt, *No Magic Bullet*, 9–11. On dread, see Edward Atkinson to Mr. Gilman, Nov. 7, 1898; on the greatest danger, see Edward Atkinson to President McKinley, Nov. 14, 1898, both in Letterbook Sept. 8, 1898–Jan. 10, 1899, Edward Atkinson Papers, MHS. Sen. Henry M. Teller, *CR* 35, pt. 2, Feb. 11, 1902, 1576; on syphilis in Britain, see Richard F. Pettigrew to Mr. F. W. Cox, Jan. 25, 1899, Richard F. Pettigrew Papers, PM.

22. Pettigrew, *The Course of Empire*, 181; Swift, *Imperialism and Liberty*, 480; see also Weston, *Racism in U.S. Imperialism*, 97; on American household, see Benjamin F. Trueblood to George F. Hoar, Nov. 2, 1898, George F. Hoar Papers, MHS.

23. William Lloyd Garrison, "Indictment by Mr. Garrison," *The Anti-Imperialist* 1, Oct. 1, 1900, 39; Edward Atkinson to Lawrence E. Sexton, Dec. 23, 1898, Letterbook, Sept. 8, 1898–Jan. 10, 1899, Edward Atkinson Papers, MHS; on social purity, see Bordin, *Woman and Temperance*, 3; on Indian campaign, see Pivar, *Purity Crusade*, 166, 218–19; "Proposed Reintroduction of the C.D. Acts in India," *Union Signal* 23, April 29, 1897, 8.

24. On home boys, see Susanna Fry, "Vice in the Philippine and other Islands, and Our Duty to our New Possessions," *Union Signal* 27, Sept. 5, 1901, 3; on brutalizing conditions, see "The Home vs. Militarism," *Union Signal* 26, March 8, 1900, 8; on debauched, see Ella M. Thacher, "The Philippines," *Union Signal* 27, Nov. 28, 1901, 10. LMS, "Against Territorial Expansion," *WJ* 29, Sept. 10, 1898, 296.

25. On lobbying efforts, see "The Philippines," *Union Signal* 27, Nov. 28, 1901, 10; Cornelia C. Moots, "A Plea from Manila," *Union Signal* 26, Aug. 30, 1900, 6; on frowzy natives, see Lester Hazlett, cited in *Affairs in the Philippine Islands* 2:1736–38. Margaret Dye Ellis cited by Sen. Benjamin R. Tillman, *CR* 35, pt. 3, Feb. 22, 1902, 2081, 2084–85; Rachel Aldrich Bailey, "War and Its Effects on Woman," "Report of the Seventeenth Annual Convention of the Michigan Equal Suffrage Association," 1901, folder 5: Michigan Equal Suffrage Association Reports, box 1, Alde L. T. Blake Papers, SL; Anthony cited in Harper, *The Life and Work of Susan B. Anthony* 3:1238.

26. Rep. John S. Williams, *CR* 35, pt. 7, June 24, 1902, 7331. Sen. Benjamin R. Tillman also played on women's concerns by claiming that the United States was waging war on women and children, *CR* 35, pt. 1, Jan. 27, 1902, 1005. On American women in the Philippines, see Moses, *Unofficial Letters of an Official's Wife*, esp. 61, 125, 158, 269; Russel, *A Woman's Journey through the Philippines*, esp. 40, 134; Jenks, *Death Stalks the Philippine Wilds*, 3, 16, 153; Condict, *Old Glory and the Gospel in the Philippines*, 35, 81, 117; May, *Social Engineering in the Philippines*, 85; Bowe, *With the 13th Minnesota in the Philippines*, 116; Rafael, "Colonial Domesticity," 639–66. Tyrrell argues that WCTU members regarded Western imperialism as conducive to their reforms, *Woman's World, Woman's Empire*, 148, 220. Similarly, Brumberg argues that American women's concern for "heathen" women led them to view imperialism favorably, "Zenanas and Girlless Villages," 371. Despite their concern for intemperance and prostitution in the British empire, late-nineteenth-century American women often applauded the British for protecting and elevating colonized women, see Miss Armstrong, "Report," in *Third Biennial of the General Federation of Women's Clubs*, 129.

27. On starvation and exposure, see Rep. Joseph A. Conry, *CR* 35, pt. 7, June 21, 1902, 7174; on torturing women, see Herbert Welsh, "An Address to the People of the United States, Relative to the Use of Torture and Uncivilized Methods of Warfare in the Persecution of the Philippine Campaign," folder, Philippines, box 1892–1902, Herbert Welsh Collection, HSP; on crippled women, see *Affairs in the Philippine Islands*, 3:2239; on attacking women, see Jordan, *Imperial Democracy*, 69; on spoils of war, see Foster, *William McKinley and the G.O.P.*, 276.

28. Rep. John W. Gaines, *CR* 35, pt. 8, Jan. 13, 1902, 91; Jordan, *Imperial Democracy*, 97. Mother Hubbards were associated with prostitutes, Blanchard, "Boundaries and the Victorian Body," 26, 31; on imperialists' doubts that white women could live in the tropics, see White, *Our New Possessions*, 163; *Affairs in the Philippine Islands* 1:391; Anderson, "'Where Every Prospect Pleases,'" 86.

29. Sen. Richard F. Pettigrew, *CR* 34, pt. 2, Jan. 31, 1901, 1715; on prizefighters and reports of carnage, see Smith, *Commonwealth or Empire*, 20, 25; on the barbaric instinct, see Jane Addams cited in "The Chicago Liberty Meeting," 39; see also Sen. Augustus O. Bacon, *CR* 32, pt. 1, Jan. 18, 1899, 734. "Militarism and Public Morals," clipping from *Scribner's Magazine*, in scrapbook of William Lloyd Garrison, Jr., "Anti-Imperialism," vol. 8, 1899–1901, Garrison Family Papers, SSC.

30. On polygamous beast, see Sen. Edward W. Carmack, *CR* 35, pt. 2, Feb. 3, 1902, 1239; on sacred names and shame, see Foster, *William McKinley and the G.O.P.*, 279. Henry B. Blackwell, "Manlier Men—More Womanly Women," *WJ* 30, Sept. 14, 1901, 292. Similarly, G. B. Stebbins warned that "ignorant, prejudiced, even barbarous" new citizens or

subjects in the islands would oppose women's equality, "Imperialism a Hindrance to Woman Suffrage," *WJ* 30, Feb. 4, 1899, 34.

31. On the Boers, see Rep. John J. Lentz, *CR* 33, pt. 8, March 27, 1900, 187; on the Spaniards, see Smith, *Commonwealth or Empire,* 79. On the push to bring soldiers home in the spring of 1899 and the growing discontent with the war, see Schirmer, *Republic or Empire,* 149–51, 172–73; Thomson, Stanley, and Perry argue that after the election of 1900 a "mood of apathy and disenchantment" over imperial policies took hold, *Sentimental Imperialists,* 115. Although he cites different causes (party politics and the monetary costs of empire), Rystad agrees that imperial policies lost public support, *Ambiguous Imperialism,* 23, 167.

32. Moorfield Storey, "Nothing to Excuse our Intervention," *Advocate of Peace* 60, May 1898, 112, folder Printed Matter, 1891–1900, box 8, Moorfield Storey Papers, LC; Jordan, "Imperial Democracy," 15.

33. Rep. Claude A. Swanson, *CR* 32, pt. 1, Jan. 6, 1899, 451; Anna Howard Shaw, "The White Man's Burden," Oct. 1899, folder 426, Anna Howard Shaw Papers, Women's Studies Manuscript Collections, reel 16, SL. Said Senator Hoar, "A nation is made up of human homes, and the glory of a nation and the value of its possessions are in its humble homes. I do not agree with the Senator who thinks that a home is made better by the loss of its boys or the crippling for life of its head," "Justice and Humanity," 5.

34. Stanton, diary entry of Sept. 30, 1899, *Elizabeth Cady Stanton,* Stanton and Blatch, eds., 2:341; Hall, *Julia Ward Howe,* 148–49. NAWSA, "Reply of the National Officers," n.p.; Alice D. Le Plongeon, "A Thought on Government," *Woman's Tribune* 16, Jan. 14, 1899, 4; A.S.B. [Alice Stone Blackwell], *WJ* 29, June 18, 1898, 193; Carrie Chapman Catt, "Annual Address," *WJ* 32, June 8, 1901, 177–78. See also Garrison, "The Nature of a Republican Form of Government," n.p.; Elnora Monroe Babcock, "Why Cannot Women Vote?" *A True Republic,* Feb. 1902, 32; Craig, "Lucia True Ames Mead," 75; Elshtain, "Women as Mirror and Other," 41; Alonso mentions that many women's rights activists believed that women could attain equality only in a nonmilitaristic world, *Peace as a Women's Issue,* 20.

35. Ellen Martin Henrotin, "The Home and the Economic Waste of War," ca. 1905, folder 12, box 1, Ellen Martin Henrotin Papers, SL; Papachristou, "American Women and Foreign Policy," 502–03. I think that the association between feminine values and civilized progress was widespread even outside of suffrage circles—that some late-nineteenth-century men tried to associate civilization with manliness in order to counter this conventional wisdom. On gendering civilization as male, see Bederman, *Manliness and Civilization.*

36. Rep. John S. Williams, *CR* 35, pt. 7, June 24, 1902, 7333; "Civilization vs. Barbarism," *Nation* 68, June 1, 1899, 410–11. Antis did not deplore strenuosity per se, they just objected to its militarist incarnation, Jordan, *The Call of the Twentieth Century,* 3; Townsend, *Manhood at Harvard,* 244–45.

37. Swift, *Imperialism and Liberty,* 3; William Lloyd Garrison quoted in "Garrison's Fiery Peace Speech," clipping, 1899, Scrapbook, "Peace and War, Anti-Imperialism, The Philippines and Spanish War," Garrison Family Papers, SSC.

38. On military scourge, see Urbain Gohier, "The Danger of Militarism," *Independent* 52, Jan. 25, 1900, 233–36, 233–34. Ernest Howard Crosby, "The Military Idea of Manliness," *Independent* 53, April 18, 1901, 873–75, 874; Ernest H. Crosby, "Thinking and Obeying," printed in "The Hell of War and its Penalties," *The Anti-Imperialist* 1, July 4, 1899, 39.

39. On freedom of opinion, see Chief Justice Story, cited in Gookin, "A Liberty Cate-chism," n.p.; Schurz, "Militarism and Democracy" (1899), *Speeches* 6:74; said David Starr Jordan, "To let blood for blood's sake is bad in politics as it is in medicine. War is killing, bru-tal, barbarous killing, and its direct effects are mostly evil. The glory of war turns our atten-tion from civic affairs. Neglect invites corruption," "'Lest We Forget,'" 11.

40. Schurz, "For the Republic of Washington and Lincoln" (1900), *Speeches* 6:235; on the glory of the republic, see Jordan, *Imperial Democracy*, 41–42; on self-governing man-hood, see Jordan, "'Lest We Forget,'" 32.

41. Charles F. Adams to Moorfield Storey, Feb. 24, 1902, Storey/C. F. Adams Corre-spondence, Moorfield Storey Papers, MHS; Sen. Edward W. Carmack, *CR* 35, pt. 5, April 25, 1902, 4670–71; on man-factory, see Tolman, "Mr. McKinley's Declaration of War," n.p.; similarly, Justice David J. Brewer said that "government by the consent of the governed de-velops the best men," "The Spanish War," 18.

42. Adams, "Imperialism," 33; on British examples, see Morrison Swift, "Expansion, for the Sake of God, Love and Civilization," 1900, folder, Printed Matter: Pamphlets on Philippines and Anti-Imperialism; box 18, William A. Croffut Papers, LC; Hoar, "Letter from the Hon. George F. Hoar," 12. Schurman, *Philippine Affairs*, 99.

43. Walters, *The Antislavery Appeal*, 64–66; Laughlin, "Patriotism and Imperialism," 4; Jordan, *Imperial Democracy*, 9–10.

44. Jordan, "The Question of the Philippines," 58. On anti-imperialists' commitment to domestic reform, see Zimmerman, "Who Were the Anti-Imperialists?" 600; Cherry, "Anti-Imperialism on the Middle Border," 23.

45. In 1917, American troops routed about fifteen hundred Moros in Mindanao, Hur-ley, *Swish of the Kris*, 234; Gowing, *Mandate in Moroland*, 278. Filipino troops organized in the U.S.-run constabulary fought resistors until 1935, Sturtevant, *Popular Uprisings in the Philippines*, 232–42; Roth, *Muddy Glory*, 36. Linn writes that after 1913, there was an un-easy peace, "broken by endemic piracy, homicides, and tribal wars—but these were now the problems of the constabulary, and occasionally the Scouts. The army had established colonial authority," *Guardians of Empire*, 41–42. On disenchantment, see Thomson et al., *Sentimental Imperialists*, 115; Rystad, *Ambiguous Imperialism*, 23.

46. On softening of fibre, see Theodore Roosevelt to Whitelaw Reid, Sept. 11, 1905; on fighting qualities, see Theodore Roosevelt to General Hamilton, Jan. 24, 1906; on mar-shaling public opinion, see Theodore Roosevelt to William Howard Taft, Sept. 28, 1906; on spoiling for a fight, see Theodore Roosevelt to Edward Grey, Dec. 18, 1906, all in *Letters of Theodore Roosevelt* 5:19, 139, 432, 529. After Venezuela seized the property of some U.S. firms, Roosevelt pressed for intervention. But when it considered the matter in March 1908, the Senate refused to go along with his proposal, Hendrickson, "Roosevelt's Second Venezuelan Controversy," 486–87, 494–95; Healy, *Drive to Hegemony*, 134. Roosevelt also tempered his own commitment to empire, saying in 1904 that he wanted to annex Santo Domingo as much as a gorged boa constrictor wanted to swallow a porcupine wrong end to, Roosevelt cited in Langley, *The Banana Wars*, 30; on his desire to make men better, see Theodore Roosevelt to Joseph Lincoln Steffens, June 5, 1908, *The Letters of Theodore Roo-sevelt* 6:1052.

47. On Caribbean interventions, see Langley, *The United States and the Caribbean;* Langley, *The Banana Wars;* Nearing and Freeman, *Dollar Diplomacy;* Musicant, *The Ba-nana Wars;* Munro, *Intervention and Dollar Diplomacy in the Caribbean;* even the turn-of-

the-century U.S. intervention in China seems to have been motivated primarily by a desire to protect expatriots rather than by dreams of adventure, Young, *The Rhetoric of Empire*, 153–70; McCormick, *China Market*, 114.

Conclusion: Engendering War

1. As Cott has argued, we can no longer consider men the "*un*marked sex," "On Men's History," 206.

2. On nongovernmental contacts, see Hunter, *The Gospel of Gentility*; Hill, *The World Their Household*; Brumberg, "Zenanas and Girlless Villages"; Boyd, *Emissaries: The Overseas Work of the American YWCA*; Tyrrell, *Woman's World*; Enloe, *Bananas, Beaches, and Bases*. On extending international relations beyond "high politics" and paying attention to gender in international relations, see Whitworth, *Feminism and International Relations*, xi, 158; Tickner, *Gender in International Relations*, 126–27; Grant and Newland, eds., *Gender and International Relations*, 5; Foot, "Where are the Women?" 615–22; Rosenberg, "Explaining the History of American Foreign Relations: Gender," 116–24; Peterson, ed., *Gendered States*.

3. On gender and high politics, see Scott, "Gender: A Useful Category of Historical Analysis," 1070–73. Other studies that address traditional security issues with gender in mind include Cooke and Woollacott, eds., *Gendering War Talk*; Rotter, "Gender Relations, Foreign Relations"; Costigliola, "'Unceasing Pressure for Penetration'"; Mart, "Tough Guys and American Cold War Policy"; Doty, *Imperial Encounters*; Gullace, "Sexual Violence and Family Honor."

4. Iriye, "Culture and Power," 117, 121.

5. On British concerns about manhood, see MacDonald, *Sons of the Empire*, 8, 16; on youth groups, see Springhall, *Youth, Empire and Society*, 17; on imperialist novels which presented empire as something that turned men into heroes, see Green, *Dreams of Adventure*. See also Dawson, *Soldier Heroes*, 1, 146–48; Richards, ed., *Imperialism and Juvenile Literature*; Reader, "*At Duty's Call*," 27–28, 42; Mangan, *The Games Ethic and Imperialism*, 17. Price argues that concerns about competition from women made lower-middle-class male clerks more receptive to jingoism as a means of asserting their manhood, "Society, Status and Jingoism," 104. Field shows how the British linked empire to individual character. Although he does not elaborate on the gendered dimensions of Victorian understandings of character, his work is suggestive in this respect, *Toward a Programme of Imperial Life*, 27, 30, 77, 91–92; on imperial mothers, see Davin, "Imperialism and Motherhood," 12, 20, 56. The attention paid to gender concerns in British imperial debates suggests the need to broaden the social-imperial theory to encompass more than class. According to this theory, policymakers diverted public attention to colonial affairs in order to preserve elites' political power. But it appears that elites saw empire as a way not only of solidifying class hegemony but also of promoting a particular gender order. On the social-imperial theory, see Wehler, "Bismarck's Imperialism," 119–55; Semmel, *Imperialism and Social Reform*. It also appears that a consideration of gender would add a new dimension to the "official mind" discussed by Robinson and Gallagher with Denny, *Africa and the Victorians*, 20–22.

6. On perceptions of India and the Orient, see Greenberger, *The British Image of India*, 11, 13, 42–43, 51, 55; Said, *Orientalism*, 182, 207, 220; Sinha, "Gender and Imperi-

alism," 218; Sinha, "'Chathams, Pitts, and Gladstones in Petticoats,'" 99–112; Sinha, *Colonial Masculinity*. On women, see Strobel, *European Women and the Second British Empire*, 49. Burton argues that British feminists believed they had a "white women's burden" to save their helpless Indian "sisters" and that the most effective way to fulfill their mission was through empire, "The White Woman's Burden," 137, 152; Burton, *Burdens of History*. Imperial historians have not stopped with studying how gender beliefs shaped imperialist motives—they also have shown how they affected the functionings of empire. Ballhatchet finds that British officials considered sexual access to Indian women essential to maintaining British troops' virility and hence fighting strength, *Race, Sex, and Class Under the Raj*, 162, 164, 165, 167. Similarly, Stoler considers how sexual relations in an imperial context helped define "the boundaries of privilege between the colonizer and the colonized," "Carnal Knowledge and Imperial Power," 54–55, 68, 75, 85.

7. On the War of 1812, see Watts, *The Republic Reborn*, 154, 168–69; Risjord, "1812," 200, 209; Hatzenbuehler and Ivie, *Congress Declares War*, 85, 131. Adams, *The Great Adventure*, 135; Gardner quoted in Kulhman, "The Feminist Pacifist Challenge to Progressive Hegemony," 144–45, see also 193–94; on Gardner, see Garraty, *Henry Cabot Lodge*, 191; on World War I, see also Mosley, *Julian Grenfell*, 51, 213; Fussell, *The Great War and Modern Memory*, chap. 8. On fascism, see Koonz, *Mothers in the Fatherland*, 53, 112, 392; Theweleit, *Male Fantasies* 2:406. Theweleit argues that Freikorps members' efforts to differentiate themselves from women and effeminate men contributed to a *"psychic compulsion* to domination," 1:171. Later in the century, a disdain for male softness appears to have contributed to U.S. involvement in the Vietnam War, for the New Frontiersmen of the Kennedy administration, viewing themselves as muscular, potent, vigorous realists, pursued policies consistent with their gendered self-image, Baritz, *Backfire*, 102. Etheredge comments on the machismo of foreign policy elites, *A World of Men*, xiii–xv, 9–10, 61–62. Hartsock comments on the "crucial links between masculinity and the making of war," "Masculinity, Heroism, and the Making of War," 133, 147–48. On U.S. policymakers' efforts to appear masculine during the Cold War, see also Smith, "National Security and Personal Isolation," 328. Crawford argues that an admiration for "macho" men who adhered to a code of honor in "a world gone soft" contributed to the New Right's opposition to surrendering the Panama Canal, *Thunder on the Right*, 81. See also Cohn, "Wars, Wimps, and Women," 242; Boose, "Techno-Muscularity and the 'Boy Eternal,'" 67–108; Stiehm, "The Protected, the Protector, the Defender," 367–76; Hartsock, "Prologue to a Feminist Critique of War and Politics," 121–50; Reardon, *Sexism and the War System*.

8. On women's peace advocacy, see Degen, *The History of the Woman's Peace Party*; Papachristou, "American Women and Foreign Policy"; Steinson, "'The Mother Half of Humanity'"; Steinson, *American Women's Activism in World War I*; Zeiger, "Finding a Cure for War"; Swerdlow, *Women Strike for Peace*; Alonso, *The Women's Peace Union*; Alonso, "Suffragists for Peace During the Interwar Years"; Alonso, *Peace as a Women's Issue*; Craig, *Lucia Ames Mead*. McEnaney investigates a more conservative thread of women's peace activism in "He-Men and Christian Mothers." On the spirit of militarism, see Grace Isabel Colbron, "Militarism the Foe of Woman's Progress," in "Woman and War: Julia Ward Howe's Peace Crusade," pamphlet published by the World Peace Foundation, Boston, Oct., 1914, p. 11, reel A5, Julia Ward Howe Papers, SL.

9. On the Revolution, see Bailyn, *The Ideological Origins of the American Revolution*, 51, 87, 136, 311, 313; Hamilton quote from 137; Wood, *The Creation of the American*

Republic, 52–53; Jordan elaborates on the revolutionary shift from filial loyalty to fraternal solidarity in "Familial Politics," 294–308. On England as a deranged mother, see also Yazawa, *From Colonies to Commonwealth,* 3, 94, 96. Like imperialists, Revolutionary propagandists insisted that the nation and its people had come of age and that this had certain policy implications, Fliegelman, *Prodigals and Pilgrims,* 3; on gendered understandings of political virtue in the Revolutionary era, see Bloch, "The Gendered Meanings of Virtue," 44–58; on continental expansion, see Horsman, *Race and Manifest Destiny,* 233–34, 258; Rogin, *Fathers and Children,* 6, 9, 12; on the importance of honor in Western conflicts stretching back to the Peloponnesian War, see Kagan, *On the Origins of War,* 569.

10. On secessionists, see Wyatt-Brown, *Yankee Saints,* 205; McCurry, *Masters of Small Worlds,* 283. Lyndon B. Johnson quoted in Kearns, *Lyndon Johnson,* 253. Halberstam has argued that Johnson was "haunted by the idea that he would be judged as being insufficiently manly," *The Best and the Brightest,* 531–32; see also Fasteau, *The Male Machine,* chap. 12, esp. 163–88.

11. McGlen and Sarkees find some differences between contemporary men and women in foreign policy making positions, but they describe these as small and predict that gender differences will disappear if societal attitudes toward men and women converge and organizational barriers to women's advancement in the State Department and military are eliminated, *Women in Foreign Policy,* 306.

Bibliography

Manuscript Collections

Alabama Department of Archives and History: Wheeler Family Papers

Cincinnati Historical Society: Joseph Benson Foraker Papers

Connecticut State Library: Orville H. Platt Papers

General Federation of Women's Clubs Archives: President's Papers

Historical Society of Pennsylvania: Herbert Welsh Papers

Harvard University Houghton Library: Theodore Roosevelt Collection, Charles Eliot Norton Papers

Library of Congress: Clara Barton, Albert Jeremiah Beveridge, William E. Chandler, Grover Cleveland, George B. Cortelyou, William A. Croffut, William McKinley, John Basset Moore, John Tyler Morgan, Richard Olney, John Coit Spooner, and Moorfield Storey Papers

Massachusetts Historical Society: Edward Atkinson, George S. Boutwell II, George F. Hoar, Henry Cabot Lodge, John Davis Long, and Moorfield Story Papers

University of Michigan Bentley Library: Frederick Family, Chase S. Osborn, and Jabez T. Sunderland Papers

University of Michigan Clements Library: Calvin Mixter Papers

Minnesota Historical Society: John Lind, St. Paul Red Cross Aid Society, and James A. Tawney Papers

National Archives: Records of U.S. Senate, Record Group 46 and Records of the U.S. House of Representatives, Record Group 233

New-York Historical Society: Howard Townsend Papers

University of North Carolina Wilson Library, Southern Historical Collection: Edward Ward Carmack Papers

Pettigrew Museum: Richard F. Pettigrew Papers

Proctor Free Library: Redfield Proctor Papers

Schlesinger Library, Radcliffe College: Addie M. Billings, Blackwell Family, Alde L. T. Blake, Ellen Martin Henrotin, Julia Ward Howe, Mary Hillard Loines, Maud Wood Park, and Woman's Relief Corps Papers

Smith College Library, Sophia Smith Collection: Garrison Family Papers

Swarthmore College Peace Collection: Hannah Johnston Bailey Papers

U.S. Army Military History Research Institute: Howard S. Greene Papers in the Spanish-American War Survey

Western Reserve Historical Society: Theodore E. Burton Papers

Widener Library, Harvard University: Immigration clippings

Newspapers and Magazines

Advocate of Peace, American Home Magazine, Anti-Imperialist, Arena, Atlanta Constitution, Atlantic Monthly, Baltimore Sun, Boston Globe, Boston Journal, Boston Transcript, Century Magazine, Chautauquan, Chicago Tribune, Congressional Globe, Congressional Record, Forum, Godey's Magazine, Harper's Weekly, Independent, Journal of the Knights of Labor, Judge, Leslie's Weekly, Literary Digest, Living Age, Los Angeles Times, McClure's, Nation, National Geographic Magazine, National Suffrage Bulletin, New England Magazine, New Orleans Picayune, New York Journal, New York Sun, New York Times, New York Tribune, New York World, North American Review, Outlook, Overland Monthly, Pennsylvania School Journal, People's Party Paper, Philippine Monthly Magazine, Political Science Quarterly, Popular Science Monthly, Remonstrance, Review of Reviews, Rochester Democrat and Chronicle, Scribner's Magazine, Union Signal, Washington Post, Woman's Column, Woman's Journal, Woman's Standard, Woman's Tribune, World's Work, Yale Review

Published Primary and Secondary Sources

Abbot, Willis J. *Watching the World Go By*. Boston: Little, Brown, 1933.

Adams, Brooks. *The Law of Civilization and Decay*. 1896. Reprint. New York: Vintage, 1955.

Adams, Charles Francis. "'Imperialism' and 'The Tracks of Our Forefathers.'" Boston: Dana Estes, 1899.

Adams, Michael C. C. *The Great Adventure: Male Desire and the Coming of World War I*. Bloomington: Indiana University Press, 1990.

Affairs in the Philippine Islands: Hearings Before the Committee on the Philippines of the U.S. Senate. 57th Congress, 1st session, Senate Doc. #331, pts. 1–3. Washington: Government Printing Office, 1902.

Agoncillo, Teodoro A., and Oscar M. Alfonso. *History of the Filipino People*. Quezon City, Philippines: Malaya Books, 1967.

Alger, Russell A. *The Spanish-American War*. New York: Harper, 1901.

Alonso, Harriet Hyman. *Peace as a Women's Issue: A History of the U.S. Move-*

ment for World Peace and Women's Rights. Syracuse: Syracuse University Press, 1993.

———. "Suffragists for Peace During the Interwar Years, 1919–1941." *Peace and Change* 14, July 1989, 243–62.

———. *The Women's Peace Union and the Outlawry of War, 1921–1942*. Knoxville: University of Tennessee, 1989.

American National Red Cross Relief Committee Reports. New York: Knickerbocker, 1899.

Anderson, Warwick. "'Where Every Prospect Pleases and Only Man is Vile': Laboratory Medicine as Colonial Discourse." In *Discrepant Histories: Translocal Essays on Filipino Cultures*, Vicente L. Rafael, ed., Manila, Philippines: Anvil, 1995, 83–112.

———. "The Trespass Speaks: White Masculinity and Colonial Breakdown." *AHR* 102, Dec. 1997, 1343–70.

Anthony, Susan B., and Ida Husted Harper, eds. *The History of Woman Suffrage*. Vol. 4, *1883–1900*. Reprint. New York: Arno and the New York Times, 1969.

Avery, Rachel Foster, ed. *Proceedings of the Twenty-Eighth Annual Convention of the National-American Woman Suffrage Association*. Philadelphia: Alfred J. Ferris, 1896.

Ayers, Edward L. *The Promise of the New South: Life After Reconstruction*. New York: Oxford University Press, 1992.

———. *Vengeance and Justice: Crime and Punishment in the Nineteenth-Century American South*. New York: Oxford University Press, 1984.

Babcock, Elnora Monroe. "Why Cannot Women Vote?" *A True Republic*. N.p. 1902.

Bailyn, Bernard. *The Ideological Origins of the American Revolution*. Cambridge: Belknap, 1967.

Bain, David Haward. *Sitting in Darkness: Americans in the Philippines*. Boston: Houghton Mifflin, 1984.

Baker, Jean H. *Affairs of Party: The Political Culture of Northern Democrats in the Mid-Nineteenth Century*. Ithaca: Cornell University Press, 1983.

Baker, Paula. "The Domestication of Politics: Women and American Political Society, 1780–1920." *AHR* 89, June 1984, 620–47.

———. *The Moral Frameworks of Public Life: Gender, Politics, and the State in Rural New York, 1870–1930*. New York: Oxford University Press, 1991.

Ballhatchet, Kenneth. *Race, Sex, and Class Under the Raj: Imperial Attitudes and Policies and their Critics, 1793–1905*. London: Weidenfeld and Nicolson, 1980.

Baritz, Loren. *Backfire: A History of How American Culture Led Us into Vietnam and Made Us Fight the Way We Did*. New York: William Morrow, 1985.

Barrett, John. *Admiral George Dewey: A Sketch of the Man*. New York: Harper, 1899.

Baron, Ava. "Questions of Gender: Deskilling and Demasculinization in the U.S. Printing Industry, 1830–1915." *Gender and History* 1, Summer 1989, 178–99.

Barton, Clara. *The Red Cross in Peace and War*. Washington: American Historical Press, 1906.

Beale, Howard K. *Theodore Roosevelt and the Rise of America to World Power*. Baltimore: Johns Hopkins University Press, 1956.

Beall, M. E., Leonard Wood, William H. Taft, Charles H. Allen, and Perfecto Lacoste. *Opportunities in the Colonies and Cuba*. New York: Lewis, Scribner, 1902.

Becker, George F. "Conditions Requisite to our Success in the Philippine Islands. Address delivered before the American Geographical Society, Feb. 20, 1901." N.p. [1901].

Bederman, Gail. "'Civilization,' the Decline of Middle-Class Manliness, and Ida B. Wells's Antilynching Campaign (1892–94)." *Radical History Review* 52, Winter 1992, 5–30.

———. *Manliness and Civilization: A Cultural History of Gender and Race in the United States, 1880–1917*. Chicago: University of Chicago Press, 1995.

Beede, Benjamin R., ed. *The War of 1898 and U.S. Interventions, 1898–1934*. New York: Garland, 1994.

Beisner, Robert L. *From the Old Diplomacy to the New, 1865–1900*. Rev. ed. Arlington Heights, Ill.: Harlan Davidson, 1986.

———. "AHR Forum: American Imperialism: The Worst Chapter in Almost Any Book: Comments." *AHR* 83, June 1978, 672–78.

———. *Twelve Against Empire: The Anti-Imperialists, 1898–1900*. New York: McGraw-Hill, 1968.

Benedict, Charles E., ed., *William McKinley: Character Sketches of America's Martyred Chieftain*. New York: Blanchard, [1901].

Benjamin, Anne M. *A History of the Anti-Suffrage Movement in the United States from 1895 to 1920: Women Against Equality*. Lewiston, N.Y.: Edwin Mellen, 1991.

Beveridge, Albert J. *The Meaning of the Times and Other Speeches*. Indianapolis: Bobbs-Merrill, 1908.

———. *The Russian Advance*. New York: Harper, 1904.

———. *Work and Habits*. Philadelphia: Henry Altemus, 1905.

———. *The Young Man and the World*. New York: D. Appleton, 1905.

Bigelow, John J., Jr. *Reminiscences of the Santiago Campaign*. New York: Harper, 1899.

Blake, George W., ed. *Sulzer's Short Speeches*. New York: J. S. Ogilvie, 1912.

Blake, Nelson M. "The Olney-Pauncefote Treaty of 1897." *AHR* 50, Jan. 1945, 228–43.

Blanchard, Mary W. "The Soldier and the Aesthete: Homosexuality and Popular Culture in Gilded Age America." *Journal of American Studies* 30, April 1996, 25–46.

———. "Boundaries and the Victorian Body: Aesthetic Fashion in Gilded Age America." *AHR* 100, Feb. 1995, 21–50.

Blight, David W. "'For Something Beyond the Battlefield': Frederick Douglass and the Struggle for the Memory of the Civil War." *JAH* 75, March 1989, 1156–78.

Bloch, Ruth H. "The Gendered Meanings of Virtue in Revolutionary America." *Signs* 13, Autumn 1987, 37–58.

Blodgett, Geoffrey. "The Mugwump Reputation, 1870 to the Present." *JAH* 66, March 1980, 867–87.

Bonsal, Stephen. *The Fight for Santiago.* New York: Doubleday and McClure, 1899.

———. *The Real Condition of Cuba To-Day.* New York: Harper, 1897.

Boose, Lynda E. "Techno-Muscularity and the 'Boy Eternal': from the Quagmire to the Gulf." In *Gendering War Talk,* Miriam Cooke and Angela Woollacott, eds., Princeton: Princeton University Press, 1993, 67–108.

Bordin, Ruth. *Woman and Temperance: The Quest for Power and Liberty, 1873–1900.* Philadelphia: Temple University Press, 1981.

Bowe, John. *With the 13th Minnesota in the Philippines.* Minneapolis: A. B. Farnham, 1905.

Bowers, Claude G. *Beveridge and the Progressive Era.* Cambridge: Riverside, 1932.

Boyd, James P. *Men and Issues of 1900.* N.p. 1900.

Boyd, Nancy. *Emissaries: The Overseas Work of the American YWCA, 1895–1970.* New York: Woman's Press, 1986.

Braeman, John. *Albert J. Beveridge: American Nationalist.* Chicago: University of Chicago Press, 1971.

Brands, H. W. *Bound to Empire: The United States and the Philippines.* New York: Oxford University Press, 1992.

Brandt, Allan M. *No Magic Bullet: A Social History of Venereal Disease in the United States Since 1880.* 1985. Expanded ed. New York: Oxford University Press, 1987.

Brewer, David J. "The Spanish War: A Prophecy or an Exception? Speech at the Liberal Club in Buffalo, Feb. 16, 1899." N.p. [1899].

Brooks, Elbridge S. *The Story of Our War with Spain.* Boston: Lothrop, 1899.

Brown, Charles H. *The Correspondents' War: Journalists in the Spanish-American War.* New York: Charles Scribner's Sons, 1967.

Brown, Thomas H. *George Sewall Boutwell: Human Rights Advocate.* Groton: Groton Historical Society, 1989.

Brown, Wendy. *Manhood and Politics: A Feminist Reading in Political Theory.* Totowa, N.J.: Rowman and Littlefield, 1988.

Brumberg, Joan Jacobs. "Zenanas and Girlless Villages: The Ethnology of American Evangelical Women, 1870–1910." *JAH* 69, Sept. 1982, 347–71.

Bryan, William Jennings. *The First Battle: A Story of the Campaign of 1896.* Chicago: W. B. Conkey, 1896.

———. *Speeches of William Jennings Bryan.* Vol. 2. New York: Funk and Wagnalls, 1913.

Buechler, Steven M. *The Transformation of the Woman Suffrage Movement: The Case of Illinois, 1850–1920.* New Brunswick: Rutgers University Press, 1986.

Buel, Richard, Jr. *Securing the Revolution: Ideology in American Politics, 1789–1815*. Ithaca: Cornell University Press, 1972.

Burton, Antoinette M. *Burdens of History: British Feminists, Indian Women, and Imperial Culture, 1865–1915*. Chapel Hill: University of North Carolina Press, 1994.

Burton, David H. *Theodore Roosevelt: Confident Imperialist*. Philadelphia: University of Pennsylvania Press, 1968.

Busbey, L. White, Willis J. Abbot, Oliver W. Stewart, Howard S. Taylor. *The Battle of 1900*. Chicago: Monarch, 1900.

Cabrera, Raimundo. *Cuba and the Cubans*. Philadelphia: Levytype, 1896.

Campbell, Charles S. *The Transformation of American Foreign Relations, 1865–1900*. New York: Harper and Row, 1976.

Carnes, Mark C. *Secret Ritual and Manhood in Victorian America*. New Haven: Yale University Press, 1989.

Cartoons of the War of 1898 with Spain. Chicago: Belford, Middlebrook, 1898.

Cashin, Herschel V., Charles Alexander, William T. Anderson, Arthur M. Brown, Horace W. Bivins. *Under Fire with the Tenth U.S. Cavalry: Being a Brief, Comprehensive Review of the Negro's Participation in the Wars of the United States*. New York: F. Tennyson Neely, 1899.

Celebration of the Two Hundredth Anniversary of the Naming of Worcester, Oct. 14 and 15, 1884. Worcester: Charles Hamilton, 1885.

Chauncey, George. *Gay New York: Gender, Urban Culture, and the Making of the Gay Male World, 1890–1940*. New York: Basic Books, 1994.

Cherny, Robert W. "Anti-Imperialism on the Middle Border, 1898–1900." *Midwest Review* 1, Spring 1979, 19–34.

"The Chicago Liberty Meeting." Chicago: Central Anti-Imperialist League, 1899.

Church, A. M. *Picturesque Cuba, Porto Rico, Hawaii and the Philippines*. Springfield, Ohio: Mast, Cromwell, and Kirkpatrick, 1899.

Cisneros, Evangelina. *The Story of Evangelina Cisneros Told by Herself*. New York: Continental, 1898.

Clark, James Hyde. *Cuba and the Fight for Freedom*. Philadelphia: Globe Bible Publishing, 1896.

Clawson, Mary Ann. *Constructing Brotherhood: Class, Gender, and Fraternalism*. Princeton: Princeton University Press, 1989.

———. "Nineteenth-Century Women's Auxiliaries and Fraternal Orders." *Signs* 12, Fall 1986, 40–61.

Clinton, Catherine. "'Southern Dishonor': Flesh, Blood, Race and Bondage." In *In Joy and In Sorrow: Women, Family, and Marriage in the Victorian South, 1830–1900*, Carol Bleser, ed., New York: Oxford University Press, 1991, 52–68.

Cohn, Carol. "Wars, Wimps, and Women: Talking Gender and Thinking War." *Gendering War Talk*, Miriam Cooke and Angela Woollacott, eds., Princeton: Princeton University Press, 1993, 227–46.

Coletta, Paolo E. *William Jennings Bryan*. Vol. 1. *Political Evangelist, 1860–1908*. Lincoln: University of Nebraska Press, 1964.

Condict, Alice Byram. *Old Glory and the Gospel in the Philippines*. New York: Fleming H. Revell, 1902.

Coolidge, Louis A. *An Old-Fashioned Senator: Orville H. Platt*. New York: G. P. Putnam's Sons, 1910.

Cosmas, Graham A. *An Army for Empire: The United States Army in the Spanish-American War*. Columbia: University of Missouri Press, 1971.

Costigliola, Frank. "'Unceasing Pressure for Penetration': Gender, Pathology, and Emotion in George Kennan's Formation of the Cold War." *JAH* 83, March 1997, 1309–39.

Coston, W. Hilary. *The Spanish-American War Volunteer*. Harrisburg: Mount Pleasant, 1899.

Cott, Nancy F. "On Men's History and Women's History." In *Meanings for Manhood: Constructions of Masculinity in Victorian America*, Mark C. Carnes and Clyde Griffen, eds., Chicago: University of Chicago Press, 1990, 205–11.

Craig, John M. "Lucia True Ames Mead: American Publicist for Peace and Internationalism." In *Women and American Foreign Policy: Lobbyists, Critics, and Insiders*, 2d ed., Edward P. Crapol, ed., Wilmington: Scholarly Resources, 1992, 67–90.

———. *Lucia Ames Mead (1856–1936) and the American Peace Movement*. Lewiston, N.Y.: Edwin Mellen, 1990.

Crawford, Alan. *Thunder on the Right: The 'New Right' and the Politics of Resentment*. New York: Pantheon, 1980.

Creelman, James. *On the Great Highway: The Wanderings and Adventures of a Special Correspondent*. Boston: Lothrop, 1901.

Croly, Jennie Cunningham. *The History of the Woman's Club Movement in America*. New York: Henry G. Allen, 1898.

Cullen, Jim. "'I's a Man Now': Gender and African American Men." In *Divided Houses: Gender and the Civil War*, Catherine Clinton and Nina Silber, eds., New York: Oxford University Press, 1992, 76–91.

Cullom, Shelby M. *Fifty Years of Public Service*. Chicago: A. C. McClurg, 1911.

Cunliffe, Marcus. *Soldiers and Civilians: The Martial Spirit in America, 1775–1865*. New York: Free Press, 1968.

Curtis, Francis. *The Republican Party, 1854–1904*. New York: G. P. Putnam's Sons, 1904.

Dalton, Kathleen M. "Theodore Roosevelt, Knickerbocker Aristocrat." *New York History* 67, Jan. 1986, 39–65.

Damiani, Brian P. *Advocates of Empire: William McKinley, the Senate, and American Expansion, 1898–1899*. New York: Garland, 1987.

Darwin, Gertrude B. *Second Report of the National Society of the Daughters of the American Revolution, Oct. 11, 1897–Oct. 11, 1898*. Washington: Government Printing Office, 1900.

Davies, Wallace Evan. *Patriotism on Parade: The Story of Veterans' and Hereditary Organizations in America, 1783–1900*. Cambridge: Harvard University Press, 1955.

Davin, Anna. "Imperialism and Motherhood." *History Workshop*, issue 5, Spring 1978, 9–65.

Davis, Allen F. *American Heroine: The Life and Legend of Jane Addams*. New York: Oxford University Press, 1973.

Davis, Calvin D. "Arbitration, Mediation, and Conciliation." In *Encyclopedia of American Foreign Policy*. Vol. 1. Alexander DeConde, ed., New York: Charles Scribner's Sons, 1978, 33–42.

———. *The United States and the First Hague Peace Conference*. Ithaca: Cornell University Press, 1962.

Davis, Richard Harding. *Cuba in War Time*. New York: R. H. Russell, 1897.

———. *The Cuban and Porto Rican Campaigns*. New York: Charles Scribner's Sons, 1898.

Dawes, Charles G. *A Journal of the McKinley Years*. Bascom N. Timmons, ed., Chicago: Lakeside, 1950.

Dawson, Graham. *Soldier Heroes: British Adventure, Empire, and the Imagining of Masculinities*. New York: Routledge, 1994.

Dearing, Mary R. *Veterans in Politics: The Story of the G.A.R.* Baton Rouge: Louisiana State University Press, 1952.

"Death of Senator George F. Hoar, Proceedings in the Senate." Senate Doc. #201, 58th Congress, 3d Session. Washington: Government Printing Office, 1905.

DeBenedetti, Charles. *The Peace Reform in American History*. Bloomington: Indiana University Press, 1980.

Degen, Marie Louise. *The History of the Woman's Peace Party*. Baltimore: Johns Hopkins University Press, 1939.

Depew, Chauncey M. *Four Days at the National Republican Convention, St. Louis, June, 1896, and other Political Occasions. Speeches and Addresses of Hon. Chauncey M. Depew*. N.p., n.d.

De Santis, Hugh. "The Imperialist Impulse and American Innocence, 1865–1900." In *American Foreign Relations: A Historiographical Review*, Gerald K. Haines and J. Samuel Walker, eds., Westport, Conn: Greenwood, 1981, 65–90.

De Steel, M. *The New Napoleon: A Satire*. Washington: Stormont and Jackson, 1896.

Dewey, Adelbert M. *The Life and Letters of Admiral Dewey*. New York: Woolfall, 1898.

Dierks, Jack Cameron. *A Leap to Arms: The Cuban Campaign of 1898*. Philadelphia: J. B. Lippincott, 1970.

Di Stefano, Christine. *Configurations of Masculinity: A Feminist Perspective on Modern Political Theory*. Ithaca: Cornell University Press, 1991.

Dixon, Thomas, Jr. *The Leopard's Spots: A Romance of the White Man's Burden, 1865–1900*. New York: Doubleday, Page, 1902.

Dobson, John M. *Reticent Expansionism: The Foreign Policy of William McKinley*. Pittsburgh: Duquesne University Press, 1988.

———. "Spanish-Cuban/American War." In *The War of 1898 and U.S. Interventions, 1898–1934*, Benjamin R. Beede, ed., New York: Garland, 1994, 520–24.

Doty, Roxanne Lynn. *Imperial Encounters: The Politics of Representation in North-South Relations*. Minneapolis: University of Minnesota Press, 1996.

Douglas, Ann. *The Feminization of American Culture*. New York: Knopf, 1977.

Doyle, David Noel. *Irish Americans, Native Rights and National Empires: The Structure, Divisions, and Attitudes of the Catholic Minority in the Decade of Expansion, 1890–1901*. New York: Arno, 1976.

Draper, Andrew S. *The Rescue of Cuba: An Episode in the Growth of Free Government*. Boston: Silver, Burdett, 1899.

Drinnon, Richard. *Facing West: The Metaphysics of Indian-Hating and Empire Building*. New York: New American Library, 1980.

Dubbert, Joe L. *A Man's Place: Masculinity in Transition*. Englewood Cliffs: Prentice-Hall, 1979.

———. "Progressivism and the Masculinity Crisis." *Psychoanalytic Review* 61, Fall 1974, 443–56.

DuBois, Ellen Carol. *Feminism and Suffrage: The Emergence of an Independent Women's Movement in America, 1848–1869*. Ithaca: Cornell University Press, 1978.

———. "Outgrowing the Compact of the Fathers: Equal Rights, Woman Suffrage, and the United States Constitution, 1820–1878." *JAH* 74, Dec. 1987, 836–62.

Dunn, Arthur Wallace. *From Harrison to Harding: A Personal Narrative, Covering a Third of a Century, 1888–1921*. New York: G. P. Putnam's Sons, 1922.

Dyer, Thomas G. *Theodore Roosevelt and the Idea of Race*. Baton Rouge: Louisiana State University Press, 1980.

Edwards, Frank E. *The '98 Campaign of the 6th Massachusetts, U.S.V.* Boston: Little, Brown, 1899.

Edwards, Rebecca Brooks. "Gender in American Politics, 1880–1900." Ph.D. diss., University of Virginia, 1995.

Egleston, George W. "Is a Limited Policy of Imperialism Justified?" N.p.: Published by the author, 1898.

Elshtain, Jean Bethke. "Women as Mirror and Other: Toward a Theory of Women, War, and Feminism." *Humanities in Society* 5, Winter and Spring 1982, 29–44.

Ely, Cecil Degrotte. *The Road to Armageddon: The Martial Spirit in English Popular Literature, 1870–1914*. Durham: Duke University Press, 1987.

Enloe, Cynthia. *Bananas, Beaches, and Bases: Making Feminist Sense of International Politics*. Berkeley: University of California Press, 1990.

Epstein, Barbara Leslie. *The Politics of Domesticity: Women, Evangelism, and Temperance in Nineteenth-Century America*. Middletown, Conn.: Wesleyan, 1981.

Etcheson, Nicole. "Manliness and the Political Culture of the Old Northwest, 1790–1860." *Journal of the Early Republic* 15, Spring 1995, 59–77.

Etheredge, Lloyd S. *A World of Men: The Private Sources of American Foreign Policy*. Cambridge: MIT Press, 1978.

"Expensive Expansion." Boston: Philpott-Hardy, 1900.

Fallows, Samuel, ed. *Life of William McKinley, Our Martyred President*. Chicago: Regan, 1901.

Fasteau, Marc Feigen. *The Male Machine*. New York: McGraw-Hill, 1974.

Faulkner, Harold U. *Politics, Reform, and Expansion, 1890–1910*. New York: Harper, 1959.

Fernald, James C. *The Imperial Republic*. New York: Funk and Wagnalls, 1898.

———. *The New Womanhood*. Boston: D. Lothrop, 1891.

Field, H. John. *Toward a Programme of Imperial Life: The British Empire at the Turn of the Century*. Westport, Conn: Greenwood, 1982.

Field, James A., Jr. "American Imperialism: The Worst Chapter in Almost Any Book." *AHR* 83, June 1978, 644–68.

Filene, Peter. "Between a Rock and a Soft Place: A Century of American Manhood." *South Atlantic Quarterly* 84, Autumn 1985, 339–55.

———. *Him/Her/Self: Sex Roles in Modern America*. 2d ed. Baltimore: Johns Hopkins University Press, 1986.

Fink, Leon. *Workingmen's Democracy: The Knights of Labor and American Politics*. Urbana: University of Illinois Press, 1983.

Fischer, David Hackett. *Growing Old in America*. New York: Oxford University Press, 1977.

Fletcher, Marvin. *The Black Soldier and Officer in the United States Army, 1891–1917*. Columbia: University of Missouri Press, 1974.

Flexner, Eleanor. *Century of Struggle: The Woman's Rights Movement in the United States*. Rev. ed. Cambridge: Belknap, 1975.

Fliegelman, Jay. *Prodigals and Pilgrims: The American Revolution against Patriarchal Authority, 1750–1800*. New York: Cambridge University Press, 1982.

Flint, Grover. *Marching with Gomez*. Boston: Lamson, Wolffe, 1898.

Flood, Ned Arden. "William McKinley and the Presidency." Pamphlet reprinted from *The American Magazine of Civics*, April 1896, 1–16.

Foner, Eric. *Reconstruction: America's Unfinished Revolution, 1863–1877*. New York: Harper and Row, 1988.

Foner, Philip S. *The Spanish-Cuban-American War and the Birth of American Imperialism, 1895–1902*. Vol. 1. *1895–1898*. Vol. 2. *1898–1902*. New York: Monthly Review Press, 1972.

Foot, Rosemary. "Where are the Women? The Gender Dimension in the Study of International Relations." *Diplomatic History* 14, 1990, 615–22.

Foraker, Julia B. *I Would Live it Again: Memories of a Vivid Life*. New York: Harper, 1932.

Foreman, John. *The Philippine Islands*. London: Kelly and Walsh, 1890. Rev. ed. New York: Charles Scribner's Sons, 1899.

———. "Will the United States Withdraw from the Philippines?" Chicago: American Anti-Imperialist League, 1900.

Foster, Gaines M. *Ghosts of the Confederacy: Defeat, the Lost Cause, and the Emergence of the New South, 1865 to 1913*. New York: Oxford University Press, 1987.

Foster, Henry E. *William McKinley and the G.O.P. Under the X-Ray*. Cleveland: Morley and Briggs, 1900.

Francisco, Luzviminda Bartolome, and Jonathan Shepard Fast. *Conspiracy for Empire: Big Business, Corruption, and the Politics of Imperialism in America, 1876–1907*. Quezon City, Philippines: Foundation for Nationalist Studies, 1985.

Fraser, John. *America and the Patterns of Chivalry*. New York: Cambridge University Press, 1982.

Fredrickson, George M. *The Black Image in the White Mind: The Debate on Afro-American Character and Destiny, 1817–1914*. Middletown, Conn: Wesleyan University Press, 1971.

———. *The Inner Civil War: Northern Intellectuals and the Crisis of the Union*. New York: Harper and Row, 1965.

Freidel, Frank. *The Splendid Little War*. Boston: Little, Brown, 1958.

Fry, Joseph A. "William McKinley and the Coming of the Spanish-American War: A Study of the Besmirching and Redemption of an Historical Image." *Diplomatic History* 3, Winter 1979, 77–97.

Fuller, Paul E. "An Early Venture of Kentucky Women in Politics: The Breckinridge Campaign of 1894." *Filson Club History Quarterly* 63, April 1989, 224–42.

Fulton, Robert I., and Thomas C. Trueblood, eds. *Patriotic Eloquence Relating to the Spanish-American War and its Issues*. New York: Charles Scribner's Sons, 1900.

Fussell, Paul. *The Great War and Modern Memory*. New York: Oxford University Press, 1975.

Garraty, John A. *Henry Cabot Lodge: A Biography*. New York: Alfred A. Knopf, 1953.

Garrison, William Lloyd. "The Nature of a Republican Form of Government." *Political Equality Series* 5, July 1900, History of Women Microfilm Series, reel 947.

Gates, John Morgan. *Schoolbooks and Krags: The United States Army in the Philippines, 1898–1902*. Westport, Conn.: Greenwood, 1973.

Gatewood, Willard B., Jr. *Black Americans and the White Man's Burden, 1898–1903*. Urbana: University of Illinois Press, 1975.

———. *"Smoked Yankees" and the Struggle for Empire: Letters from Negro Soldiers, 1898–1902*. Urbana: University of Illinois Press, 1971.

Gay, Peter. *The Cultivation of Hatred*. New York: W. W. Norton, 1993.

Gehring, Lorraine A. "Women Officeholders in Kansas, 1872–1912." *Kansas History* 9, Summer 1986, 48–57.

Gibson, George H. "Attitudes in North Carolina Regarding the Independence of Cuba, 1868–1898." *North Carolina Historical Review* 43, Winter 1966, 43–65.

Giddings, Franklin Henry. *Democracy and Empire*. New York: Macmillan, 1900.

Gillett, Frederick H. *George Frisbie Hoar*. Boston: Houghton Mifflin, 1934.

Gilmore, Glenda Elizabeth. *Gender and Jim Crow: Women and the Politics of*

White Supremacy in North Carolina, 1896–1920. Chapel Hill: University of North Carolina Press, 1996.

Girouard, Mark. *The Return to Camelot: Chivalry and the English Gentleman*. New Haven: Yale University Press, 1981.

Glad, Paul W. *McKinley, Bryan, and the People*. Chicago: Ivan R. Dee, 1964.

Goldberg, Michael L. "'An Army of Women': Gender Relations and Politics in Kansas Populism, the Woman Movement, and the Republican Party, 1879–1896." Ph.D. diss., Yale University, 1992.

Goldman, Eric F. *Rendezvous with Destiny*. New York: Alfred A. Knopf, 1956.

Gookin, Frederick W. "A Liberty Catechism." Chicago: American Anti-Imperialist League, 1899.

Gordon, Linda. *Woman's Body, Woman's Right: Birth Control in America*. Rev. ed. New York: Penguin, 1990.

Gorn, Elliott J. *The Manly Art: Bare-Knuckle Prize Fighting in America*. Ithaca: Cornell University Press, 1986.

Gould, Lewis L. *The Spanish-American War and President McKinley*. Lawrence: University Press of Kansas, 1982.

Gowing, Peter Gordon. *Mandate in Moroland: The American Government of Muslim Filipinos, 1899–1920*. Quezon City, Philippines: Philippine Center for Advanced Studies, 1977.

Grant, Rebecca, and Kathleen Newland, eds. *Gender and International Relations*. Buckingham, England: Open University Press, 1991.

Green, Martin. *Dreams of Adventure, Deeds of Empire*. New York: Basic Books, 1979.

Green, Nathan C. *Story of Spain and Cuba*. Baltimore: International News and Book Co., 1896.

Greenberg, David F. *The Construction of Homosexuality*. Chicago: University of Chicago Press, 1988.

Greenberg, Kenneth S. *Honor and Slavery*. Princeton: Princeton University Press, 1996.

Greenberger, Allen J. *The British Image of India: A Study in the Literature of Imperialism, 1880–1960*. New York: Oxford University Press, 1969.

Grenville, John A. S. "American Naval Preparations for War with Spain, 1896–1898." *Journal of American Studies* 2, April 1968, 33–47.

Grosvenor, Charles H. *William McKinley, His Life and Work*. Washington: Continental Assembly, 1901.

Groves, Charles S. *Henry Cabot Lodge the Statesman*. Boston: Small, Maynard, 1925.

Gullace, Nicoletta F. "Sexual Violence and Family Honor: British Propaganda and International Law during the First World War." *AHR* 102, June 1997, 714–47.

Hagedorn, Hermann. *Leonard Wood: A Biography*. New York: Harper, 1931.

Halberstam, David. *The Best and the Brightest*. New York: Random House, 1972.

Hall, Florence Howe, ed. *Julia Ward Howe and the Woman Suffrage Movement.* Boston: Dana Estes, 1913.

Halstead, Murat. *Life and Distinguished Services of Hon. Wm. McKinley.* Philadelphia: Edgewood, 1896.

———. *The Story of Cuba: Her Struggles for Liberty.* Chicago: Cuba Libre Publishing, 1896.

———. *The Story of the Philippines, the Eldorado of the Orient.* Chicago: Our Possessions Publishing, 1898.

Harper, Ida Husted. *The Life and Work of Susan B. Anthony.* Vol. 2. Indianapolis: Hollenbeck, 1898.

———. *The Life and Work of Susan B. Anthony.* Vol. 3. Indianapolis: Hollenbeck, 1908.

Harrington, Fred H. "The Anti-Imperialist Movement in the United States, 1898–1900." *Mississippi Valley Historical Review* 22, Sept. 1935, 211–30.

Hartsock, Nancy C. M. "Masculinity, Heroism, and the Making of War." In *Rocking the Ship of State: Toward a Feminist Peace Politics,* Adrienne Harris and Ynestra King, eds., Boulder: Westview, 1989, 133–52.

———. "Prologue to a Feminist Critique of War and Politics." In *Women's Views of the Political World of Men,* Judith Hicks Stiehm, ed. Dobbs Ferry, N.Y.: Transnational, 1984, 121–50.

Haskins, David Greene, Jr. "Report of the Second Annual Meeting of the New England Anti-Imperialist League, November 24, 1900." Boston: New England Anti-Imperialist League, 1900.

Hatzenbuehler, Ronald L., and Robert L. Ivie. *Congress Declares War: Rhetoric, Leadership, and Partisanship in the Early Republic.* Kent: Kent State University Press, 1983.

Healy, David. *Drive to Hegemony: The United States in the Caribbean, 1898–1917.* Madison: University of Wisconsin Press, 1988.

———. *U.S. Expansionism: The Imperialist Urge in the 1890s.* Madison: University of Wisconsin Press, 1970.

———. *The United States in Cuba, 1898–1902: Generals, Politicians, and the Search for Policy.* Madison: University of Wisconsin Press, 1963.

"Hearing of the National American Woman Suffrage Association." Jan. 28, 1896, Committee on the Judiciary, House of Representatives.

Helg, Aline. *Our Rightful Share: The Afro-Cuban Struggle for Equality, 1886–1912.* Chapel Hill: University of North Carolina Press, 1995.

Hendrickson, Embert J. "Roosevelt's Second Venezuelan Controversy." *Hispanic American Historical Review* 50, Aug. 1970, 482–98.

Herron, George D. "American Imperialism: An Address." Chicago: National Christian Citizenship League, 1899.

Hewitt, Nancy A. "Varieties of Voluntarism: Class, Ethnicity, and Women's Activism in Tampa." In *Women, Politics, and Change,* Louise A. Tilly and Patricia Gurin, eds., New York: Russell Sage, 1990, 63–86.

Higham, John. "The Reorientation of American Culture in the 1890s." *Writing American History,* Bloomington: Indiana University Press, 1970, 73–102.

———. *Strangers in the Land: Patterns of American Nativism, 1860–1925.* Westport, Conn.: Greenwood, 1955.

Higonnet, Margaret R., and Patrice L.-R. Higonnet. "The Double Helix." In *Behind the Lines: Gender and the Two World Wars,* Margaret Randolph Higonnet, Jane Jenson, Sonya Michel, and Margaret Collins Weitz, eds., New Haven: Yale University Press, 1987, 31–47.

Hill, Patricia Ruth. *The World Their Household: The American Woman's Foreign Mission Movement and Cultural Transformation, 1870–1920.* Ann Arbor: University of Michigan Press, 1985.

Hoar, George Frisbie. "American Citizenship," Address Delivered before the State University of Iowa, June 17, 1903. Iowa City: State University of Iowa, 1903.

———. *Autobiography of Seventy Years.* Vols. 1–2. New York: Charles Scribner's Sons, 1903.

———. *Book of Patriotism.* 1901. Rev. ed. Boston: Hall and Locke, 1902.

———. *A Boy Sixty Years Ago.* Boston: Perry Mason, 1898.

———. *The Character of Washington.* Boston: Society of the Sons of the American Revolution, 1904.

———. *Conditions of Success in Public Life.* New York: Thomas Y. Crowell, 1901.

———. "Justice and Humanity, not Revenge, the Only Justification for War, Senate speech, April 14, 1898." Washington: N.p. 1898.

———. "Letter from the Hon. George F. Hoar." Boston: Anti-Imperialist League, 1899.

———. "The Lust of Empire, Senate speech of April 17, 1900." New York: Tucker, 1900.

———. *Old Age and Immortality: An Address Delivered Before the Worcester Fire Society at its Centennial, Jan. 21, 1893.* Worcester: Colonel Timothy Bigelow Chapter, DAR, 1904.

———. "Oration at the Celebration of the Centennial of the Founding of the Northwest. Delivered by George F. Hoar, of Massachusetts, April 7, 1888." Washington: Judd and Detweiler, 1888.

———. "Orderly and Decorous Conduct of Foreign Relations, Senate Address of March 11, 1896." Washington: N.p. 1896.

———. "Our Duty to the Philippines." New England Anti-Imperialist League, 1900.

———. "The Place of the College Graduate in American Life: An Address delivered before the Social Union at Amherst College." Worcester: Tyler and Seagrave, 1879.

———. "A Question of Conscience." Boston: N.p. 1900.

———. "Woman in the State," address of September 24, 1891, *Political Equality Series.* Vol. 4, Warren, Ohio: National American Woman Suffrage Association, n.d.

Hobson, Richmond Pearson. *The Sinking of the "Merrimac."* New York: Century, 1899. Reprint. Annapolis: Naval Institute Press, 1987.

Hofstadter, Richard. *Anti-intellectualism in American Life*. New York: Alfred A. Knopf, 1963.

———. "Cuba, the Philippines, and Manifest Destiny." In *Essays in American Diplomacy*, Armin Rappaport, ed., New York: Macmillan, 1967, 149–70.

———. "Manifest Destiny and the Philippines." In *America in Crisis: Fourteen Crucial Episodes in American History*. Daniel Aaron, ed., New York: Alfred A. Knopf, 1952, 173–200.

Hoganson, Kristin. "Garrisonian Abolitionists and the Rhetoric of Gender, 1850–1860." *American Quarterly* 45, Dec. 1993, 558–95.

———. "The 'Manly' Ideal of Politics and the Imperialist Impulse: Gender, U.S. Political Culture, and the Spanish-American and Philippine-American Wars." Ph.D. diss., Yale University, 1995.

Holbo, Paul S. "The Convergence of Moods and the Cuban-Bond 'Conspiracy' of 1898." *JAH* 55, June 1968, 54–72.

———. "Economics, Emotion, and Expansion: An Emerging Foreign Policy." In *The Gilded Age*, H. Wayne Morgan, ed., 1963. Rev. ed. Syracuse: Syracuse University Press, 1970, 199–221.

Horsman, Reginald. *Race and Manifest Destiny: The Origins of American Racial Anglo-Saxonism*. Cambridge: Harvard University Press, 1981.

Howe, Julia Ward. *Reminiscences, 1819–1899*. Boston: Houghton, Mifflin, 1899. Reprint. New York: Negro Universities Press, 1969.

Hunt, Michael H. *Ideology and U.S. Foreign Policy*. New Haven: Yale University Press, 1987.

Hunter, Jane. *The Gospel of Gentility: American Women Missionaries in Turn-of-the-Century China*. New Haven: Yale University Press, 1984.

Hurley, Vic. *Swish of the Kris: The Story of the Moros*. New York: E. P. Dutton, 1936.

Hyam, Ronald. *Britain's Imperial Century, 1815–1914: A Study of Empire and Expansion*. London: B. T. Batsford, 1976.

———. "Empire and Sexual Opportunity." *Journal of Imperial and Commonwealth History* 14, Jan. 1986, 34–90.

———. *Empire and Sexuality: The British Experience*. New York: Manchester University Press, 1990.

Ileto, Reynaldo C. "Cholera and the Origins of the American Sanitary Order in the Philippines." In *Discrepant Histories: Translocal Essays on Filipino Cultures*, Vicente L. Rafael, ed., Manila, Philippines: Anvil, 1995, 51–81.

Iriye, Akira. "Culture and Power: International Relations as Intercultural Relations." *Diplomatic History* 3, 1979, 115–28.

———. "A Round Table: Explaining the History of American Foreign Relations—Culture." *JAH* 77, June 1990, 99–107.

Jacobson, Matthew Frye. *Special Sorrows: The Diasporic Imagination of Irish, Polish, and Jewish Immigrants in the United States*. Cambridge: Harvard University Press, 1995.

James, William. *Essays, Comments, and Reviews*. Cambridge: Harvard University Press, 1987.

Jeffords, Susan. *The Remasculinization of America: Gender and the Vietnam War*. Bloomington: Indiana University Press, 1989.

Jenks, Maud Huntley. *Death Stalks the Philippine Wilds: Letters of Maud Huntley Jenks*. Carmen Nelson Richards, ed., Minneapolis: Lund, 1951.

Jensen, Richard. *The Winning of the Midwest: Social and Political Conflict, 1888–1896*. Chicago: University of Chicago Press, 1971.

Johnson, Edward A. *History of Negro Soldiers in the Spanish-American War*. Raleigh: Capital, 1899. Reprint. New York: Johnson, 1970.

Johnson, Helen Kendrick, ed. *Why Women do not Want the Ballot*. Boston: Massachusetts Association Opposed to the Further Extension of Suffrage to Women, 1904.

———. *Woman and the Republic*. New York: D. Appleton, 1897. Rev. ed. New York: Guidon Club Opposed to Woman Suffrage, 1913.

Jordan, David Starr. *The Blood of the Nation: A Study of the Decay of Races through the Survival of the Unfit*. Boston: American Unitarian Association, 1903.

———. *The Call of the Twentieth Century: An Address to Young Men*. Boston: American Unitarian Association, 1903.

———. *The Days of a Man: Being Memories of a Naturalist, Teacher and Minor Prophet of Democracy*. Vol. 1. Yonkers-on-Hudson, N.Y.: World, 1922.

———. "Imperial Democracy." Boston: Women's Educational and Industrial Union, 1898.

———. *Imperial Democracy*. New York: D. Appleton, 1899.

———. "'Lest We Forget', an address delivered before the graduating class of 1898, Leland Stanford Jr. University, May 25, 1898." Palo Alto: John J. Valentine, 1898.

———. "The Question of the Philippines. An Address Delivered before the Graduate Club of Leland Stanford Junior University on February 14, 1899." Palo Alto: John J. Valentine, 1899.

Jordan, Winthrop D. "Familial Politics: Thomas Paine and the Killing of the King, 1776." *JAH* 60, Sept. 1973, 294–308.

"Joseph Wheeler." *National Cyclopaedia of American Biography*. Vol. 9. New York: James T. White, 1907, 19–20.

Josephson, Matthew. *The Politicos, 1865–1896*. New York: Harcourt, Brace, 1938.

Journal of the Thirty-First National Encampment of the Grand Army of the Republic. Lincoln: State Journal Co., 1897.

Kagan, Donald. *On the Origins of War and the Preservation of Peace*. New York: Doubleday, 1995.

Kammen, Michael. *A Season of Youth: The American Revolution and the Historical Imagination*. New York: Alfred A. Knopf, 1978.

Kann, Mark E. *On the Man Question: Gender and Civic Virtue in America*. Philadelphia: Temple University Press, 1991.

Kaplan, Amy. "Black and Blue on San Juan Hill." In *Cultures of United States Imperialism,* Amy Kaplan and Donald E. Pease, eds., Durham: Duke University Press, 1993, 219–36.

———. "Romancing the Empire: The Embodiment of American Masculinity in the Popular Historical Novel of the 1890s." *American Literary History* 2, Winter 1990, 659–90.

Karnow, Stanley. *In Our Image: America's Empire in the Philippines.* New York: Random House, 1989.

Karp, Walter. *The Politics of War: The Story of Two Wars Which Altered Forever the Political Life of the American Republic (1890–1920).* New York: Harper and Row, 1979.

Kearns, Doris. *Lyndon Johnson and the American Dream.* New York: Harper and Row, 1976.

Keenan, Henry F. *The Conflict with Spain.* Philadelphia: P. W. Ziegler, 1898.

Keller, Morton. *Affairs of State: Public Life in Late Nineteenth Century America.* Cambridge: Belknap, 1977.

Kelso, James Arthur. "Justifying Intervention and Imperialism: The Ideology and Rhetoric of the Spanish-American War." Ph.D. diss., University of Pittsburgh, 1977.

Kemble, C. Robert. *The Image of the Army Officer in America.* Westport, Conn.: Greenwood, 1973.

Kennedy, Dane. "The Perils of the Midday Sun: Climatic Anxieties in the Colonial Tropics." In *Imperialism and the Natural World,* John M. MacKenzie, ed., Manchester: Manchester University Press, 1990, 118–40.

Kern, Stephen. *Anatomy and Destiny: A Cultural History of the Human Body.* New York: Bobbs-Merrill, 1975.

Kett, Joseph F. *Rites of Passage: Adolescence in America, 1790 to the Present.* New York: Basic Books, 1977.

Kidd, Benjamin. *The Control of the Tropics.* New York: McMillan, 1898.

Kimmel, Michael. "The Contemporary 'Crisis' of Masculinity in Historical Perspective." In *The Making of Masculinities: The New Men's Studies,* Harry Brod, ed., Boston: Allen and Unwin, 1987, 121–53.

———. *Manhood in America: A Cultural History.* New York: Free Press, 1996.

Kleppner, Paul. *The Third Electoral System, 1853–1892: Parties, Voters, and Political Cultures.* Chapel Hill: University of North Carolina Press, 1979.

———. *Who Voted? The Dynamics of Electoral Turnout, 1870–1980.* New York: Praeger, 1982.

Klotter, James C. "Sex, Scandal, and Suffrage in the Gilded Age." *The Historian* 42, Feb. 1980, 225–43.

Koenigsberg, Sergeant M. *Southern Martyrs: A History of Alabama's White Regiments during the Spanish-American War.* Montgomery: Brown, 1898.

Koonz, Claudia. *Mothers in the Fatherland: Women, the Family, and Nazi Politics.* New York: St. Martin's, 1987.

Kousser, J. Morgan. *The Shaping of Southern Politics: Suffrage Restriction and the*

Establishment of the One-Party South, 1880–1910. New Haven: Yale University Press, 1974.

Kraditor, Aileen S. *The Ideas of the Woman Suffrage Movement, 1890–1920*. New York: Columbia, 1965. Reprint. New York: W. W. Norton, 1981.

Kriebel, Robert C. *Where the Saints Have Trod: The Life of Helen Gougar*. West Lafayette, Ind.: Purdue University Press, 1985.

Kroeger, Brooke. *Nellie Bly: Daredevil, Reporter, Feminist*. New York: Random House, 1994.

Kuhlman, Erika A. "The Feminist Pacifist Challenge to Progressive Hegemony: The Debate over U.S. Intervention in World War I." Ph.D. diss., Washington State University, 1995.

LaFeber, Walter. *The New Empire: An Interpretation of American Expansion, 1860–1898*. Ithaca: Cornell University Press, 1963.

Lamar, Mrs. Joseph Rucker [Clarinda Huntington Pendleton]. *A History of the National Society of the Colonial Dames of America*. Atlanta: Walter W. Brown, 1934.

Langley, Lester D. *The Banana Wars: United States Intervention in the Caribbean, 1898–1934*. Rev. ed. Lexington: University Press of Kentucky, 1985.

———. *The United States and the Caribbean in the Twentieth Century*. 1980. 4th. ed. Athens: University of Georgia Press, 1989.

Lasch, Christopher. "The Anti-Imperialists, the Philippines, and the Inequality of Man." *Journal of Southern History* 24, Aug. 1958, 319–31.

Laughlin, J. Laurence. "Patriotism and Imperialism." Chicago: Central Anti-Imperialist League, 1899.

Law, Robert O. *The Parties and the Men, or, Political Issues of 1896*. N.p. 1896.

Lawrence, William. *Henry Cabot Lodge: A Biographical Sketch*. Boston: Houghton Mifflin, 1925.

Lears, T. J. Jackson. *No Place of Grace: Antimodernism and the Transformation of American Culture, 1880–1920*. New York: Pantheon, 1981.

Lebsock, Suzanne. "Women and American Politics, 1880–1920." In *Women, Politics, and Change,* Louise A. Tilly and Patricia Gurin, eds., New York: Russell Sage, 1990, 35–62.

Leech, Margaret. *In the Days of McKinley*. New York: Harper, 1959.

Leffler, John Joseph. "From the Shadows into the Sun: Americans in the Spanish-American War." Ph.D. diss., University of Texas at Austin, 1991.

Legaspi, Edelwina C. "The Rhetoric of the Anti-Imperialist Movement, 1898–1900, with Special Emphasis on the Role of the Anti-Imperialist League." Ph.D. diss., Cornell University, 1967.

Leonard, Elizabeth D. *Yankee Women: Gender Battles in the Civil War*. New York: W. W. Norton, 1994.

Leonidas, Marion. *Private Smith at the Philippines*. Hammond, Ind.: Franklin, 1899.

Levere, William C. *Imperial America: The Policy of National Expansion*. Chicago: Forbes, 1898.

Lewenson, Sandra Beth. *Taking Charge: Nursing, Suffrage, and Feminism in America, 1873–1920*. New York: Garland, 1993.

Linderman, Gerald F. *Embattled Courage: The Experience of Combat in the American Civil War*. New York: Free Press, 1987.

———. *The Mirror of War: American Society and the Spanish-American War*. Ann Arbor: University of Michigan Press, 1974.

Linn, Brian McAllister. *Guardians of Empire: The U.S. Army and the Pacific, 1902–1940*. Chapel Hill: University of North Carolina, 1997.

———. "The Struggle for Samar." In *Crucible of Empire: The Spanish-American War and its Aftermath*, James C. Bradford, ed., Annapolis: Naval Institute Press, 1993, 158–82.

———. *The U.S. Army and Counterinsurgency in the Philippine War, 1899–1902*. Chapel Hill: University of North Carolina Press, 1989.

Lodge, Henry Cabot. "Address by Hon. Henry Cabot Lodge, U.S. Senator from Massachusetts, Under the Auspices of the Union League, At the Academy of Music, Philadelphia, Oct. 1, 1900," Philadelphia: Union League, 1900.

———. *Anna Cabot Mills Lodge*. Boston: privately printed, 1918.

———. *Certain Accepted Heroes and Other Essays in Literature and Politics*. New York: Harper, 1897.

———. *Early Memories*. New York: Charles Scribner's Sons, 1913.

———. *A Fighting Frigate and Other Essays and Addresses*. New York: Charles Scribner's Sons, 1902.

———. *A Frontier Town and Other Essays*. New York: Charles Scribner's Sons, 1906.

———. *Historical and Political Essays*. Boston: Houghton, Mifflin, 1892.

———. *Speeches and Addresses, 1884–1909*. Boston: Houghton Mifflin, 1909.

———. *The War With Spain*. New York: Harper, 1899.

Lodge, Henry Cabot, and Theodore Roosevelt. *Hero Tales from American History*. New York: Century, 1895.

———. *Selections from the Correspondence of Theodore Roosevelt and Henry Cabot Lodge, 1884–1918*. Vol. 1. New York: Charles Scribner's Sons, 1925.

Lutz, Tom. *American Nervousness, 1903: An Anecdotal History*. Ithaca: Cornell University Press, 1991.

McAleer, Kevin. *Dueling: The Cult of Honor in Fin-de-Siècle Germany*. Princeton: Princeton University Press, 1994.

McClintock, Anne. *Imperial Leather: Race, Gender, and Sexuality in the Colonial Contest*. New York: Routledge, 1995.

McConnell, Stuart. *Glorious Contentment: The Grand Army of the Republic, 1865–1900*. Chapel Hill: University of North Carolina Press, 1992.

McCormick, Thomas J. *China Market: America's Quest for Informal Empire, 1893–1901*. Chicago: Quadrangle, 1967.

McCullough, David. *Mornings on Horseback*. New York: Simon and Schuster, 1981.

McCurry, Stephanie. *Masters of Small Worlds: Yeoman Households, Gender Relations, and the Political Culture of the Antebellum South Carolina Low Country*. New York: Oxford University Press, 1995.

————. "The Two Faces of Republicanism: Gender and Proslavery Politics in Antebellum South Carolina." *JAH* 78, March 1992, 1245–64.

MacDonald, Robert H. *Sons of the Empire: The Frontier and the Boy Scout Movement, 1890–1918.* Toronto: University of Toronto Press, 1993.

McEnaney, Laura. "He-Men and Christian Mothers: The America First Movement and the Gendered Meanings of Patriotism and Isolationism." *Diplomatic History* 18, Winter 1994, 47–57.

McFarland, Gerald W. *Mugwumps, Morals and Politics, 1884–1920.* Amherst: University of Massachusetts Press, 1975.

McGerr, Michael E. *The Decline of Popular Politics: The American North, 1865–1928.* New York: Oxford University Press, 1986.

————. "Political Style and Women's Power, 1830–1930." *JAH* 77, Dec. 1990, 864–85.

McGlen, Nancy E., and Meredith Reid Sarkees. *Women in Foreign Policy: The Insiders.* New York: Routledge, 1993.

McGovern, James R. "David Graham Phillips and the Virility Impulse of Progressives." *New England Quarterly* 39, Sept. 1966, 334–55.

McKee, Delber L. "Samuel Gompers, the A.F. of L., and Imperialism, 1895–1900." *The Historian* 21, Feb. 1959, 187–99.

McKinley, William. *Speeches and Addresses of William McKinley from March 1, 1897 to May 30, 1900.* New York: Doubleday and McClure, 1900.

Macleod, David I. *Building Character in the American Boy: The Boy Scouts, YMCA, and their Forerunners, 1870–1920.* Madison: University of Wisconsin Press, 1983.

McMath, Robert C. *American Populism: A Social History, 1877–1898.* New York: Hill and Wang, 1993.

McNulty, Edward M. "The Cuban Crisis as Reflected in the New Jersey Press, 1895–1898." Ph.D. diss., Rutgers, 1970.

Mahan, Alfred T. *The Interest of America in Sea Power, Present and Future.* Boston: Little, Brown, 1897.

Mallan, John P. "The Warrior Critique of the Business Civilization." *American Quarterly* 8, Fall 1956, 216–30.

Mangan, J. A. *The Games Ethic and Imperialism.* New York: Viking, 1985.

March, Alden. *The History and Conquest of the Philippines and Our Other Island Possessions.* Boston: George M. Smith, 1899.

Marcus, Robert D. *Grand Old Party: Political Structure in the Gilded Age, 1880–1896.* New York: Oxford University Press, 1971.

Markowitz, Gerald E., ed. *American Anti-Imperialism, 1895–1901.* New York: Garland, 1976.

Marshall, Edward. *The Story of the Rough Riders.* New York: G. W. Dillingham, 1899.

Mart, Michelle. "Tough Guys and American Cold War Policy: Images of Israel, 1948–1960." *Diplomatic History* 20, Summer 1996, 357–80.

"Mass Meetings of Protest Against the Suppression of Truth about the Philippines. Faneuil Hall, March 19, 1903." Boston: N.p. 1903.

Matthews, Claude. "The Cuban Patriots' Cause is Just." Philadelphia: Charles F. Simmons, 1895.

May, Ernest R. *American Imperialism: A Speculative Essay*. New York: Athenaeum, 1968.

———. *Imperial Democracy: The Emergence of America as a Great Power*. New York: Harcourt, Brace, and World, 1961.

May, Glenn Anthony. *Battle for Batangas: A Philippine Province at War*. New Haven: Yale University Press, 1991.

———. *Social Engineering in the Philippines: The Aims, Execution, and Impact of American Colonial Policy, 1900–1913*. Westport, Conn.: Greenwood, 1980.

Miller, Stuart Creighton. *"Benevolent Assimilation": The American Conquest of the Philippines, 1899–1903*. New Haven: Yale University Press, 1982.

Millis, Walter. *The Martial Spirit*. Houghton Mifflin, 1931. Reprint. Chicago: Elephant Paperbacks, 1989.

Minutes of the Eighth Annual Meeting and Reunion of the United Confederate Veterans. New Orleans: Hopkins, 1899.

Monoson, S. Sara. "The Lady and the Tiger: Women's Electoral Activism in New York City Before Suffrage." *Journal of Women's History* 2, Fall 1990, 100–35.

Moore, John L., ed. *Congressional Quarterly's Guide to U.S. Elections*. 3d ed., Washington: Congressional Quarterly, 1994.

"The Moral and Religious Aspects of the So-Called Imperial Policy, Discussed by Representative Clergymen of Many Denominations." Washington: Anti-Imperialist League, [1899].

Morgan, H. Wayne. *America's Road to Empire: The War with Spain and Overseas Expansion*. New York: John Wiley and Sons, 1965.

———. *From Hayes to McKinley: National Party Politics, 1877–1896*. Syracuse: Syracuse University Press, 1969.

———. *William McKinley and His America*. Syracuse: Syracuse University Press, 1963.

Morris, Edmund. *The Rise of Theodore Roosevelt*. New York: Ballantine, 1979.

Morris, James. *Pax Britannica: The Climax of an Empire*, New York: Harcourt, Brace and World, 1968.

Moses, Edith. *Unofficial Letters of an Official's Wife*. New York: D. Appleton, 1908.

Mosley, Nicholas. *Julian Grenfell: His Life and the Times of His Death, 1888–1915*. London: Weidenfeld and Nicolson, 1976.

Mosse, George L. *The Image of Man: The Creation of Modern Masculinity*. New York: Oxford University Press, 1996.

Mott, Frank Luther. *A History of American Magazines*. Vol. 3. *1865–1888*. Cambridge: Harvard University Press, 1938.

Mumford, Kevin J. "'Lost Manhood' Found: Male Sexual Impotence and Victorian Culture in the United States." In *American Sexual Politics: Sex, Gender, and Race since the Civil War,* John C. Fout and Maura Shaw Tantillo, eds. Chicago: University of Chicago Press, 1993, 75–99.

Munro, Dana G. *Intervention and Dollar Diplomacy in the Caribbean, 1900–1921.* Westport, Conn.: Greenwood, 1964.

Musgrave, George Clarke. *Under Three Flags in Cuba.* Cambridge: Little, Brown, 1899.

Musicant, Ivan. *The Banana Wars: A History of the United States Military Intervention in Latin America from the Spanish-American War to the Invasion of Panama.* New York: Macmillan, 1990.

National American Woman's Suffrage Association. "Reply of the National Officers." May 1900, History of Women Microfilm Series, reel 947.

National Cyclopaedia of American Biography. Vol. 9. New York: James T. White, 1899.

National Cyclopaedia of American Biography. Vol. 13. New York: James T. White, 1906.

National Cyclopaedia of American Biography. Vol. 28. New York: James T. White, 1940.

Nearing, Scott, and Joseph Freeman. *Dollar Diplomacy: A Study in American Imperialism.* New York: B. W. Huebsch and Viking, 1925.

Ninkovich, Frank. "Theodore Roosevelt: Civilization as Ideology." *Diplomatic History* 10, Summer 1986, 221–45.

Nye, Robert A. *Masculinity and Male Codes of Honor in Modern France.* New York: Oxford University Press, 1993.

Official Proceedings of the Democratic National Convention, 1896. Logansport, Ind.: Wilson, Humphreys, 1896.

Ogilvie, J. S., ed. *Life and Speeches of William J. Bryan.* New York: J. S. Ogilvie, 1896.

Offner, John L. "Treaty of Paris (1898)." In *The War of 1898 and U.S. Interventions, 1898–1934,* Benjamin R. Beede, ed., New York: Garland, 1994, 544–47.

———. *An Unwanted War: The Diplomacy of the United States and Spain over Cuba, 1895–1898.* Chapel Hill: University of North Carolina Press, 1992.

Osborne, Thomas J. *"Empire Can Wait": American Opposition to Hawaiian Annexation, 1893–1898.* Kent: Kent State University Press, 1981.

Ostler, Jeffrey. *Prairie Populism: The Fate of Agrarian Radicalism in Kansas, Nebraska, and Iowa, 1880–1892.* Lawrence: University Press of Kansas, 1993.

Ownby, Ted. *Subduing Satan: Religion, Recreation, and Manhood in the Rural South, 1865–1920.* Chapel Hill: University of North Carolina Press, 1990.

The Oxford English Dictionary. Vol. 1, 2nd ed., prepared by J. A. Simpson and E. S. C. Weiner, Oxford: Clarendon, 1989.

Painter, Nell Irvin. *Standing at Armageddon: The United States, 1877–1919.* New York: W. W. Norton, 1987.

Palmer, Bruce. *"Man over Money": The Southern Populist Critique of American Capitalism.* Chapel Hill: University of North Carolina Press, 1980.

Pamphlets Printed and Distributed by the Women's Anti-Suffrage Association. Albany: Women's Anti-Suffrage Association, 1905. Reprint. Littleton, Colo.: Fred B. Rothman, 1990.

Papachristou, Judith. "American Women and Foreign Policy, 1898–1905: Exploring Gender in Diplomatic History." *Diplomatic History* 14, Fall 1990, 493–509.

Papers Relating to the Foreign Relations of the United States, 1898. Washington: Government Printing Office, 1901.

Pascoe, Peggy. *Relations of Rescue: The Search for Female Moral Authority in the American West, 1874–1939.* New York: Oxford University Press, 1990.

Patterson, David S. *Toward a Warless World: The Travail of the American Peace Movement, 1887–1914.* Bloomington: Indiana University Press, 1976.

Pérez, Louis A., Jr. *Cuba and the United States: Ties of Singular Intimacy.* Athens: University of Georgia Press, 1990.

———. *Cuba Between Empires, 1878–1902.* Pittsburgh: University of Pittsburgh Press, 1983.

———. *Cuba: Between Reform and Revolution.* New York: Oxford University Press, 1988.

Perry, Bliss. *Life and Letters of Henry Lee Higginson.* Boston: Atlantic Monthly, 1921.

Peterson, V. Spike, ed. *Gendered States: Feminist (Re)visions of International Relations Theory.* Boulder: Lynne Rienner, 1992.

Pettegrew, John. "'The Soldier's Faith': Turn-of-the-Century Memory of the Civil War and the Emergence of Modern American Nationalism." *Journal of Contemporary History* 31, Jan. 1996, 49–73.

Pettigrew, R. F. *The Course of Empire.* New York: Boni and Liveright, 1920.

Pick, Daniel. *Faces of Degeneration: A European Disorder, c. 1848–c. 1918.* Cambridge: Cambridge University Press, 1989.

———. *War Machine: The Rationalisation of Slaughter in the Modern Age.* New Haven: Yale University Press, 1993.

Pivar, David J. *Purity Crusade: Sexual Morality and Social Control, 1868–1900.* Westport, Conn.: Greenwood, 1973.

Pletcher, David M. "Rhetoric and Results: A Pragmatic View of American Economic Expansion, 1865–98." *Diplomatic History* 5, Spring 1981, 93–106.

Porter, Robert P. *Life of William McKinley, Soldier, Lawyer, Statesman.* Cleveland: N. G. Hamilton, 1896.

Pratt, Julius W. *America's Colonial Experiment: How the United States Gained, Governed, and in Part Gave Away a Colonial Empire.* New York: Prentice-Hall, 1951.

———. *Expansionists of 1898: The Acquisition of Hawaii and the Spanish Islands.* Baltimore: Johns Hopkins University Press, 1936.

Prescott, Lawrence F. *The Great Campaign.* N.p.: Loyal, 1896.

Price, Richard N. "Society, Status and Jingoism: The Social Roots of Lower Middle Class Patriotism, 1870–1900." In *The Lower Middle Class in Britain, 1870–1914,* Geoffrey Crossick, ed., New York: St. Martin's, 1977, 89–112.

Proceedings of the American Conference on International Arbitration. New York: Baker and Taylor, 1896.

Pryor, Elizabeth Brown. *Clara Barton: Professional Angel*. Philadelphia: University of Pennsylvania Press, 1987.

Pugh, David G. *Sons of Liberty: The Masculine Mind in Nineteenth-Century America*. Westport, Conn.: Greenwood, 1983.

Quesada, Gonzalo de, and Henry Davenport Northrop. *America's Battle for Cuba's Freedom*. Chicago: Dominion, 1898.

———. *The War in Cuba, Being a Full Account of her Great Struggle for Freedom*. Chicago: National, 1896.

Rafael, Vicente L. "Colonial Domesticity: White Women and United States Rule in the Philippines." *American Literature* 67, Dec. 1995, 639–66.

Ragsdale, Bruce A., ed. *Biographical Directory of the United States Congress, 1774–1989*. Washington: Government Printing Office, 1989.

Reader, W. J. *"At Duty's Call": A Study in Obsolete Patriotism*. New York: Manchester, 1988.

Reardon, Betty A. *Sexism and the War System*. New York: Teachers College, 1985.

Report of the First Annual Meeting of the Lake Mohonk Conference on International Arbitration, 1895. Martha D. Adams, reporter. N.p.: Lake Mohonk Arbitration Conference, 1895.

Report of the Third Annual Meeting of the Lake Mohonk Conference on International Arbitration, 1897. Martha D. Adams, reporter. N.p.: Lake Mohonk Arbitration Conference, 1897.

Ricard, Serge. "War and Myth: Rough Riding at San Juan." In *Interface: Essays on History, Myth, and Art in American Literature*, Daniel Royot, ed., Montpellier, France: Publications de la Recherche, 1985, 61–69.

Richards, Jeffrey, ed. *Imperialism and Juvenile Literature*. New York: Manchester, 1989.

Richards, Laura E., and Maud Howe Elliott. *Julia Ward Howe, 1819–1910*. Vol. 2. Boston: Houghton Mifflin, 1916.

Rickover, H. G. *How the Battleship* Maine *Was Destroyed*. Washington: Department of the Navy, 1976.

Risjord, Norman K. "1812: Conservatives, War Hawks, and the Nation's Honor." *William and Mary Quarterly* 18, April 1961, 196–210.

Robbins, Louise Barnum, ed. *History and Minutes of the National Council of Women of the United States*. Boston: E. B. Stillings, 1898.

Roberts, Gerald Franklin. "The Strenuous Life: The Cult of Manliness in the Era of Theodore Roosevelt." Ph.D. diss., Michigan State University, 1970.

Robinson, Ronald, and John Gallagher with Alice Denny. *Africa and the Victorians: The Official Mind of Imperialism*. 2nd ed. London: Macmillan, 1981.

Rodgers, Daniel T. *Contested Truths: Keywords in American Politics Since Independence*. New York: Basic Books, 1987.

Rogers, Joseph M. "Characteristics of Senator Hoar," pamphlet from article in *Booklovers Magazine*, N.p. 1904.

Rogin, Michael Paul. *Fathers and Children: Andrew Jackson and the Subjugation of the American Indian*. New York: Alfred A. Knopf, 1975.

——. "Liberal Society and the Indian Question." In *Ronald Reagan, the Movie and other Episodes in Political Demonology*. Berkeley: University of California Press, 1987, 134–68.

Roosevelt, Theodore. *American Ideals, the Strenuous Life, Realizable Ideals: The Works of Theodore Roosevelt*. Hermann Hagedorn, ed., New York: Charles Scribner's Sons, 1926.

——. *American Problems*. Hermann Hagedorn, ed., New York: Charles Scribner's Sons, 1926.

——. *Campaigns and Controversies*. Hermann Hagedorn, ed. New York: Charles Scribner's Sons, 1926.

——. *Letters from Theodore Roosevelt to Anna Roosevelt Cowles, 1870–1918*. New York: Charles Scribner's Sons, 1924.

——. *The Letters of Theodore Roosevelt*. Vols. 2–3. Elting E. Morison, ed., Cambridge: Harvard University Press, 1951.

——. *The Letters of Theodore Roosevelt*. Vols. 5–6. Elting E. Morison, ed., Cambridge: Harvard University Press, 1952.

——. *Literary Essays*. Hermann Hagedorn, ed., New York: Charles Scribner's Sons, 1926.

——. *Presidential Addresses and State Papers of Theodore Roosevelt, pt. 1*. New York: P. F. Collier and Son, 1905. Reprint. New York: Kraus, 1970.

——. *The Rough Riders and Men of Action*. Hermann Hagedorn, ed., New York: Charles Scribner's Sons, 1926.

——. *State Papers as Governor and President, 1899–1909*. Hermann Hagedorn, ed., New York: Charles Scribner's Sons, 1926.

Rosenberg, Emily S. "A Round Table: Explaining the History of American Foreign Relations—Gender." *JAH* 77, June 1990, 116–24.

Roth, Russell. *Muddy Glory: America's "Indian Wars" in the Philippines, 1899–1935*. West Hanover, Mass.: Christopher, 1981.

Rotter, Andrew J. "Gender Relations, Foreign Relations: The United States and South Asia, 1947–1964." *JAH* 81, Sept. 1994, 518–42.

Rotundo, E. Anthony. *American Manhood: Transformations in Masculinity from the Revolution to the Modern Era*. New York: Basic Books, 1993.

——. "Body and Soul: Changing Ideals of American Middle-Class Manhood, 1770–1920." *Journal of Social History* 16, Summer 1983, 23–38.

Rubens, Horatio S. *Liberty: The Story of Cuba*. New York: Brewer, Warren and Putnam, 1932.

Russel, Florence Kimball. *A Woman's Journey through the Philippines*. Boston: L. C. Page, 1907.

Russell, Henry B. *The Lives of William McKinley and Garret A. Hobart*. Hartford: A. D. Worthington, 1896.

Russett, Cynthia Eagle. *Darwin in America: The Intellectual Response, 1865–1912*. San Francisco: W. H. Freeman, 1976.

————. *Sexual Science: The Victorian Construction of Womanhood*. Cambridge: Harvard University Press, 1989.

Ryan, Mary P. *Women in Public: Between Banners and Ballots, 1825–1880*. Baltimore: Johns Hopkins University Press, 1990.

Rystad, Göran. *Ambiguous Imperialism: American Foreign Policy and Domestic Politics at the Turn of the Century*. Sweden: Berlingska Boktryckeriet, 1975.

Said, Edward W. *Orientalism*. New York: Vintage, 1979.

Samuels, Peggy, and Harold Samuels. *Remembering the* Maine. Washington: Smithsonian, 1995.

Sarkesian, Sam C. *America's Forgotten Wars: The Counterrevolutionary Past and Lessons for the Future*. Westport, Conn.: Greenwood, 1984.

————. "Philippine War." (1899–1902). In *The War of 1898 and U.S. Interventions, 1898–1934*, Benjamin R. Beede, ed., New York: Garland, 1994, 424–28.

Saveth, Edward N. "Theodore Roosevelt: Image and Ideology." *New York History* 72, Jan. 1991, 45–68.

Schellings, William J. "The Advent of the Spanish-American War in Florida, 1898." *Florida Historical Quarterly* 39, April 1961, 311–29.

Schirmer, Daniel B. *Republic or Empire: American Resistance to the Philippine War*. Cambridge: Schenkman, 1972.

Schott, Joseph L. *The Ordeal of Samar*. New York: Bobbs-Merrill, 1964.

Schriftgiesser, Karl. *The Gentleman from Massachusetts: Henry Cabot Lodge*. Boston: Little, Brown, 1944.

Schumpeter, Joseph A. "The Sociology of Imperialisms." *Imperialism and Social Classes,* trans. Heinz Norden, New York: A. M. Kelley, 1951, 3–130.

Schurman, Jacob Gould. *Philippine Affairs: A Retrospect and Outlook*. New York: Charles Scribner's Sons, 1902.

Schurman, Jacob Gould, George Dewey, Elwell S. Otis, Charles Denby, and Dean C. Worcester. *Report of the Philippine Commission to the President*. Vol. 3. Washington: Government Printing Office, 1901.

Schurz, Carl. "For American Principles and American Honor." New York: Anti-Imperialist League, 1900.

————. "For the Republic of Washington and Lincoln." Chicago: American Anti-Imperialist League, 1900.

————. *Speeches, Correspondence and Political Papers*. Vols. 5–6. Frederic Bancroft, ed. New York: G. P. Putnam's Sons, 1913.

Scott, Joan Wallach. "Gender: A Useful Category of Historical Analysis." *AHR* 91, Dec. 1986, 1053–75.

Second Report of the National Society of the Daughters of the American Revolution. Washington: Government Printing Office, 1900.

Semmel, Bernard. *Imperialism and Social Reform: English Social-Imperial Thought, 1895–1914*. Cambridge: Harvard University Press, 1960.

Sewall, May Wright, ed. *The World's Congress of Representative Women*. Chicago: Rand, McNally, 1894.

Sexton, William Thaddeus. *Soldiers in the Sun: An Adventure in Imperialism.* Harrisburg: Telegraph, 1939.

Shulman, Mark Russell. *Navalism and the Emergence of American Sea Power, 1882–1893.* Annapolis: Naval Institute Press, 1995.

Silber, Irwin. *Songs America Voted By.* Harrisburg: Stackpole, 1971.

Silber, Nina. *The Romance of Reunion: Northerners and the South, 1865–1900.* Chapel Hill: University of North Carolina Press, 1993.

Simundson, Daniel. "The Yellow Press on the Prairie: South Dakota Daily Newspaper Editorials Prior to the Spanish-American War." *South Dakota History* 2, Summer 1972, 211–29.

Sinha, Mrinalini. "'Chathams, Pitts, and Gladstones in Petticoats': The Politics of Gender and Race in the Ilbert Bill Controversy, 1883–1884." In *Western Women and Imperialism: Complicity and Resistance,* Nupur Chaudhuri and Margaret Strobel, eds., Bloomington: Indiana University Press, 1992, 98–116.

——. *Colonial Masculinity: The "Manly Englishman" and the "Effeminate Bengali" in the Late Nineteenth Century.* Manchester: Manchester University Press, 1995.

——. "Gender and Imperialism: Colonial Policy and the Ideology of Moral Imperialism in Late Nineteenth-Century Bengal." *Changing Men: New Directions in Research on Men and Masculinity,* Michael S. Kimmel, ed., London: Sage, 1987, 217–31.

Skocpol, Theda. *Protecting Soldiers and Mothers: The Political Origins of Social Policy in the United States.* Cambridge: Belknap, 1992.

Slotkin, Richard. "Buffalo Bill's 'Wild West' and the Mythologization of the American Empire." In *Cultures of United States Imperialism,* Amy Kaplan and Donald E. Pease, eds., Durham: Duke University Press, 1993, 164–81.

——. *Gunfighter Nation: The Myth of the Frontier in Twentieth-Century America.* New York: Atheneum, 1992.

Smith, Edwina C. "Southerners on Empire: Southern Senators and Imperialism, 1898–1899." *Mississippi Quarterly* 31, Winter 1977–78, 89–107.

Smith, Joseph P. *McKinley's Speeches in August.* N.p.: Republican National Committee, 1896.

——. *McKinley's Speeches in September.* Canton: Repository Press, [1896].

Smith, Ephraim K. "William McKinley's Enduring Legacy: The Historiographical Debate on the Taking of the Philippine Islands." In *Crucible of Empire: The Spanish-American War and its Aftermath,* James C. Bradford, ed., Annapolis: Naval Institute Press, 1993, 205–49.

Smith, Geoffrey S. "National Security and Personal Isolation: Sex, Gender, and Disease in the Cold-War United States." *International History Review* 14, May 1992, 307–37.

Smith, Goldwin. *Commonwealth or Empire: A Bystander's View of the Question.* New York: Macmillan, 1902.

Smith, Joseph. *The Spanish-American War: Conflict in the Caribbean and the Pacific, 1895–1902.* New York: Longman, 1994.

Smith, William Henry. *The Life and Speeches of Hon. Charles Warren Fairbanks*. Indianapolis: Wm. B. Burford, 1904.

Spector, Ronald. *Admiral of the New Empire: The Life and Career of George Dewey*. Baton Rouge: Louisiana State University Press, 1974.

Spence, Jonathan D. *The Search for Modern China*. New York: W. W. Norton, 1990.

Springhall, John. *Youth, Empire and Society: British Youth Movements, 1883–1940*. Hamden: Archon, 1977.

Sproat, John G. *"The Best Men": Liberal Reformers in the Gilded Age*. New York: Oxford University Press, 1968.

Stanley, Peter. *A Nation in the Making: The Philippines and the United States, 1899–1921*. Cambridge: Harvard University Press, 1974.

Stanton, Theodore, and Harriot Stanton Blatch, eds. *Elizabeth Cady Stanton as Revealed in Her Letters, Diary and Reminiscences*. Vol. 2. New York: Harper, 1922.

Staudacher, Rosemarian V. "Richard Harding Davis." *Dictionary of Literary Biography*. Vol. 23. *American Newspaper Journalists, 1873–1900*, Perry J. Ashley, ed., Detroit: Gale Research, 1983, 81–94.

Steinson, Barbara J. *American Women's Activism in World War I*. New York: Garland, 1982.

———. "'The Mother Half of Humanity': American Women in the Peace and Preparedness Movements in World War I." In *Women, War and Revolution*. Carol R. Berkin and Clara M. Lovett, eds., New York: Holmes and Meier, 1980, 259–84.

Stepan, Nancy Leys. "Race and Gender: The Role of Analogy in Science." *ISIS* 77, June 1986, 261–77.

Stevens, William Oliver. *Pistols at Ten Paces: The Story of the Code of Honor in America*. Boston: Houghton Mifflin, 1940.

Stewart, William Rhinelander. *The Philanthropic Work of Josephine Shaw Lowell*. New York: Macmillan, 1911.

Stickney, Joseph L. *Admiral Dewey at Manila*. Philadelphia: Elliott, 1899.

Stiehm, Judith Hicks. "The Protected, the Protector, the Defender." In *Women and Men's Wars,* Judith Stiehm, ed., New York: Pergamon, 1983, 367–76.

Stoddard, Henry L. *As I Knew Them: Presidents and Politics from Grant to Coolidge*. New York: Harper, 1927.

Stoler, Ann Laura. "Carnal Knowledge and Imperial Power: Gender, Race, and Morality in Colonial Asia." In *Gender at the Crossroads of Knowledge: Feminist Anthropology in the Postmodern Era,* Micaela di Leonardo, ed., Berkeley: University of California, 1991, 51–101.

Storey, Moorfield. "Is It Right?" Chicago: American Anti-Imperialist League, 1900.

[———]. "'Marked Severities' Secretary Root's Record in Philippine Warfare." Boston: Geo. H. Ellis, 1902.

———. "What Shall We Do with Our Dependencies? The Annual Address before the Bar Association of South Carolina Delivered in Columbia January 16 1903." Boston: Geo. H. Ellis, 1903.

Strobel, Margaret. *European Women and the Second British Empire*. Bloomington: Indiana University Press, 1991.

Sturtevant, David R. *Popular Uprisings in the Philippines, 1840–1940*. Ithaca: Cornell University Press, 1976.

Sullivan, Mark. *Our Times: The United States, 1900–1925*. Vol. 2. New York: Charles Scribner's Sons, 1927.

Summers, Festus P., ed. *The Cabinet Diary of William L. Wilson, 1896–1897*. Chapel Hill: University of North Carolina Press, 1957.

Swanberg, W. A. *Citizen Hearst*. New York: Charles Scribner's Sons, 1961.

Swerdlow, Amy. *Women Strike for Peace: Traditional Motherhood and Radical Politics in the 1960s*. Chicago: University of Chicago Press, 1993.

Swift, Morrison. *Imperialism and Liberty*. Los Angeles: Ronbroke, 1899.

Sylvester, Christine. *Feminist Theory and International Relations in a Postmodern Era*. New York: Cambridge University Press, 1994.

Taft, Rev. Stephen H. "Letters Regarding McKinley's War Upon the Philippinos." Santa Monica: Los Angeles Herald, 1899.

Takaki, Ronald. "The Black Child-Savage in Ante-Bellum America." In *The Great Fear: Race in the Mind of America*, Gary B. Nash and Richard Weiss, eds., New York: Holt, Rinehart, and Winston, 1970, 27–44.

———. *Iron Cages: Race and Culture in 19th-Century America*. 1979. Rev. ed., New York: Oxford, 1990.

Taylor, Charles Carlisle. *The Life of Admiral Mahan*. London: John Murray, 1920.

Testi, Arnaldo. "The Gender of Reform Politics: Theodore Roosevelt and the Culture of Masculinity." *JAH* 81, March 1995, 1509–33.

Theweleit, Klaus. *Male Fantasies*. Vol. 2. *Male Bonds: Psychoanalyzing the White Terror*. Trans. Erica Carter and Chris Turner in collaboration with Stephen Conway. Minneapolis: University of Minnesota Press, 1989.

———. *Male Fantasies*. Vol. 1. *Women, Floods, Bodies, History*. Trans. Stephen Conway. Minneapolis: University of Minnesota Press, 1987.

Third Biennial of the General Federation of Women's Clubs. Louisville: Flexner, 1896.

Third Report of the National Society of the Daughters of the American Revolution, Oct. 11, 1898–Oct. 11, 1900. Washington: Government Printing Office, 1901.

Thomson, James C., Jr., Peter W. Stanley, John Curtis Perry. *Sentimental Imperialists: The American Experience in East Asia*. New York: Harper and Row, 1981.

Thurner, Manuela. "'Better Citizens Without the Ballot': American Antisuffrage Women and their Rationale During the Progressive Era." *Journal of Women's History* 5, Spring 1993, 33–60.

Tickner, J. Ann. *Gender in International Relations: Feminist Perspectives on Achieving Global Security*. New York: Columbia University Press, 1992.

Tolman, Albert H. "Mr. McKinley's Declaration of War." Chicago: American Anti-Imperialist League, 1900.

Tompkins, E. Berkeley. *Anti-Imperialism in the United States: The Great Debate, 1890–1920*. Philadelphia: University of Pennsylvania Press, 1970.

———. "The Old Guard: A Study of the Anti-Imperialist Leadership." *The Historian* 30, May 1968, 366–88.

Townsend, Kim. *Manhood at Harvard: William James and Others*. New York: W. W. Norton, 1996.

Trask, David F. *The War with Spain in 1898*. New York: Macmillan, 1981.

Turner, Frederick Jackson. *Rereading Frederick Jackson Turner*. With commentary by John Mack Faragher, New York: Henry Holt, 1994.

Turton, Peter. *José Martí: Architect of Cuba's Freedom*. London: Zed, 1986.

Tyrrell, Ian R. *Woman's World, Woman's Empire: The Woman's Christian Temperance Union in International Perspective, 1880–1930*. Chapel Hill: University of North Carolina Press, 1991.

Vance, Norman. *The Sinews of the Spirit: The Ideal of Christian Manliness in Victorian Literature and Religious Thought*. Cambridge: Cambridge University Press, 1985.

Vanderbilt, Kermit. *Charles Eliot Norton: Apostle of Culture in a Democracy*. Cambridge: Belknap, 1959.

Varon, Elizabeth R. "Tippecanoe and the Ladies, Too: White Women and Party Politics in Antebellum Virginia." *JAH* 82, Sept. 1995, 494–521.

Walters, Everett. *Joseph Benson Foraker: An Uncompromising Republican*. Columbus: Ohio History, 1948.

Walters, Ronald G. *The Antislavery Appeal: American Abolitionism after 1830*. New York: W. W. Norton, 1978.

Watterson, Henry. *History of the Spanish-American War*. St. Louis: L. F. Smith, 1898.

Watts, Steven. *The Republic Reborn: War and the Making of Liberal America, 1790–1820*. Baltimore: Johns Hopkins University Press, 1987.

Waugh, Joan. "Unsentimental Reformer: The Life of Josephine Shaw Lowell." Ph.D. diss., University of California, Los Angeles, 1992.

Wehler, Hans-Ulrich. "Bismarck's Imperialism, 1862–1890." *Past and Present* 48, Aug. 1970, 119–55.

Welch, Richard E., Jr. *George Frisbie Hoar and the Half-Breed Republicans*. Cambridge: Harvard University Press, 1971.

———. "Organized Religion and the Philippine-American War, 1899–1902." *Mid-America* 55, July 1973, 184–206.

Weston, Rubin Francis. *Racism in U.S. Imperialism: The Influence of Racial Assumptions on American Foreign Policy, 1893–1946*. Columbia: University of South Carolina Press, 1972.

Wheeler, Marjorie Spruill. *New Women of the New South: The Leaders of the Woman Suffrage Movement in the Southern States*. New York: Oxford University Press, 1993.

White, Trumbull. *Our New Possessions*. Chicago: Monarch, 1898.

Whites, LeeAnn. "The Civil War as a Crisis in Gender." In *Divided Houses: Gen-*

der and the Civil War, Catherine Clinton and Nina Silber, eds., New York: Oxford, 1992, 3–21.

Whitney, William Dwight, ed. *The Century Dictionary.* Vols. 3–4. New York: Century, 1895.

Whitworth, Sandra. *Feminism and International Relations: Towards a Political Economy of Gender in Interstate and Non-Governmental Institutions.* London: Macmillan, 1994.

Why Women do not Want the Ballot. Boston: Massachusetts Association Opposed to the Further Extension of Suffrage to Women, 1903.

Widenor, William C. *Henry Cabot Lodge and the Search for an American Foreign Policy.* Berkeley: University of California Press, 1980.

Wiebe, Robert H. *The Opening of American Society: From the Adoption of the Constitution to the Eve of Disunion.* New York: Alfred A. Knopf, 1984.

———. *Self-Rule: A Cultural History of American Democracy.* Chicago: University of Chicago Press, 1995.

Wilkerson, Marcus M. *Public Opinion and the Spanish-American War: A Study in War Propaganda.* Baton Rouge: Louisiana State University Press, 1932.

Wilkinson, Rupert. *American Tough: The Tough-Guy Tradition and American Character.* Westport, Conn.: Greenwood, 1984.

Williams, Walter L. "United States Indian Policy and the Debate over Philippine Annexation: Implications for the Origins of American Imperialism." *JAH* 66, March 1980, 810–31.

Williams, William Appleman. *The Roots of the Modern American Empire: A Study of the Growth and Shaping of Social Consciousness in a Marketplace Society.* New York: Random House, 1969.

———. *The Tragedy of American Diplomacy.* Cleveland: World, 1959. Rev. ed., New York: Dell, 1962.

Williamson, Joel. *The Crucible of Race: Black-White Relations in the American South Since Emancipation.* New York: Oxford University Press, 1984.

Wilson, Charles Reagan. *Baptized in Blood: The Religion of the Lost Cause, 1865–1920.* Athens: University of Georgia Press, 1980.

Wisan, Joseph E. *The Cuban Crisis as Reflected in the New York Press, 1895–1898.* New York: Columbia University Press, 1934.

Witherbee, Sidney A., ed. *Spanish-American War Songs.* Detroit: Sidney A. Witherbee, 1898.

Wolff, Leon. *Little Brown Brother: How the United States Purchased and Pacified the Philippine Islands at the Century's Turn.* Garden City, N.Y.: Doubleday, 1961.

Wood, Gordon S. *The Creation of the American Republic, 1776–1787.* New York: W. W. Norton, 1969.

———. *The Radicalism of the American Revolution.* New York: Alfred A. Knopf, 1992.

Worcester, Dean C. *The Philippine Islands and their People.* New York: Macmillan, 1898.

Wrobel, David M. *The End of American Exceptionalism: Frontier Anxiety from the Old West to the New Deal*. Lawrence: University Press of Kansas, 1993.

Wyatt-Brown, Bertram. *Southern Honor: Ethics and Behavior in the Old South*. New York: Oxford University Press, 1982.

————. *Yankee Saints and Southern Sinners*. Baton Rouge: Louisiana State University Press, 1985.

Yazawa, Melvin. *From Colonies to Commonwealth: Familial Ideology and the Beginnings of the American Republic*. Baltimore: Johns Hopkins University Press, 1985.

Young, Louis Stanley. *Life and Heroic Deeds of Admiral Dewey*. Philadelphia: Globe Bible Publishing, 1899.

Young, Marilyn Blatt. *The Rhetoric of Empire: American China Policy, 1895–1901*. Cambridge: Harvard University Press, 1968.

Zeiger, Susan. "Finding a Cure for War: Women's Politics and the Peace Movement in the 1920s." *Journal of Social History* 24, Fall 1990, 69–86.

Zimmerman, James A. "Who Were the Anti-Imperialists and the Expansionists of 1898 and 1899? A Chicago Perspective." *Pacific Historical Review* 46, Nov. 1977, 589–601.

Index